An Untractable Country

The History of

KENNER,

Louisiana

An Untractable Country

The History of

Kenner, Louisiana

Craig A. Bauer

University of Louisiana at Lafayette Press
2016

University of Louisiana at Lafayette Press
P.O. Box 43558
Lafayette, LA 70504-0831
http://ulpress.org

ISBN 13 (paper): 978-1-935754-84-8

Printed in the United States on acid-free paper.

Library of Congress Cataloging-in-Publication Data:

Names: Bauer, Craig A., author.
Title: An untractable country : the history of the city of Kenner, Louisiana / by Craig A. Bauer.
Description: Lafayette, LA : University of Louisiana at Lafayette Press, 2016. | Includes bibliographical references.
Identifiers: LCCN 2016024824 | ISBN 9781935754848 (alk. paper)
Subjects: LCSH: Kenner (La.)--History.
Classification: LCC F379.K44 B38 2016 | DDC 976.3/38--dc23
LC record available at https://lccn.loc.gov/2016024824

Front Cover (top) - "Carte Particuliere du cours du fleuve st. louis depuis le village sauvage jusqu'au dessous du detour aux anglois" (1749) by Francois Saucier; courtesy of the Library of Congress.

Front Cover (Bottom) - Kenner, Louisiana, including Armstrong Airport; courtesy of Aero Photo.

Rear Cover - all images are courtesy of the City of Kenner, except: future expansion of Armstrong Airport, which is courtesy of the City of New Orleans; and author photo, which is courtesy of Craig Bauer.

Contents

For Betsy and Charlotte
and
In Loving Memory of
Dad and Mom

Preface

"It is an untractable country." Spoken by the French explorer Pierre Le Moyne, sieur d'Iberville, in 1699, these words are among the earliest recorded observations of the area on the east bank of the Mississippi River that has become the site of modern Louisiana's sixth largest city. With the 2010 Federal Census showing a population of 66,702 residents, the city of Kenner currently ranks behind Lake Charles, with its count of 71,993, as one of the state's largest communities. Today, Kenner is primarily known as a suburban community where the New Orleans Armstrong International Airport is located. Few realize that it has a long history which dates back to times prior to the arrival of Europeans in the region. Long visited by Indian tribes native to the area, the "untractable" nature of the area mentioned by Iberville referenced the abundant and thick canes that choked the lands along the bank of the Mississippi River. It was the presence of these canes and the Indian practice of burning them that gave the region its original European name of Cannes Brûlées or "burnt canes." The flammable nature of the reeds convinced Iberville and other Europeans that the area could be easily cleared and opened for settlement. By the time the French took their first census of the Louisiana colony in 1721, Cannes Brûlées was the site of large agricultural concessions. Hence, beginning with the early Indian inhabitants of the area to today's modern suburban community, for more than three centuries an historic tableau of people and events has unfolded and today makes up the mosaic that is Kenner's history.

Though the chronology of Kenner's long history has some similarities to that of its large urban neighbor, the city of New Orleans, in most ways Kenner's story is unique and does not begin to dovetail with that of the Crescent City until modern transportation conveniences joined the two. Over its three-century history, the Kenner area experienced a transition from primitive agricultural concession to one of Louisiana's largest cities. This three hundred-year metamorphosis occurred in three dramatic phases: the colonial/antebellum period when large-scale commercial agriculture dominated; the small-town period when Kennerville became a reality and gradually grew in the twentieth century to become a city with home rule; and finally the modern period following World War II when the community experienced a rapid population expansion and evolved to become primarily a suburban bedroom community.

In spite of its long and unique story and its stature as one of the state's largest cities, historians have largely overlooked Kenner. Frequently mentioned in sections of works on the history of Jefferson Parish, until this book, no stand-alone manuscript-length narrative of the history of Kenner has been produced. In the 1970s, Raconteur Mel Leavitt released a short historical sketch as a publicity piece for Kenner's Merchant's Bank and, more recently, Troy Broussard and Frank Borne, Jr. produced a book of photographs of the community as part of the popular Images of America series. Yet, in spite of these works, much of Kenner's story has remained untold until now.

The origin of this book goes back multiple decades to a sunny but cold February day in 1956. On that day my parents, my siblings, and I loaded up a large moving van at our shotgun double home on Willow Street in the Uptown section of New Orleans and headed for our recently constructed new family home "in the country." Our new "country" home was on Maine Street and was located just barely within the city limits of Kenner. The other side of the street was Metairie. To my brothers and me it was truly country living. Having lived our lives to date in the crowded urban neighborhood of shotgun houses and limited open spaces of New Orleans, our new life in Kenner, with its areas of large undeveloped woodlands and newly developing subdivisions, made for a boyhood full of exploration and adventure.

The smallness of the Kenner of the 1950s meant that both old and new residents of the city got to know a large portion of the people who lived in the community. City officials were on a first name basis with many, if not most, of their constituents. It was because of the closeness and friendliness of the community that at the young age of ten or eleven I became interested in the story of Kenner. When a childhood friend of my parents who had resided in Kenner for some time—and who had suggested to my parents that they look into moving from our shotgun home in the city to a new modern ranch-style house in Kenner—ran for the elective office of city alderman, I got work delivering political literature to homes across the community. Being "bitten" by the political bug and the excitement that working in a campaign brought, I continued to work and volunteer in political campaigns, including the one that resulted in Joe Yenni being elected mayor at a time in Kenner's history when the city was at the height of its transition from small town to a modern-suburban community.

As a history major in college, I read as much as possible about Kenner and its history. I was disappointed to discover that, with the exception of a few short articles over the years in the *Jefferson Parish Yearly Review* and an unpublished copy of the late Mayor Joseph S. Kopfler's historical sketch written for the city's centennial celebration, there was relatively little known about Kenner's history. In graduate school, I selected Kenner as my thesis topic and eventually produced a 114-page manuscript titled "The History of the City of Kenner, Louisiana." Although the work was the first full-length history of the city, I realized at the time that there was much more to the story. Over the next four decades I continued my interest in "all things Kenner." My research eventually resulted in the writing and publication of two monographs on aspects of the Kenner family, including *A Leader Among Peers: The Life and Times of Duncan Farrar Kenner* (1993) and *Creole Genesis: The Bringier Family and Antebellum Plantation Life in Louisiana* (2011). In the researching and writing of these works and a journal article on Kenner, as well as serving as co-chair of the Heritage Committee of the City of Kenner's American Revolution Bicentennial Celebration Committee, I continued to collect a wide range of materials about Kenner's history that form the basis of much of this work.

Over the decades material was collected for this work, advances in technology greatly enhanced the effort of uncovering the story of

Kenner. Among the greatest roadblocks faced by researchers of Kenner's past is the lack of a community newspaper of record. In modern times there have been periods when weekly newspapers have appeared; however, none have survived for an extended period of time, thus denying the researcher a continuity of information concerning most periods of Kenner's history. This lack of a local press was no doubt the result of Kenner's proximity to its neighbor New Orleans, whose newspapers sometimes offered stories about events in Kenner or Kennerville. The weakness of that scenario is that there was little consistency in the coverage of Kenner's news by the New Orleans papers. If a story was sensational enough, they may have carried it for a day or so. But seldom did they give Kenner's news the detail and length of coverage a local paper would have provided. Fortunately, modern database technology provides the researcher the tools to mine the large daily papers of New Orleans, such as the *Times-Picayune*, for the small snippets of news about events in Kenner that easily could have been overlooked in the old research method of physically having to read each page of the old-yellowing newspapers that were often found on dusty shelves stuck away in seldom visited sections of libraries. Additionally, the lack of municipal records for Kenner's history prior to 1908, when the city's charter was revoked, also creates a difficult hurdle for historians to surmount. All city records prior to the time the charter was canceled by the state were transferred to Jefferson Parish and have since been lost, forcing the researcher to rely mostly on unofficial sources for the story of Kenner during the city's early years.

A work such as *An Untractable Country: The History of Kenner, Louisiana* in which materials for inclusion in the work were collected for a period of decades could only have been accomplished with the help and encouragement of many individuals. Regretfully, some of the people who assisted in providing materials and encouragement for this work are no longer with us. Among those who were instrumental in providing valuable assistance to me and now have gone to their supernal reward are: Engel H. Schmidt, a descendant of the Kenner family who graciously provided me with access to the Kenner family bible and other materials, and Chris Lochbaum and Raphaella Maggiore, two early researchers into Kenner's history who, early in my research, convinced me that the story of Kenner was unique and interesting and deserved to be told. There were also civic leaders including the late mayor Joseph Yenni and the late city clerk Dora Mae Aucoin, former mayor Louis Congemi, former police chief Nick Congemi, and mayor Mike Yenni and his staff, who gave generously of their time and who were instrumental in providing me access to important archival materials held by the City of Kenner.

Special thanks is extended to Kay Fowler who, as secretary to mayor Joseph Yenni and later as my colleague at the Jefferson Historical Society, has been a faithful supporter and provider of materials for this work. Two other individuals deserving of a special note for their generosity in providing materials for this work are Mr. J. P. Walker of Metairie, who supplied me with a copy of an 1855 real-estate map based on W.T. Thompson's plan of early Kennerville, and Shirley Hay, who kindly provided me with a copy of her family's papers, which were instrumental in shedding light on the turbulent political times in Kenner at the end of the nineteenth century. I am also indebted to private investigator DeeDee Denise DiBenedetto, whose assistance in locating rare and difficult to find database materials helped to make this work possible. Thanks also to Judith Stiebel for her suggestions and comments on the early draft of this manuscript. Though the identities of most of them remain unknown to me, I am grateful to the numerous librarians, archivists, and record keepers at the many public and academic institutions where research for this work took place. In particular, I want to thank for their assistance Sr. Helen Fontenot, M.S.C., and Diana Schaubhut of the Blaine S. Kern Library at the University of Holy Cross in New Orleans.

Finally, and most importantly, a heartfelt and special debt of gratitude goes to my wife Betsy, whose support and encouragement have been instrumental in the completion of this work. Special appreciation and gratitude are also extended to my daughter Charlotte for her patience and understanding of the time and effort demands that the research and writing of this project placed upon the family.

Historical marker celebrating the colonial settlement of Cannes Brûlées..

1
Cannes Brûlées

The first Europeans to set their eyes on the beauty of the natural landscape of what would become modern southeast Louisiana did so from their small boats traversing the turbulent and murky waters of the Mississippi River. While the Spaniard Luis de Moscoso Alvarado led the tattered survivors of Hernando De Soto's ill-fated expedition to safety in 1543, and nearly a century and a half later when Frenchman Rene-Robert Cavalier, sieur de La Salle, led his epic expedition to the mouth of the great river in 1682, the two groups of early explorers floated and paddled past mile upon mile of low-lying shoreline that bordered the great river. As they traversed the southern portions of the waterway in the region that would one day become the urban landscape of one of America's great cities, they found the banks of the river frequently in a state of inundation. When they did locate dryer landscape along the river, it turned out to be a source of rich alluvial soils and home to a wide variety of wildlife and vegetation. Included among the plentiful varieties of native-plant life in the region were large masses of reeds, great thickets of canes and tall grasses, palmettos, and numerous types of trees including stands of cypress, tupelo, hickory, sweetgum, beech, maple, cottonwood, black willow, magnolia, sweet bay, hackberry, and live, water, pin, and willow oaks.[1]

The interest in the lower Mississippi River, which resulted from the early visits of European explorers to the region, over time led to consequences far in excess of anything the sixteenth and seventeenth-century adventurers ever could have imagined. Subsequent appearances by other explorers in the region revealed the area's geography and environmental character and its potential for large-scale settlement. Additionally, their contacts with the region's native peoples, who made the region their home long before the first Europeans made even their early tentative visits to the area, played an important role in determining the nature and location of the future settlements of the Europeans. The date of the arrival of the first Indians to the area is not known with great accuracy. Archaeologists place the first arrival of nomadic Paleo-Indians in Louisiana to the late Pleistocene or early Holocene times, a period roughly 12,000 years ago. These first arrivals found a Louisiana far different from today. Because of the lingering effects of the Ice Age, the sea level was lower and much of the area was covered with broad grasslands and was populated with mammoths, ground sloths, and other now extinct mammals.[2]

With the end of the Ice Age, great changes occurred in both the region's climate and geography, and over time they gradually assumed their contemporary nature. In spite of the disappearance of the large Pleistocene-era animals that their early ancestors hunted, the post-Ice-Age Indians adapted their hunting tactics, which allowed them to pursue and survive off of the region's abundant smaller wildlife, such as deer, bear, and at later times bison, as well as the wide variety of seafood found in the area's lakes and waterways. The natural environment of the lower delta of the Mississippi River and the lifestyles of the region's first inhabitants have resulted in relatively few tangible archaeological traces of their presence. The oldest sites in the region where archaeological evidence has been discovered date to circa 2000 B.C. and reveal continuous occupancy in the area until long after the arrival of the Europeans.[3]

Over the centuries that humans resided in Louisiana before the arrival of the Europeans, the environment and geography of the region changed dramatically, and the paleo-residents and their descendants successfully adapted to and even exploited the changes. As the Ice Age drew to a close and temperatures increased, the great ice sheets, which at one time reached as far south as present-day Cairo, Illinois, melted, sending great volumes of water and sediments into an immense downwarping in the Earth's crust known as the Mississippi Embayment. When the volume of water increased, it flowed south and over time created the great Mississippi River. As the river carried the Ice-Age remnants southward, it delivered enormous quantities of sediment-laden waters into the Gulf of Mexico. When the Ice-Age flood waters met the calmer waters of the gulf, the river lost the kinetic energy needed to continue its drive southward and dumped its sediment load of water, waste, silt, sand, loam, and vegetation. Approximately 7,200 years ago, the sediments accumulated creating the modern Mississippi River Delta, which gradually protruded into the Gulf of Mexico. As the alluvial deposits increased in elevation, the mighty river, on more than one occasion, sought paths of less resistence around the deposits and formed new channels, moving either east or west of the old channel. One consequence of the river's wandering and spreading of its alluvial deposits was the creation of the land area that would one day become the city of New Orleans and its surrounding environs. The land building of the New Orleans region by the Mississippi is estimated by geologists to have started about 4,300 years ago.[4]

One meander of the mighty river from its present channel ran roughly west to east through the center of what are today the east-bank portions of Louisiana's Jefferson and Orleans Parishes. Abandoned long before the arrival of the Europeans, the channel is known as the Bayou Metairie-Gentilly-Sauvage system. Originating between 2600 and 2300 B.C., the system formed when a break or crevasse in the Mississippi River's natural banks occurred slightly east of the present day city of Kenner. Sediments from the crevasse carried over the low banks of the distributary and gradually built up to form ridges on each side of the new waterway. When the great river meandered once more, the distributary became separated from the main channel thus creating the bayous of Metairie and Gentilly (also referred to as Bayou Sauvage). The abandoned distributaries together took a meandering path through the future location of the New Orleans community. Roughly paralleling the track of the Mississippi River, the eastern end of the sluggish waterway started near the location of modern Kenner, about thirteen miles upriver from the future site of the French settlement of New Orleans, and stretched eastward to the vicinity of Chef Menteur Pass in today's eastern Orleans Parish.[5]

Over time the Indian population comfortably adapted to the region's ecological and landscape changes. The Indians of the area generally were members of the Chitimachan and Muskhogean linguistic groups, with the Colapissas (also Acolapissa) being the most common tribe on the east bank of modern Jefferson Parish during the time of the early European settlements in the region. Although it is known that the area near the future site of the city of Kenner was used for hunting by several Indian tribes, including the Colapissa and Choctaw tribes from the north shore of Lake Pontchartrain, it is not clear if there were any villages of note at Kenner. In 1682 scouts from La Salle's expedition did observe the presence of a village located in the marshes near the area that eventually became the city of Kenner. However, since they were unable to visit the site because of the hostile reaction of the Indians and the conditions of the marsh, there is little evidence of the size of the hamlet they spotted. As later explorations showed, the larger villages of the region were typically located on higher ground rather than in marshlands. With the area frequented by Indians from other regions, the village noted by the French may have been a small temporary camp established by Indians who sometimes visited the region to fish or hunt the abundant game found there and used their camps to serve as bases to trade with other settlements in the area. However, French explorers who came after La Salle, including Andre Penicaut and Pierre de Charlevoix, did note the presence of Colapissa villages not far from the site of today's Kenner. One of these areas may have been the site spotted by La Salle's scouts.[6]

It is from Penicaut, among the earliest of French explorers to visit the area, that we obtain an interesting portrait of the lifestyle of some of the Kenner area's earliest residents. In 1708 he visited a village of the Colapissas and observed that:

> The Colapissas' bodies, men's and women's, are all tattooed. They prick almost their entire bodies with needles and rub the pricks with willow ash crushed quite fine, which causes no inflammation of the punctures. The arms and faces of the Colapissas women and girls are tattooed in this way which disfigures them hideously . . . .
>
> As for their religion, they have a round temple before which they appear morning and evening rubbing their bodies with white mud and lifting their arms on high; they mutter some words very low for a quarter of an hour. At the portal of the

temple there are some wooden likenesses of birds; within the temple are numerous little idols, of both wood and stone, representing dragoons, snakes, and some toad-like creatures, which they keep locked up in three chests inside the temple, the key being held by the Grand Chief.

When a savage dies, a kind of grave is prepared, or, rather, a platform raised two feet above the grounds, on top of which the dead man is placed. He is covered completely with mud, and further, bark is put on top of that, for fear of animals or birds of prey; and down below is put a little jug filled with water with a platter full of meal. Every morning and evening fire is lighted beside the platform, and here they come and weep. The richest people hire women to weep besides the platform. After six moons, the body is uncovered; if the flesh is consumed, the bones are put in a little basket and carried to their temple; if it is not yet consumed, the bones are taken from the flesh, and the flesh is burned.[7]

They are rather cleanly with their food: they have an individual pot for each thing that they cook—that is, the meat pot is never used for fish. They cook all their food with bear fat, which is white in winter, when it is congealed, like lard, and is like olive oil in summer. It does not have a bad taste. They eat it with salad, use it in making pastry, in frying, and usually in everything they cook.

As for fruits, they happen to be few. They have, however, peaches in season that are even bigger than those in France, and sweeter; strawberries; plums; and a grape that is a bit sour and not so big as the grapes of France. There are also nuts which they pound into flour, using it with water to make pap for their children and mixing it with corn meal to make sagamite, or bread.

These savages have no hair on them whatever except the hair on their heads. The men as well as the women and girls remove the hair from their faces as well as from other parts of the body; they remove hair with shell ash and hot water as one would remove the hair from a suckling pig.

They have an unusual way to light a fire. They take a small piece of cedar wood, the size of one's finger, and another

> small piece of mulberry wood, which is very hard. They put them side by side between their hands and by spinning them together, like making chocolate froth, they make a little piece of fuzz come out of the cedar wood and catch fire. This can be done instantly.
>
> When they go hunting, they go dressed in deer skins with the antlers attached. They make the same motions that a deer makes; and when the deer notices this, he charges them; and when he gets in good musket range, they shoot at him and kill him. With this method they kill a great many deer; and it should be acknowledged that in hunting buffalo as well as bear and deer they are more skillful than the French. When winter came, we went out to the channel and into the woods to kill bustards,[8] ducks, and wild geese[9] that are much bigger than the geese in France.[10]

The Colapissas and other tribes that visited the area were typically highly mobile and sometimes moved their villages or established temporary camps. The Kenner area not only drew Indians because of its abundant food sources, but also because of its nearness to the headwater of Metairie Bayou. The little stream allowed them to use the site as a convenient portage to the great river and also provided them the opportunity to avoid the sometimes treacherous waters of Lake Pontchartrain and the strong currents of the Mississippi by allowing them to travel the inland water route from the Kenner area eastward as far as the Chef Menteur, a distance of approximately thirty miles. The area also afforded a means to get conveniently back and forth between the river and the lake. Bayous Piquant and LaBranche, which were located slightly west of present-day Kenner in St. Charles Parish, also served as connecting waterways between the lake and river. The trip from the lake to the river on the bayous required an individual to ascend either waterway as far as they could and then portage approximately a league's (3.5 miles) distance to the river. Though the site was often frequented by Indians, the actual number of natives who resided in or visited the swampy lands along the lower Mississippi River is not known. Archaeological and historic evidence suggests that the number was relatively small. Nevertheless, their presence and use of the landscape for their villages, portages, trails, shell middens, and hunting ranges did result in permanent alterations to the environment of the area. However, it was the sharing with, some would say the appropriation by, the Europeans of their knowledge of the environment and geography of the area that proved to be the Indian's most lasting contribution to the history of the region and opened the door to the incredible transformation of the virgin forest, swamp, and marshlands of the area into the modern city of Kenner.[11]

The first known arrival of Europeans at the future location of Kenner occurred during La Salle's historic first voyage down the Mississippi. The event also marked the initial encounter between native Indians and the French in the lower delta of the great river. La Salle's small expedition of twenty-two Frenchmen and thirty-one friendly Indians, including ten women and three children, from regions further to the north, arrived in the area as the river experienced its yearly spring rise. On April 3, 1682, a notary with the expedition named Jacques de La Metairie[12] memorialized in his journal the details of the meeting with the following observation:

> At ten in the morning we saw in the canes thirteen or fourteen pirogues. M. de La Salle debarked with some of his company. We noticed a number of traces; a little farther down, we saw some Savages who were fishing but who, having detected us, left the place and fled. We touched ground on the edge of a marsh caused by the flooding of the river. M. de La Salle sent two Frenchmen on reconnaissance and then two Savages who reported that there was a village close by; that, to reach it, one had to cross this whole marsh covered with canes; that they had been attacked with flying arrows by those in the place who did not dare engage themselves in the marsh and had fallen back, despite the fact that neither the French nor the Savages with them wished to fire their arms, according to the instructions that they were to do no such thing except in an emergency. Soon we heard the beating of a drum in the village, and shouts and abusive cries with which these barbarians are accustomed to attack [their enemies]. We heard them for three or four hours, and since we could not camp in the marsh, [after] seeing no one and hearing nothing more we embarked.[13]

La Salle did not linger long in the area. Continuing to the mouth of the Mississippi, La Salle claimed the river and its surrounding lands for France and its monarch. His subsequent effort to return to the area and enter the river directly from the Gulf of Mexico ended in failure with La Salle's murder by his men in 1687. Fortunately, the La Salle calamity did not end France's interest in the area. Twelve years later in 1699, the king sent Pierre Le Moyne, sieur d'Iberville, to continue with the mission of establishing a colony on the Gulf Coast in order to secure France's claim to the great river and its surrounding lands. On his initial ascent of the river during the first week of March in 1699, Iberville and his men explored the future site of Jefferson Parish and Kenner and noted that:

> This entire area floods to a depth of one foot as far as one-half league[14] into the woods. From the sea to my present location, both riverbanks are almost without exception, so densely lined with cane of all sizes, one, two, three, four, five, and six inches in circumference, that it is impossible to walk along the riverside. It is an untractable country, which will be easy to clear. Most of the foliage is dry; setting it afire, it burns easily and makes much noise aflame as a pistol shot.[15]

The Kenner area was visited again several months later when in August of the same year Iberville's younger brother Jean-Baptiste Le Moyne, sieur d'Bienville led an expedition to explore along the entire shoreline of Lake Pontchartrain. When the small group of explorers passed along the shoreline of the lake a short distance west of the present western boundary of Kenner, their Indian guides showed the Frenchmen what Bienville's ship carpenter and recorder Andre´ Penicaut called "a stagnant body of water that the savages called *bayouque*." After camping on the lakeshore near the small waterway, the party and their Indian guides followed the slow-moving stream, which most historians believed to have been either Bayou Piquant or Bayou Labranche[16] in St. Charles Parish, to the Mississippi River. As did Iberville before them, they found the riverbanks covered with "tall reeds, or canes" and "everywhere else . . . along the river appeared . . . to be covered with all kinds of forest trees . . . such as oaks, ash, elms, and others whose names we did not know."[17] The discovery of the portage between the river and lake "greatly delighted"[18] the explorers. As the French made additional efforts to explore the area around the bayou,

Pierre Le Moyne, sieur de Iberville was a French-Canadian explorer who in 1699 founded the first permanent French settlement in Louisiana. It was during his search for a settlement site along the Mississippi River that he visited the Cannes Brûlées area and called the location of the future city of Kenner as being an "untractable country."

they also learned of the portage a few miles to the east, near the boundary of modern-day Kenner, where the headwaters of Metairie Bayou offered relatively easy passage through the interior to the Bayou St. John area. The name of the first European to learn of and make use of this Indian passage is not known. However, the Indians who used the area sometimes set the thick canes, which grew in such great abundance, on fire. Whether to make it easier to traverse the cumbersome reeds that grew densely in the area or to assist in hunting game or perhaps even as one earlier explorer noted "to obtain better access to aim and shoot at us,"[19] the Indian practice of burning cane resulted in the area being given the name by the French of Cannes Brûlées, literally, "Burnt Canes." The area and its name quickly became a landmark for the French and an important point of reference for early map makers of the region, making Cannes Brûlées the oldest identified site in eastern Jefferson Parish. As neighboring areas were given identities of their own by later map makers, Cannes Brûlées was often the designation given to the region immediately to the upriver side of the region that was called Chapitoulas (also Tchoupitoulas) and sometimes the Chapitoulas Coast.[20]

Although Cannes Brûlées and the lower Mississippi River region remained an area of exploration interest to the French, with the exception of a few farms along Bayou St. John, for several years they failed to make a serious effort at moving settlers into the area. That situation changed in late 1717 when John Law's Company of the West acquired proprietorship of Louisiana. In return for its twenty-five-year control of the colony, the company was required to send 6,000 colonists and 3,000 African slaves to Louisiana within a ten-year period. The company also promised to build churches and furnish clergymen to man the new ecclesiastical parishes that were to be created to serve the new colonists. To meet their obligation, company leaders decided that the colony's agricultural potential was the key to attracting new settlers. The company worked to find people in Europe who were willing to relocate to Louisiana. An elaborate publicity campaign was launched using great exaggeration about the riches of the colony. Because of the campaign, many honorable people and soldiers of fortune made their way to Louisiana. However, when it was unable to meet its quotas of new settlers, the company lowered its standards and resorted to the sending of exiles, jail inmates, deserters, and most any other individual they could get to move to the colony.[21]

The Company of the West, popularly known as the Company of the Mississippi, and later known as the Company of the Indies, did not want to repeat mistakes previously made by Antoine Crozat, Louisiana's first proprietor, who had failed in his efforts to make the colony a financial success. The directors of the new company decided that instead of focusing on developing trade with the Spanish, searching for mines of precious metals, or establishing exclusive trade restrictions for the thinly populated province, the future of the colony depended upon its ability to exploit its agricultural potential. The company's leaders determined that the nature of the colony's agricultural economy would best be maximized by the creation of large land grants to wealthy and influential individuals. These great land holdings were known as concessions, with the individual to whom the lands were granted called "concessionaries." Each land grantee was obligated to have his lands cleared and tilled and was responsible for transporting a number of settlers proportioned to the extent of his concession.[22]

The Cannes Brûlées and Chapitoulas areas were among the first places where concessions were granted along the great river. The first census of the region around the new settlement of New Orleans was taken in 1721 by Bernard Diron d'Artaguiette, the Inspector General of the Troops in Louisiana and himself a concessionaire. He noted in the census that there were two concessions at Cannes Brûlées. One was owned by Jean-Baptiste Martin d'Artaguiette, the older brother of the Inspector General, and the other by Count d'Artagnan, Joseph de Montespuiou. The two properties were located adjacent to each other. D'Artagnan's stood on the Mississippi River six leagues above New Orleans. A member of the prominent French family who were related to the real-life d'Artagnan, Charles de Batz-Castelmore, Comte d'Artagnan, whose novelized and highly fictionalized memoirs were the source material for Alexander Dumas when he wrote his classic novel *The Three Musketeers*, D'Artagnan was an absentee landlord. There is no evidence that he ever traveled to the colony to visit his concession. Instead he relied upon managers, including M. d'Artiguiere and M. de Benac, to oversee his holdings at Cannes Brûlées, with de Benac and a M. Chevalier actually directing the daily operations at the settlement. In many cases where the concessionaires were absent from their holdings, their properties were not efficiently managed; however, this does not seem to have been the situation at Cannes Brûlées. By 1721 the concession grew to thirty arpents[23] along the river and had a population of eighty residents, including forty-seven Frenchmen, eight Frenchwomen, three children, and twenty Africans. By 1724, the workforce on d'Artagnan's holdings at the settlement grew to include thirty slaves and five white workers. By that time the estate had expanded to a cultivated area between 160 and 200 arpents. With only two horses and no cattle, the property was worked almost entirely by the labor of d'Artagnan's small workforce. By 1724, the small settlement was producing a successful harvest of 360 barrels of rice and corn, fifteen barrels of indigo, and sixty barrels of sweet potatoes.[24]

Unlike his partner and investor Count d'Artagnan who never visited the colony or his concession, Martin d'Artaguiette visited the Cannes Brûlées site early in 1708. A naval commissioner who played a prominent role in the then ongoing investigation of the accounts of the colony, he was accompanied on his first visit to the area by the early pioneers Jean-Baptiste Le Moyne, sieur de Bienville, and Louis Juchereau de St. Denis. A man of deep insight and vision, d'Artaguiette quickly recognized the great potential that the area and the colony in general offered. His contributions to the colony and its history were more than the fact that he was quick to recognize the potential offered by the Cannes Brûlées site, which led him and d'Artagnan to become the first European owners of the site. During his four-year sojourn of 1708 to 1712 in the colony, he gathered valuable first-hand information that he shared with officials upon his return to France. D'Artaguiette aptly recognized that if the colony was to have any chance of success, more government aid for settlers was needed, as well as higher quality settlers. He believed that, instead of the soldiers and workers who made up a large portion of the population during the early colonial period, experienced farmers were needed to help clear the virgin land and convert it to productive farmland. This was pivotal if the French colony was to become self-sufficient. D'Artaguiette also promoted the granting of land not only to nobility and large companies but to ordinary organizations that possessed the financing to send to the colony stable families who possessed needed skills and who were willing to commit long term to living in Louisiana. Even with the additional farmers, he realized that the French and Indian population was not sufficient to perform all of the heavy labor required to make the colony a success. To address the problem, he became an early supporter of the importation of African slaves to the colony. After John Law obtained his proprietorship of the colony through the Company of the West, d'Artaguiette returned to France in 1717 and became a member of the board of the joint-stock venture company. His years of experience in Louisiana proved to be a valuable asset to the company, and d'Artaguiette was able to use his position to advance his ideas as to what was needed for the colony's success. The only board member to have ever set foot in Louisiana, d'Artaguiette's opinions and observations soon ranked him among the most influential members of the board. He was given the important responsibility of overseeing the purchase of staples and merchandise for the colony and was made head of the company's office that concerned itself exclusively with Louisiana. So significant were his contributions that even after Law's financial fiasco and the end of the Company of the West and the bursting of the "Mississippi Bubble," d'Artaguiette survived to become a member of the Company of the Indies that assumed control of the Louisiana colony. His office or bureau at the Company of the Indies grew in importance and influence. D'Artaguiette worked to centralize all correspondence relating to the colony and the status of the troops stationed there. He also coordinated and centralized the transport of passengers on ships heading to Louisiana and the land grants made by the company in the colony. Hence, Martin d'Artaguiette, and to a lesser degree his younger brother Bernard Diron, played pivotal roles in strengthening the French colonial experience in Louisiana.[25] Perhaps the most telling analysis of the significance of the d'Artaguiette family's contributions during the early years of France's colonization of Louisiana was written by their contemporary, noted Jesuit historian Pierre Francois Xavier de Charlevoix:

> Indeed, there could scarcely be said to be a colony in Louisiana, or at least it did not begin to take shape till the arrival of Diron d'Artaguette [*sic*][26] . . . . This magistrate's first care was to enable the settlers to cultivate the soil . . . so that they might not be obligated to wander about, living by hunting or with the Indians whenever the ships from France were late in bringing provisions, as it happened on several occasions.[27]

Although Martin d'Artaguiette's stay in Louisiana lasted for only four years, even after his return to France, he not only remained deeply involved in events in the colony but also in developing a land concession at Cannes Brûlées. In 1720 he sent his younger brother, Diron, the colony's inspector-general of troops, and a workforce of forty-five to cultivate the family's land holdings at Cannes Brûlées. Like other concessions in the area, the Cannes Brûlées properties stretched from the Mississippi to Lake Pontchartrain and required considerable labor to convert the area from virgin forest and swamp lands to productive cultivated fields. Nevertheless, within a year of the arrival of workers at Cannes Brûlées, Diron d'Artaguiette was able to make ample progress in cultivating a large section of the concession. Though smaller in numbers and size, twelve arpents as opposed to thirty arpents at the neighboring d'Artagnan property, by the time he took his census in 1721, Diron had successfully located a group of settlers at the Cannes Brûlées concession. The inhabitants at the concession at the time of the census included d'Artaguiette and a "Frenchman, six Frenchwomen, one child, twenty French domestics, twenty Negroes, and two Indians."[28] Three years after the census, Diron's concession grew to include eighty arpents under cultivation and a harvest of 250 to 300 barrels of rice and corn, twenty of indigo, and thirty to forty barrels of sweet potatoes. Additionally, the concession in 1724 included fifteen cows and an enlarged workforce of twenty-five slaves and two white workers.[29]

The task of clearing and tilling the land was not easy. The early settlers to the area suffered greatly from having the area frequently inundated by the river and the difficult chore of preparing the soil for crops. In the early days of the settlements along the river, only the land fronting on the river was cultivated. Once that was accomplished, the area under cultivation gradually expanded away from the river. To clear the dense forest settlers began by peeling off a large piece of the bark from around the trunks of the trees to be felled. The best time to perform this task was in March when the sap was running. Once the trunks became dry, approximately fifteen days after the girdling took place, fires were built around the tree to kill it and to burn off its branches. Once burned, the remaining portion of the tree was easily removed, leaving a stump to be cleared at a later date. In some instances the settlement's crops were simply planted around the old stumps.[30]

Added to the drudgery of clearing virgin lands was the constant threat to the workers and residents of attacks from venomous snakes and hordes of mosquitoes and other insects. Tragedy and even death was never far away. Bad weather, Indians, venomous creatures, malnutrition, overwork, or the general nature of the dangers of attempting to live in a primitive environment all posed deadly menaces to the colony's settlers. Conditions in the region were so poor that the majority of children that came to the colony from Europe did not survive.[31]

In spite of their efforts to improve their living conditions, the early residents at Cannes Brûlées lacked many of the essentials typical of community life of the period, including a church and a chaplain to staff it. As part of the conditions included by the Company of the West in its issuing of land concessions in the colony, the beneficiaries of the grants were obligated by the company to not only clear and till the land but also to make certain other improvements, including providing a chaplain to look after the spiritual welfare of the concession's residents. Efforts to staff the concessions with chaplains met with only limited success. The Company of the West and its successor the Company of the Indies were lax in meeting their obligations of providing the Cannes Brûlées concessions with churches and clergy. Those that did arrive in the colony tended to have short tenures because of high mortality rates or their being recalled by officials. Others became overwhelmed with the magnitude of their task in the frontier colony and simply quit. So few were the number of chaplains in the region that when Father Charlevoix made his long trip in 1721-1722 from Canada down the Mississippi to the region, he noted that upon arriving at Cannes Brûlées, "the first object that attracted my notice, was a large cross erected on the banks of the river, round which I found them singing vespers. This is the first place of the colony, after leaving the country of the Illinois, where I saw this ceremony of our religion."[32] The Jesuit chronicler also noted that the Cannes Brûlées residents remained faithful despite the fact that "They have no priest" because "there having been one sent them, whom they were obliged to send away for his drunkenness, wisely concluding, that more harm than good was to be expected from a bad priest, in a new settlement, where there was no superior to watch over his conduct."[33] Subsequently, the inhabitants at Cannes Brûlées were ministered to through the chapel that was constructed in 1729 at Chapitoulas, two leagues down river from their concession. Years later, near the end of the century when the Chapitoulas chapel fell into disrepair, the families of both the Cannes Brûlées and the Chapitoulas turned to the "red church" of St. Charles Borromeo upriver at the German Coast in St. Charles Parish for their religious needs.[34] The paucity of religious services for the residents of the area had the not unexpected result of a loss of fervor among the residents of the area. After touring the settlements along the lower Mississippi River, the first bishop of the newly created Diocese of Louisiana and the Floridas, Luis Ignacio Maria de Penalver y Cardenas, bemoaned that, "The inhabitants do not listen to, or if they do, they disregard, all exhortations to maintain in its orthodoxy the Catholic faith, and to preserve the innocence of life." He went on to note the treatment of young boys in the settlements and complained that "they leave school when very young, and return to the houses of their parents . . . , where they hear neither the name of God nor the King, but daily witness the corrupt morals of their parents."[35]

The success of the French in establishing concessions along parts of the lower Mississippi River had a great effect upon the native peoples of the region. Unfortunately for the local Indians, the changes brought by the Europeans permanently altered the culture of the region's first residents. Either from being forced to move their villages to less desirable locations or from being decimated by European-carried diseases, the tribes of the region suffered from having to compete with the French for use of the land. Nevertheless, Indian and French relations on the east bank of the Mississippi in the region of New Orleans and Cannes Brûlées remained friendly. The local indigenous people helped the early colonists survive and become acclimated to their new surroundings. Of the various tribes found in the region around the French settlement at New Orleans, the Colapissa, who lived north of the lake and on the east bank of the river were the closest to the French.[36] During the early years of the settlements on the east bank, Bienville found the natives there to be "very brave and excellent hunters" who furnished "all the fresh meat that [was] consumed in New Orleans." However, he went on to note that, with the exception of their supply of meat, there were not many other items that the Indians had that were of value to the French and concluded that the Colapissa, without "neglecting the culture of their lands which produced a quantity of merchandise[,] . . . do not take much trouble to trade their pelts, [and] there is not very much return for France."[37]

In spite of the generally friendly relations the French enjoyed with the Indians of the Cannes Brûlées area, the fact remained that they lived in a frontier community and danger was ever present. To protect the area a small stockaded fort was constructed in the center of the settlement. It was designed so that in case of attack the inhabitants of the settlement had a place to retreat and defend themselves. Although there is no record of the area being threatened, there was one occasion when the residents feared a major uprising. In 1729 the Natchez Indians killed or captured a large number of settlers at the French concession near one of their villages approximately 125 miles upriver. Word of the assault spread panic throughout much of the colony. At Cannes Brûlées, the settlement fortified its fort with additional arms and ammunition, which were distributed by the company's magazine in New Orleans. Although the community was gripped with terror for some time, the difficulties with the Natchez remained upriver and the settlement at Cannes Brûlées fortunately remained safe without incident.[38]

Many of the survivors of the Natchez massacre sought residence elsewhere in the colony. Some chose the safety of Cannes Brûlées for their new home, including Jacques Cantrelle. A native of France, Cantrelle had arrived in Louisiana in 1720 and settled with his wife at the Natchez concession. Among the first to realize that the Natchez were attacking the settlement, Cantrelle escaped detection by the Indian warriors by hiding with his wife in their corn field. Remaining in the field until dark, Cantrelle and his wife attempted to flee the area. Realizing that he needed to return to their house to retrieve important articles, he sent his wife ahead to a designated place to wait for him. To Cantrelle's horror, upon his return to the rendezvous spot, she was gone. A desperate search proved fruitless. Finally giving up, he located a pirogue and made his escape down the river to New Orleans. There he found four of his slaves who had also managed to escape the uprising. The Superior Council provided him with thirty barrels of rice and a cow to start over again. This time he established himself at Cannes Brûlées. Shortly thereafter, on April 16, 1730, he married Marguerite Larmusiau LeChoux, a widow whose first husband, a store keeper and interpreter at Yazoo, had been killed in the Natchez attack. Cantrelle and his new family prospered at their new home site. By 1731, the census showed that his farm on the river had grown to include a wife, a stepdaughter, two children, one workman, four slaves, two horses, and two armed guards. In 1735 he purchased a lot in New Orleans and built a house. Shortly thereafter he moved his family to the city and became an employee of the Superior Council. Nearly three decades later in 1763, he again moved, this time to St. James Parish, where he developed an indigo plantation and became a leading resident.[39]

Although the Company of the West and later the Company of the Indies only partially achieved its goal of populating the colony with the number of colonists needed to make Louisiana financially viable, over time there was a gradual increase in the population along the lower Mississippi River. By 1730 the population of New Orleans and its surrounding area numbered about one thousand people. There were also a handful of settlements along the river not far from the city. The concessions at Tchoupitoulas, Cannes Brûlées, and the German Coasts joined each other in an almost continuous belt of well-cultivated farms along the upriver banks of the Mississippi. Over the years the choice of crops grown in the concessions changed. In the early years of the settlements because of the difficulty it was having in providing a reliable supply of food for the colonists in the area around New Orleans, the Company of the West instructed inhabitants of the early settlements in the region to plant gardens as a source of fresh food. This plan was discarded after a couple of years when the newly arrived colonists at the German Coast, located upriver from Cannes Brûlées, began producing garden vegetables in large enough quantities to meet the region's needs. Even with the successful German truck gardening, food supplies for the colony always remained tight resulting in most settlers spending much time and effort in producing essential foodstuffs for local consumption. Among the popular crops grown on the local farms were Indian corn (the most popular of the local crops), peas, beans, potatoes, pumpkins, melons, mirlitons, cabbage, and tomatoes.[40]

As the colony matured, French horticulturists worked to identify which crops performed best in the various regions of Louisiana. The soil at Cannes Brûlées proved to be productive and ideal for a large variety of crops favored by the French. In their 1721 census of the colony, officials noted that the soil of the province was ideal for such crops as indigo "as fine as that of St. Dominque," tobacco, rice, corn, and "every sort of vegetable." They even optimistically suggested that silk could become "an important object of cultivation" because of the "prodigious quantity of mulberry trees" found in the area. Horticulturists also reported that the area provided "great quantities of herbs suitable for all kinds of sickness" as wells as "several sorts of good woods" such as white and live oaks, cottonwood, and cypress. Census officials also reported that although the Cannes Brûlées settlement boasted "great clear fields which are to be sown" and that the ground there was "very good," they lamented that, even though levees had been built, the area was susceptible to "great overflows [which]. . . flooded [the fields] from eight to ten inches." So great a problem was the flooding at the settlement, officials offered the concessionaires additional land several leagues up the river where flooding was not as great a problem.[41]

In the areas around New Orleans and Mobile, extensive effort was placed on growing a wide variety of fruit trees—including fig, cherry, lemon, orange, plum, apple, and peach—alongside grapevines and pineapple plants. Although there was some success in the New Orleans area with the growing of pineapples, figs, grapes, oranges, and peaches, overall the effort to produce a commercial fruit crop returned disappointing results. Similar disappointing results were achieved in the attempt to grow wheat in the concessions along the lower Mississippi River. Even with nearly every farm in the area following Company of the West instructions to grow at least some wheat, the grain crop of the region was overly susceptible to rust disease, ruining its commercial viability.[42]

The search by the French for a staple crop that would both be commercially viable and feed the colony's growing European population led Bienville to import cattle from Cuba as a means of improving the meat supply. The large quantity of canes that grew along the river and gave Cannes Brûlées its name proved to be an ideal source of food for the livestock.[43] Over time the herd gradually increased, eventually providing the colony's inhabitants with a self-sufficient supply of beef. Cattle-raising grew to become a significant part of the economy of every settlement along the river, including Cannes Brûlées. By 1724 the d'Artaguiette concession at Cannes Brûlées included, for the time, a relatively large herd of fifteen cows.[44]

The food supply situation in the concessions along the river gradually improved to such a state that by 1723 the Company of the West relaxed its emphasis on the production of market gardening, and farmers and planters at Cannes Brûlées began to concentrate on the production of staples. According to one colonial administrator, except for new arrivals, the colony's residents had "sufficient stocks of provisions, so nothing prevents them from producing tobacco and rice."[45] French officials looked forward to the day when their settlements along the Mississippi River produced enough tobacco to break their countrymen's reliance on tobacco produced by the British in their East-Coast colonies. It was this desire to establish a slave-powered tobacco society along the fertile banks of the Mississippi that became a leading consideration for the French decision to move the colony's economic center from their Gulf Coast settlements to the lands along the great river. Though tobacco was grown somewhat successfully in areas upriver near the concessions at Baton Rouge, Natchitoches, Natchez, and

Pointe Coupée, its need for high, dry land made it a poor choice for the concessions along the lower regions of the river. Because of the wet conditions at the settlement, the planters at Cannes Brûlées gave up on trying to produce successful tobacco crops and instead turned to the growing of rice as a staple.[46]

The arrival of rice in the colony actually predated the establishment of both the New Orleans and Cannes Brûlées settlements. The first rice harvest occurred on the farms along Bayou St. John. The crop proved successful, and officials encouraged its growth elsewhere. So extensive did its production become that by 1733 Bienville reported, "Three-fourths of the inhabitants live on [rice] and have forgotten wheat bread."[47] The grain proved itself to be highly adaptable to the lower Mississippi region. It could withstand better than most other crops the heavy rains and flooding common to the area. A relative easy crop to cultivate, the chief drawback to its production was that at times during the growing process it was labor-intensive, which during the early years of the settlement was a major impediment. The cultivation process required the grower using only primitive mattocks, hoes, and plows to prepare the ground to accept the seed. Once the prepared soil was seeded, the area was gently flooded and would remain so until the seeds sprouted and took roots. Then the field was drained and was allowed to dry out over a period of ten to twelve days. During the drying period planters had to watch and work continuously to protect the young seedlings from flocks of marauding birds that cherished the taste of the young sprouts. Once the shoots matured to three or four inches, the fields were flooded again in order to protect them from birds, insects, and weeds. Over the growing season, the fields would be drained and flooded as needed and as determined by the presence of pests and weeds, which if left unaddressed could endanger the entire crop. For those working the crop, the process of weeding and hoeing in the wet fields while fighting off the hordes of mosquitoes that swarmed throughout most of the year was not only an unpleasant but also unhealthy experience. Finally, in the early fall the labor-intensive harvesting process took place. To harvest the grain the farmer cut the stalks with a sickle and then collected, bundled, stacked, threshed, hulled, and stored the crop. All of these steps were done by hand.[48]

Although a labor-intensive crop, extended periods, during both the growing season of rice and afterwards, provided times of idleness for the workers. Because of the down periods, the growing of rice was profitable only when it was farmed in conjunction with other crops. Hence, the rice growers at Cannes Brûlées and elsewhere typically coupled the crop with others, such as the fruit trees mentioned earlier. Among the other secondary crops grown in the area were some small amounts of tobacco[49] and, more likely, cotton and myrtle trees. The French introduced cotton to the colony as early as 1719-1720. They grew a variety that was known for its whiteness called "white Siam." However, the gins available in Louisiana were not very efficient in cleaning the cotton. Because of a very short staple and the expense required to separate the lint from the seeds, the popularity of the crop stalled during the French regime. Nevertheless, cotton continued to be grown by locals to make cloth for their own use. Another important crop in the colony that was sometimes grown in association with rice was the myrtle tree. Grown by most farmers and planters, the wax myrtle produced a berry that was used to make a wax for candles. The wax was highly prized by the French in their colony at Santo Domingo and in France.[50]

Another of the important staple crops grown at Cannes Brûlées was indigo. Although a native variety existed in Louisiana, the French preferred an imported variety that performed well in the colony and produced a product superior in quality and color to that grown in France's other major producer of indigo, Santo Domingo. The crop proved to be exceedingly profitable and by 1725 was being grown by most planters in the colony. Because of its value, planters often favored it to the exclusion of other crops. However, as it tolerated other crops and could be grown along with other staples, farmers and planters frequently alternated their fields between indigo and other crops. The processing of indigo was an unpleasant and tedious task. A three vat steeping system was used. The three vats included a "rotting" vat, a "beating" vat, where the liquid was beaten with wooden paddles, and the final or "settling" vat. After being processed in the vats, the product was placed in cloth bags and hung up to drain. Once dry, it was packed into casks and was ready for shipment. The crop was not without its problems. Though it eventually became the colony's leading export by the end of the French regime, it remained susceptible to the uncertain-

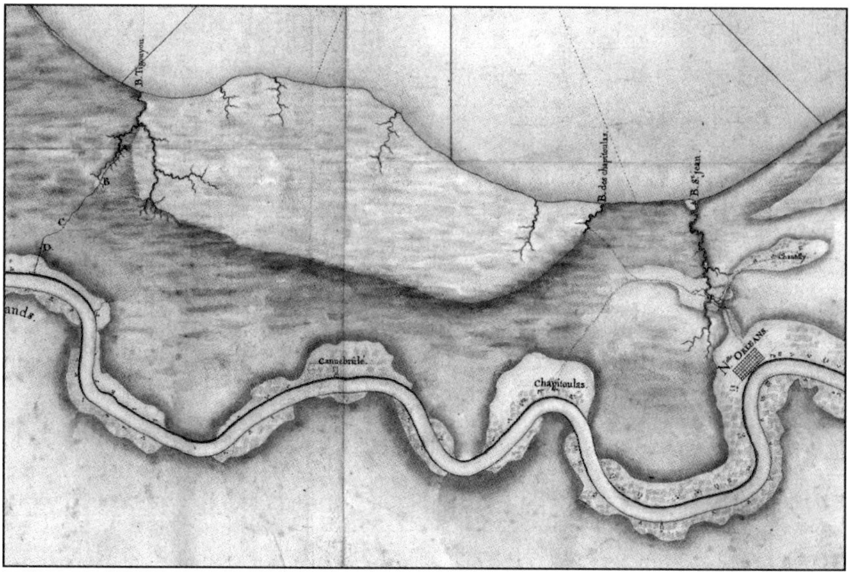

Pictured is a portion of the 1749 map by Francois Saucier titled "Carte Particuliere du cours du fleuve st. louis depuis le village sauvage jusqu'au dessous du detour aux anglois." The detail shows the early settlement at Cannes Brûlées and its location in relation to New Orleans, the Chapitoulas and the des Allemands districts. The chart also reveals the extent of the marsh and woodlands at Cannes Brûlées during the colonial period.

ties of the region's weather. Farmers were also hindered by the collapse of the indigo market which had resulted from Spain's acquisition of the colony and the subsequent departure of French trade for the product. Indigo, however, remained a major crop in Louisiana until the 1793-1794 season when the crop was destroyed by swarms of locusts.[51]

Though it eventually became a major crop in the region, during the early years of the Cannes Brûlées settlement sugar was not produced in large quantities. Sugar cane was brought to Louisiana by Iberville during the opening years of the French colonization. The first efforts at producing a sugar crop were disappointing. What was able to be produced was a liquidy, raw sugar that was primarily used for local consumption. Hence, the crop was produced in small quantities on most of the farms and plantations of the area. Furthermore, the early crop was vulnerable to the harsh winters that frequented the area during the early years of the colony. Not until the failure of the indigo crop during the 1793-1794 growing season did interest turn to the large-scale production of sugar. Growers began in earnest to look for ways to improve the product. In 1795 Etienne de Boré,on his plantation near New Orleans, developed an improved and commercially viable method to granulate sugar. This achievement quickly transformed the economy of the plantations along the river from a somewhat diversified crop structure of indigo and other crops to a dependence on the growing of sugar.[52]

A natural agricultural product that the inhabitants of Cannes Brûlées and other areas made use of was the abundant lumber found in the cypress-tupelo swamps that dominated much of the land of the region and at spots extended to within a mile of the river. Although not familiar at first with the beneficial characteristics of cypress lumber, the French soon discovered its usefulness and the demand for the wood grew. It came to be regarded as an ideal product for building purposes and thus became in great demand in the Caribbean region. Thus residents at Cannes Brûlées and elsewhere along the Mississippi River, supplemented their economies by lumbering the areas around their concessions during the periods when their labor was not needed for their other crops. Most notably in the autumn, settlers began cutting down and squaring the timber for sawing into boards and scantling. Since the timbers were usually taken from the rear areas of the concession, it was necessary to find a convenient and inexpensive means of transporting the logs to a place where they could be processed. This was accomplished by digging a ditch from the lumbering area to the river. The ditch was filled with water from the back swamps, making it relatively easy to conduct the felled timbers to the river. Once the logs reached the river they were bound together in large rafts and floated down to New Orleans. Over the years, great quantities of cypress wood were exported to the West Indies. So important was lumbering in providing building materials for residents of the colony and as a commercial commodity that, though unintentionally, it became the primary source of revenue for the colony throughout most of the eighteenth century.[53]

By the end of the French regime, the Cannes Brûlées settlement had endured the trial and difficulties of the French colonial period and was gradually developing its agricultural economy. Established in an area frequented by local Indians, the settlement was one of the earliest by the French along the lower Mississippi. It started as part of the Company of the West's effort to establish a self-sufficient agricultural economy along the fertile banks of the great river. The emphasis by the company on agriculture made commercial development of the area inevitable and was a prime factor in the prosperity enjoyed by the settlement at Cannes Brûlées. Additionally, the concession's location on the banks of the Mississippi River provided its inhabitants a convenient and important means of communication and trade between the various settlements located along the river, and the important port of New Orleans. Hence, by the time France signed the secret Treaty of Fontainbleau in November 1762 transferring control of much of the Louisiana colony to Spain, the community at Cannes Brûlées was among the handful of commercially successful settlements along the lower Mississippi River.[54]

2

William Kenner, Oakland Plantation, and the Slave Rebellion

Immigrants to colonial Louisiana found an environment largely made up of untamed marshes, swamps, grassy and wooded lands sprinkled with a handful of towns, trading posts, and small military outposts. To survive in their new land, colonial settlers faced a variety of hardships ranging from a lack of an adequate supply of food to flooding from occasional storms or high-river levels. Included among the most persistent of problems colonial Louisianans faced was the task of moving about the colony. Ordinarily a simple enough task, early settlers along the lower Mississippi River traveled as individuals either on foot or in small boats along the area's waterways. However, the shipping of goods and supplies was another matter and usually was a major undertaking. The nearly impenetrable forests and swamp lands found during the early colonial period required that most of the movement of the region's products and goods be transported by water. Because of the nearby Bayou Metairie to the east, the Bayou Labranche (Piquant) portage to the west, and the Mississippi River to the south, the residents of the Cannes Brûlées settlement had access to multiple waterways to handle their transportation needs. Nevertheless, the difficulty associated with moving about the colony did affect the development of the area. Although during the early days of the colony the concession attracted more settlers than its neighboring settlements, over time, because of its distance upriver from New Orleans and the extra difficulty it took to fight the great river's current in order to reach it, the little

Cannes Brûlées community gradually declined in importance to the one at Chapitoulas, which was located roughly midway between New Orleans and Cannes Brûlées.[1]

With the Mississippi River and the region's bayous serving as their primary transportation routes, the early settlers at Cannes Brûlées were dependent upon an assortment of boats to carry on communications and trade with the other settlements in the colony. Before the arrival of the wood-fired, self-propelled steamboat in the early part of the nineteenth century, the most common vessels found in the colony included skiffs, pirogues, rafts, flatboats, bateauxs, keelboats, and other similar craft propelled by men with oars, paddles, or poles. When possible and practicable, sails were utilized on the vessels. When descending the river, there was little difficulty. However, when making the return trip upstream and against the current, travel was often arduous and sometimes required sending people ashore with ropes to tow the vessel upstream. As settlements gradually spread throughout the colony, the Mississippi River became a veritable highway of vessels from the North hauling products to New Orleans. By the early years of the American regime, the parade of craft floating past their settlement afforded the residents of Cannes Brûlées the access to an almost endless variety of products, including such things as molasses, rice, cotton, flour, pork, bacon, whiskey, apples, cider, corn, oats, cheese, beans, lumber, butter, lard, onions, potatoes, hemp, yarn and cordage, linen, tobacco, beer, bear meat, horses, hogs, poultry, and a wide variety of other items. In 1810 alone, 679 flatboats and 392 keelboats brought their goods down the river past Cannes Brûlées to New Orleans. Frequently, the passing vessels took time to stop to sell some of their goods and to purchase or barter with the residents of Cannes Brûlées for items produced at the concession.[2]

The reliance on the river and other waterways for transportation by colonial settlers was a necessity resulting from the lack of usable roadways. The first trail to reach Cannes Brûlées was located on the Mississippi's raised bank, which had been built up by years of overflow silt being deposited alongside the river. Improvements to the roads that passed through the dense vegetation along the river took place slowly. So primitive was the colony's road network that it took several decades for wheeled vehicles to make a presence in the settlements along the lower Mississippi. It was not until 1730 that the first carriage was brought to New Orleans. Recognizing the need for an improved road system, colonial officials addressed the issue of roads and flood protection by requiring landowners in the New Orleans region to build a six-foot wide and two-foot high levee along the river that was also to double as a foot and bridle path. Over time, the path was expanded in both width and length. As wheeled vehicles became more common, it was broadened to handle wagon traffic and connected New Orleans with its neighboring settlements at the Chapitoulas Coast, Cannes Brûlées, and the German Coast. By 1784 the Chemin Royal (Royal Road), as the route was named by officials, stretched from several miles downriver of New Orleans to the German Coast, a distance of more than fifty miles. Landowners along the road were required to maintain it and any bridges that passed over ditches.[3]

The Cannes Brûlées area was also served by a second road that actually predated the Chemin Royal. From the earliest colonial times, French settlers had followed a path along the banks of Bayou Metairie. By the 1720s the path had widened into a road inhabitants called the Chemin des Chapitoulas, as it followed the bayou to its headwaters near the Mississippi River between the Chapitoulas Coast and Cannes Brûlées. As noted, the construction of the early roads in the colony went hand-in-hand with the effort to control flooding through the construction of levees. The first organized effort at flood control was started by the French in New Orleans shortly after the city was first settled. The French, and later the Spanish, continued the building of levees throughout the colonial era. The early attempts at flood control and the extension of the levees was largely the work of the private landowners who resided along the banks of the river and the region's bayous. Most levee work was supervised by local colonial officials. Though the first levees were primitive in design when compared to today's massive structures, by 1732 the line of levees extended from twelve miles below to thirty miles above the city and provided at least a modicum of flood protection for both Cannes Brûlées and the German Coast.[4]

In spite of the effort during the colonial era to construct levees and roads, the results on both items were less than impressive. The levees often broke or were overtopped, with the result that for decades the roads remained little more than mud paths. Hence the area's roads were of little importance in the region's greater transportation scheme. The Mississippi River and the area's larger bayous remained the primary transportation routes for the region's inhabitants. Because of the importance of having a convenient means of shipping and receiving products to and from their farms and estates, colonial settlers made every effort to obtain properties that fronted on navigable waterways. Also, unlike British and American settlers who liked to establish their farms singly and at scattered locations because of their aspiration of becoming property owners, French colonists favored locating in small compact settlements, such as at Cannes Brûlées.[5]

During the early years of the Louisiana colony, the French also built their houses differently than did the British colonists in America. Whereas the British built their wood structures by laying the logs one on top of another, in Louisiana the first settlers used a method they called *maison de poteaux en terre*, a house of posts in the ground, which involved the standing of logs for the house's walls on end. The space between the logs was then filled with bousillage, a mixture of moss, straw, or grass and earth or clay that was commonly known as *bousillage entre poteaux*. Later, as the colony matured, bricks and sawed lumber began to make their appearance. The colony's early houses typically had steep roofs of straw, grass, or wooden shingles and floors of either earth or roughhewn boards. Glass was scarce so most windows in houses were protected by wooden shutters and often had scraped skins or oiled papers nailed over the openings. The house's chimney stood on the outside of the building and was made of wood and clay, with a small fireplace opening into the structure. Most early dwellings used by the common folk of the colony were small and typically consisted of only one or two rooms.[6]

Over time the French colonists began to modify their construction techniques. With the increased availability of bricks in the colony, settlers gradually came to rely on their use in the construction of their homes, both large and small. *Briquette entre poteaux*, brick between posts, became a common building technique that involved constructing the walls of a house by placing bricks between square posts and then sealing the wall with plaster or boards. As conditions gradually improved in the colony and some residents accumulated wealth, the homes they built were improved and enlarged. It was not long before the distinctive French colonial plantation house appeared. These houses typically fronted on waterways where they were almost always located. By the mid-eighteenth century, when their presence became fairly common, the plantation house assumed a more-or-less standardized architectural style with a raised house and large galleries. An extended, double pitched, hipped and dormered roof typically covered both upper and ground-level galleries, which surrounded the house. The floor plan of the structures also followed the familiar pattern of three rooms wide and one or two rooms deep. Small cabinet rooms often flanked the main part of the house and most rooms opened directly onto the large shaded galleries so as to provide the maximum cross ventilation to the hall-less interior room design. Stairs to the upper level were located on the exterior of the house. The walls of the ground floor were constructed of brick nearly two feet thick; whereas, the walls of the upper level were usually of plaster over *bousillage entre poteux*. The structure's upper level was supported by round Tuscan columns, usually constructed of brick and plaster, and slender wooden colonettes helped to uphold the galleries on the second floor.[7]

At Cannes Brûlées during the colonial period, most of the houses built were of a simple and small design. As the economy of the colony expanded, the demand for land facing on the river increased. Eventually the concession holdings of D'Artagan and Diron D'Artaguiette were subdivided into plantations. During the Spanish regime, Louis Trudeau acquired a large tract of land at the site. By the end of the period several other plantations joined Trudeau's. Included among the early planters to settle at Cannes Brûlées were individuals that the Spanish maps of the time simply identified as Meuillon,[8] Mather, Bellechasse, and Fortier. Within a few years these holdings at Cannes Brûlées were consolidated into plantations owned by Louis Trudeau, Jacques Fortier, and John R. Holliday. As the plantations developed and their owners began to reap the financial rewards that successful large-scale commercial agriculture offered, planters placed increased resources into the construction of larger and grander manor homes. Two such large plantation-style houses were eventually located at the future location of the city of Kenner. Constructed on the property of John R. Holliday, the Bell Grove Plantation house was the centerpiece of a 193-acre tract of land that stretched from the river to the

William Kenner (1776 to 1824), the first member of the Kenner family to acquire property in the Cannes Brûlées area along the Mississippi River where he purchased property for his Oakland Plantation.

shore of Lake Pontchartrain. Located downriver from the present-day intersection of Jefferson Highway and Williams Boulevard, the property was originally situated between the downriver property of Jacques Fortier and the upriver holdings of Louis Trudeau. Completed in 1814 by Jacques Fortier, the house was large with a raised brick basement and over time was modified to include between eighteen and twenty rooms. A drawing of the house as it existed in 1837 is located in the New Orleans Notarial Archives. It shows the details of the classic French colonial plantation house located on the Holliday family's Belle Grove estate. Galleries with Tuscan brick columns encircled the ground floor and matching colonettes were found on the second floor. Three shuttered dormers extended on the front of the hipped roof and a single dormer on each side. Also on the second level were three sets of double-shuttered doors that opened onto the gallery, while on the lower gallery, the central entrance to the house was located. The door was topped with a fanlight and was matched on each side by a single double-hung window.[9]

Immediately upriver from the Belle Grove property was Oakland

Plantation, the estate of William Kenner and his family. Shortly before Louisiana was granted statehood, William Kenner became interested in making an investment in the region's growing sugar industry. Joining with Benjamin Morgan and later with Stephen Henderson he acquired property at Cannes Brûlées. Shortly thereafter when Kenner and Henderson decided to dissolve their partnership, William Kenner acquired sole ownership of his holdings at Cannes Brûlées and decided to make it the site of his country estate and the center of his commercial-agricultural efforts. Perhaps more than any other individual's, William Kenner's interest in Cannes Brûlées had far-reaching consequences for the future development of the region. Among the most prominent Americans living in New Orleans at the time of the Louisiana Purchase in 1803, Kenner had risen to a position of influence in the city during the final years of the Spanish regime when he was among the earliest Americans to establish a successful mercantile business in the Crescent City. Born at Staunton in Augusta County, Virginia, one month before the Declaration of Independence was signed, Kenner abandoned his native state at an early age and migrated to the Natchez area of Adams County, Mississippi.[10] Although Spanish territory at the time he arrived at the settlement, the area was populated predominantly by Anglo-Americans along with a few Frenchmen and an even smaller number of Spaniards. To promote settlement, Spanish officials in the little town located on bluffs above the Mississippi River were lax in the enforcement of colonial trade regulations.[11]

The favorable business climate at Natchez offered an opportunity that William Kenner was quick to capitalize upon. The majority of settlers in the region cultivated the rich soils found there and exported bountiful crops of tobacco, indigo, and cotton to a ready market by way of New Orleans. The planters used the assistance of merchants to get their crops to market. Seeing the potential in each activity, William invested in both endeavors, becoming both land owner and a mercantile proprietor. Possessing sharp business acumen, young William, while he lived in Natchez, joined in a mercantile business partnership with James C. Wilkins. The partnership prospered and the business eventually controlled much of the commerce in the region. William also prospered financially by speculating in real estate. One of his holdings on St. Catherine's Creek in Mississippi alone totaled 764 arpents of valuable land. As late as 1805, years after he had moved to New Orleans, he continued to maintain large land holdings in the area, including a tract located across the Mississippi River from Natchez in Concordia Parish, Louisiana. There a workforce of thirty-two slaves was maintained to work the property.[12]

As a successful merchant and planter, Kenner became associated with the social and political leaders of Natchez. Like other regions of the Old South, political leadership in the Natchez community was mostly limited to a small number of wealthy individuals who had both the leisure time and inclination necessary to sustain a position of influence. During the period of Spanish control of the region, Kenner established a close relationship with the Spanish adjutant major, Stephen Minor. A native of Pennsylvania, Minor was a close friend of the Spanish governor and was chosen to serve as the interim governor during the final months of Spanish possession of the area. With the signing of the Treaty of San Lorenzo on October 17, 1795, Spain relinquished its control of the Natchez District to the United States. When the Americans assumed control of the newly created Territory of Mississippi and gave it essentially the same boundaries as the old Natchez District, Kenner continued to be recognized as a community leader.[13]

The new American governor of the territory was Winthrop Sargent, a New Englander and Federalist. Appointed by President John Adams, the new governor turned to the local citizenry for assistance in organizing his administration and government. Seeking recommendations for suitable men for local offices, Sargent conferred with Andrew Ellicott, who had served as the U. S. boundary commissioner during the transfer of territorial ownership with Spain. Among Ellicott's suggestions was a recommendation of William Kenner. Soon after, on April 6, 1799, Governor Sargent appointed the twenty-two-year-old native Virginian to the influential position of justice of the peace for Adams County. A hold-over office from colonial America, the position of justice of the peace was such an essential component of government in the Old South and held such great influence upon the lives of a community's residents that historian Clement Eaton labeled those who held the job in early America as the "ruling oligarchies of the counties." Impressed with Kenner's abilities, the governor also appointed him to the post of captain in the Adams County militia.[14]

As a prominent official and an important merchant in the community, young Kenner's relationship with Stephen Minor grew closer. So fond of his young associate did the former Spanish official become that he offered to him the hand of his young daughter Mary. A delicate young girl only fourteen years-old at the time of her marriage, Mary was the only surviving child from her father's marriage to Martha Ellis, who had died in 1791. Bringing into her marriage a sizeable dowry of $70,000, Mary married William on November 19, 1801, in a wedding at the Minor family's estate at Concord Plantation at Natchez.[15]

In addition to being the date of his marriage, the year 1801 was an important milestone in the life of William Kenner for other reasons. The national election of 1800 was a political disaster for Governor Sargent's Federalist Party. Not only did they lose control of Congress to the Republicans but President Adams was defeated by Thomas Jefferson, who shortly after taking office replaced Sargent with William C.C. Claiborne. The change in political control marked a decline in the influence of the supporters of the Federalists, including Kenner. However, simultaneously with the political changes in Mississippi, economic opportunities elsewhere caught the interests of young Kenner. Pinckney's Treaty of 1795 between the United States and Spain granted the Americans the right of deposit in New Orleans. Though the treaty allowed American goods to transit the city, it stipulated that nothing was to be sold by Americans in the city. Fortunately, lax Spanish enforcement of trade restrictions offered ambitious Americans prospects for handsome profits. With his father-in-law's connections with the Spanish officials in New Orleans, opportunity called. William and his young bride made the decision to leave their family, friends, and comfortable lifestyle in Natchez to begin a new business venture and life in New Orleans. Though the exact date of the move is not known, it likely occurred after the couple's marriage in late 1801 and before 1803.[16]

At the beginning of the nineteenth century, New Orleans was becoming one of the leading urban centers in North America. Spain's lenient trade policies energized the city's economy and attracted new residents, including the Kenners. A cosmopolitan settlement with a population of approximately five thousand whites, three thousand slaves, and two thousand free-persons of color, most residents of New Orleans were of French descent. Upon arriving in New Orleans, William and Mary settled in the Vieux Carré section of the city and acquired a home at Number Seventeen on Bienville Street. Kenner established his business office at Number Nine Chartres Street, a short distance from his home, and he entered into a partnership with Stephen Henderson in a general mercantile and commission business. First called William Kenner and Company, the name was later changed to Kenner and Henderson and still later, when additional partners were added, to Kenner, Henderson, and Company. Eventually, once William ended his partnerships, he reverted the name of the company back to its original William Kenner and Company. Because of the limited volume of business in the city and the vagaries and unreliability of shipping, specialization in business was rare at the time in New Orleans. Like most merchants of the period, Kenner and Henderson were involved in a wide variety of services including the buying and selling of goods, assisting in the procuring of building materials that were not produced locally and other manufactured goods such as machinery, fine furniture, and fancy goods from the East Coast and Europe. Many of his business dealings involved his friends and former neighbors around Natchez, including John Bisland. A store owner in Cross Creek close to Natchez, Bisland sold cotton to Kenner and used his company's services to ship his crop out of New Orleans. Kenner's services to him included the loading and storing of Bisland's cotton in the Crescent City for a fee of $640 and an overall cost for Kenner's services of $2,638 or approximately $12 a bale. Kenner's business also engaged heavily in the western trade and provided arrangements for the shipping of the crops and products of the region's planters to northern and overseas markets. This was the situation in January 1811, when William Kenner & Company advertised in the *Le Courrier de la Louisiane* that the vessel *Mary* under the command of a Captain Robinson was to carry to Philadelphia a shipment of the company's goods that included locally produced sugar and molasses, as well as packing fabric and cases of Madeira and other wines. The company also organized lines of credit, wrote insurance, collected bills of exchange, and operated a retail business. For example on August 4, 1819, William Kenner and Company advertised in the *Orleans Gazette* that the company had ninety-five kegs of chewing tobacco for sale to the public at its location on Chartres

Street. Even after the death of William Kenner, his company remained in business and continued to offer an eclectic range of services. Nearly a year and a half after Kenner's death on November 3, 1825, the managers of the company made a large loan in the amount of $61,195.39 to John R. Holliday, Kenner's neighbor at the family's Cannes Brûlées property, for the operation of his Bell Grove Plantation.[17]

Another example of Kenner's business prowess was demonstrated in 1812, when he was no longer in partnership with Stephen Henderson, with the arrival of the first steamboat in the Crescent City. When the side-wheeler vessel *New Orleans* completed its historic trip to the city, it contained a consignment for his William Kenner and Company. In a letter to his father-in-law Stephen Minor at Natchez, William marveled at the impressive appearance the vessel had on the residents of the city. In his letter, he noted that, "He [the vessel] has been astonishing and amusing the multitude here by going down to the extremity of the English turn, returning in five hours, without setting any sail." He added that the vessel's "manouvring [*sic*] in the River . . . has exceeded the most sanguine expectations that had been formed by any person here."[18]

Because of the labor shortages that were ever present on the area's plantations, among the most unsavory, yet profitable, endeavors of the company was the buying and selling of slaves. The demands of large-scale commercial agriculture as practiced on the plantations along the Mississippi River required a large capable workforce. The native Indians of the area and many of the French settlers brought to the colony during the colonial era proved to be poor workers. Officials turned to the importation of slaves to address the colony's labor shortage. As early as the 1720s, slavery had become the dominant labor system on the plantations of Louisiana. This was true for the Cannes Brûlées concessions. However, the little settlement had some difficulty during its early years in obtaining enough slaves to meet its labor needs adequately. This fact was noted by government officials in a 1724 report on military conditions in the colony when they wrote that the concessions at Cannes Brûlées were "very well built" and had "very fine land" but lamented that because the d'Artaguiette estate had "but twelve" slaves the settlement was "not very rich in negroes [*sic*]."[19]

As immigration to the area increased with the American purchase of Louisiana and as the production of sugar cane proved profitable and spread across the southeastern portion of the territory, the demand for agricultural workers multiplied. As one of the leading commercial merchants in New Orleans at the time the demand for workers increased, William Kenner actively participated in the unsavory yet profitable trade of human merchandise. For those merchants who served as brokers in the slave trade, payment was typically 1.5 percent of the purchase price for both the seller and purchaser. A slave owner himself who kept a slave force on his properties at Natchez, Kenner showed no misgiving over his participation in the buying and selling of bondsmen. Indeed, in 1806, when it was still legal to import slaves into America directly from Africa, his company Kenner and Henderson went so far as to outfit the sixty-ton schooner *Reliance* in New Orleans for an African voyage, ostensibly to acquire slaves for the New Orleans market. Even after the foreign slave trade was ended in the United States in 1808, William continued for years to import slaves from other American cities for his company to sell. For example, in 1819 his company received a shipment by sea of ninety-nine slaves from Abner Robinson in Baltimore. The exact number of slaves handled by Kenner's company is unknown. However, records for a single nine-month period between 1821 and 1822 show that at least 322 slaves were processed by Kenner's company. In June, he acquired from John L. Tabb in Norfolk, Virginia, 116 slaves ranging in age from infancy to forty-one years, with the fifty-two males and sixty-four females being shipped to the Crescent City by sea on the brig *Dumfrees*. Four months later in October, the company received a second shipment from Tabb of 106 slaves. This time they were transported on the vessel *Brazillian*. Finally, four months later in February a shipment of one hundred slaves, insured for the value of $40,000, were brought to the city by the company in the brig *Fame*. These numbers of imported slaves by Kenner and his company made him a very active player in the perfidious slave trade and among New Orleans's leading slave importers during the early years of the nineteenth century.[20]

An ambitious entrepreneur, Kenner was always interested in expanding his business activities. A leading businessman in the rapidly expanding New Orleans of the time, he on occasion was called upon by others in the business community for advice and leadership. Over the years he operated his business in New Orleans, Kenner was selected to serve as a director on the boards of many of the city's most important businesses. Serving on as many as thirteen different boards, he was appointed to the directorships of some of the city's leading insurance companies and banks, including the Bank of New Orleans and the Louisiana branch of the prestigious Bank of the United States, where he was one of only thirteen local citizens appointed to the board of directors of the important national financial institution. Well respected by his business colleagues, he continued to be reelected to the directorship for years. With his Kenner and Henderson Company owning a large section of property along Bayou St. John, William was also selected to serve as a director of the bayou's improvement company. Similarly, in 1808, he was appointed to the directorship of the Orleans Navigation Company, which later acquired control from Congress of the Old Basin Canal (Carondelet Canal), a mile-and-a-half long channel which connected Bayou St. John to the rear of the Vieux Carré.[21]

Kenner's success in the business community in New Orleans led to his and Mary's acceptance among the political and social elite in the city. The acquisition of Louisiana by the Americans in 1803 opened the door to expanded freedom and openness in the city. During the Spanish regime authorities restricted all non-Catholic services. At the time of the Louisiana Purchase there was not a single Protestant church or Jewish synagogue in the territory. This quickly changed with the arrival of American authorities in New Orleans. On June 2, 1804, fifty-three Protestant residents of the Crescent City held a meeting in which they agreed to establish an Episcopal congregation in the city. Although this first Protestant church never appealed to more than a small fraction of the people of the region, it was an important organization. Naming itself Christ Church, the congregation included among its membership many of the most influential Americans who lived in early nineteenth-century New Orleans. Joining Kenner as a member of the congregation were prominent citizens John McDonogh; Edward Livingston; Maunsel White, a leader among the commercial and banking interest of the city; Thomas Urquhart, president of the Louisiana Bank; and B. Chew and R. D. Shepherd, both directors of the Bank of the United States. So respected was Kenner among the church's members that he was selected in 1805 to be a member of the congregation's original vestry.[22]

William's ability was also recognized by governmental leaders. Shortly after Louisiana was acquired by the United States, Congress divided the new territory into two areas: the Territory of Louisiana and the Territory of Orleans. The latter territory covered below the 33rd degree of latitude and approximated the current boundaries of the modern State of Louisiana. The same act of Congress provided for a temporary government of the new territories and called for the president to appoint a governor and a legislative body consisting of "thirteen of the most fit and discreet persons of the territory."[23] In response to the law, President Thomas Jefferson appointed William C. C. Claiborne governor of the new territory. Legislative authority in the territory was vested in the governor and in a unicameral body called the Legislative Council. The thirteen members of the council were appointed annually by the president. President Jefferson relied heavily on Governor Claiborne's recommendations in making his appointments to the legislative body. In a letter to the governor dated July 7, 1804, Jefferson directed that the council should be "composed of men of integrity, of understanding, of clear property and influence among the people, well acquainted with the laws, customs, and habits of the country." He added that the majority of the council should be "of sound American characters long established and esteemed there, and the rest of French and Spaniards, the most estimable and well affected." However, in spite of the broadness of the guidelines, Claiborne had difficulty in finding individuals to recommend to the president for appointment to the Legislative Council. Because they were not allowed to elect any officials in the new government, many residents of the territory opposed the plan and refused to participate. As late as December 1804, the governor was only able to find eight individuals willing and qualified to serve on the lawmaking council. Among those who accepted appointment to the council was William Kenner.[24]

Claiborne and Kenner were acquaintances from their time in Mississippi. Although there had been differences between the two men because of Kenner's support in Mississippi of Claiborne's political opponent, Governor Sargent, the relationship between the two men while in New Orleans was one of respect and a willingness to put their past political differences behind them. In a letter to the president on October 5, 1804, Claiborne recommended the appointment of Kenner to the legislative post as being "a native of the United States, an honest man and a respected merchant." Jefferson agreed and Kenner was duly appointed to the Legislative Council. However, his political career was short lived. The dissatisfaction in the territory over the form of the new government led the president to move quickly to find a more acceptable format. On March 2, 1805, Congress authorized Jefferson to establish a new government patterned after that of the Mississippi Territory. As such, a new bicameral legislature was created, comprising a twenty-five member house, with its members elected by the people to two-year terms, and a five-member legislative council appointed by the president. Whether by his choice or the president's is not known; nevertheless, Kenner was not selected to serve on the new legislative council, thus ending his career in public office.[25]

His short career as one of the first members of the territory's legislative council did not mark the end of Kenner's community service. Until his death he remained an active and concerned citizen. This was demonstrated during the War of 1812 when he provided valuable assistance to the government. The commander of American forces protecting the Gulf Coast from British attack, General Ferdinand Leigh Claiborne, often found himself without the needed resources to carry out his responsibilities. When ordered to provide the necessary medicine and supplies required to transfer a force of six hundred soldiers from Baton Rouge to the Alabama River, the general did not have the means to carry out his orders. Learning of the general's plight, Kenner joined with his wife's relatives, John and Stephen Minor, to advance sufficient funds to cover the cost of the troop transfer.[26]

An ambitious entrepreneur, Kenner was not content with only operating his merchant business in New Orleans. As he had done at Natchez, Kenner invested in large land tracts in the city and the region. In addition to the tract of land his company owned along Bayou St. John, he joined in partnerships with Theophilus Minor, his wife's uncle, in acquiring a three-quarter interest in the large Linwood Plantation in Ascension Parish and with Benjamin Morgan in obtaining a section of land at Cannes Brûlées. The relationship between Kenner and Morgan was more than just a business partnership. Before joining in their joint land ownership, the two men had known each other and worked together for some time. Both had served together as members of the

Legislative Council and as members on various business directorships, including the Louisiana branch of the Bank of the United States.[27]

Kenner and Morgan acquired their tract of real estate at Cannes Brûlées from Louis Trudeau, who had obtained rights to the property during the Spanish period. The property fronted along the Mississippi River for a distance of twenty arpents and abutted the St. Charles Parish line all the way back to Lake Pontchartrain, a distance slightly less than five miles. However, only the section closest to the river to a depth of approximately forty arpents or three-quarters of a mile was developed during the plantation period. Existing records do not reveal the specific date of Kenner's and Morgan's purchase of the property. Neither do they reveal the date nor the circumstances of Kenner's acquisition of Morgan's share of the estate. It is known that by 1811 ownership of the property had changed, with the Cannes Brûlées estate still being owned by William Kenner but now with a new business partner, Steven Henderson. It was under the Kenner and Henderson ownership that sugar became the primary crop of the estate. In 1811, Kenner and Henderson divided their operations between two companies, William Kenner and Company and Stephen Henderson and Company. With the split, William acquired sole ownership of the Cannes Brûlées property and soon after decided it was an ideal site for a country home.[28]

A leading merchant in New Orleans, Kenner became an active player in Louisiana's agricultural industry. As a commercial agent he assisted the region's planters in many activities, including helping them find markets for their crops, the purchasing and selling of slaves, and the obtaining of supplies and equipment. Agents such as Kenner also assisted in performing the valuable service of furnishing credit to planters until their crops were sold at market. Kenner's skill as a commercial agent as well as his professional and personal contacts helped him to establish an impressive list of clients ranging from his brother-in-law John Minor to several members of the prominent Bringier family who owned multiple properties in both New Orleans and along the Mississippi River in St. James and Ascension parishes. Dealing with some of the area's most successful planters stirred Kenner's entrepreneurial interest and led him to turn his attention towards acquiring rural lands at both Cannes Brûlées and in Ascension Parish that could be used for commercial crop agriculture. His focusing on rural properties coincided with the movement among the region's planters of switching from a diversified crop structure with an emphasis on the growing of indigo and other crops such as cotton to the large-scale production of sugarcane. It took some time for this transition to be completed. In spite of crop failures in the production of indigo during the period of Spanish dominance, early attempts in Louisiana at sugarcane cultivation had also ended in failure. However, planters in colony continued to work on improving the crop until the final years of the eighteenth century, when they produced a successful and profitable sugar crop and gave birth to the Louisiana's sugar industry.[29]

Kenner was among the earliest growers to realize the economic potential sugar offered to the region. He was soon growing the crop at both of his rural properties. Both of his plantations, Linwood in Ascension Parish and Oakland at Cannes Brûlées, appear to have been named by him after estates he knew and admired in Natchez, with Oakland apparently being named for the Natchez plantation of Dr. William N. Mercer, the husband of Mary Kenner's cousin Anna Farrar. Located less than twenty miles upriver from the center of New Orleans, the Cannes Brûlées property could be conveniently reached by riverboat by the Kenners and eventually became the preferred estate of the family. As such, it was where William constructed his country home. When constructed, the Cannes Brûlées plantation house was similar in design to that of the Belle Grove and other manor houses of the time. What is known of the Oakland house is largely derived from a brief description of the property published in 1876 and old photos taken of the building shortly before it was abandoned and consumed by the Mississippi River in the later years of the nineteenth century. The house included many of the elements of the classical French-style plantation home common to the time. The structure included multiple levels where the family resided. Its roof was high pitched with two dormers in the front (and probably rear) and one on each side of the house to promote ventilation. Both levels of the house included a center entrance that opened to a central hallway that ran back to front through the house. A single double-hung window was located to the left and right of each entrance into the house. The lower gallery was supported by the traditional brick and plaster Tuscan columns that circled the house. However, the design of the upper-level gallery somewhat broke with tradition of instead of using colonettes, which was the common practice of the time. Kenner used a more substantial Tuscan column on the second level of his house, which presented the appearance of a tapered sturdy column running from the ground to the roof line. Having eight rooms in total, the large two story structure would have been considered quite a home for the period in which it was constructed.[30]

As a favorite of the Kenner family, they spent many happy times at the Cannes Brûlées estate enjoying life away from the city. The family's attachment to their country home was evident in a note written by William in 1813 from his home in New Orleans to his wife's father at Natchez. In the note, he yearned for a return to his Oakland home "where things really look charmingly." Kenner proudly concluded his comments to his father-in-law with the boast that his Cannes Brûlées estate possessed "the finest crop of corn in Louisiana and about ninety acres of prime cane."[31] Being one of the first Anglo-Americans to become involved in the growing and making of sugar, Kenner's effort at producing the crop proved to be both successful and lucrative. He soon became one of the major producers of the crop in the New Orleans area. As a successful sugar plantation, the Oakland property encompassed a variety of structures, including the family's raised manor home and a sugar mill, office building, multiple slave quarters, and barns for

The Kenner family's Oakland Plantation house as it appeared in the late nineteenth century, shortly before being abandoned.

the work animals.[32]

Despite serious financial reverses towards the end of his life, at the time of his death in 1824, Kenner's estate at Oakland had grown in value to $80,257, and his total assets amounted to $277,288. These figures included the value of the sizeable workforces and livestock he maintained at his two Louisiana plantations. At his death, Kenner maintained a workforce at Linwood of 148 slaves, while at the smaller Oakland estate he kept sixty-three slaves, eight of whom were house servants. Because each estate was essentially a self-sufficient operation, a successful plantation operation required a wide variety of materials and items as demonstrated by an inventory of items kept at the Oakland Plantation. Made shortly after Kenner's death, the inventory included an office, sugar mill, sundry other buildings, twenty-two horses and mules, thirty oxen, twenty cows and calves, fifty sheep, fifteen hogs, one dray, two ox carts, three horse carts, seven ploughs, five harrows, forty-six hoes, thirty-six spades, twenty-four axes, a set of blacksmith's tools, some carpenters' tools, and a four-wheel carriage.[33]

When Kenner was joined at Oakland by his wife and children, the plantation became a beehive of family activities. William and Mary had seven children, three girls and four boys. All save one of the children lived to middle age. The couple's first born, Maria, died in October 1806, when she was only three-years old. Their other daughters were Martha and Frances Ann. Martha was born on September 28, 1804, while her mother was visiting with her family at their Concord Plantation in Natchez. Before her death in 1873, she would have three husbands, including John B. Humphreys, a nephew of John Brown, the owner of Roseland Plantation in St. Charles Parish and one of Louisiana's first U. S. senators. Her second husband was a Mr. Brice of whom scant information is known. Her third spouse was Charles Oxley, an Englishman from Liverpool who was a merchant in New Orleans. Frances Ann, who was born in New Orleans in 1806, married John Dick, an attorney who became U. S. Attorney for Louisiana. Following his death, she married George Currie Duncan, another Englishman who was one of the region's leading bankers. Until she died in 1875, Frances Ann remained a leading socialite in New Orleans.[34]

William and Mary's first son was born on February 18, 1808. Stephen Minor Kenner was named for his grandfather. Known throughout his life as Minor Kenner, he married Eliza Davis and operated Bell Grove Plantation, which was located slightly down river from his family's Oakland property. William and Mary's second son, William Butler, was born on March 11, 1810. Called Butler, he married Ruhamsh Riske of Cincinnati, Ohio and, after his parents died, lived at Oakland Plantation. On January 18, 1812, George, the third son of the Kenners was born. He was the only child of Mary and William to leave Louisiana permanently. As a young man, after spending some time at the family's Linwood Plantation (later renamed Ashland by Duncan Kenner) in Ascension Parish, he moved to Kentucky where he met and married Charlotte Riske Jones, the sister to Butler's wife Ruhamsh. The couple eventually moved to Matagorda County in Texas, where they lived growing sugar until his death in 1852.[35]

As with his older brothers, the family's youngest son, Duncan Farrar, was a native son of New Orleans. Born on February 11, 1813, Duncan eventually became the most successful and famous member of the family. Owner of Ashland, one of Louisiana's largest and grandest plantations, Duncan became a leading figure in both the state's sugar industry and the thoroughbred horse racing and breeding industry. In addition to his business and sporting ventures, he had a notable political career. Winning election to the state legislature at age twenty-three, Duncan rose in influence to become a leader in the Whig political party in Louisiana. In 1852, he was chosen president of Louisiana's 1852 Constitutional Convention. A fervent supporter of secession, Duncan held a seat in the provisional Congress of the Confederacy and the Confederate House of Representatives, where he served as chair of the important Ways and Means Committee. In 1865 he was appointed minister plenipotentiary by Confederate President Jefferson Davis and was sent on a perilous mission to Europe to offer the abolition of slavery in the South in exchange for diplomatic recognition by the major European powers.[36]

Although comfortable in comparison to the lifestyles and living conditions experienced by most other residents of the New Orleans and Cannes Brûlées regions, the lives of the members of the Kenner family were far from the serene and leisured experience sometimes depicted in the romantic legends and literature of the Old South. In reality, the great majority of plantation owners were working farmers who managed the day-to-day activities of their properties. Aided by an overseer and several slave drivers, William Kenner took a more direct hand in the operations of his Oakland property in Jefferson Parish than he did at his upriver Linwood Plantation in Ascension Parish. There he seemed to have used a manager to supervise the day-to-day operations of the plantation. The close proximity of the Cannes Brûlées site to New Orleans allowed the Kenners to easily travel by steamboat back and forth to the property from their home in the city.[37]

Even for members of the elite class, including the Kenners, life in old Louisiana during the first decades of the nineteenth century was at times dangerous and a threat to both the health and fortune of those who chose to live there. Danger came in many forms, some natural and some manmade. Among the most persistent dangers, which remain to this day as a shadow over the residents of the region, was the threat of flooding. Sometimes endangered by high waters brought by either the visit of powerful tropical storms from the Gulf of Mexico or more regularly by the annual rise of the Mississippi River, the people of the Cannes Brûlées area had to remain on vigilant guard to protect against the arrival of high water. To threaten the Cannes Brûlées settlement, storm waters typically traveled from the un-protected shores of Lake Pontchartrain across miles of swamp and grasslands before reaching the settled area along the river. Though not as damaging as river floods, lake floods were much more numerous. The more feared threat of flooding came from the great river. Although the Mississippi River itself built natural levees by depositing sediments during its annual high-water periods, from the earliest days of European settlement along the river, efforts were made to build higher levees. The endeavor never stopped. By the time William Kenner acquired Oakland Plantation, the levee system along the river ran from slightly below the city upriver for approximately 155 miles on the east bank and 180 miles on the west bank. Though these manmade structures protected the region during most high-water periods, they also produced a sense of security which could produce tragic consequences when they failed and residents had to deal with the dreaded disaster of a levee collapse or crevasse. The sudden release during periods of high-river levels of racing torrents of water from the mighty river through a breech in the levee could have calamitous consequences for not only the plantation where the break occurred but also for neighbors in areas for miles around.[38]

On at least two occasions William Kenner had to handle the devastation wrought by levee breaks at his Oakland property. The first crevasse at the Kenner plantation occurred in 1813. Following the practice of the time, the Orleans Police Jury, the local governing authority, ordered the planters in the area to supply slave workers to help Kenner repair the levee break. Planters who failed to send the requisite number of workers were fined five dollars a head for each worker they were short. Closing the 1813 crevasse was more difficult than expected and in order to be completed required additional slaves from Metairie estates being called to work the repairs. So expensive and difficult was the effort to repair the levee at Oakland that ten-years later when a second crevasse took place at almost the same location, the police jury demurred from aiding Kenner with an expensive work force. Instead, it established a committee of planters who were experienced in levee repair to prepare a report on the crevasse at Oakland. In spite of the lack of mandated assistance from the police jury, William, using mostly his own resources, was able to repair successfully the damage to the levee in 1823.[39]

Though danger from floods and levee breaks remained a recurring threat to their safety, the event that brought the greatest threat to the safety of the planters living in the region of Cannes Brûlées did not come as a result of a natural disaster. Late in the evening of January 8, 1811, the largest slave rebellion in North American history erupted on the plantation of Colonel Manuel Andry, a little over twenty miles upriver from the Cannes Brûlées property of Kenner and his partner Steven Henderson. Court records from the time suggest that perhaps the primary leader of the revolt, Charles Deslondes, planned the event, which originated on the plantations located between present-day communities of Norco in St. Charles Parish and LaPlace in St. John the Baptist Parish. Although the exact number of participants remains uncertain, historians estimate that participants in the event probably ranged between two and three hundred.[40] Once the group organized, it began a march along the levee down the east bank of the river towards New Orleans. Nearly all of the participants in the revolt made their homes on the various plantations and farms that were located along the east bank of the Mississippi River. As the group moved down the river road, additional slaves joined the effort. They pillaged or destroyed several homes, including three plantations, and other holdings of the area's white families they came across. Unaccountably, they left other properties, including some of the largest manor homes located along their route, such as the large manor house at the Destrehan estate, undamaged. Word of the uprising spread quickly. Terrified whites in the path of the advancing slave force hastily retreated to the safety of New Orleans. It is not known if at the time of the event any members of the Kenner family were at the Kenner and Henderson property at Cannes Brûlées.[41] No doubt, with the angry slave force approaching the western boundary of the plantation, any members of the family at the property fell in with most of the whites who lived in the region and joined the exodus of refugees who were in the process of fleeing the area in advance of the approaching slave force.[42]

When the rebel slaves reached the Kenner and Henderson plantation, they were met with enthusiasm by some members of the estate's slave force. Harry Kenner, a twenty-five year-old light-skinned mulatto who was a native of Virginia, was an early participant in the revolt, having met previously with leaders of the rebellion while they were still at the Andry plantation. A passionate supporter of the effort, he was later identified by other slaves as one of the "most outstanding brigands" of the revolt.[43] With the arrival of the rebellious slaves, Harry quickly obtained the active support of other members of the Kenner and Henderson slave force. At least a dozen males from the plantation joined the rebellion. Among those whose identities are known were plowmen and carters, Peter, Croaker, Smillet, Nontoun, and Charles. Skilled laborers who also joined the effort included a slave driver named Elisha, the blacksmith Jerry, the stableboy Major, the coachmen Joseph and Guiam (also a sugar worker), and the skilled sugar hand, Harry. Lindor, another coachman and carter, acted as the group's drummer and helped to organize a charge against the nearby home of Cadet Fortier, which was led by Guiam waving a saber while on a horse commandeered from his masters.[44]

With the exception of recruiting some members of the estate's slave force to join their ill-fated venture of marching on New Orleans, the rebellious slaves appear to have done relatively little damage to the property at Cannes Brûlées. Some tools that could be used as weapons and a few animals were taken, but there is no record of any structures on the estate being destroyed. After reaching the Kenner and Henderson estate, the rebel force continued a short distance down river to the plantation of Jacques Fortier, near the eastern boundary of the modern city of Kenner. It marked the spot closest to New Orleans that the slave force reached and the location where the slaves were first confronted by the armed force sent to meet them. Prompt mobilization by volunteer forces, the militia, and regular army units in the region and their tactic of moving on the slaves from different directions resulted in a bloody crushing of the revolt. Though superior in numbers, the slave army, armed with cane knives, axes, other farm tools, and a few small arms, was no match for the well-armed counter force. When confronted at the Fortier plantation by the better equipped forces of militiamen and planters under the command of U.S. General Wade Hampton,[45] the slave force retreated upriver where they made a stand at the plantation of Francois Bernard Bernoudi (Bernoudy)—near modern day New Sarpy in St. Charles Parish. Caught in a flanking movement by the militia and volunteers under the command of Manuel Andry, the larger slave army was soon crushed by the bloody attack of the counter force. Dozens were killed and many others were wounded and captured, with one leader of the attacking force later proclaiming, "We made considerable slaughter."[46] The official numbers on the revolt included two whites killed by the slaves prior to the battle and sixty-six slaves killed or summarily executed, seventeen missing, and sixteen captured and held for trial. Over the next days and weeks, additional participants were captured and added to the those standing trial. Eventually twenty-one of the captured slaves were found guilty by a tribunal of local officials and planters and were sentenced to death. Some were taken to their home plantations where they were shot by a militia firing-squad. Their heads were cut off and placed upon poles placed at plantations and along the river as a warning to other slaves. Others were executed by hanging with their heads and bodies left on display as a gruesome warning to others as to the consequences of rebellion.[47] One eyewitness to the events surrounding the trials and punishments of the rebels noted the gruesome nature of events by commenting that "executions by hanging and beheading are going on daily."[48] Edward Palfrey, another visitor in the city at the time of the trials, wrote home to family in Massachusetts and observed:

> Poor wretches! They are now suffering the punishment of their foolish wickedness. Government has hung one every day since their trial commenced. They hung one yesterday and one today. After they have hung the negroes, [sic] they cut off their heads and stick it on a pole, and set it up in the street.[49]

Months after the trials and executions had ended the decaying remains of the executed slaves remained on public display as a lesson for all to see.

Not all slaves accused of participating in the revolt were found guilty and punished with execution. Some faced lessor punishments, including being lashed and forced to witness the executions of friends. For example, the St. Charles Parish tribunal found one of Kenner and Henderson's slaves, Bausson, to be innocent and returned him to his masters. However, of the dead, at least eleven are known to have been individuals owned by Kenner and Henderson. Of this number, three, including Harry, Guiam, and Joseph were executed after being found guilty by a court in St. Charles Parish and four others, Charles, Lindor, Nontoun, and Smillet were executed on orders of the court in St. John the Baptist Parish. In the end, it is estimated that a total of 115 slaves were killed, jailed, or went missing during the event. Once the revolt's participants were captured and punished, the territorial legislature reimbursed the planters for their losses in manpower by providing a payment of $300 to each plantation owner for every slave lost in the insurrection.[50]

The abortive slave rebellion of 1811 was not the last of William Kenner's problems.[51] International tensions concerning the ongoing war in Europe between France and England created difficulties for the planter-merchant. The prewar embargo imposed by President Jefferson and Congress on trade and the coming of the War of 1812 resulted in a serious decline to Kenner's business. Because it was so heavily dependent upon commerce and trade, the war and the British blockade wreaked havoc on William's ability to carry on his business, However, it was not the war and its negative economic effects nor even the actual invasion of the area by British troops that brought the greatest upheaval and forlornness to the Kenners. In the autumn of 1814 as the people

The daughter of an influential Spanish official in Natchez, Mary Minor Kenner married William Kenner at age fourteen. The mother of seven, Mary died in 1814 at the family's Oakland Plantation at Cannes Brûlées.

of Louisiana and the rest of the United States fretted over the status of the war with Great Britain, William and his family confronted a far more meaningful reality and tragedy that forever altered the close and happy ways members of the Kenner family had long enjoyed. Death was no stranger to the residents of nineteenth-century Louisiana. The effects of the area's climate on the population were noted by the traveler Josiah Gregg when he wrote that, "it is no wonder that the air of New Orleans should be generally so unhealthy, and in autumn quite pestilential, for the town was built in a complete swamp." He prophetically concluded his observation that the area was so unhealthy that it was "never intended by nature [to be] the abode of men . . . . It is the Churchyard of the United States."[52]

Although Mary Kenner had grown up in the region and enjoyed a standard of living that few women of the South of that period got to experience, the unavoidable burdens of being a wife and mother in early nineteenth-century Louisiana took their toll on the delicate body of the twenty-seven-year-old mother of seven. For months leading up to the fateful day, she was in declining health. In June, William wrote to Mary's father that nearly everyone in his family was "sick with violent colds and soreness in the breast." He added that Mary was the sickest because her illness was accompanied by fever. After having seemingly recovered from her June illness, she again fell ill in late summer while at the family's

Oakland home at Cannes Brûlées. The family's physician, Dr. Cochrane, was summoned, and he reassured the family that although "severe," Mary's condition "was not very dangerous." In spite of the doctor's optimistic diagnosis, her condition did not improve. By early October, so serious had the situation become that Dr. Flood, a more experienced physician, was summoned from New Orleans. His arrival brought hope and though at first she seemed to respond to the new treatment, soon it was evident to all that death was near. Her six living children were called to her bedside, where they remained with their father until Mary's death came at approximately three o'clock on the afternoon of October 5, 1814. As she had wished, Mary was laid to rest the next morning in a grave in the Protestant section of the Old St. Louis Cemetery in New Orleans. An observer at the funeral later recalled that, "perhaps no event of the same nature has occurred here for many years which excited more sensibility, or was generally lamented."[53]

William was disconsolate over the loss of Mary. Family members and friends offered their assistance to him and his surviving six children, all of whom were under the age of ten. Friends attempted to persuade Kenner with his children to accompany them to their homes for rest. When he refused to leave his home, friends and relatives arranged for a week of alternating visits among themselves so that the family would not be left without companionship. In spite of the burden of single parenting such a large family, William kept his family together until they were old enough to attend boarding schools. With educational opportunities limited in Louisiana, Kenner, as did many other parents in his social class, eventually enrolled his children, both daughters and sons, in schools out of state.[54]

With the end of the war with Great Britain in 1815, Kenner's business ventures once again returned to prosperity. So successful was his economic rebound that he was able to purchase 1,200 acres from Wade Hampton and add it to his Linwood Plantation in Ascension Parish and construct for his family in 1822 a new elegant three-story brick city home in New Orleans at No. 13 Royal Street in the Vieux Carré. Unfortunately, Kenner's good fortune in his business operations did not last. Sometime before the start of his financial troubles William had brought into his business two trusted associates. Richard Claque had joined Kenner in his business operations during the period prior to the death of Mary Kenner. John Oldham was brought into the company in 1819 with Kenner's expectation that his "mercantile knowledge, ability, and activity [would] afford . . . great additional aid in transacting to the best advantage the concerns of our friends."[55] Unfortunately, this enthusiasm for Oldham's ability was not fulfilled. After only a year, the relationship between the two men fell apart and Oldham's actions led to a loss of a large portion of the company's assets and valuables.[56] The quarrel between the two continued for some time, with both Oldham and Claque becoming entangled in legal actions which went on for years, including after Kenner's death when both men were recognized by the courts as creditors of and syndics for the company. The business dispute greatly disrupted Kenner's ability to carry on his mercantile operations. Unable to meet his business partnership's financial responsibilities, William was forced to declare bankruptcy.[57]

The failure of the business that he had worked so diligently to build placed a great deal of stress upon Kenner. Fortunately, friends and relatives assisted him in his effort to survive the financial crisis. Among those who aided in the effort was William's very able attorney, Etienne Mazureau. A state senator and attorney general (1820-1823), Mazureau was able to save a sufficient portion of William's resources to allow him and his family to continue to live comfortably. Though mortgaged heavily, both of his valuable sugar plantations, Linwood and Oakland, remained in his possession. Even William Kenner and Company survived the crisis and continued to operate in a reorganized mode until after Kenner's death. Kenner was even able to complete for his family the new house on Royal Street mentioned above. Nevertheless, despite his success in surviving the financial crisis that threatened his company, financial obligations resulting from the crisis continued to weigh both financially and personally upon him. A stout, florid gentleman, with mild blue eyes and large spectacles, Kenner always carried out his dealings energetically. Though he was not legally obligated to do so, he set himself the goal of rebuilding his finances and to pay back anyone who may have lost money from the bankruptcy of his company. Unfortunately, he would not be able to carry out his plan. On March 2, 1824, as the family happily made preparations for the marriage in a few days of his eldest surviving child Martha, the forty-seven-year-old planter and businessman suffered a paralytic stroke.

The stroke affected the left side of his body, his speech, and his mind. Though in the days after the attack some improvement took place, it was evident to his children and friends that there would be no meaningful recovery.[58]

Realizing the gravity of her father's illness, Martha decided to proceed with her wedding so that he could witness the event. On the day of the nuptials, William remained partially paralyzed and mentally confused, and he asked that the ceremony take place in the morning. This was done. Sadly, by mid-afternoon he had no recollection of the morning's event and asked when the marriage would take place. Never regaining his presence of mind, his health gradually worsened over the next months. Finally, less than a month before his forty-eighth birthday, on May 10, 1824, at eleven-thirty in the evening at his home on Royal Street, he breathed his last.[59]

3
Kennerville

William Kenner's death in 1824 shook the Kenner and Minor families to their roots. In the space of a single decade the young children of William and Mary Kenner lost both of their parents. With the climate and conditions of the region being as they were, it was not an uncommon event for young children to be orphaned. Fortunately, the Kenners had resources and options that few families of the time and place could utilize. When William died, his two oldest daughters, Martha and Frances Ann, were married. Among his four sons, Stephen Minor was the eldest at age sixteen. He was followed by William Butler age fourteen, George Rappele age twelve and, at age eleven, Duncan Farrar. The adolescents were hardly prepared to assume independence and the operation of their father's business and his plantations. Relatives and friends in both New Orleans and Natchez offered their help to the young men. However, the court turned to their new brother-in-law, John B. Humphreys, Martha's husband and sugar planter at Roseland plantation in St. Charles Parish, to serve as the Kenner boys' "curator and tutor." Also coming to the aid of the family was their father's attorney, Etienne Mazureau. A native of France and a respected lawyer in the state who had served as Louisiana's attorney general and secretary of state, Mazureau had been instrumental in helping William survive his financial crisis of a few years prior. Though William endured the worse consequences of his financial misfortunes, aspects of the crisis continued to plague his estate up until the time of his death.[1]

In spite of their father's financial problems at the time of his death, each of William Kenner's six surviving children received substantial assets from his estate, which totaled $277,288. In his will, written in July 1823, he simply requested that everything he possessed be equally divided among his children "under the direction and friendly care of my worthy friends Philip Minor, Abner S. Duncan, and John Dick."[2] Estate assets, large and small, were either liquidated or divided among the children. Items ranged in uniqueness and value from his Oakland property and house at Cannes Brûlées, which was valued at $80,257, to his pew in Christ Episcopal Church, which carried a price of $500. During the time that their father's estate was being settled and for some time thereafter, the Kenner boys focused their attentions on their schooling, with all of them eventually going north to attend college.[3]

As they matured, the Kenners' interest turned to their land holdings in both Jefferson and Ascension parishes. Once the estates of their parents were settled and the boys had completed their schooling, the Kenner children began to consolidate their shares of the family's estate. The two sisters of the family were married to wealthy men with interest separate from their brothers. Martha was married to a well-to-do St. Charles Parish sugar planter, John B. Humphreys, and Frances Ann was married to George Currie Duncan, an Englishman by birth and one of New Orleans's leading bankers. Her first husband, John Dick, who served as U. S. Attorney for Louisiana and who had been named in her father's will as an executor of his estate, had died near the same time as her father in 1824. With their own families and business issues to manage, both sisters sold or transferred their shares of the Kenner properties to their four brothers. The brothers decided it was beneficial for them to reorganize their holdings in order that each of them receive a sufficient sized property that would allow each to be able to establish an estate of their own. It was decided that the two older Kenner brothers, Stephen Minor and William Butler, would concentrate their efforts on the family's holdings at Cannes Brûlées. The youngest two boys, George and Duncan, who were only a year apart in age and were much attached to each other, decided to unite together to further develop their father's Linwood Plantation in Ascension Parish. Over time they acquired neighboring lands and soon had an estate of nearly

2,500 acres that they renamed Ashland. Duncan eventually acquired sole ownership of the property when George married and moved away to establish his own sugar plantation in Matagorda County, Texas.[4]

At Cannes Brûlées, Stephen Minor and William Butler—known throughout their lives as Minor and Butler—continued to consolidate their holdings. By 1836, each brother owned an undivided half interest in Oakland Plantation.[5] The two men then acquired three one-arpent lots from the neighboring Bell Grove Plantation owned by Maria Holliday, the widow of John Robert Holliday. The lots extended from the river all the way back to the shoreline of Lake Pontchartrain. On June 15, 1840, Minor Kenner sold his share of the plantation to his brother, making Butler Kenner full owner of Oakland Plantation with its buildings, machinery, livestock, and a slave force of eighty-three. At the time of the sale, Oakland stretched twenty-three arpents (21.16 acres) along the Mississippi.[6]

After selling his share of the Oakland estate, Minor remained in the area[7] and eventually married Eliza Davis, the daughter of Mrs. Holliday and her first husband William Davis. When Maria Holliday died in 1842, Minor and Eliza acquired her mother's Bell Grove

Sketch by Philip Chadwick Foster Smith of Minor Kenner's Bell Grove Plantation house based on a fragile 1837 drawing of the structure archived in the New Orleans Notarial Archives.

Plantation located a short distance down river from Oakland. Slightly larger than Butler's Oakland property, with a frontage along the river of twenty-four and a half arpents, the property also stretched all the way to the lake. Minor extended his holdings even further down river with the purchase of Aimme Durel's (the widow of Jacques Fortier) Pasture Plantation, which lay adjacent to Belle Grove.[8] The Kenners had been interested in the Pasture property for some time. Minor's brothers, Butler, Duncan, and George had acquired three parcels of the property in 1835, 1840, and 1843. However, by 1845 the brothers had decided on the division of their father's holdings, with the siblings dividing their interest between their father's Jefferson and Ascension Parish properties. As a result of that decision, the Pasture property was consolidated under the sole ownership of Minor. Hence, as early as 1843, all of the lands which would one day comprise the modern city of Kenner were owned by members of the Kenner family.[9]

By the time William Kenner's sons assumed control of their inheritance, the growing of sugar cane dominated the agricultural industry along the lower Mississippi River in southeast Louisiana. The good times and large profits earned by the sugar planters resulted in the industry spreading westward in the state to the Teche and Vermillion watersheds and as far north as Pointe Coupée Parish and the Red River Valley above Baton Rouge. As noted in the items included in the succession of William Kenner, the operation of a successful sugar plantation required a wide variety of materials and equipment. Including such items as simple hand tools, livestock, support buildings, workers, and a mill, a sugar plantation such as the ones operated by the Kenner brothers required an investment of many thousands of dollars. The price of equipping an average-size sugarhouse for a plantation alone cost approximately $50,000. Added to that sizeable expense was the cost of acquiring workers for the plantation. With the exception of a few skilled artisans and mechanics whose specialized services were required from time to time, the hard, daily work of a sugar plantation was performed by a workforce of purchased slaves. The rapid expansion of the sugar industry in Louisiana led to an increased demand for slaves—and a profitable business opportunity for William Kenner. The increased demand also resulted in a rapid increase in the prices planters were forced to pay in expanding their labor forces. Most slaves on the

Kenner plantations were obtained on the New Orleans slave market. Prices at the market varied from about $600 for a prime field hand at the end of the 1820s to $1,200 to $1,500 in the 1850s. Skilled slaves such as carpenters and blacksmiths brought even higher prices, with some selling for as much as $2,000 to $3,000 dollars in the period shortly before the Civil War.[10]

Although there were larger sugar-producing estates upriver from the Butler and Minor Kenner's plantations, in Jefferson Parish the Kenners were among the top sugar growers. As noted in the following chart, except for times when the their lands were flooded, in the years prior to the Civil War the Kenner plantations annually produced respectable sized sugar crops. One reason for the success of their sugar plantations was their dedication to the use of technology and improved farming methods. For example, they were among the first planters in Jefferson Parish to acquire a vacuum-pan system for processing the juice of the cane into sugar. Considered to be the most revolutionary development in the sugar-making process in the period prior to the Civil War, the vacuum pan was more complicated and expensive to purchase than the older steam and open kettle method of sugar making used by most planters in the state. The progressive nature of the Kenner brothers' dedication to technology is highlighted by the fact that in 1853, almost two decades after the improved device became available, they were the only planters in Jefferson with the superior vacuum-pan equipment. At that time across the state, out of the 1,481 sugar mills in operation, only fifty-three had adopted the new advanced equipment. So successful were their efforts that by 1850, Butler's Oakland Plantation alone was valued at the notable sum for the time of $200,000.[11]

As was the situation on plantations across the sugar-growing regions of Louisiana, production totals on the Kenner estates varied widely from year to year. Production figures from one year to another could double in size or fall by fifty percent or more. During the antebellum years for which production figures are available, the two Kenner brothers produced an average annual crop of 476 hogsheads (1,000 pound barrels) of sugar. Of the three Kenner family properties in Jefferson Parish, the largest sugar yield in any one year came in 1854 when their Pasture property produced 1,145 hogsheads of sugar. Over the years that the family produced sugar on their properties in Jefferson

Table 1:
Antebellum Sugar Production at Kenner Family Plantations in Jefferson Parish

Harvest Year	Name	Plantation	Yield in 1000 lb hogsheads
1845	**Butler Kenner**	**Oakland**	**675**
	Minor Kenner	**Belle Grove**	**756**
1846	**Butler Kenner**	**Oakland**	**328**
	Minor Kenner	**Belle Grove**	**201**
	Minor Kenner	**Pasture**	**400**
1850	**Butler Kenner**	**Oakland**	**500**
	Minor Kenner	**Belle Grove**	**409**
	Minor Kenner	**Pasture**	**302**
1851	**Butler Kenner**	**Oakland**	**95 (overflowed)**
	Minor Kenner	**Belle Grove**	**0 (overflowed)**
	Minor Kenner	**Pasture**	**350 (overflowed)**
1852	**Butler Kenner**	**Oakland**	**300**
	Minor Kenner	**Pasture**	**875**
1853	**Butler Kenner**	**Oakland**	**625***
	Minor Kenner	**Pasture**	**820***
1854	**Butler Kenner**	**Oakland**	**650**
	Minor Kenner	**Pasture**	**1145**
1855	**Mrs. W. Butler Kenner**	**Oakland**	**640**
1856	**Mrs. W. Butler Kenner**	**Oakland**	**640**
1857	**Mrs. W. Butler Kenner**	**Oakland**	**150**
1858	**Mrs. W. Butler Kenner**	**Oakland**	**260**
1859	**Mrs. W. Butler Kenner**	**Oakland**	**475***
1860	**Mrs. W. Butler Kenner**	**Oakland**	**150**
1861	**Mrs. W. Butler Kenner**	**Oakland**	**490**
1862	**Mrs. W. Butler Kenner**	**Oakland**	**550**

- **Years when the Kenners were the largest sugar producers in Jefferson Parish.**

Parish, Oakland Plantation served as the center of the family's sugar operations. Between 1845 and 1862—the years for which reliable production figures are available—Oakland produced twenty-three seasonal sugar crops; whereas the Belle Grove estate was used only for three seasons and Pasture Plantation produced for only six seasons. The ups and downs of the Kenners' production figures highlight the fact that in spite of the industry's profitable nature, there was no guarantee of yearly success. Profits and successful crops were dependent upon a large variety of factors including plant diseases, rainfall, floods, hurricanes, freezing temperatures, and manufacturing and labor difficulties. For example, in 1851, the difficulties began in February with the destruction by fire of Minor's sugarhouse and all of its expensive equipment. Later the same year the spring high-water levels brought flooding from a crevasse on Minor's plantation. So catastrophic were his losses that they led Minor to begin to look elsewhere for a means to make his Belle Grove property profitable. After the fire and flood of 1851, Minor never again produced a sugar crop at Belle Grove.[12]

The desperation and toil that planters faced when dealing with levee breaks was a part of life for all who lived along the Mississippi River. The heroic aspects of the struggle to keep the mighty river in its banks were aptly captured by an un-named reporter who, while visiting the region in the spring of 1849, was able to witness firsthand a break in the levee at Butler Kenner's Oakland Plantation and the fevered battle to prevent the break from becoming a full-blown disaster. Originally written for the *New Orleans Delta*, the dramatic story was reported in papers in other states, including the *Davenport Gazette* under the title "A Night at a Crevasse." According to the reporter:

> We had just risen from the tea table, about eight o'clock on the evening of the 13th of May. I was lighting my segar [*sic*] at the lamp . . . when I heard a loud about, as if of someone calling for aid. In a second it was repeated, in a still more piercing tone. We rush to the door . . . , when we heard distinctly that most fearful of all cries to a planter, "A crevasse, a crevasse—the levee has given way!" It was a man rapidly riding by on a mule. The negroes [*sic*] had retired to rest. In an instant the shrill sound of the quarter bell was ringing on the air its notes of alarm. We rushed on the levee. The bearer of the evil tidings was directed to hurry along, to arouse the

coast planters, and seek aid.

The crevasse was on the upper line of Butler Kenner's plantation. I hurried to the spot with one or two negroes [sic], who, on the first stroke of the bell, had rushed out to the river bank. The road was already under water, but guided by the roar of the crevasse, we found the breach. It was caused by the undermining of that shell little animal, the seemingly insignificant crawfish—for the levee was unbroken. We had noticed the hole only an hour previous, and it was only an inch in diameter, and but little water running out and not the slightest danger was apprehended. When we reached the spot, the water was pouring out in a fountain about the size of a hogshead, with a roar that shook the ground. The suck outside the levee was like a young maelstrom, carrying drift, and everything in its neighborhood, down before it. A hundred negroes [*sic*] were now gathering to the spot, wailing and moaning, but each had sufficient presence of mind to seize a stake, an axe, and a handful of brush, or something that might be serviceable, as they came along.

A huge fire soon blazed upon the high ground, and the fight began. The old "Father" for a while, had it all his own way—he roared, he foamed, he dived under the levee, he bit out a huge mouthful—he tore up grass, he caved in the sides, he broke down the fence, and the cane, and the corn—everything that opposed him; but the "boys" soon began to pitch into him. The levee fell in. The break was now ten feet wide and six feet deep. A reinforcement, under Mr. Labranche—an able captain—now arrived. Each had brought an armful of bags. An old negro [sic], who had fought such battles for half a century, plunged into the rapid current with a stake in his hand, brandishing it like a spear. For a second he stood his ground, when I saw a streak, that looked like the blending of a white wooly head and a red jacket, pass like lightening down the breach—the water passing at an angle of forty-five degrees. The next instant the old fellow was about two hundred yards off in a cornfield—shook himself as he walked out—gathered a fence rail, and with a yell of defiance was at his post again. The scene, though truly appalling, was now picturesque in the extreme. A line of fires blazed along the bank. The "forces" of Minor Kenner, always

> indefatigable when his neighbors are in distress, now swelled the number of combatants to about three hundred, and they met the enemy with skill and courage. The stakes began to hold, but the breach in thirty minutes was thirty feet wide, and ten feet deep. An immense beam was thrown across the stream—it seemed for a moment that it must yield, though it barely touched the water—lines were fastened to it, and it was secured. One line of negroes [*sic*] passed stakes, another brush, another hay—the most efficient thing of all. The fight was now at its hottest. They crammed hay into the old "Father's" mouth, they speared him with stakes, they lashed him with tree tops, they shouted and they swore, but they worked . . . . The odds . . . were in their favor. The old "Father" had now rooted up a portion of the first palisade, and another, and still another is washed away . . . . The stake for which they fight, is 10,000 hogsheads of sugar, besides perquisites. The bottle holders cheer their man. "A little more hay, Capt. Kenner," is the cry. About twenty haystacks and a wilderness of willows are thrust into the breach, gunny bags are throne upon them and keep them in their place. The old "Father" begins to lose ground; he throws the water through the stakes like a Kentucky boatman ejecting his "amber" between his teeth. A hundred loads of dirt are tumbled in—it is like a pinch of snuff in his nostrils; sneezed out in a second; but he is getting "cowed;" with his mouth full of gunny bags, haycocks, and tree tops, he draws his breath like a man in a state of suffocation—now he only whimpers like a whipped hound—he is baffled at last—his roar has no longer any terror to his brave foes, who, though worn out and exhausted by their labors at the Sauve crevasse, to a man, are all night at their posts. Eight hours have passed, and they are victorious; the day is their own and the crops are saved. The breach is closed by daylight; at the earliest dawn the old Father of Waters gives up to despair.[13]

Though their herculean efforts saved their crop in 1849, it was only a temporary victory for the Kenners. A short distance down river from the Kenner properties at Cannes Brûlées, at Pierre Sauve's plantation (near the present day Little Farms area), a second break in the levee occurred at around the same time as had the one at Oakland. Unfortunately the effort to close the levee break at the Sauve property

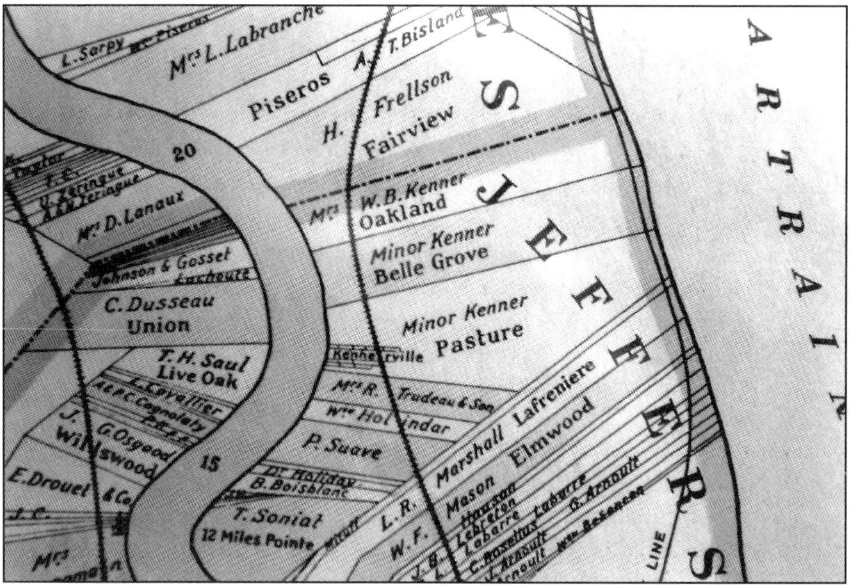

Detail from Adrian Persac's 1858 "Norman's Chart of the Lower Mississippi" showing the early layout of Kennerville as well as the Kenner family's plantations of Oakland, Belle Grove, and Pasture.

was not as successful as the one at the Kenner plantation. The flood waters from the new Sauve crevasse flowed along the Metairie Ridge all the way to New Orleans where it caused a great deal of damage. Eventually becoming 150-feet wide with a depth of six feet, the levee break soon attracted tourists who for the cost of fifty cents each way could board steamers in New Orleans and take a sightseeing trip upriver to see the devastating crevasse. To help promote the venture, passengers were accompanied while on their river trip by the sounds of a "splendid band of music."[14] Though tourists at the crevasse may have been entertained, the newspaper lamented the serious nature of the situation by reporting that as a result of the crevasse's flooding 12,000 people were homeless and that ". . . the terrible inundation made the streets [of New Orleans] look like the Canals of Venice."[15]

Unfortunately, the crevasses of 1849 were not the last of the Kenners' struggles with the forces of nature. The very next year, a cold spring and dry summer were followed by an early hard frost. This triple blow of nature was followed once again by flood waters from the river. This time the crevasse was at Bonnet Carré, several miles upriver from the Kenner plantations. Nevertheless, in spite of the distance, flood waters inundated much of the Kenners' crops, resulting in Minor's crop at Belle Grove being totally destroyed and the yields at Oakland and Pasture being greatly compromised with only a fraction of their normal totals being produced.[16]

Besides being prominent sugar growers in the community, Butler and Minor Kenner also were involved in local politics. As had their father before them, the Kenner brothers believed in the importance of public service, both as a way to serve the community and to protect their business interests. Throughout most of the antebellum period in Louisiana, government was dominated by the wealthy planters and merchants of the state. Among William Kenner's sons, his youngest child Duncan F. Kenner of Ashland Plantation in Ascension Parish was the most successful politician in the family. An active politician throughout most of his adult life, Duncan eventually rose to become a major figure in both Louisiana and Confederate politics. Butler and Minor, however, only were interested in holding local office. Both men held public office as members of the Jefferson Parish Police Jury.[17] Minor was the first to sit on the local governing body, being elected in June of 1835. Serving only a few years, he was followed on the Police Jury in February 1838 by his brother Butler. During the antebellum period in most southern states the local governing authority was the county court. In Louisiana the police jury exercised local authority in each of the state's parishes. Except for the president of the body, police jury members were elected from the various wards in the parish. The president's position was filled by the parish judge who was appointed by the governor for a four-year term. As the local governing authority, the police jury was invested with a variety of powers including the authority to levy taxes, to establish a schedule of fines for violators of its regulations, to appoint officials, to police the parish's slave population, to regulate taverns, to make and repair roads, to establish ferries, to remove obstructions from navigable waterways, to control livestock ranging, and to regulate the form and height of fences.[18]

In spite of their service on the Jefferson Parish Police Jury, Minor and Butler Kenner did not savor the political arena to the degree of their younger brother Duncan. Their service on the local governing body was limited with them focusing their energies on their plantations and their families. While Minor resided at Bell Grove Plantation with his wife Eliza and their two sons, William and Minor, Butler Kenner and his family continued to work the family's old homestead at Oakland Plantation. As a young man in his early twenties, Butler and his younger brother George spent some time in Cincinnati where they became acquainted with two sisters Ruhamah and Charlotte Riske. The young couples soon fell in love and Butler married Ruhamah in 1832 and George married her sister Charlotte, the widow of George W. Jones. Although both couples eventually returned to their homes in Louisiana (George and Charlotte later relocated to Matagorda County in Texas), they spent a fair amount of time in Ohio. Butler and Ruhamah's first two children, Philip Minor and Sarah Belle, were born in Cincinnati. In years to come, five other children were born at Oakland, including Josephine ("Josey"), Charlotte ("Lotty"), Butler, Mary Minor, and Frederick Butler. Unfortunately for the family, the happiness enjoyed by Butler and Ruhamah at their beloved Oakland home did not last.[19]

The incertitude, including fluctuating prices, bad weather, and broken levees, that sometimes attended the growing and the production of the annual sugar crop in antebellum Louisiana led both Minor and Butler Kenner to explore additional sources of revenue. Butler invested heavily in the Citizen's Bank in New Orleans. As required by the bank's charter, he was obligated to mortgage Oakland as security for his participation in the bank's business dealings. When the bank was unable to meet its obligations and failed to pay promised dividends to its bondholders, the interest owed by the bank became the obligation of its stockholders, including Butler Kenner. The family found itself facing financial ruin.[20]

Just as things appeared as if they could not become worse for Butler and Ruhamah, they did—much worse. New Orleans had a justly earned reputation for being a dirty and diseased city. The most deadly consequences of the unsanitary conditions that afflicted the city was the annual arrival with the warmer summer months of the yellow fever season. Unaware of the connection of the deadly disease to the hordes of *aedes aegypti* mosquitos that frequented the area, the people of New Orleans suffered greatly from the menace, particularly in the years when the spread of yellow fever became epidemic. The most deadly of the periodic epidemics to strike the city took place in 1853 when as many as 269 people a day died from the disease. Before the 1853 epidemic ran its course, approximately 40,000 cases of the deadly illness were reported in the city and some 11,000 to 12,000 persons died. Tragically included among this number was forty-three year-old Butler Kenner and his twelve year-old second son Butler. Both succumbed within days of each other in September 1853.[21]

At age thirty-eight, having to deal with the loss of her husband, young son, and pending financial ruin, as well as having the responsibility of caring for her surviving five children and the management of a large, working plantation, Ruhamah Kenner found herself overwhelmed. In February 1854, she hired a new overseer to supervise the operations of the plantation and then left the estate for an extended tour that lasted for months visiting friends and relatives away from Oakland. In the years that followed, she continued to make extended trips away from the plantation. Before her death in 1885, she would spend most of her elder years living with a married daughter in Philadelphia, rarely returning to Oakland.[22]

Though Ruhamah's overseer handled most of the day-to-day management activities at Oakland, the task of saving the family from complete financial ruin fell to her brother-in-law Minor, who was the official executor of Butler's estate. During the next few years bumper sugar crops were produced on the plantation providing the family with the funds needed to save the estate from bankruptcy. The added responsibility of having to deal with his late brother's affairs seems to have been a major factor in Minor's decision to end sugar production at his Belle Grove and Pasture properties. With the death of Butler, Minor focused on the growing of sugar at Oakland. For example, the 1860 census revealed that Minor owned forty slaves (twenty-four males and sixteen females), while at Oakland, Butler's widow maintained a force of only ten slaves, of which nine were females. Considering that the Oakland property, in the years following Butler's death, produced an average-annual sugar crop of 395 hogsheads and in 1859 even led all other plantations in Jefferson Parish in the production of sugar, it is highly unlikely that the Oakland slave force of nine women and one male could have performed the entirety of the backbreaking labor required to produce the large amount of sugar production achieved at the Kenner property without considerable assistance from Minor's workforce. With Oakland being only a short distance upriver from his properties, it appears that Minor used the slave force at Belle Grove and Pasture to work the sugar crop at his late brother's plantation.[23]

Having to deal with Butler's financial difficulties as well as his own problems associated with bad weather, levee breaks, fire, floods, and the threats these dangers posed to the family's sugar crops, led Minor to explore other investment and business options. In the months prior to his being stricken with his fatal illness, Butler had discussed with Minor the opportunities which would become open to them if and when the then proposed railroad approached their properties. Because of its reliance on the commercial opportunities offered by the Mississippi River, the New Orleans community was slower than most large cities in the country to embrace the technology and prospects offered by the newly developing railroad industry. Although New Orleans and the state had supported an effort to establish the New Orleans and Nashville Railroad in the mid-1830s, the effort failed with the onset of the financial panic of 1837. Only roughly twenty miles of track were laid, which reached an area near present day Causeway Boulevard and Metairie Road—several miles short of the Kenner plantations. Thus by 1850, New Orleans had only a few short intra-urban lines designed to meet local needs. In early 1852, efforts began in New Orleans to sell stock in the New Orleans, Jackson, and Great Northern Railroad. When completed, the railroad was to connect New Orleans with Jackson, Mississippi. Unlike the failed New Orleans and Nashville, which planned to run its tracks through the marshlands near the lake, the proposed path of the new railroad was designed to pass through the Kenner plantations not far from the river.[24] Approximately $2,000,000 was subscribed for the railroad stock by the people of New Orleans and the new company began to obtain the required servitudes to start laying track bed. Butler was so enthusiastic for the new railroad that he donated a right-of-way across his Oakland Plantation. The railroad jumped at the opportunity of the use of the 150-foot right-of-way and promised that it would be used for ". . . the ordinary purpose of hauling and carting dirt, stone, timber, iron, free of cost on condition [there would be] no unnecessary waste or damage." Butler also made the railroad promise to make "necessary bridges across my land and any drainage canals and ditches at their expense."[25]

Though not completed all the way to Jackson, Mississippi until the spring of 1858, by August 1854 construction of the New Orleans, Jackson, and Great Northern Railroad reached a degree of completion where trains passed on a regular basis along the tracks that crossed the plantations of the Kenner brothers and traveled as far north as the Mississippi state line at Osyka. This time frame coincided with Minor becoming the executor of his brother's estate. Faced with the calamities of recent times, including his crop failures, crevasses, barn fire, the death of his brother and his assumption of the executorship of Oakland Plantation, Minor began to formulate a plan for a bold new business venture that would focus on the needs of the region as well as the opportunities offered by the arrival of the railroad. He would build a town![26]

The devastating loss of his brother and nephew to yellow fever, along with the catastrophic consequences that the periodic epidemics

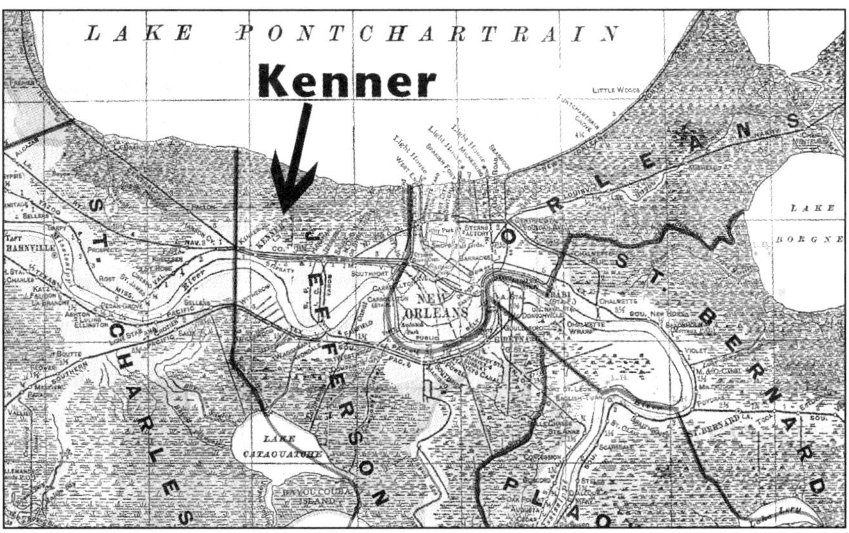

This detail taken from the 1918 map of the Department of Agriculture and Immigration shows how the railroad track bed turned to the north at Kenner. Being located at the spot where the railroad's track turned to the north to pass through the region's swamp and woodlands proved to be an essential determinant in the location and success of the Kenner(ville) community.

brought to New Orleans, led Minor to explore ways for the people of the city to escape the deadly menace. Though it is known today that the cause of the disease is a virus which damages the liver and is spread through the bite of mosquitoes, before the cause of the disease was discovered in the early years of the twentieth century, it was generally believed that the deadly fever was caused by poisonous vapors in the atmosphere, water contagions, or droplet infections that accompanied the arrival of hot weather. Doctors fought the disease with traditional treatments, such as the bleeding and purging of patients. Also, barrels of tar were burned throughout the city, cannons were fired, the clothing and bedding of infected individuals were burned, homes and privies were disinfected with carbolic acid and sulphate of iron, and homes were protected by fumigation with sulphuric acid. Yet, in spite of determined efforts to deter the disease, the death and dying in the city continued until the arrival of cool weather in the fall and winter. One of the few successful methods used to defend against the deadly disease was the practice among many of the area's residents of fleeing the city for healthier climates. As soon as rumors of the return of the killer began to be whispered in the city, those who could afford the expense of leaving the city began to take action. Though normally a city of approximately 150,000 people—placing it among the nation's largest metropolitan areas of the time, when word of the return of the disease spread, thousands of residents headed out of New Orleans for healthier environs in the North or along the Mississippi Gulf Coast. During the 1853 epidemic as many as one-third of the residents of the city fled its borders. Many others—members of what locals called the "Can't-Get-Away-Club"—simply could not afford to make the escape. These merchants, tradesmen, and laborers paid a heavy price for remaining in one of America's dirtiest and sickliest cities. During the 1853 epidemic as many as one out of every ten who remained in the city died, while thousands more were struck by the disease and survived.[27]

The idea of starting a town on their plantations had been discussed by the two Kenner brothers from the time word of the plans to build a railroad through the area first began to be discussed. As planned, it was to be at the Kenner properties where the future railroad would begin its turn towards the north so as to skirt the western edge of Lake Pontchartrain as its tracks passed through the Manchac swamp lands to places north. Minor and Butler both figured that their lands offered an ideal location for a residential community that could provide both service to and be serviced by the new railroad. With Butler's death and the catastrophic epidemic of 1853, Minor began to take action on the plan that he and his brother had long discussed. For decades the population of New Orleans gradually spread westward from the heart of the city. The crowded and unsanitary conditions of the city led many of its residents to seek improved living conditions in the less populated faubourgs located on the outskirts of New Orleans. The suburban faubourgs, including St. Mary, Lafayette, Jefferson, and Carrollton, grew in popularity and eventually were all annexed by their larger neighbor. Because of the lack of transportation facilities which would have enabled the residents of the suburban areas convenient access to the city, the faubourgs never expanded any further than a few miles from center city.[28]

Minor was convinced that the rural setting of a town—located a little over ten miles to the west of the city and serviced by a railroad that would supply quick and convenient transportation to the city offered the large number of residents of New Orleans who in the past could not escape the city and its deadly summers—would provide an ideal opportunity for a new healthier lifestyle. So sure was Minor of the venture's potential success that he hired W.T. Thompson to survey his Belle Grove and Pasture properties. At Minor's direction, Thompson completed his survey and laid out a plan for a town, including streets, avenues, and building lots. When completed on March 2, 1855, Thompson's ambitious plan involved a large portion of the area adjacent to the Belle Grove manor house and Pasture Plantation. The plan called for the future town to be formed around a large empty rectangular plot of land centered on the Belle Grove house. Beginning with the river and running back towards the lake, Thompson's plan called for a series of residential lots neatly laid out in perfectly shaped blocks. A street grid was designed that called for the future streets that paralleled the river to be simply identified by numerical sequence. Beginning with First Street and running north, the plan ended with Nineteenth Street. Roadways that ran perpendicular to the river carried two types of names. Streets formed to the east of the Belle Grove house were given names of events and political figures of the time. Hence, running eastward, the main east-side streets and their namesakes included Compromise (the Compromise of 1850), Clay (Henry Clay), Webster (Daniel Webster), Jackson (Andrew Jackson), Taylor (Zachary Taylor), Fillmore (Millard Fillmore), Calhoun (John C. Calhoun), and a street of relative short length called Maury (namesake unknown). To the west of the house, the important streets were mostly given names of family members. Running westward from the manor house was William Street (named for William Kenner), Minor (Minor Kenner), Daniel (namesake unknown), Oxley (Charles Oxley—Minor's brother-in-law and third husband of Martha Kenner), Maria (Maria Kenner—the younger sister of Minor who died in childhood at age three), Duncan (Duncan Kenner), Butler (Butler Kenner), George (Minor's brother George Kenner), Hollandey (namesake is unknown, perhaps a misspelling of Minor's wife's family name of Holliday). The plan also

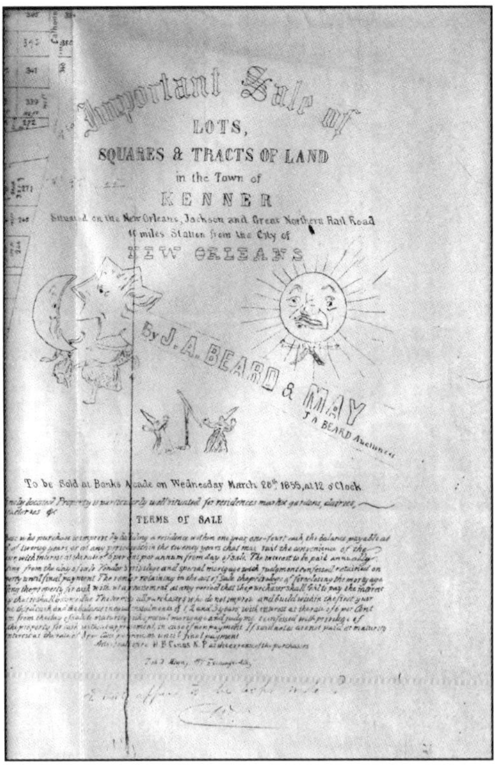

Detail from J.A Beard & May advertisement announcing the original sale of homesteads at the new town of Kenner.

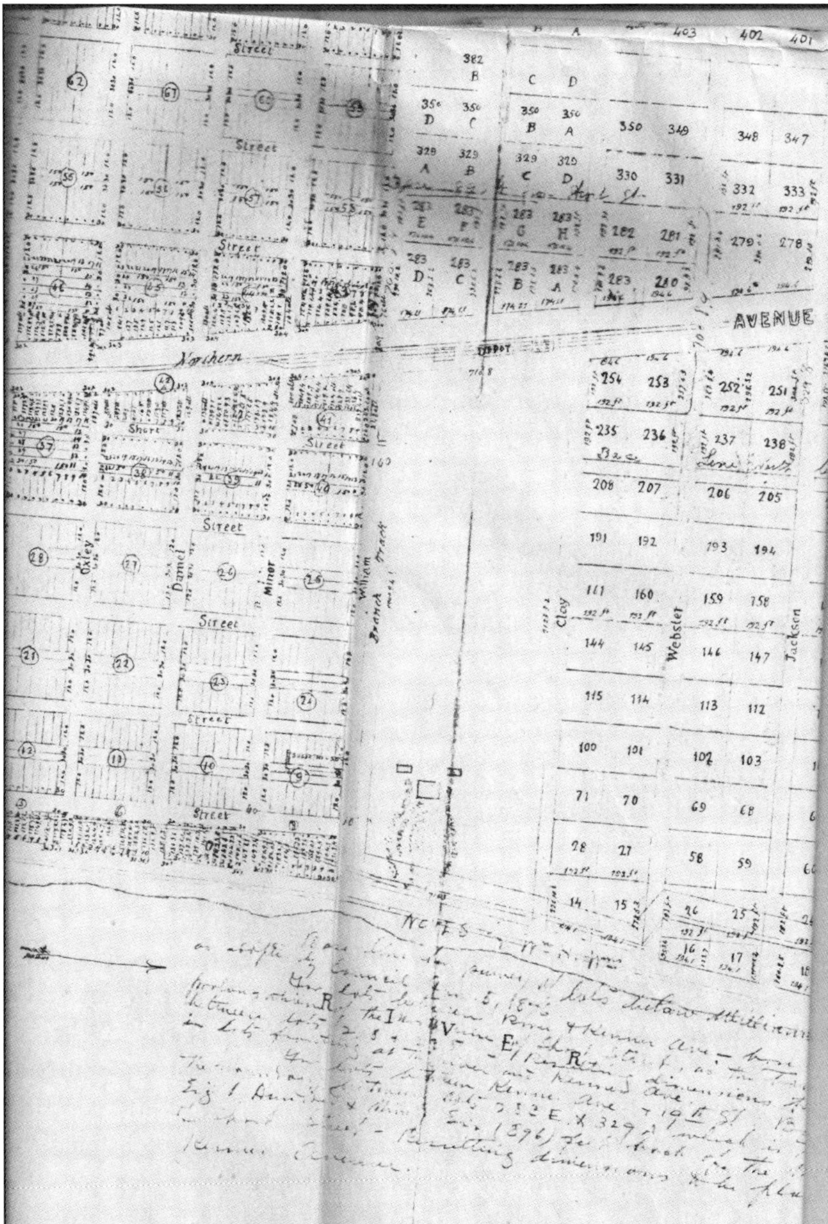

Detail from the J.A. Beard & May copy of the 1855 Thompson plan for the town of Kenner, shows the location of the Bell Grove Plantation house and its gardens and open area as well as the street layout and real estate plots.

contained areas of possible future development, which included the streets of Worth, Warren, Decatur, Perry, Scott, Franklin, and Fulton. Finally, Thompson included on his plan a drawing depicting the location and design of the new town's railroad depot.[29]

With Thompson's plan in hand, Minor moved quickly to get the project underway. Within days of receiving the layout of the future town, he employed the firm of J.A. Beard & May, an auctioneer company in New Orleans, to handle the sale of the town's lots. Shortly thereafter on March 28, 1855, the "Important Sale of Lots, Squares & Tracts of Land in the Town of Kenner" began. Minor was anxious to get construction started, so special consideration was given to those buyers who committed to constructing their new home promptly. For those individuals who purchased a lot and built a house within one year, they were required to put a one-fourth down payment and were given a twenty-year mortgage with a six-percent interest rate; whereas, those who bought land and did not "improve and build within the first year" were required to pay one-third of the purchase price up front and were required to pay off the mortgage at six percent within three years.[30]

Though events progressed according to Minor's plan with streets being laid out and broad fields, which once held acres of sugar cane, now subdivided into tracts and building lots, Minor and his supporters anxiously awaited the expected influx of New Orleans residents looking for the healthier lifestyle of country living. Unfortunately, the hoped-for migration never occurred. Perhaps it was the fact that the worst of the yellow fever epidemic of the previous years had passed and the fear that had grasped the city just a few months before had dissipated, or perhaps it was the new concept of commuter living which required a daily railroad commute for workers who held jobs in the city. Whatever the reason, people did not flock to the new village on the railroad. Even following mostly positive comments by a reporter for the *Daily Picayune* newspaper in New Orleans, interest in the venture remained limited. Published in June 1854, several months before Thompson's plan was finalized, an unnamed reporter noted the bucolic nature of the area and concluded that:

> Here an open, marshy plain, covered with rank, low, gramineous vegetation, with tangled, brushwood-like clumps,

> occasionally bordered with patches of bulrushes ever and anon dotted with palmettos. There were woods. . . tall black shafts of cypress with tresses of Spanish moss and other trees. . . well tilled expanses; large fields of waving corn; strongly springing rattoons and vigorous plants of sugar cane; contented peasants wielding sturdy hoes, guiding and driving plough and barrow; laborious immigrants toiling in the drains. . . in the distance, plantation works and houses spoke but industry, hope, and happiness.[31]

Unfortunately, only limited interest in the new homesteads took place. However, those who did have an interest in the project included several German and Italian families, who were interested in using the newly opened lots to establish small truck farms from which they hoped to provide fresh produce for the residents of New Orleans. For Minor, the venture did not bring the financial success he had expected. Nevertheless, he remained dedicated to the project. At the time of his succession in 1864, an inventory of his holdings revealed hundreds of unsold lots, which were appraised at a total value of $30,000. The succession also showed that Minor held promissory notes on mortgaged lots totaling $136,208.34. Although the footprint of the new town covered only a portion of his Belle Grove and Pasture plantations, once he began work on his real-estate project, he never produced another sugar cane crop on either of his two properties. In addition to his real estate venture, Minor looked to other business opportunities to supplement his income. Most notable of his other business enterprises was the establishment of a foundry at his new settlement on the river. Details of the size of the foundry are not known. However, Minor appears to have focused his effort on the manufacturing of what he promoted as "Coleman's Patent Superior Corn Mills." In advertisements placed in the New Orleans newspaper, Minor boasted that his foundry's eighteen inch machines could mill corn and flour at a rate better than his competitor's thirty-six inch mills.[32]

The Coleman Foundry was not the only business enterprise to be established in the new settlement on the railroad. In 1858 Victor Scheliha, with the endorsement of Minor Kenner and other prominent citizens in New Orleans, opened the Kenner Academy. The new educational institution was not intended for the children of the farmers of Kennerville. Instead, it was open to receive "a limited number of Young

Gentlemen" who were to be provided "a solid and superior education." In addition to Mr. Scheliha, the faculty included "a resident English and French Tutor" and had a staff of the "most competent Professors in the different branches of Education." The academy promised to design a plan of study for each student that was to be "strictly adhered to." To meet the students' physical education needs, a "complete Gymnasium [was] erected on the play ground [sic] of the institution." Building on the theme used by Minor Kenner to sell his home sites, the Kenner Academy advertised the convenience of its location by noting that, "the location of the establishment in the town of Kenner offers many . . . [advantages, including] . . . being within half an hour's ride from New Orleans, by the New Orleans, Jackson, and Great Northern Railroad, combines all the advantages of a rural retirement, with the utmost facility of supplying any immediate wants from the city, and parents have the opportunity of visiting their children at all times."[33] The actual location of the academy within the village is not known for the only address advertised for the school was the Kenner post office. The number of students who attended the academy is also not known. However, with the onset of the Civil War and the turmoil and hardships it brought to the area, it is unlikely that the Kenner Academy prospered for long.

In spite of not being the real-estate success the Kenners had expected, small numbers of farmers continued to move to the area. Some of the new residents were freshly arrived Irish, German, Italian, and other foreign immigrants who were coming to New Orleans in increasing numbers. Among the new arrivals in the settlement were thirty-two year old Samuel Baumann and his thirty-eight year old wife Barbara, natives of Switzerland. They were the fourth family to purchase a lot in Minor's new real-estate development. Fortunately, preserved reminisces by members of the family give interesting details of life in Kenner during the early years of its development. The Baumanns left their native country for life in the New Orleans area in 1848. When land became available at the new development on the Kenner plantations, they purchased two plots of land and built their family a new home. The family was not wealthy and had to work several jobs in order to make ends meet. Samuel conducted a livery stable in the village for several years and farmed his land. The Baumann's hard work led to

Samuel's livery stable growing to a respectable value of $15,000 and included ten horses, two mules, carriages, wagons, and sundry support materials. The livery business in the village was very competitive, and when the Baumann's uninsured business was destroyed by fire in December 1865, the family lost everything. Though they were personally convinced that the fire was set by their competitors, not enough evidence existed for authorities to make an arrest. Purchasing a second piece of land in Kennerville at the corner of 2nd and William streets in 1866 for $4,000 from Minor Kenner's brother-in-law John B. Humphreys, Samuel reopened his livery business. When fire again struck the operation in 1868, the loss was limited because Samuel had learned from his first fire experience and had his new business fully insured.[34]

The fires were not the only misfortune to strike the Baumanns. Shortly after their move to Kennerville, Samuel sent to Switzerland for his four children of a former marriage. The four young Baumanns, Elisabeth, Rosa, Rosallia, and Albert, found the climate of south Louisiana to be much more difficult to take than that of their home country. The children's acclimation difficulties proved tragic with the arrival of the yellow fever season of 1857. Just as the deadly ailment had struck down Butler Kenner and his young son four years earlier, young Elisabeth and Rosa succumbed to the disease. Death revisited the family several years later when Albert was crushed to death when a large sugar-house chimney fell on the young man.[35]

The Baumann family's papers also provide insight that not all of the neighbors of the Kenner family were comfortable with the Minor's new real-estate venture and the arrival of the new residents it brought into their area. Barbara Baumann supplemented her family's income by picking and selling blackberries, which grew wild in great abundance in the area. Typically, she and her seven year old son worked in the morning to pick the berries. In the afternoon they would take them for sale in New Orleans and return at the end of the day. On one of their picking expeditions, Mrs. Baumann and her young boy were about two miles away from their home. In an attempt to save time and effort, the pair decided to take a plantation road that ran through the center of the neighboring Trudeau plantation. The morning had been productive and the pair carried a heavy load of berries, including a full basket on Mrs. Baumann's head and another full bucket in her arms, while the boy hauled two small tin buckets full. When they traveled approximately a half mile down the road, the pair were approached on horseback by the property's owner, Zeno Trudeau. Baumann explained that she was taking a shortcut back to her home and that she and her little son were doing no harm to the property. Trudeau angrily gave her only ten minutes to get off of his property by turning around and heading back from where she came. If she did not, he threatened to call his slave driver to give her twenty-five lashes for he "did not want any poor trash trespassing on his plantation."[36]

Though the effort to attract residents such as the Baumanns to the new settlement met with some limited success, for the most part the endeavor was hampered by the failure of the railroad to build a promised depot, which was needed for the community's farmers and residents to be able to transport their products to the city. The delay in the construction of the depot was caused by the New Orleans, Jackson, and Great Northern Railroad's policy of only serving stations and depots of recognized communities. Hence, to overcome the railroad's hesitancy in building a depot, the residents of the new little community decided to take action. Bonding together, the people of the settlement selected several of their members to serve as the leaders of their local government and formally organized themselves into a village. As to a name for their new village, the residents decided to honor their most prominent resident and founder and designated the first new community on the newly opened New Orleans, Jackson, and Great Northern Railroad as the village of Kennerville.[37]

4
War and Occupation

The little village of Kennerville grew slowly. For years after its founding, hundreds of lots remained unsold. By the time of the 1860 census, the new village was not large enough to be identified as a community by the U.S. Census Office. Even the limited growth the community had enjoyed since its founding slowed as the threat of hostilities over the secession crisis loomed. Across Louisiana the presidential campaign of 1860 was followed with enthusiasm and deadly seriousness by the residents of the state. Most realized that the results of the historic vote would have far-reaching consequences. The race in Louisiana was largely a contest between John Breckinridge, the nominee of the Southern Democrats; Stephen Douglas, the Northern Democrat; and John Bell, the nominee of the Constitutional Union Party.[1] Abraham Lincoln had nearly zero support in the state. When the vote was taken, Breckinridge, the most conservative of the nominees, narrowly won in the state. The majority of the voters in Jefferson Parish favored the more unionist positions of the nominees of the Constitutional Union Party (61.9 percent of the votes cast in the parish) and the Northern Democrats (25.6 percent of the votes cast in the parish). John Breckinridge, the conservative statewide winner and leader of the Southern Democrats, captured only 12.5 percent of the vote in Jefferson Parish. Though he came in third in the state with a vote total far lower than Breckinridge and Bell, forty-five percent of Douglas's pro-union vote in Louisiana was cast in the two neighboring parishes of Orleans and

Jefferson.[2]

The national election results giving victory to the disliked Lincoln increased apprehension across the state. Public opinion soon evolved into two general positions, those who favored "Immediate Secession" and those who considered themselves "Cooperationists" because they wanted to wait and see what actions Lincoln would take when he assumed office before taking any drastic steps. As in the rest of Louisiana, in Jefferson Parish and Kennerville individuals took to both sides of the debate. However, as in the presidential election a few weeks earlier, when the citizens of Jefferson Parish and Kennerville voted in early January for delegates to the secessionist convention they voted nine hundred against secession and only two hundred in favor. Nevertheless, despite the fact that results from the presidential and secessionist convention elections reveal that the majority of the residents of the area favored the "Cooperationist" position, most members of the Kenner family sided with those who favored secession. Minor's younger brother Duncan was a strong advocate for secession and later represented Louisiana as a delegate to the Convention of Southern States at Montgomery, Alabama, where the Confederacy was organized. He was later elected to the House of Representatives of the Confederate congress. Once the outbreak of hostilities between the North and South broke out, other members of the Kenner family readily offered their service to the Southern cause.[3]

Louisiana's secession and the formation of the Confederacy met with enthusiasm throughout the state. Even areas like Jefferson Parish, which had been tepid to the idea of immediate secession, warmed to events. The *Picayune* noted that in New Orleans "every one [sic] seemed to breath more freely, every one's heart beat with a more rapid and pleasurable pulsation." All stood ready to "defend the sovereignty of Louisiana, come what might," and so it was in Jefferson Parish and the village of Kennerville.[4] Several military units were organized in the vicinity of the settlement. Among the more popular ones were the Jefferson Mounted Guards (they would later serve as General P.G.T. Beauregard's body guard), the Jefferson Rifles, and the Jefferson Rangers.[5] The rangers were considered to be an elite cavalry unit that was provided special funding allotments from the Jefferson Parish Police Jury. Closer to the village, the Kenner Guards were organized by Captain

John B. Humphreys, a nephew of Minor Kenner. The date the Guards organized is not known. Existing records reveal that Humphreys and his twenty-one-year-old cousin Minor Kenner[6] were among the privates reported by the *Daily Picayune* in early 1862 as being among the new recruits who enlisted for ninety days in the Fifth Company of the Washington Artillery, so it is likely that Humphreys organized the Kenner Guards sometime after his service with the Washington Artillery.[7]

Kennerville's excitement over secession and the formation of the Confederacy continued as the region prepared for war with the North. Events at Ft. Sumter in South Carolina and other skirmishes in the east resulted in thousands of the troops mobilized in Louisiana being sent east. Many of these soldiers passed through Kennerville as they were transported on the railroad on their way eastward. The passage of troops through the village increased in May 1861 when Confederate authorities decided that the living conditions at Camp Walker, the Confederate's post at the Metairie Race Course and their main military camp in New Orleans, were unsuitable for the large number of troops congregated there. Officials decided to move most of the troops from Camp Walker by railroad through Kennerville to the newly established Camp Moore at the village of Tangipahoa, approximately eighty miles north of New Orleans. Within days of the completion of the transfer of the troops to their new camp in the piney woods north of the city, the severity of the South's struggle with the North hit home for the region's residents with word of the arrival of the *USS Brooklyn,* the first of the Federal blockaders to take up position, on May 27 at the mouth of the Mississippi River. With news of the arrival of Federal warships in the Gulf and knowledge of the transfer of large numbers of Confederate troops out of New Orleans, the confidence so loudly proclaimed by the residents of the Crescent City and its suburbs only a few weeks prior was soon replaced with apprehension and anxiety.[8]

In October 1861, Major General Mansfield Lovell of the Confederate army assumed command of New Orleans and the surrounding area. He immediately went to work improving the area's defenses, focusing on Forts Jackson and St. Philip on the Mississippi River seventy-five miles below the city, and on Camp Parapet, a fortified defensive line located west of the city three-quarters of a mile above

Shortly after New Orleans was taken by Federal forces in April 1862, the USS Kineo (above pictured with the USS Hartford with sails) and the USS Richmond (below) were directed to take positions in the Mississippi River at Kenner with orders to protect Union forces occupying the town and to prevent the return of Confederate forces on the railroad by, if necessary, firing upon its track bed as it exited the swamps.

the Carrollton community. In spite of Lovell's efforts to build up the city's defenses, as word of the growing size of the Federal forces in the Gulf of Mexico and at Ship Island off of the Mississippi coast spread, apprehension of a pending attack increased among the residents of the region. The fear of invasion and possibility of the presence of Federal spies and sympathizers led both state and Confederate authorities to appeal to President Jefferson Davis to declare martial law in the area. On March 13, 1862, the Confederate president authorized General Lovell to declare martial law in Orleans, Jefferson, St. Bernard, and Plaquemine parishes. Within a week, the orders were issued, along with the directive that all white males above the age of sixteen, except unnaturalized foreigners, appear before a provost marshal and register. Residents claiming Confederate citizenship had to take an unconditional oath of allegiance to the Confederacy. Aliens were required to swear obedience to the laws of the Confederacy and the Southern states, and those individuals "unfriendly" to the cause were ordered to leave the district "without delay."[9]

The apprehension and gossip concerning invasion that engulfed the residents of the region around New Orleans during the spring of 1862 proved portentous. Within a month of the declaration of martial law, a large Federal force that had gathered off of the mouth of the Mississippi River under the command of Flag Office David G. Farragut began its advance up the waterway. Blocked at first by Confederate forces located at Forts Jackson and St. Philip and a small fleet located on the river to the south of the Crescent City, the Federal flotilla managed to fight its way past the rebel fortifications on the evening of April 24, 1862. Once past the Confederate forts, Farragut's fleet faced no other formidable fortifications in its advance on New Orleans. In the city, General Lovell believed he did not have sufficient forces or heavy guns capable of contending with the approaching Federal fleet. Furthermore, because of high water in the area surrounding the city, there was no viable evacuation route for the citizens of the city to escape the approaching battle. The only plausible outlet by land was through Kennerville on the New Orleans and Jackson Railroad. Not able to carry the area's civilian population of 170,000, the railroad was however a viable route of evacuation for the approximately 3,000 rebel soldiers and their equipment still in the city. Determining that the city and its residents would be better off with a military evacuation than with a fruitless defense and its accompanying destruction, and that his forces in the city could be easily trapped by the simple placement by the Federals of one or two of their gunboats in the river at Kennerville that could block his troops' evacuation by rail, Lovell ordered the destruction of all war materials that could not be carried away. He also ordered his soldiers to evacuate by rail through Kennerville and by lake vessels to the Confederate garrison at Camp Moore. Not realizing the peril that a battle for the city would cause for them, many of the people of the city and region were angered by the collapse of the Confederate defenses at New Orleans. They had been assured by Confederate officials and the press of the Crescent City that the defenses of the area were adequate to stop any Federal attack. All such illusions ended forever at approximately noon on April 25, 1862, when Farragut's flotilla dropped anchor in the Mississippi River at New Orleans and demanded the surrender of the Confederacy's queen city.[10]

Although it took Federal forces several days to consolidate their hold on the city of New Orleans, their troops soon moved into the countryside around the city. Federal officers realized that if the city would ever be threatened by Confederate forces in the future, the attack would have to come by way of the Mississippi River or the railroad. Kennerville's location on the river and at the spot where the New Orleans and Jackson railroad exited the swamps and began to parallel the river into the Crescent City led the Federals to identify the village as a strategic point of defense for protecting the area from Confederate attack. So vital did Federal authorities consider the village that it was among the first objectives taken by Union forces when they moved out of the city. Just as General Lovell had feared, on May 7, a little over twelve days after the arrival of Farragut's flotilla in New Orleans, two naval vessels—the *USS Richmond* and the *USS Kineo*—were ordered to take up positions in the river just above Kennerville so as to be able to restrict use of the railroad, which was located only 1,500 feet from the river and in easy range of the warships' canons. The next day when the *Richmond* was ordered elsewhere, the *Kineo* was ordered to remain at Kennerville to assist in the landing of Federal troops who were directed to either occupy the railroad at the village or, if problems arose, to destroy the railway in order to prevent it from being used by the Confederates.[11]

Coinciding with the stress brought about by the arrival of Federal gunboats with their menacing cannons directed towards their home and the occupation of the plantation and surrounding community by Union troops, the members of the Kenner family confronted the devastating event of the death of the family's surviving patriarch, Minor Kenner, founder and leading resident of Kennerville. Other than the date of his death on May 10, 1862, at age fifty-four, little is known of Minor's demise. Whether the result of an accident, an illness, a sudden medical attack precipitated by the stress of the onset of the Federal occupation of his village, or the victim of some military action, the cause of his death is unknown. A death notice published in the *Daily True Delta* newspaper several days after the event simply announced his death at his home and gave no additional details. However, the fact that Minor's death occurred at the time of the arrival of Federal forces in the area suggest that his passing could very possibly have been related to the event.[12]

The Federal occupation of Kennerville met with no serious resistance from either Confederate military units or from the civilian population of the area. Federal forces from Michigan and Wisconsin landed at the village, easily took control of the railroad, and established a camp at the settlement. However, the occupation was not completely without incident. Among the troops involved in the occupation of the village were individuals that a Federal officer later labeled as being "wholly destitute of the moral sense." Upon taking possession of the village, troops from a Wisconsin regiment, who apparently regarded "pillaging not only [as a] right in itself but a soldierly accomplishment," began to forage and plunder the private homes of Kennerville's residents. Their actions included the killing of chickens, robbing sugarhouses, and insulting the female residents of the village. Butler Kenner's widow, Ruhamah, noted in her journal that Federal troops arrived on her Oakland Plantation on the night of May 11 and gave her "such a fright" that in the morning she personally traveled to the city to complain in person to the Federal commanding officer, General Benjamin Butler. Ruhamah remained in the city until the May 19 when she observed in her journal that "all being quiet at Oakland I returned home. No white female on the place but my self [*sic*]."[13]

General Butler angrily labeled the actions of the marauding

troops at Kennerville an "instance of gross outrage" and let it be known that he considered the incident a disgrace to the flag and country. He ordered steps to be taken immediately to prevent a reoccurrence of the practice. The general directed that a sergeant and six men be stationed at Kennerville as a guard for the inhabitants and that these soldiers be "held responsible for the safety and quiet of the neighborhood." To allay the complaints of the people of Kennerville concerning the plundering, Butler also ordered the establishment of a three-man board of inquiry to determine the damage caused by the marauding soldiers and the appropriate compensation for the victimized residents. Two of the members of the inquiry board were military officers and the third was a civilian resident of the village named P. Soniat.[14]

General Butler's assertive response to the plundering at Kennerville by his troops brought a quick end to the practice. Nevertheless, the occupation by Federal troops brought other changes to the lives of the region's residents—both whites and blacks. At the time the area was occupied, Brigadier General John W. Phelps of Vermont was made commander of the earthwork fortification known as Camp Parapet, located a little over five miles east of Kenner near present day Causeway Boulevard. Phelps was an ardent abolitionist who interpreted broadly the terms of the Confiscation Act passed by Congress concerning the status of slaves in occupied areas of the South. He took a particularly aggressive stand on offering assistance to the black residents of the region. Word of his generosity and abolitionist feelings spread throughout the area and soon hundreds of blacks from the region's plantations as far away as the Teche country began to flood the camp. The numbers of "freed" slaves or freedmen soon overwhelmed the resources and facilities Phelps had on hand to provide for the new arrivals. The Yankee general attempted to ameliorate the situation by putting as many of the slaves as he could to work and even organized infantry units for them to join. The numbers were so great that Phelps' efforts were only partially successful. Given only limited access to the military's camp, the freedmen were forced to live along the old River Road that ran along the levee. However, a lack of food, clothing, proper housing, and other necessities resulted in many of the former slaves living in squalor and being forced to survive off of the land. Hungry and idle, many of the ex-slaves returned to their plantations and plundered them for food.[15]

Complicating matters even further was Phelps's policy of protecting the area's blacks from the actions of local authorities. Whenever a slave or freedman was caught and punished for committing a crime, General Phelps dispatched a party of his soldiers to free the individual and had him brought to the Federal camp where he was protected from further punishment. This was the situation shortly after the Federal occupation of the Kennerville area began in 1862 when a slave on Oakland Plantation harassed Mrs. Butler Kenner. Caught after burning the plantation's barn and other "riotous conduct," the slave was confined in stocks to await an opportunity to send him to the city for trial. On hearing of the incident and disregarding the fact that Mrs. Kenner was personally given a "safe guard" order by General Butler, in which all officers and soldiers were commanded to respect her property and "to afford her every protection," Phelps sent a company of soldiers to the plantation who freed the troublesome slave and removed him to the safety of Camp Parapet.[16]

As word of General Phelps's generosity towards blacks spread, it became increasingly difficult to get the area's slaves to perform their duties. When ordered to do work by their masters, they often refused their assignments with the comment that they only had to go to Parapet to be free. As a result, crops were not harvested on time and more importantly the conditions of the levees deteriorated seriously. So troublesome became the issue that complaints concerning Phelps's policies were made to General Butler by both civilians and military officials. W. Mitthoff, the president of the Police Jury for the Left [east] Bank of Jefferson Parish, wrote on May 29, 1862, to the commanding general that "I feel it is my duty to call to your attention to the demoralizing effect on the serving population, not alone of this Parish, but of the whole state, by the course General Phelps adopted in refusing to return our servants. . . ."[17] More telling was the complaint filed by Captain Edward Page of the 31st Massachusetts, who was ordered to the area to "prevent the commission of excesses on the part of soldiers or laborers." In his report on the situation to General Butler dated May 27, 1862, Page complained that because of Phelps' actions "it is utterly impossible to call upon the negroes [sic] for any labor." In regards to his orders to protect the community, he noted that, "I shall find impossible to do if the soldiers from Camp Parapet are allowed to range the country, insult the planters, and entice negroes [sic] away from their plantations, and I regret I must report this conduct on the part of soldiers from that camp."[18] The complaints against Phelps eventually had some effect on curbing some of the worst abuses of his troops. Nevertheless, the issue of large numbers of idle former slaves milling around the region continued throughout most of the war. As late as February 1865, the commander of the Federal army camp at Kennerville had to address the issue when he contacted the provost marshal at Carrollton and noted that, "it is necessary that the negroes [sic] should be removed from the vicinity of my camp at this place. Where shall I send them to?" He then added, "They have no honest means of getting a living."[19]

Though he had some issues with General Phelps's zealous handling of the freedmen's issue, General Butler took the Federal confiscation acts seriously and issued sweeping enforcement policies to Federal authorities in New Orleans. The passage by Congress of the Second Confiscation Act in the summer of 1862 broadened the authority of Federal officials to confiscate the property of Confederate supporters and sympathizers. In September 1862, General Butler enthusiastically implemented the terms of the new law and mandated that the property of citizens in the region who did not register their allegiance to the United States was subject to confiscation. The citizens of Kennerville and its surrounding areas were now forced to proclaim their loyalties. Because the oaths of allegiance at the village were recorded by signature only, without accompanying address, it is impossible to know the numbers of citizens who refused to take the oath. However, with the community described at the time by one Federal soldier stationed there as including "a small cluster of houses" and another soldier's contemporary description of the village as being "a place of a dozen houses," its population was not large. Records of the names and signatures of the residents (no addresses are listed) of the Kennerville area who took the oath of allegiance include such a large number of individuals that it is probable that a sizeable majority of the village swore their support to the United States. It is not known if any resident of Kennerville had their property confiscated as a result of their refusal to take the oath.[20]

With the exception of the abusive incident by the Wisconsin troops during its early stages, the Union occupation of the village saw the local citizenry and soldiers at Kennerville generally cooperate with one another. In a January 1865 report, Lt. Colonel John M. Wilson noted that the troops camped in the community were "respectful, tractable, and obedient."[21] Alfred A. Rigby, a soldier with the 24th Regiment of the Iowa Infantry, gratefully noted in his diary in June 1864 that the troops at Kennerville were able to supplement their monotonous military fare with the generosity of "citizens [who] supply us with plenty of vegetables at reasonable prices . . . ." Similarly, when his camp was inundated by the heavy showers that muddied the living arrangements of the Federal troops, Rigby penned with appreciation that, "A citizen very kindly loaned us some fencing to make bunks" so the soldiers would not have to rest in the mud.[22]

Indeed, the mud of Kennerville remains the most common theme among the handful of surviving remarks of soldiers who were stationed in the community during the Civil War. They all probably agreed with Alfred Rigby, who observed that when the weather was dry the military camp located on the fallow sugar-cane fields of Kennerville was "a very pleasant camping ground with pleasant accommodations."[23] However, when the rains came it was a very different situation. The combination of the soft alluvial soil of the area, poor drainage, and the traffic of the weighty equipment and the number of troops associated with a large military camp and the heavy rainfall common to the area produced a quagmire at times. Carl Ketzle of Company A of the 37th Illinois Volunteer Infantry complained in his journal as he was departing the area in mid-February 1865 that "everything [at Kennerville] seemed to be underwater" and that before living conditions at the camp improved "the water [had to be] squeezed out of the ground."[24] John J. Bigbee of Company H of the 47th Indiana Infantry who was in Kennerville in early January 1865 noted in a letter home that his military camp had "mud nee [*sic*] deep to a mule."[25] In another unit at the camp about the same time, Elias P. Risshel of Company G of the 46th Illinois Volunteer Infantry recorded in his journal that the "rainy season made [the camp] exceedingly muddy." So much so that he considered Kennerville to have become a "stick in the mud camp." A month later, after his unit was transferred to Dauphin Island in Alabama to take part in the Federal campaign around Mobile, Risshel, with his former camp's muck remaining a vivid memory, happily compared the conditions of his new camp to his former post: "While the camp at Kennerville was pure mud, at this place it [is] pure white sand."[26] So hampering did the mud problem become at Kennerville that the Assistant Inspector General for Federal forces in the region, Lt. Colonel John M. Wilson, wrote on January 26, 1865, to the commanding general about the situation:

> The ground is naturally exceedingly flat, low, and damp, and the violent and continued rain-storms that have prevailed since the arrival of the troops have so softened it that with the little drainage the whole surface is transferred to yielding mud, greatly increasing the difficulties of transportation and almost annulling the usual requirements of troops in military drills and exercises.[27]

Even the commanding officer at Kennerville, Major General Frederick Steele lamented in early February 1865 in a report to his command headquarters in New Orleans that conditions had seriously deteriorated in his camp because "The mud is so deep that we can scarcely move here."[28]

Although the muck and mire that frequently accompanied the rainy seasons during the occupation of Kennerville soured the opinions of some of the soldiers posted there, from the earliest days of their occupation of the area, Federal officials were high on the strategic and military importance of the little village. If New Orleans was ever to be threatened by Confederate attack on the east bank of the Mississippi, it would have to come by way of Kennerville. Because of the strategic location, the village was made one of the Federal army's permanently garrisoned posts designed to protect New Orleans.[29] As an important garrison, Kennerville remained continuously occupied by sizeable numbers of Union troops throughout the war. With the primary mission of the garrison being the defense of the railroad at the point where it turned north and entered the swamp, the camp was also used throughout the war as a major troop transfer center for Federal units coming and leaving the region. Some soldiers remained stationed at the village for weeks and others for only days or even hours.

The large size of the garrison at Kennerville kept Confederate forces in the region from ever making a serious threat against either New Orleans or the camp itself. With so many soldiers gathered in the limited camping space located between the river and the swamp, there were, not unexpectedly, deaths among the soldiers brought about by accidents, illness, and natural causes.[30] However, as far as is known, there was only one soldier killed at the camp during the occupation of the village and his death was an accident. On May 27, 1863, Corporal John P. Coen of the 9th Regiment of the Connecticut Volunteer Infantry fell fatally when the train he was boarding unexpectedly lurched, causing him to slip and strike his head. Though Kennerville never faced the danger of a major Confederate attack, on occasion rumors circulated among the troops and residents of the village that warned that the rebels were about to carry out an assault. The most serious of these took place in March 1863 when an erroneous rumor reached Federal forces in New Orleans that the feared Confederate General Stonewall Jackson had arrived at Camp Moore seventy-five miles to the north and was preparing to move against New Orleans. General Nathaniel Banks, who had replaced Butler as commander of the Federal forces in the region, ordered the 6th Michigan Volunteers to Kennerville and from there to advance up the New Orleans and Jackson Railroad to the town of Ponchatoula located on the railroad north of Lake Pontchartrain. With Union forces in possession of Pontchatoula and Kennerville, it would have been impossible for the rebels to attack New Orleans from the north along the western shore of Lake Pontchartrain. The Union advance up the railway from Kennerville was made by foot instead of rail. Confronted with very bad weather and the difficult task of marching along the raised wooden trestles that traversed the swamp, many of the Michigan soldiers suffered injuries by falling through the trestle work and had to be returned to the military camp at Kennerville for treatment. With reinforcements from New York and Connecticut regiments, the remaining force continued its advance and was able to seize control, without much difficulty, of Ponchatoula and its surrounding area. With control of the railroad at the spots where it both entered the swamp at Ponchatoula and exited it at Kennerville, the city of New Orleans was secured from the threat of Confederate attack from the north side of the lake.[31]

There were no other threats of any real consequence by the Confederates against the Federal camp at Kennerville. Nevertheless, Federal officials continued to keep the camp at Kennerville as a major camp and garrison and a strategic part of the defense of the region.

Major General Frederick Steele in late 1864 and early 1865 served as commander of the Union's reserve forces stationed at Kenner. He later commanded a division in the Union campaign against Mobile.

On May 27, 1863, Corporal John P. Coen of the 9th Regiment of the Connecticut Volunteer Infantry became the first known casualty among Federal forces stationed at Kenner during the Civil War. He died when he was injured fatally boarding a train which unexpectedly lurched causing him to slip and strike his head.

During the final months of the war, Kennerville continued to serve as a major transfer station for Federal units and was chosen as the site of the Union army's cavalry camp of instruction and distribution under the command of Colonel Charles Everett. Additionally, in late 1864, the Kennerville camp was chosen as the site for the region's important reserve corps. This corps had the responsibility of housing the Union army's reserve units for the region and for preparing and re-equipping the troops stationed there for future field operations. So important was the task of overseeing the reserve corps, that the camp was placed under the command of a major general, Frederick Steele.[32] As a camp of instruction and base for the reserve corps, Kennerville swelled in size and marked the period when the garrison accommodated the largest number of Federal troops it had at any single time during the war. At the end of January 1865, the force of Union troops at Kennerville consisted of four brigades of infantry, numbering nineteen regiments and four batteries of artillery. In addition to the large force of combat troops crowding the small community, there were also support units and a large number of animals for both the cavalry camp and transport troops. The transportation units at Kennerville alone included 147 wagons and 938 mules.[33]

Having their little village occupied by thousands of soldiers undoubtedly affected the lives of the residents. However, in spite of the fact that the presence of large numbers of troops camping on the once productive sugar cane and vegetable fields of the settlement and the accompanying turmoil, noise, dust, muck, and mire associated with a large military encampment, the presence of Federal troops in the village also provided benefits to the Kennerville residents. Unlike areas of the state that suffered from combat and economic calamity because of the war, the little village was spared combat damage. Furthermore, Federal forces stationed in the village made an effort to maintain the settlement's infrastructure. For example, although not entirely successful because of their inexperience in dealing with the problem, Union troops and workers attempted to construct a new levee to safeguard the area from flooding. The maintenance on the old levee had been seriously neglected when many of the local slaves who possessed experience in levee repair abandoned their plantations upon the arrival of Federal troops. The lack of experience in levee construction and maintenance of northern troops became painfully obvious with the arrival of stormy and wet weather in early 1865; heavy rains resulted in the near collapse of the newly repaired levee at Kennerville. The threat of levee failure remained throughout the period of Federal occupation. Fortunately for the people of the village, not all developments brought to the area by the occupation were as big of a problem as the levees. On January 5, 1865, Federal troops established the village's first telegraph office, which gave residents the ability to communicate directly with the outside world. Finally, thanks to maintenance provided by Union soldiers, the railroad through the village was kept in good order and a reliable schedule was kept of a daily departure from New Orleans to the village at 8:00 a.m. and from Kennerville back to the city sometime between two and four p.m. With the residents of the area supplying the soldiers with fresh vegetables and other trade commodities, the commerce provided the people of the settlement with a modest income that helped them offset the losses caused by the war. It is not known how long the village remained a base for Federal forces. Presumably, with the end of hostilities between the North and South in mid-1865, Union forces at Kennerville gradually withdrew from the little village.[34]

5
After the War

Louisiana paid a heavy price for its membership in the ill-fated Confederacy. Although many parts of the state were spared from prolonged large-scale military actions during the war, much of Louisiana experienced wide-spread occupation by Union forces. The state also suffered the loss of a great many of its young men who died while in service to the Southern cause. Only Virginia, South Carolina, and Georgia suffered greater property destruction and casualties during the conflict than did Louisiana. In addition to what it paid in the blood of its bravest sons, the state suffered devastating financial damages from its war costs as a result of its losses in both agricultural production and its slave workforce. Added to these losses was the near ruin of its banking and railroad industries. For example, the New Orleans, Jackson, and Great Northern Railroad that was so vital to the Kennerville community suffered the devastating loss during the war of 90 percent of its rolling stock. When financial losses from all causes in the war are included, historians calculate that the Civil War cost Louisiana more than one-half of its prewar wealth.[1]

Included among the hardest hit by the war were the great sugar plantations of the state. As a result of the conflict, the number of sugar-producing plantations in Louisiana dropped from a prewar total of 1,200 to only 175 by the last year of the conflict. Oakland at Kennerville was not among the producing plantations at the end of the war. Though spared the large-scale looting and destruction so many of the once grand sugar estates experienced during the war, Oakland by the end of the conflict was largely a scene of desolation. Following Minor Kenner's death and the arrival of Federal troops at Kennerville, Butler Kenner's widow, Ruhamah, largely abandoned her Oakland property to the management of her son Philip Minor and an overseer and moved north to Philadelphia to live with her daughter Charlotte and her husband George Harding. It was not until December 1867 that she returned to the plantation for an extended stay in order to spend time with her ill daughter Josey (Josephine) and her husband Charles Moses Shepherd Jr. When Josey died in April 1868, Ruhamah once again left Oakland for her surviving daughter's home in Philadelphia, never again to take up long-term residence at the plantation.[2]

With Ruhamah's absence from the plantation, responsibility for the property shifted to her son Philip Minor. A difficult task in normal times, management of Oakland during the postwar years was made all the more difficult by the fact that he also had the responsibility for operating his and his wife Ella Humphreys's Roseland Plantation in St. Charles Parish some eighteen miles upriver from the family's plantation at Kennerville. Because of the changes wrought by the conflict, operating a sugar estate in the months following the end of the war was a daunting task. Lands, tools, and machinery had been neglected and once productive sugar cane fields were now choked with weeds and broken equipment. However, the greatest hurdle to overcome by the postwar planter was the securing of an adequate labor force to perform the backbreaking work associated with the production of a sugar crop. First with the arrival of Federal soldiers during the war and then the formal end of the institution of slavery that accompanied the end of the conflict, the war fractured forever the labor arrangement which had dominated life and work on the South's plantations in colonial and antebellum times. Both the freedmen and their former masters struggled to adopt to the vagaries of the wage-labor system. Freedmen refused to return to the deferential master/slave relationship and white planters were slow to extend to their former wards the respect and demeanor reserved for equals.[3]

Philip Minor's effort to regenerate sugar production at Oakland met with only limited success. Few records remain of the size of the sugar crops produced on most Louisiana plantations during the first years following the war. At Oakland, family records indicate that sugar production was inconsistent and that the estate remained in financial jeopardy throughout the period. The growing financial problems of the plantation and those faced by members of the family were noted by Ruhamah in August 1868 when she wrote Philip Minor from her daughter's home in Philadelphia and noted that

> I am very glad the Cane [sic] is good but indeed I must *insist* on your grinding cane enough to give some money . . . . To carry on the place next year appears to be all that can be done; but where the money is to be gotten is more than I know. As to the repairs & fixing up the plantation generally . . . I don't see how it can be done, & to keep it in tolerable order will be sufficient.[4]

With his cane crops not producing the funds needed to keep the plantation in good order, Philip Minor was open to other options, including turning to the growing of rice. Because it was cheaper to produce, during the postwar period many sugar growers in the southern part of the state switched to rice cultivation on all or part of their properties. As technology improved over the next few decades, rice gradually expanded to become a major agricultural product for Louisiana. Unfortunately for Philip Minor and Ruhamah, their effort at rice growing did not prove satisfactory. During the 1869-1870 season they reported no sugar grown and only fifty hogsheads of rice. Frustrated with the rice experiment, in the next crop season the Kenners gave up on rice and returned to the production of sugar; once again their efforts met with disappointing results, producing a meager crop of only forty-two hogsheads of sugar.[5]

Unexpectedly, in the midst of their growing financial crisis at Oakland, the plantation became the site of one of the most famous sports events of the time—America's first, if unofficial, World Heavyweight Boxing Championship. At the time, because there were no professional boxing associations, rankings, or procedures, for determining a single champion, individuals claiming the title of champion issued challenges to others who claimed the designation. In 1870 two Englishmen claimed champion status. Jem Mace, later known as the father of the modern school of British scientific boxing, was accepted at

On May 10, 1870, in a hastily arranged event on the Kenner family's Oakland Plantation, Englishman Jem Mace (shown) defeated his fellow countryman Tom Allen in a bare-knuckle boxing match. The bout between the two world-famous boxers drew hundreds of spectators who traveled to the site in a special train from New Orleans. The match, in which the winner obtained a purse of $2500, is considered by many to be the first World Heavyweight Championship prizefight to take place in America.

the time by the British as world champion; whereas, at the same time, Tom Allen claimed the American boxing title. To settle the question of who really was champion, the two boxers looked for a venue to settle the issue and agreed upon New Orleans. The city was chosen because although bare-knuckle fighting was illegal across the United States, it was believed that the Crescent City would be tolerant of the event.[6]

When the fighters arrived in the city, they were chagrined to find that officials in Orleans Parish would not allow the fight. With members of the public anxious for the fight to take place, on the day of the scheduled fight a special train was readied and passengers began loading at 3 a.m. Over a thousand passengers, including General Philip Sheridan, commander of the Fifth Military District, which included Louisiana and Texas, boarded the train for its undisclosed destination. Only a few of the fight's promoters knew where the train was heading. They planned a short trip to neighboring Jefferson Parish, where officials were known to be more accommodating for the bare-knuckle event. However, when the train reached Camp Parapet, where the promoters expected to be able to stage the fight, New Orleans Metropolitan policemen refused to let the fight take place. With that, the train and its riders moved further west down the tracks looking for a suitable spot for the match. Moving slowly pass the Kennerville depot the train continued to Oakland Plantation. Evidently without any prior arrangements with Philip Minor Kenner, fight promoters walked the plantation road and decided the area near the estate's sugar house was "a beautiful spot" for the ring to be pitched and the fight held.[7] Somewhat carried away with hyperbole, the reporter for the *Daily Picayune* wrote:

> The scene at this moment was most picturesque. Down the narrow road filed about a thousand people. The field hands left off hoeing corn, mounted their mules and dashed toward the house like squads of Moorish cavalry, their long hoe-handles in the distance looking like so many lances, while the sun, which had risen gloriously, was now gleaming over field and forest.[8]

Others did not find the scene so colorful. Several years after the match in a short remembrance of the event, a newspaper reporter who was present at the fight recalled his trip from the train station to the ring "in wagons with mules, huddled together like pigs at a swill trough, jostled and jammed as well as jawed."[9]

The ring was set up near the sugar house, about one hundred yards back from the Mississippi River, and two cabins of field hands were chosen to serve as ready rooms for the fighters. The two contenders arrived shortly thereafter in a separate train and at 9:05 a.m. the bout began. The contest continued for forty-four minutes and lasted for ten rounds. Throughout the fight, Tom Allen took a beating. Mace's punches broke Allen's nose, cut him severely under his left eye and closed his right eye. Towards the end of match, Allen, realizing he was losing the boxing contest, desperately tried to wrestle Mace to the mat, which resulted in his dislocating his own left shoulder—effectively ending the match. Jem Mace was declared the winner and champion and was awarded the winner-take-all victor's purse of $2,500. By midafternoon the event labeled by the *Daily Picayune* as "one of the most scientific encounters ever witnessed" was over and the ring, the crowd, the fighters, and the train were all gone from Oakland and the Kennerville community. Interest in the sport remained high in the area. In 1890, Louisiana was among the first states to legalize prize fighting, which led to New Orleans becoming the center of the sport in the nation.[10]

In spite of the fact that the details of the fight were covered by newspapers around the country, the notoriety the event brought to the Kennerville community had little effect upon the financial difficulties at Oakland. So serious was the situation becoming that Ruhamah was forced to sell personal items to have any money on which to survive. For example, while staying with her daughter in Philadelphia, she wrote to Philip Minor and complained of the depths of her financial problems: "I had to sell my diamond broach to Lotty for $300 to enable me to have any money at all. I never was so poor since I was married, and I feel it greatly."[11] Months later she again complained to her son that "I am literally out of money of my own."[12]

So serious was the financial situation becoming that Philip Minor was forced to turn to his uncle Duncan Kenner for help. Although he played an active and leading role in the Confederate government during the war, Duncan managed to survive the conflict with much of his prewar fortune intact. With his resources, Duncan generously aided several members of both his and his wife Nanine's families during the difficult postwar years. When the situation worsened to a point that Philip Minor faced the loss of his Roseland Plantation in St. Charles Parish at a sheriff's sale, Duncan stepped in and protected the property by purchasing a half interest in the estate. Aware of Philip Minor's obligations to his mother in Philadelphia and the family's Oakland Plantation, Duncan for months provided Philip Minor and his wife Ella a stipend of $300 a month and on another occasion in early 1872 a loan of $2,600. Over time Duncan's assistance to Philip Minor amounted to over $12,000, a notable sum when it is considered that at the time, because of the depressed status of the sugar industry in the state, once bountiful and proud sugar plantations were being sold for as little as $10 to $30 an acre.[13]

Although Duncan's assistance helped to stabilize the situation at Roseland Plantation, the problems at Oakland continued. Of all family members, Butler Kenner's widow, Ruhamah, seems to have suffered the most from the crisis at Oakland. In an undated letter to Philip Minor, she made it clear that she hoped that the plantation would supply her with some financial support. She explained that, "It is only my business to spend the income in paying debts interest & taxes & if there is any money left it is mine." Perhaps realizing that her words were overly covetous, Ruhamah added that with the exception of the money, she had little interest in whatever else remained of Oakland. She wrote:

> The property is really yours & the other children, so if you choose, you can make the proposition to Mr. H [probably her son-in-law George Harding] that you spoke of . . .if there are any carpets at Oakland that will be of any use to Ella [Philip Minor's wife] or Martha [her husband's sister] I beg you to make use of them. I think one of them could be made long enough for a pretty good cover to your hall. They will never be of use to me.[14]

After essentially giving away much of what remained of her family's home and furnishings, she concluded her comments on Oakland with the sad and melancholy sigh, "Oh how I long for a home of my own."[15]

George Harding, in whose house Ruhamah lived while she was in Philadelphia, was a successful patent attorney. In the years following the end of the war, he had joined Duncan Kenner in providing support for several members of the Kenner family. In addition to opening his house to his mother-in-law, he generously financed the failed business ventures of his young brother-in-law Frederick. As the financial crisis at Oakland worsened in 1871 and members of the family were asked to dig deeper into their pockets to support the family's homestead near Kennerville, George and Lotty Harding had enough. In a letter to her brother Philip Minor, Lotty forcefully let him know that things needed to change by noting:

> The question is who is to be benefitted by keeping Oakland, Mother certainly not for she had better have a little now while she can enjoy it—Fred [their younger brother] could do better with his money North—Mary [their younger sister] don't [*sic*] want to sell. My share no matter now I[t] would be of more benefit to me here—Now the only two interested down there are you, & Shep, & I do not think it is worthwhile, for Mr. Harding to worry, for two who can

> take care of themselves. I want you to understand it is not only the $5000 he is asked for now . . . or the $5000 already loaned.[16]

Word of Lotty and George's decision to cut their assistance to the effort to keep Oakland financially viable was received with frustration by family members back in Louisiana. Perhaps the most agitated of all was Duncan Kenner who at the time was providing large financial subsidies to both Philip Minor and several members of his wife's family. Duncan strongly favored retaining the Oakland homestead in the family's hands. He had long worked to have all members of the family contribute to the effort to save the place and did not hesitate to apply pressure to win their participation as he did when he heard about the Hardings' decision. As one family member noted at the time, "Uncle Kenner put it to him [George Harding], that as an heir, he ought to protect the property."[17]

Duncan's request was to no avail. Within months of the dispute over the contributions of members of the family, ownership of Oakland Plantation slipped from the control of the Kenner family. In addition to the labor difficulties the end of slavery brought to the sugar growers, the cane crop at the time also suffered severe damage from the appearance of the destructive mosaic disease. So damaging was the blight to the cane crop that during the final months of Kenner ownership, sugar production on the property totaled only forty-two hogsheads and 10,500 gallons of molasses in 1871. Even efforts to lease the land failed to change the situation. Increasingly the Kenners fell farther and farther behind with their creditors until finally, in April 1873, Oakland was adjudicated at a sheriff's sale to the Citizens Bank of Louisiana.[18]

Citizens Bank kept ownership of the property for the next sixteen years. During that time it leased the land to various individuals who, as had the Kenners, struggled to make the property a profitable venture. Charles Hodges, a native of England, was the first to lease the plantation's lands. Having previously leased land at the Belle Grove estate, when Oakland became available he added the property to his lease holdings. With sugar production totals of twenty-eight hogsheads in 1872 at Oakland and twenty-two hogsheads in 1873 from Belle Grove, Hodges' efforts proved as disappointing as had the Kenners' attempts to turn the situation around. When the bank took over ownership,

Hodges lost the use of Oakland's lands and focused his efforts on Belle Grove, where he continued to work the land until 1879.

Although Hodges produced a few small sugar crops on his Kennerville properties, his most successful crop was rice. First grown in 1870 at Oakland by Philip Minor and Belle Grove by Hodges, rice increasingly became the area's primary crop for the large-scale farms in the postwar period. The first crop of rice was modest with a production at Oakland of fifty hogsheads and at Belle Grove of 250 hogsheads. Over the next decade the planters of the region became more comfortable with the crop and improved their yields. By 1877 Hodges's company at Belle Grove had increased its yield to 1,190 hogsheads. Improved technology and techniques resulted in even larger yields. The largest crop produced came in 1887 at Belle Grove, now renamed Boisblanc, by planters only identified as Thompson and Wilkinson who produced a yield of 6,600 hogsheads. Regretfully for the planters around Kennerville, in spite of their improved crop yields, in the 1880s large numbers of middle-western grain farmers settled on the flat fertile areas of southwest Louisiana. Using their experience and the latest rice-producing technology, they created larger and more efficient farms and revolutionized the rice industry in Louisiana. Unfortunately, the competition created by the modern rice farms located in the southwest portion of the state proved to be too much for local planters, and the once profitable rice industry at Kenner came to an end. With the demise of the rice industry in the area, the Citizens Bank of Louisiana decided to rid itself of its holdings at Kennerville and sold its Oakland property to John Deloss Rouse and a local political leader, James Conner Baumann, on April 5, 1889. The two men held the land for two months before selling it to The Oakland Land Company for only $11,000. The company then subdivided the property. Thus, by 1890, the large-scale-plantation agriculture that had dominated the economy of the Cannes Brûlées/Kennerville area since its earliest colonial days was no more.[19]

In the waning years of plantation agriculture in Kenner, some of the land at Oakland Plantation was put to a different use than simply producing a commercial crop. The influential Sugar Planter's Association acquired the rights to use a section of the Oakland property for a new agricultural endeavor. In an effort to improve their industry, the sugar planters of the state organized in 1877 a professional association. As the organization grew in power and influence it joined forces with the Louisiana Scientific and Agricultural Association to establish the Sugar Experiment Station in 1885. Formed to promote progress in the sugar culture of the state, a site needed to be obtained for the station. With the influence of Duncan Kenner, who at the time served as president of the association, a portion of his brother's estate at Oakland was selected as the site for the first experiment station in Louisiana. Although the station remained at Kenner for only four years before being moved to a site at Audubon Park in New Orleans, it played an integral role in the early effort to use science to improve agriculture in Louisiana. During its first year of operation alone, the station performed over 400 field experiments in such areas as the use of improved fertilizers, germination studies, and "desuckering." The station's efforts were not limited to sugar. During its first months of existence it also performed studies on sorghum, corn, rice, and cowpeas.[20]

When the experimental station moved to New Orleans and The Oakland Land Company began subdividing the property, the old-plantation-manor house that William Kenner constructed and lived in at Oakland fell into misuse and was soon abandoned. Shortly thereafter,

William Kenner's Oakland Plantation house as it appeared near the end of the nineteenth century and its destruction by rising waters of the Mississippi River.

when it appears that the house was left unprotected by a new levee system, the old house was consumed by the high waters and currents of the Mississippi River. The other large Kenner manor home, Belle Grove, suffered a fate even more destructive than did the Oakland house. Leased by Minor Kenner's widow, who had moved to Mobile, Alabama, to Charles Hodges, the old Belle Grove house and its contents was "entirely destroyed" by a fire that started in its basement at 4:30 on the morning of March 17, 1870. Uninsured, the twenty-room house was a total loss.[21]

Though the postwar decades brought tough times to the plantations of the area, the small farms at Kennerville and the surrounding area survived the war largely intact. As most of them had not been dependent on slave labor before and during the war, emancipation did not have the economic consequences for the small farmer that it had on the plantation owners. In fact, as most of the farmers in the area had concentrated their efforts at growing food crops for sale in New Orleans, the occupation of the area by large numbers of Federal troops provided a ready market for their agricultural products. In the postwar period when the region's planters and the producers of staple crops suffered greatly from the economic decline of the time, the small truck farmers of Kennerville prospered. For though the large-scale agricultural operations in Louisiana were severely damaged by the war, in the postwar years there was a demand for food products in New Orleans and elsewhere in the state. With food more important than staples, the farmers of Kenner were able to prosper in spite of the economic and political problems that dominated life in postwar Louisiana.[22]

It was during the postwar era that the little community increasingly became known simply as Kenner. As early as the late 1850s, references to Kenner instead of Kennerville made their way into the New Orleans newspapers and onto maps prepared at the time. During the war, military reports, maps, and communications used both titles in referring to the village. Kennerville remained the dominant reference for the village and Kenner to the overall area formerly referred to as Cannes Brûlées. In the years following the end of the war, the village continued to be known by both terms, with Kenner gradually growing in popularity. Nevertheless, as late as 1892 the papers in New Orleans continued to refer frequently to the town as Kennerville.[23]

The slow pace of settlement that had stalled Minor Kenner's plans for a real-estate bonanza in the months leading up to the war continued after the conflict ended. One major difference in the residents of the area was that after the war a large percentage of the new inhabitants of the village were the former slaves who once worked and lived on nearby plantations. By 1870, the U. S. Census[24] showed the greater Kennerville area having a population of 2,008 residents. Of this number, 81 percent (1,635) were listed in the census as being black and only 15 percent (298) as white. The remaining 4 percent (75) were listed as mulattos. As the population increased, the village began to take on the trappings common to larger towns. At the time of the census, the town boasted a growing number of businesses, including several agricultural related companies, a bakery, a butcher shop, several small grocery stores, a shoe repairman, a livery stable, a variety store, and a coffee house. In addition to these businesses, the village also boasted several carpenters, a mechanic, a stock dealer, a brick mason, and its own place of worship. Officially, the village was part of the church parish of St. Mary of the Nativity at Carrollton (now Mater Dolorosa in New Orleans). Because of the size of the Kenner community and its distance from Carrollton, the Archdiocese of New Orleans in 1868 began to hold services in the village at the community's first church, St. Mary's Catholic Church. Father F. X. Ceuppens was the first Catholic priest to offer services in the village in the postwar period. So well received were the services that the archdiocese moved to establish an independent parish at the village. By 1872, Father J. Scollard was appointed the first resident pastor of the new parish. In addition to serving the residents of Kenner, the new parish became the center of all missionary activities in both the Florida Parishes and in areas as far as seventeen miles upriver from Kenner. Although the church was built and operated for years prior, it was not until 1877 that the archdiocese canonically recognized its organization. Not long afterwards, the parish began being referred to as Our Lady of Perpetual Help.[25]

Many of the new residents of the village in the years following the war were not unlike those who had arrived when Minor Kenner first offered his lots for sale. As it had in antebellum times, New Orleans during the postwar period remained among the nation's leading ports for the arrival of immigrants to America. Adding to the issues associated with the arrival of new immigrants to the area was the presence of growing labor difficulties between planters and their laborers that had accompanied emancipation of the region's sizeable slave population. In an attempt to replace the freedmen who, when given a chance, abandoned plantation work, in 1866 the Louisiana legislature passed legislation that created a commission of immigration to promote migration to the state. Although some immigrants continued to arrive in the area, by the late 1880s the flow of Irish and other northern Europeans slackened because the opportunities in postbellum Louisiana could not compete with those offered in the rapidly industrializing North. However, as the arrival of immigrants from northern Europe diminished, political and economic changes in Italy led to a large migration of residents from the island of Sicily to Louisiana. When they arrived in America, typically poor, uneducated, and unskilled, the Italians, as the Irish before them, largely found work as the stigmatized working class who were forced to begin at the bottom of the economic ladder and who along with members of the black community performed the menial labor of the region.[26] Over time, many of the new Sicilian immigrants to New Orleans made their way to the Kenner area. Few of the new arrivals brought any type of trade or professional skills other than their experience of working the land back in their homeland. Some of the more fortunate families were able to save enough money to acquire land at Kenner. Along with the families that had settled the area before the war, newly arrived Italian and German migrants along with the region's former slaves developed a thriving agricultural community at Kenner. With a three hundred day growing season and an annual rainfall of sixty-two inches, it was possible as soon as one crop was harvested to plant another immediately. Unlike their neighbors on the Belle Grove and Oakland estates, the farmers on their small plots of land concentrated on dairy farming and the growing of vegetables. With the Italian farmers of the area focusing on vegetable production, a number of German families concentrated their efforts on the growing of flowers and ornamental shrubbery. For years the German farmers at Kenner were the primary providers of the thousands of chrysanthemums used by the florists of New Orleans.[27]

The Italian migration to the Kenner area continued throughout the latter half of the nineteenth century. In time, the Italian/Sicilian

Undated photo probably taken in the final years of the nineteenth or early days of the twentieth century depicting the rural nature of early Kenner with its sparsely placed housing and open vegetable fields.

Originally named as St. Mary's, the name of Kenner's Catholic parish was changed to Our Lady of Perpetual Help in 1936. Pictured in this 1928 photo is the old school house and church (which also served as a classroom building for a time) where hundreds of Kenner's children were educated before a modern school was constructed in the early 1960s.

Shortly before its destruction by hurricane Katrina, Cristina's packing shed, located near the intersection of William's Blvd. and the Illinois Central Railroad's tracks, once served as the center of Kenner's thriving truck-farming industry.

population of the town gradually increased to a point where they began to dominate the truck-farming industry of the region. The Italian dominance of the local economy put pressure on the other farmers of the community to such a degree that some sold their properties because they did not like dealing with the Italian competition. Gradually the Italian population gained a near monopoly in the truck-farming industry in Kenner.[28]

Hard work by its farmers, fertile alluvial soil, warm temperatures, a long growing season, plentiful rainfall, and increasing demand for their products all led the Kenner area to become one of Louisiana's richest and most productive agricultural communities. By 1900, with the continued arrival of new residents who took up truck farming on their small family plots, the once sluggish little town at the height of the growing season produced on average three railroad carloads daily of fresh produce that was shipped across the nation. Much of the town's produce was processed for market at Cristina's depot, operated by Joseph Cristina, a town grocer and treasurer of the Kenner Truck Farmers Association. The president of the farmers' group was John Clancy, whose son Frank would later serve as sheriff of Jefferson Parish and become one of the most powerful politicians in the history of the parish. By 1913, the size of the local produce crop had increased to such an amount that the number of vegetable packaging companies grew to twenty-one. In the early years of the new century as many as sixty refrigerated railcars a day left Kenner for points across the nation.[29]

Other farmers in the community continued to focus their efforts on meeting the needs of the local produce market in New Orleans. On the small farms of Kenner it was common practice that each day a member of the family took a wagon or truck load of their produce to the farmers' section of the old French Market in the Crescent City. There they would remain until the cargo was sold before making the long road trip back to Kenner to prepare another load to be taken to the city on the next day. Because of the climate and the near year-long growing season, it was possible to have almost non-stop crop production. During the long growing season, the Kenner farms produced a varied list of products. Among the variety of crops grown on the town's farms and shipped to New Orleans and other parts of the country were bell peppers, tomatoes, red beets, broccoli, collards, cabbages, carrots, corn, cucumbers, endive, escarole, Creole peas, eggplants, field peas, potatoes, lima beans, mirlitons, mustard, lettuce, onions, okra, parsley, snap beans, yellow and white squash, chards, spinach, red and white radishes, shallots, sweet potatoes, turnips, and cauliflower.[30]

Although in the months and years following the end of the Civil War the economy of the Kenner area centered primarily around small-scale-truck farming, towards the end of the century some large-scale manufacturing ventures also moved into the area. Among the earliest companies to be established at Kenner was Rogers and Ballintine Company Limited. This business at first leased and later purchased a section of the western portion of Oakland Plantation, where they harvested timber for the purpose of cutting crossties for use by the railroad. Other manufacturers also interested in the abundant timber supply in the area soon followed. One of the oldest and largest of these companies was the Sutherland Innis Company, which in 1904 became the Southwestern Box and Lumber Company. The firm was later sold and became J.P. Morgan's Louisiana Box and Lumber Company. Also involved with making product from the area's timber was the Anchor Sawmill, which later became the Ipik Plywood Company. Additionally, the Mancuso Barrel and Box Company worked with the town's farmers providing special packing designed to ship safely the vegetables produced by the local farmers. Kenner's farmers believed that because their vegetables were better packed than competing produce they could command better prices for their products in the North. Finally, to meet the demand of the town's produce industry, in 1908 the state-of-the-art Kenner Ice and Cold Storage Company opened to service the area's farmers.[31]

Among the most ambitious projects to come to the area during the period prior to the turn of the twentieth century was a real-estate venture intended to create an entirely new suburban community a short distance to the west of the upriver boundary of Kennerville. Designed to take advantage of the location of the Illinois Central railroad line, the plan for the new community essentially followed the one originally put into place by Minor Kenner when he first tried to establish a residential community on his plantation lands. Engineered by Horace W. Sessions, the new community was given the name of Hanson City in honor of a popular passenger agent of the Illinois Central named

A.H. Hanson. Designed as a modern suburban community with its own passenger depot on the railroad, the development was divided into 550 residential lots, which ranged in price from $29 to $125 per lot. Preceding its grand opening on November 10, 1894, the Hanson City Land Company ran extensive an public relations campaign in New Orleans newspapers, promoting the development as "The New Industrial City of the South." The developer offered special trains, which provided free transport from New Orleans, for the several thousand prospective homeowners who made the trip to the site during the projects' grand opening. Unfortunately, in spite of an enthusiastic opening in which the owners boasted that they sold over three hundred lots, the project never achieved the success its planners expected. Only a smattering of the lots ever had homes constructed on them. Nevertheless, though the "prosperous little city" promised by the developers never came to be, the area of the location of the project has continued to modern times to be known as Hanson City.[32]

The overall prosperity enjoyed by the small farmers of Kenner during the decades of the late nineteenth century was accompanied by an array of problems. As in the years before the war, the condition of the area's levees evoked constant concern. Of all the physical damage caused by the Civil War to Louisiana, the longest lasting was the degradation of the state's levee system. The combination of the neglect that occurred during the war and the loss after emancipation of laborers who had experience in levee repair and upkeep resulted in the levees of the region being in such disrepair that they provided little protection from flood waters. Before the war, levee maintenance was the responsibility of the owners of lands subject to flooding. After the war ended, the large landowners, without their slaves and largely lacking the needed capital, were unable to restore or maintain the levees. With the planters unable to fulfill their obligations, the state and parish governments were forced into providing levee maintenance and repair. Yet, in spite of government involvement with the levees, the resources available for the job were so limited that little was accomplished in flood protection. The ineffectiveness of local and state government levee management was evident just a few months after the end of the war when Kennerville was dangerously threatened by flood waters after it took over a month for local officials to address a one hundred-foot cave-in of a vital section of the levee at the Bell Grove Plantation. The condition of the levees continued to be a major concern for the residents of the Kenner area and elsewhere until Congress established the Mississippi River Commission in 1879. The Federal takeover of flood control finally brought real flood protection to the region. Unfortunately, one result of the Federal participation in levee construction and maintenance was the loss of a large portion of the Kennerville river front. Because the town was situated on the cutbank or outer bend of a Mississippi River meander, the natural levee was gradually eroded by the river's currents. For years, as the river eroded the bank next to the town, efforts were made to maintain the levee in such a manner that it veered in an almost crescent design around the little town. However, with the Federal management of levee construction and the arrival of larger and more effective levees, the town could no longer be spared from a loss of land. The new stronger levee required a direct line of construction which did not allow for the veer around the town, and as a result nearly two and a half blocks of the old Kennerville ended up outside of the new levee and were soon lost to the river, thus making Third Street the southernmost roadway in modern Kenner.[33]

It took some time for the new federally sponsored Mississippi River Commission to implement improved levees. During the period of levee upgrading Kennerville continued to face the danger of river flooding. Twice in 1880, once in February and once in May, the town was endangered by crevasse flooding. On both occasions, poorly constructed rice flumes succumbed to high river levels and caused area flooding. The May crevasse, which took place four miles upriver from the town, was approximately thirty-feet wide and four-feet deep. Although most houses in Kennerville were spared from serious damage by the crevasse, many of the agricultural fields of the community were inundated with flood waters. As late as 1892, the area continued to face potential flooding from breaks in the river's levee. In May of that year flooding from a break at Bonnet Carré once again dangerously threatened but fortunately spared Kennerville from serious damage.[34]

Besides the issues of the area's weakened levees and occasional flooding they brought to the vegetable fields of Kenner, the farmers of the town also had to deal with several years of extremely cold winters. Some of the worst of the cold arrived on Mardi Gras day, February 14,

1899, when the thermometer dropped to seven degrees and a large ice flow miles in length actually floated down the Mississippi to Kenner. Though the river ice was a novelty that drew Kenner citizens to the levee to view the once-in-a-lifetime occurrence, the farmers of the town faced losing the results of much of the hard labor they had put into their fields during the recent planting season. The *Daily Picayune* lamented at the time that, "everything outdoors was dead, not even excepting the cabbages, which are the hardiest of all vegetables. Truck farmers who had worked hard to keep the freeze out of their hotbeds had most of them failed [*sic*] and their young plants were all gone."[35]

The killer freeze of Mardi Gras was not the only disaster to befall the farmers of Kenner in 1899. Several months after the freeze, when the area's agriculture was still recovering from the killer cold of the previous winter, a deadly anthrax plague struck the area's livestock. The disease destroyed many of the cattle and mules that were essential to the livelihood of the small farms of the town. With many of the farmers in the area being of Italian or Sicilian descent, they held a special reverence for St. Rosalie, the patroness of Palermo in Sicily. In the 1600s when the livestock of Sicily were threatened by the plague, the residents of the Mediterranean island prayed to the saint for assistance. Shortly thereafter the plague broke. Hence, with the disease ravaging livestock in Kenner, the people prayed to St. Rosalie for help and promised to honor her for her assistance by placing a statue of the saint in their church (then called St. Mary's) and by having an annual event to honor her intercession. When the plague ended and the farmers of Kenner returned to prosperity, the people of the town kept their word and started the tradition of honoring the saint on a yearly basis.[36]

The first festival honoring St. Rosalie attracted only a handful of participants. But in 1902 a large number of residents of the town organized the St. Rosalie Society and began making plans for a festival that would truly do honor to its patron. On September 2, 1902, over a thousand visitors and residents of the town came together in a day-long celebration that began with a 7:00 a.m. mass and ended with a large fireworks display at 7:30 in the evening. The highlight of the celebration was a 4:00 p.m. procession by hundreds of residents in which the large statue of the saint was paraded through the streets of the town. Ever since that time, each year during the first or second

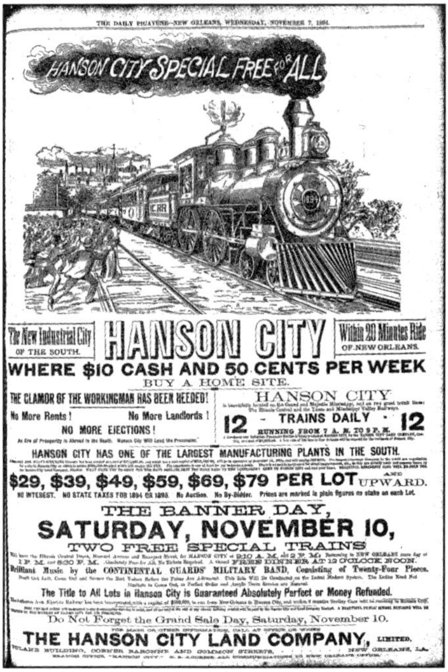

1894 advertisement promoting the opening of the Hanson City real estate.

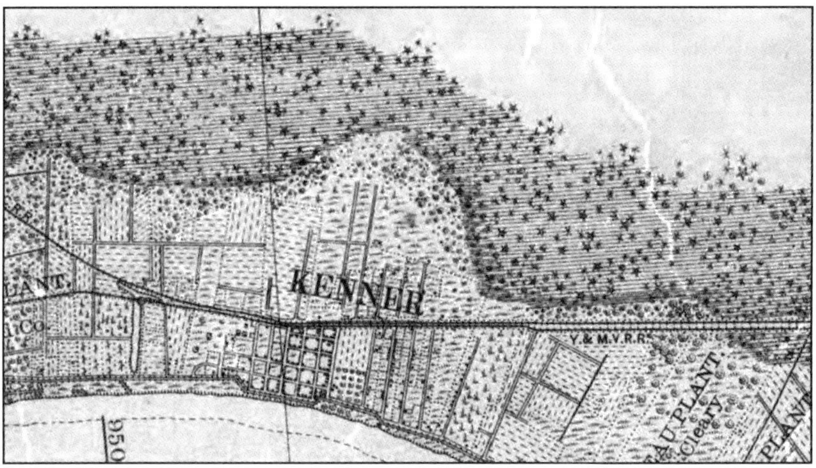

This Mississippi River Commission map shows the settlement pattern in Kenner at the end of the nineteenth century. Housing and adjacent agricultural plots and the large Oakland Land Company holdings are laid out. Also visible is the zigzag nature of the Mississippi River levee at the town. With the strengthening and straightening of the levee to create its modern footprint, several blocks and streets in the town were lost to the mighty river.

Among the more unique natural phenomenon to affect the people of Kenner occurred on Mardi Gras day, February 14, 1899, when residents awoke to seven degree weather and three inches of snow covering the region. Most amazing of all was the situation on the Mississippi River at Kenner where a huge ice floe, stretching miles in length, clogged the mighty waterway as far as the eye could see.

On the first or second weekend every September, residents of Kenner celebrate the feast of St. Rosalie by processioning the saint's statue through the streets around Our Lady of Perpetual Help Catholic Church. The event dates back to 1899 as an annual thanksgiving honoring the saint's intercession in a crippling anthrax epidemic which was killing the community's livestock. Pictured is the 1929 celebration leaving Our Lady of Perpetual Help church at the start of the procession.

week of September the people of Kenner continue to celebrate the feast of St. Rosalie. Although the crowds of the past, which numbered in the thousands, have slackened in modern times, hundreds of people from throughout the area continue to take part in the celebration. After a mass dedicated to the patroness, the statue of Saint Rosalie is carried from the now-named parish of Our Lady of Perpetual Help Catholic Church on a traditional three-mile walk through the streets of the older areas of modern Kenner. Traditionally some walk in the procession barefoot and others carry lighted candles which they place in the church when the procession returns to the location where it began for benediction of the Blessed Sacrament. With the end of the procession and services, a celebration takes place. Although for decades the event was celebrated with a parish fair, in recent times it has taken the form of a large community dinner held on the grounds of the parish church.[37]

The annual church festival was not the only social activity enjoyed by the people of Kenner. As discussed previously, the town was the site of several important boxing events, which brought large crowds of visitors to the community. Additionally, the large open area that separated the old Bell Grove Plantation house site from the neatly laid out homestead plots of the town became a popular gathering spot for community activities. Known as the "Kenner Lawn" the open green area was sometimes used for large picnics. For example, in late May 1871, the New Orleans Jackson and Great Northern Railroad Beneficiary Association advertised in the *Daily Picayune* its plans for a grand picnic at the location and promised that, "There will be horse racing and field sports generally, refreshments in abundance, music by Portune's band. With good weather, a fine time is to be expected."[38] On other occasions the town's people were entertained by traveling performing groups. Among the most popular of these groups was the occasional visit to the town by the circus. So it was in February 1872 when Dan Rice with his "monster circus company" stopped at the town to give a one-day performance of "arenic [*sic*] entertainment" so grand that "nothing has ever been seen to surpass it." Advertised as "Dan Rice's Pavilion," the circus company promised the people of Kennerville a wide range of entertainment, including "wonderfully trained horses, . . . comic mules, educated dogs, . . . acrobats, gymnasts and trapeze performances . . . ."[39]

6
Ugly Tensions and Violent Vigilantism

Fortunately for the farmers of Kenner, during most of the postwar period they were spared the worst aspects of the economic devastation that afflicted most of the rest of the agricultural community in Louisiana. Because the farmers of Kenner focused their postwar efforts on truck farming and the supplying of fresh-food products to the markets in the city of New Orleans and elsewhere rather than of on large-scale commercial crops, they were able to minimize the economic problems faced by farmers and planters in other parts of the state. Unfortunately, their success in avoiding some of the worse aspects of the poor economic conditions that people of the state faced was not repeated in regards to the social and political crisis that gripped Louisiana during the same postwar period. With the end of the Civil War came the formal emancipation of the state's slave population. White Louisianans, for the most part, accepted the defeat of the Confederacy and the freeing of the slaves. What the majority of the white population was not willing to accept was the political and social equality of the Negro. They did not think that the loss of the war and the legal end to slavery required them to change the social and cultural traditions and values they had practiced throughout their lives.[1]

Shortly after the end of the war, statewide elections were held, and the voters overwhelmingly elected officials who had served in the Confederate effort or enthusiastically supported it. The newly elected leaders then passed legislation designed to regulate and limit the freedom and social standing of the state's African American residents. Though the former slaves were to be given new privileges, the parameters and extent of their new rights and freedoms had to be determined. Whites across the South were intent on seeing that the former slaves were kept in a place of manual labor and of social and political subservience. To accomplish this, Black Codes were passed by the Louisiana legislature and other law-making bodies across the South. As noted by historian Kenneth Stampp, these codes, in spite of cries by white Southerners that they were simply an effort to bring order to postwar chaos, were simply an attempt to "keep the Negro, as long as possible, exactly what he was: a propertyless rural laborer under … strict controls, without political rights, and with inferior legal rights."[2] Many of the new codes resembled legislation that was in effect during the antebellum period, including limiting areas in which former slaves could purchase or rent property. Other laws imposed vagrancy restrictions that levied heavy penalties designed to force freedmen to work, whether they desired to or not. For example, if a black man quit his job, he was subject to arrest and imprisonment for breach of contract.[3]

At the end of the war and after all Federal troops withdrew from the area, the little town of Kennerville soon reverted to its prewar appearance of a few commercial enterprises and a handful of residences and small truck farms. It was still dirty and dusty when the sun was shining and became a muddy quagmire with the slightest rain. Among the most dramatic changes brought by the war was the presence of large numbers of former slaves in the area. As was the case with freedmen across the postwar South, in the months following emancipation the black population of the Kenner area generally found themselves without money, land, jobs, schools, or businesses. These uncertain conditions led to a large number of blacks roaming and foraging the area for supplies. To some, their newly granted liberty meant freedom to do as they pleased. When combined with their increasingly difficult living conditions, some freedmen used their liberty to roam the region committing petty crimes. On the other hand, many of the white residents of the Kenner area, like white Southerners elsewhere, had during the antebellum period long harbored deep fears of what would happen if blacks were ever able to escape the controls of the plantation. Now in the months after emancipation with hundreds of former slaves foraging the area, the white residents of Kenner were forced to face the problem they had dreaded for so long. Unhappy wartime experiences, such as the incident involving the burning of the Kenner family's barn at Oakland Plantation by a disgruntled black man as discussed above, and the knowledge that they were now greatly outnumbered by the area's former slaves, reinforced the fears and insecurities of the region's whites.[4]

The differences, anxieties, and economic problems faced by the white and black residents of the Kenner area led to increased tensions and at times open hostility between the two groups. One such incident occurred in late October 1865 at Kennerville. According to a complaint he sent to Governor J. Madison Wells, W.P. Coleman, a white resident of the town, claimed that he was afraid for his safety as his life and that of his family had been threatened by a group of blacks. The governor ordered an immediate investigation by the Provost Marshall of Jefferson Parish. The investigation revealed the complicated and increasingly hostile nature of race relations at the time in Kennerville. The blacks involved in the incident were laborers on the Bell Grove Plantation who were picking pecans from trees located near Coleman's property. On seeing the blacks, Coleman angrily ordered the workers off his land. When they refused, he threatened them with a gun, which resulted in their leaving the area. One of the threatened men retrieved his own gun and returned to the tree and resumed picking pecans. On seeing his return, Coleman began shooting at him, and he returned fire. No injuries resulted from the exchange of gunfire and the matter was turned over to the civil authorities for settlement.[5]

Although the pecan-tree incident in Kennerville was relatively minor, it exemplified the growing tension between the races in the entire region. The more freedmen pushed for political and social equality the more the whites of the region felt threatened and the more harshly they responded. Tensions worsened to such a degree that in 1866 and 1868 there were large-scale bloody clashes between the races on the streets of New Orleans resulting in the deaths of numerous blacks and a lesser number of whites. Smaller and less violent race-related disturbances soon spread into surrounding areas including Jefferson Parish. The increasing violence against blacks in Louisiana and elsewhere led to growing concern among members of Congress and people throughout the North. Convinced that African Americans in the South needed additional protections, Congress passed multiple pieces of legislation designed to protect blacks in the South. Once in place, the Reconstruction Acts brought fundamental political changes to Louisiana and the rest of the South.[6]

The Federal legislation, which came about as a result of Radical Republicans taking the reins of reconstruction following their success in the Congressional elections of 1866, had the effect of declaring the governments of the former Confederate states, excluding Tennessee, to be illegal and that they were to be henceforth governed by Federal authorities. The South was divided into five military districts, with Louisiana and Texas making up the Fifth District under the command of General Philip H. Sheridan. Under the new Radical regime, a drastic reorganization based upon the expansion of African American suffrage and political power with the simultaneous disfranchisement of ex-Confederates brought about a historic altering of the long-standing power structure in Louisiana and the rest of the South. By the time Federal authorities extended the franchise to include Louisiana's African American population and eliminated most ex-Confederates from the voter rolls, two-thirds of the total number of the voters of the state were black. Furthermore, Federal authorities continued to push for a new order in the state by pressing for constitutional changes that resulted in the adoption in 1868 of a new state charter that granted blacks political, civil, and social rights. As expected, in the election of state officials that coincided with the vote to ratify the new Constitution of 1868, Republicans, with the support of the state's African American voters, seized control of state government. Though the transfer of power in Louisiana was now complete, the takeover of the government by the Radical Republicans quickly resulted in a broadening of the breach between the races and the formation of a powerful counter coalition between poor whites and the remains of the old-guard planter-merchant oligarchy that had long dominated power in the state. [7]

It did not take long before the shift in political power in the state brought changes to the local political scene. With the rise of African American political power and the approaching 1868 presidential election, there came increased occasions of tension and street violence and intimidation between the races in and around New Orleans, including in Jefferson Parish. In an effort to increase control and security for the area's Republican supporters, the new Republican governor Henry Clay Warmoth encouraged the legislature to create the Metropolitan Police District. The legislation stripped control of the New Orleans area's all-white and heavily Democratic police departments from local officials and merged the departments of Orleans, Jefferson, and St. Bernard into a single multi-racial force under the direction of a five member racially mixed board appointed by the governor. This new force was supposed to act as the primary law enforcement agency in the New Orleans region. It was financed by taxation on the municipalities within the district and, much to the loathing of most whites, superseded the authority of local police organizations, including those that maintained order in the Kenner area.[8]

Radical rule also brought other important changes to the lives of the people of Kenner. The desire of the convention delegates who wrote the new constitution of 1868 for bringing social and civil equality to the state's freedmen led them to make changes in Louisiana's educational system. Though there was an understanding among many of the convention's delegates that the equal accommodations and directives to integrate all schools would take some time to implement, the convention, nevertheless, mandated important changes in the schools of the state. A minimum of one public school was required to be established in every parish and children from ages six to eighteen years were to be eligible to attend, regardless of race. It was this new interest in public education in Louisiana that led to the establishment of Kenner's first public school.[9]

During antebellum times, public schools in Jefferson Parish were mostly the responsibility of the small municipalities located in the parish, including the city of Jefferson and the town of Carrollton. Though a private academy was located for a time in Kennerville, no public schools were operated in the village during the prewar period. With the coming of the Civil War and the arrival of Federal authorities in the area, which sparked renewed interest in public education and for the first time a desire to provide schooling for the region's black children. Nathaniel Banks, the commander of Federal troops in the region, promoted the education of African Americans in the arena under his command and in the fall of 1863 authorized the establishment of schools for blacks. The general continued to push the issue, and by September 1864 schools for African American children were in operation in most of the parishes under Federal control, including Jefferson. In July 1865, the black schools were placed under the authority of the Freedmen's Bureau, the newly created Federal agency with the mission of aiding the transition of former slaves to freedom. As for white children in Jefferson, in the months following the end of the war, education was much as it was before the conflict with the municipalities in the parish operating the few schools that managed to open.[10]

In spite of the fact that the schools operated by the Freedmen's Bureau in the parish were eventually turned over to the state to operate and that schools remained open in the city of Carrollton for white children, the availability of public education for most who lived on the east bank (left bank) of Jefferson Parish before the adoption of the 1868 Constitution was limited. A change in the political leadership that accompanied the adoption of the new constitution evidently resulted in an improvement in the schooling offered to children who resided on the east bank of the parish. In his 1871 annual report, the school superintendent praised the schools of the area for being "better supervised and cared for than any others" and for local school-board members for having "manifested a zealous interest in the fostering of their schools." By the time the quote was made, East Jefferson could boast of having one school open in each of its six wards. However, with the decrease in Federal oversight in the region over the postwar years, money became increasingly tight for the operation of local schools and their operation remained sporadic for a long time. So frustrating did the lack of financial support for public education become that in 1873 the parish treasurer lamented that "the police jury [the governing authority of the parish] had never manifested any disposition to foster the educational interest of the parish, having been too much interested upon gleaning for their own coffers."[11]

The lack of adequate financial support from the state and local governments slowed but did not end support for public education in Jefferson Parish and Kennerville. By 1874 East Jefferson had four schools in operation, including Kenner No. 1 and Kenner No. 2. In spite of the existence of state laws calling for integrated schools, the two Kenner schools were segregated by race, with the school for blacks having an enrollment of seventy and the white facility being smaller with a daily attendance of twelve students. When compared to other public schools in the area, both Kenner schools won the commendation of locals, including the *Daily Picayune*, which praised the two schools for what it noted as "the liberal munificence [the way] public money is applied to education in that [Kenner] booming and progressive burg." The paper gave credit for the schools' success to Mr. and Mrs. Connor, the schools' two teachers. Mrs. Connor taught the children in the school for whites, and Mr. Connor at the school for black children. In addition to serving as a teacher, Mr. Connor also served as the mayor of Kenner, its justice of the peace, and as the local school board member. When questioned by a local reporter about his many duties, he noted that he added the role of teacher to his busy schedule because he was not willing "to see the youth of Kenner grow up in ignorance."[12]

Despite the dedicated efforts of the Conners to educate all the children of Kenner, money issues and competition from both a nearby private school and from newly opened Catholic schools led the following year to the operation of only one of the community's two schools—Kenner No.1. The school served the combined populations of the previous two Kenner schools and enjoyed an integrated-student enrollment of eighty-three pupils. The custom at the time among the Catholic parishes of the region was to establish denominational schools in each community served by the parish. Being a poor church parish, the Catholics of Kenner had to look elsewhere for the money needed to build and operate a Catholic school. Help came from the Society of the Holy Spirit, an organization of Catholic men formed to spread Catholic literature and to help the archbishop in his duties. The organization was successful in finding funding for Catholic education in Kenner and opened St. Agnes School for white children and St. Benedict for the area's black children to attend. The two schools prospered, for all Catholics were required, under pain of sin, to send their children to a Catholic school. As the Catholic schools were free, their existence and competition placed a burden on the area's public school and slowed the growth of public education in the community. Nevertheless, by 1908 three public schools were in operation in Kenner, including two for whites and one for blacks. Five teachers were employed in the schools and earned from thirty to forty dollars per month.[13]

The challenge presented by Kenner's parochial schools was not the last major problem faced by the community's supporters of public education. In 1881, financing of public education in Jefferson Parish was accomplished by a property tax, which assessed a fee of one-fourth of one percent on taxable property. Over time the levy gradually increased until it reached three mills in 1914. It was a dispute over this tax that resulted in one of the most serious crises in the effort to bring quality public education to the residents of Kenner. Because of a technicality in the city charter of Kenner, residents of the community were not legally obligated to pay their share of the education tax. In 1884, after lengthy negotiations, town and parish officials were unable to reach an agreement on how much the residents of Kenner needed to pay. With the deadlock, the city of Kenner simply stopped paying its share of the tax. The police jury responded by refusing to allot any funds for the operation of the schools in Kenner, which resulted in their closing. Because of the dispute, the Kenner community remained without public education for more than two years before the issue was settled and the schools in the town reopened.[14]

Unfortunately, the school tax debate and the subsequent loss of public education in Kenner was only one consequence of the tarnished relations between the residents of the community and others in Jefferson Parish. As will be discussed in the following chapter, the political, social, and racial discord between people in Kenner and powerful political forces in Jefferson Parish not only led to the closing of public schools, but also brought about decades of tension and violence in Kenner and other parts of Jefferson Parish and would eventually lead to the demise of the City of Kenner itself. Meanwhile, the political changes ushered in during the Reconstruction period temporarily gave political power and control to what most white Southerners considered to be radical forces. These individuals were considered radical because they included the newly enfranchised freedmen of the South and their benefactors in the Republican Party. The racial and political tensions of the postwar years continued to divide the residents of Kenner for decades.

As long as Federal military forces remained present, it was impossible for the anti-radical forces in the state to overthrow Radical rule using legal methods. Growing frustration among white Southerners resulted in racial antagonisms becoming increasingly fierce and led whites to turn to subterfuge and extralegal means, including terror tactics, to challenge Radical authority. Even with the end of Radical Reconstruction following the presidential election of 1876, the political process in Louisiana remained enmeshed in violence for decades. As in the past, the Democratic Party in Louisiana during the postwar years remained under the domination of the state's white elites. Using fraud, violence, and intimidation of blacks, the Democrats by 1878 were able to achieve the final overthrow of the Republican Party as a cogent political power in Louisiana. Rewriting the Constitution in 1879, the Democrats made as their priority in the new document the formal reaffirmation of white supremacy in Louisiana.[15]

In spite of the success of the Democrats in reasserting their control in the state, areas persisted where Republicans and their African American supporters remained embedded in the local political structure. Jefferson Parish was one of the places in the state where blacks outnumbered whites and remained an area of Republican influence. Democrats were confident that the African Americans in the state could be controlled politically and socially by means of labor constraints, violence, and other methods of intimidation, provided the alliances between the Republicans and blacks could be broken. However, with the whites in Jefferson being outnumbered by the African American population, the effort of the whites to take political and social control in the parish was not a simple matter. The struggle between the two political and racial groups continued for decades and on occasion degenerated into violence, intimidation, and vigilantism. Racism and violence became an all-too-familiar occurrence in Jefferson Parish during the second half of the nineteenth century. So tumultuous became the struggle between the blacks and whites that the parish eventually earned a reputation that one modern-day historian labeled it as having a "virulently racist white sub culture"[16]

With the Kenner community having one of the largest populations of African American residents in Jefferson Parish, it was one of the central battlegrounds for political control of the parish. As personified by the dispute over the payment of school and parish taxes discussed above, the political fight in Jefferson was wide ranging and long lasting. The effort by whites to manipulate the situation in the parish began even before the end of Reconstruction and the withdrawal of Federal forces from the region. For example, in the elections of 1874, Charles Hodges, a white candidate for mayor of Kennerville and tenant of the old Belle Grove manor house at the time it was destroyed by fire, publicly attempted to intimidate African American voters by proclaiming in his campaign speech that "if the colored people in his employ did not vote the Conservative ticket they could, after the election, seek employment elsewhere."[17]

The tactics proved successful. State Senator T.B. Stamps gave testimony before a Congressional investigating committee that between two and three-hundred African Americans in his district, which included Jefferson Parish, voted for the Democratic ticket because of the fear of discharge from their job. He added, "I don't suppose there is one colored man in my district that will vote the Democratic ticket of his own volition." Finally, he noted that "The people were afraid they would be murdered like their friends—shot down in the streets."[18] Similarly, whites who voted Republican in elections also faced intimidation. Such was the situation noted by the Associated Press at the time when it reported in one of its releases on the elections that "a white man could not vote the Republican ticket without being ostracized, called a nigger, and anything else but a responsible gentleman."[19]

The bitter and personal nature of the struggle in the final years of the nineteenth century between the political factions in both Jefferson Parish and Kenner is demonstrated by the political career of James C. Baumann. The son of one of Kennerville's first settlers, as a youth James focused on his formal education. After completing his schooling, in 1867 he established himself as a druggist in the town. Not satisfied with his new career, he decided to take advantage of the prosperity that truck farming offered in Kenner in the years that followed the end of the war. He opened a mercantile business and began truck farming and sugar cane production on his land. In addition to his business dealings, Baumann also had an interest in the changing political events of the time. In late 1868, he took part in the national election, supporting the Republican nominee Ulysses Grant for president. Serving as the clerk of the election at Kennerville, Baumann got an eye-opening introduction to the politics which would dominate events in Jefferson Parish for decades to come. In the 1868 election, Democrats ran several special trains to Kenner filled with men under orders to intimidate voters going to the polls. So tense became the situation that by the end of the election a near riot took place when at the closing of the polls at 6 p.m. a group of the protesters broke down the doors of the polling place and proceeded to destroy ballots and threaten the election clerks with being shot. [20]

After the election, Baumann received his first political job when he was appointed by the president of the State Board of Education to be the representative of the 6th Ward (left bank) on the Jefferson Parish School Board. Chosen as the treasurer of the board, he continued to serve until 1871 and was among the strong proponents for a viable public-school system in the parish. In 1873 Baumann was selected to serve as a member of the Jefferson Parish Police Jury where he served as chairman of the Finance Committee. Later in that same year, he was elected secretary and treasurer for the City of Kenner. In the same election, he successfully worked to replace incumbent mayor O.T. Connor, who, with his political ally Charles Hodges, had run the city into thousands of dollars of debt. Even with the end of Reconstruction in 1877, Republican Baumann continued to win the support of the voters of Kenner. In 1879, he won election to the office of Second Justice of the Peace for Jefferson Parish. Given a salary of fifty dollars per month, Baumann donated his pay to the hiring of two teachers at the monthly salary of twenty-five dollars each. The two teachers were hired to provide instruction for the African American children of the area. Claiming that they only had enough funds for the operation of the school for white children, the parish school board had denied funding to educate the area's black children. Thanks to Baumann's generosity 125 African American children of Kenner were provided with schooling.[21]

Remaining a loyal member of the Republican Party throughout his decades-long political career, Baumann served in both appointed and elected political positions. Included among his elected offices were four years (two, two-year terms from 1880 to 1884) as mayor of Kenner and several years as clerk of court for Jefferson Parish. Additionally, Baumann often served in non-elected political positions at the parish, state, and national levels, including serving as a local election commissioner and as a delegate to the national Republican nominating convention. During his years of political activity, he came to know firsthand the dangerous nature of Jefferson Parish politics in the latter half of the nineteenth century. Even the relatively minor job of serving as an election commissioner brought with it threats of bodily harm as was discovered by Baumann during one of his first stints as an election official. When he attempted to enforce a new law that required all voters to have re-registered by denying Thomas McManan his vote because his registration papers were outdated, McManan, angered over his rejection, threatened Baumann with physical harm. So serious was the threat that for six months following the election—until McManan apologized for his threats—Baumann was forced to remain at home after dark for he feared coming into contact with his angry neighbor.[22]

On another occasion while giving a speech at the Baptist Church in Kenner to a crowd he later estimated to have been around five hundred people, Baumann barely escaped injury once again. Things got out of hand when an individual, Emanuel King, under the influence of liquor, made offensive remarks to others in the crowd. The offended parties drew their guns and opened fire. Over one hundred shots were exchanged between the two groups. King was killed, and Baumann had to be pulled by his friends from the riot. At the time, he served as the justice of the peace, so he immediately swore in several deputy constables who restored order.[23]

The individual who caused Baumann his greatest difficulties as a public servant and political activist was Henry Long, a leading Democrat in the Kenner area. Baumann's and Long's differences dated to two incidents in the 1880s when Baumann was called upon, because of his position as justice of the peace, to handle issues involving Long's behavior. The first incident took place in March 1880 when Leon Meyers of New Orleans, while he was on a visit to Kenner, filed a complaint for assault and harassment against Long, Paul Felix, Martin Donnelly, and a Mr. Ryan. Baumann accepted the complaint and issued warrants for the arrest of the accused men. The second incident came in 1886, when Long and several buddies entertained themselves one night by shooting up and down the streets of Kenner. One of the shots hit a young boy in the head. The victim was not mortally wounded, and he was able to identify Long as the shooter. Baumann issued a warrant for the arrest of Long and his friends. Finding them guilty of the municipal offense of shooting in town, Baumann fined each of them $2.50 and referred the more serious charge of shooting the victim to the district court for trial. In a trial by judge, the accused shooters were found not guilty because the judge doubted the eyewitness testimony due to the distance involved and the darkness of the night. The next day, Long met Baumann at his office in Kenner and had words. He questioned why Baumann had pressed the case and promised to see that the seventeen Democrats who had previously voted for Baumann would not do so in the future.[24]

An influential Democrat, Long began to work tirelessly to undermine Baumann's political support in the parish. When Baumann stood for re-election as clerk of court in 1888, Long and his fellow Democrats organized a plan against him. On the morning of the election, word circulated among Democratic voters to get to the polls in Kenner as early as possible. As soon as the Democrats voted, the election commissioners, the majority of whom were Democrats and included Long, A. Felix, and H.A. Stahl, ordered the polls closed on the pretext that there was an imminent threat of a riot taking place. Over two hundred Republicans appeared at the closed polls and remained standing in the sun in protest. With the same tactics being used by Democrats at other voter precincts in the parish, Baumann supporters were unable to cast their ballots and he failed to win re-election. Shortly thereafter the Democrats made inroads with the African American population in Kenner by orchestrating a black political organization called the "Progressive League of Kenner." With the support of the new African American political group, the Democrats successfully put together a multi-racial political ticket for the municipal elections that were held later in the year. In the election the Democrats were successful in getting Philip Holliday, a black man, elected mayor along with a multi-racial council.[25]

With the Democrats increasing their political presence in Kenner, Baumann turned to his Republican political contacts in Washington, D.C., and filed complaints against Henry Long's mother, who held the position of Postmistress of Kenner. Tying Mrs. Long to her son's vote manipulations in recent elections, Baumann urged that Mrs. Long be removed from her job. Shortly thereafter, Mrs. Long lost her position on orders of the U.S. Postmaster General. She was replaced with one of Baumann's allies, Dr. J.D. Faucett. The success of Baumann in having Mrs. Long replaced unleashed a fury and a desire for revenge that brought to politics in Kenner a dark virulence that surpassed anything else to date. Soon after Dr. Faucett assumed his duties, he was assaulted by Long, who was arrested and later placed under bond by a Federal judge. In January 1890, Dr. Faucett was again assaulted, this time by a man named Tucker who worked in the railroad office with Long. Although the attack was merciless and was witnessed by Long, the mayor, and several policemen, no attempt was made by the officials to rescue the victim. No arrests were made and the attacker was able to leave town without consequence. The unfortunate victim was seriously injured and was confined to bed for months before passing away.[26]

Tensions grew even worse in Kenner when the parish grand jury filed indictments in December 1889 for extortion, oppression, and malfeasance against several of the town's officials, including the mayor, who had been elected on the Democratic ticket. Baumann was soon approached by citizen groups in Kenner and urged to run for mayor in the November 1890 elections on an anti-corruption platform. When Long and the Democrats placed on the ballot the same ticket of officials who had been accused of corruption, Baumann made the decision to run. With the recent scandals fresh in voters' minds and with the history of Republican political support in Kenner, it looked increasingly apparent that the Republican candidates were heading for an election victory.[27]

As Baumann later recalled, Long and his allies in the parish's Democratic party realized that if strong measures were not taken immediately, the Republicans would recapture control of the municipal government in Kenner. Hence, on the evening before the election, a committee of Democratic leaders from around the parish traveled by train to Kenner. The committee included L.H. Marrero,[28] police jury president and future sheriff; Dr. L. Lebeauf, coroner; Dr. C.W. Settoon, parish physician; J.W. McCunethe, notary public and school board member; H. Keilman, police jury member; William Strelle, deputy sheriff and jailer; and several others. They were all heavily armed. In Kenner they approached Baumann, with Marrero acting as spokesman. They informed the Republican candidate that he would simply have to take himself out of the race for mayor and that they were in Kenner to see that it would be done—even if there had to be some bloodshed to accomplish their goal. The group went on to explain that if Baumann did not withdraw from the race, their committee would not be responsible for what might happen during the night. They suggested that his family and property would not be safe. Realizing the serious nature of the threat and the fact that he had no law enforcement official he could turn to for immediate help, Baumann gave in and the next day retired from active politics in Jefferson Parish—or so he thought.[29]

Though he dropped out of active politics,[30] the fact that Baumann and his family continued as a respected member of the Kenner community remained a problem for his political and personal enemies. In November 1891, Baumman received the following anonymous letter:

> J.C. Baumann,
> Kenner, Jefferson Parish
> The white people of Jefferson Parish consider your presence here perfectly obnoxious: still they do not believe in blood shed, unless they are forced to it. One thing they are decided to maintain: Their supremacy. You have had warning enough, we tell you now for the last time to leave, this parish, and if you do not do it immediately—BEWARE BEWARE
>
> Executive Committee of the
> White People of Jefferson Parish[31]

Baumann took the letter to the authorities but all mistakenly agreed, including Baumann, that the letter was only an idle threat. Several days later on the night of December 5, 1891, the Baumann home was visited by Thomas Ryan who asked for medical assistance to help his ill sister from Mrs. Baumann, who was well known for being a talented nurse. An attempt to call the nearest doctor who lived at Carrollton, ten miles away, failed when the Baumann's phone was found to be dead. So Mrs. Baumann departed to go give aid to the ill woman. Shortly after midnight, Mr. Baumann was awakened by someone attempting to open his front door. Thinking it was his wife, he went to the door to open it, but before he did he caught the sight of two suspicious looking men in heavy overcoats with hats pulled down over their faces. When he challenged the men's presence they informed him that they wanted to use the Baumann's phone. As he was explaining that his telephone was out of order (later to discover that the line had been cut), a shot rang out, splattering glass into Baumann's face and nearly hitting his head. Not totally unprepared for such an event, Baumann managed to jump from the hall where he was standing into a bedroom and retrieved his gun. With that, shotgun blasts of ten to fifteen loads began to shatter rooms throughout his house. One load of buckshot even entered the room where his children slept, missing them by eighteen inches. With the house riddled, the attackers left after about five minutes of shooting. Mrs. Baumann, who was a short distance away, heard the shots and hurried home to find her family in a panic. Baumann met her and told her all were safe. The couple then agreed that they would not remain in the house or Kenner for another day. After decades of service to the community, Baumann and his family packed their belongings and abandoned their property and moved the next day to New Orleans. The Democrats now had full control of Kenner.[32]

The change in political fortunes for the Democrats in Kenner did not end the enmity in the community between the supporters of each party. Although Baumann and his family figured that the change in address from his long-time Kenner home to a new residence in New Orleans would free them once and for all from the dangerous morass of the partisan politics of Kenner and Jefferson Parish, they soon discovered that they were wrong. With Baumann's exit from the political

James G. Baumann and his family. Baumann was the son of one of Kennerville's first residents. A loyal member of the Republican Party, he held multiple political positions, including mayor (1880-1884), during turbulent times in post-reconstruction Jefferson Parish and Kenner. He was also among the last owners of the Oakland Plantation estate.

arena in Jefferson, Henry Long and his colleagues filled the political void, including his assuming the position of local judge. In spite of the success of the Democrats taking political control, many in the community remained loyal to their Republican beliefs. Tensions between the political camps continued to rise until a sultry evening in July 1892. According to Judge Long, while walking to his home after returning on the evening train to Kenner from a visit with friends in Gretna, he was confronted, by "a negro [sic] [who] jumped from behind a tree and fired." Struck by two bullets which hit his arm and right breast near his collar bone and lung, the leader of the local Democrats was quickly given aid by several witnesses of the attack and was rushed by special train to New Orleans for medical care. The would-be assassin escaped into the night and in spite of the efforts of as many as twenty search parties to capture him, he avoided apprehension.[33]

The attack opened the door to a release of the political and racial frustrations that had been building for months in the Kenner community. Seemingly ignoring municipal authorities in Kenner, the investigation of the shooting was immediately taken over by Long's political allies in Jefferson Parish, including L.H. Marrero, now parish sheriff; Captain Landridge, the clerk of court; and Captain Fiesch of the Gretna police.[34] Within days of the attack the *Daily Picayune* reported that the shooting had "aroused considerable bitterness" and that the "vigilant officers of Jefferson parish" had learned that prior to the shooting several meetings had been held and that a plot was launched in Kenner by "several negroes [*sic*] and white men to force a number of white residents out of the place." According to the newspaper, the conspiracy called for the burning of the businesses of several of Long's Democratic allies, including that of his mother. Parish authorities began rounding up numerous suspects who were supposed to be members of the plot to set the fires and were thought to have been involved in the attack on Long. The paper noted that the arrested suspects "had given details of the plot, the names of the ringleaders and the name of the party who shot Judge Long."[35]

Racial tensions in Kenner now escalated dangerously. The 1890 census showed that whites now held the majority in Jefferson Parish, reinforcing their belief in racial dominance over their African American neighbors and their growing willingness to use violence to demonstrate to blacks the dangerous repercussions of defying the racial order.

When word circulated that "the negroes [*sic*] of the town had been holding secret meetings. . . [and] had agreed to first kill Judge Long . . . a leading citizen and politician, . . . [who was] feared by them, and then . . . [planned to] kill the other white citizens and burn their residencies and stores," angry whites decided to act. [36]

Supposedly identified by co-conspirators as the shooter of Long, Henry Dixon was arrested for the crime and held in the Gretna jail. Upon being granted bail, Dixon was released. However, once he crossed the river, he was arrested again for burglary in New Orleans by Kenner police at the corner of St. Charles and Jackson avenues. He was immediately returned to Kenner where he was placed in the city's old dilapidated jail alongside three other African American men being held for the plot to burn the town. Left without a guard, the prisoners were jarred awake around two o'clock in the morning by blows on the door by a gang of masked men. When the old door was breached, the men entered and took only the frightened Dixon. The mob re-nailed the door to the jail shut. The hapless prisoner was taken about four blocks from the jail and was quickly lynched from the branch of a large oak tree near the home of a member of the parish police jury. A volley of shots was fired to give warning to the community and then the masked murderers disappeared into the night. Demonstrative of the racial attitudes of many whites of the time, the *Daily Picayune* made little criticism of the killers by giving a more-or-less straightforward narrative of the lynching; however, when it came to the murdered victim, the paper focused on his reputation and practically vindicated the actions of the vigilantes by labeling the dead man as a person of "bad character" who was a "negro [sic] thief, desperado, and would-be assassin."[37]

The tragedy of Dixon's murder was compounded just a few days later when Dennis Richards confessed to the attack on Long. One of several individuals arrested by parish authorities in the wake of the assault, Richards told the sheriff that he was alone when he did the shooting, thus exonerating the lynched Dixon as a suspect. However, according to the sheriff, a close ally of the wounded Long, Richards confessed that he was given one thousand dollars by the Republican politician and former mayor J. C. Baumann to kill Long. Richards reportedly claimed that Baumann had explained that the reason he wanted Long killed was because "he has got to be put out of the way, for I [Baumann] can do nothing in Kenner as long as he is there." The startling statement led quickly to Baumann's arrest at his new home in New Orleans. Within hours he found himself incarcerated in the jail in Gretna.[38]

The fraud and manipulation that permeated much of the political arena in late nineteenth-century Jefferson Parish all came to forefront in Baumann's arrest. Baumann was soon moved to New Orleans because it was feared by his supporters that he could be lynched in Gretna, where he had been in the custody of his political enemies. In December 1892 the grand jury in Jefferson Parish indicted Baumann as an accessory before the act and for conspiracy to kill. The grand jury report also revealed that there was more to the story than what had been reported concerning the case. Long and his allies, including law-enforcement officials in the parish, had spread the word that they had located witnesses who supported the charges against Baumann. The grand jury report also noted that supporters of Baumann had charged Long and several of his Democrat colleagues with the bribery of Wilbert Williams—the individual who gave testimony supporting the charges against Baumann. However, the jury disregarded Baumann's claim of being framed and failed to take action against the Democratic machine in Jefferson Parish. Nevertheless, the grand jury's report exposed that there were unanswered questions concerning the evidence against Baumann. His attorneys continued to vigorously challenge the evidence against their client as well as the venue of the case.[39]

As word spread to the general public that the case against Baumann was not as clear cut as had been reported, concern among the public and Democratic political leaders in the parish began to be voiced. Realizing that the outcome of the case could result in an acquittal, supporters of Long and the Democrats circulated talk that violence might be necessary for them to receive their desired outcome. So serious did the threat become that the press reported the potential for violence. The uniqueness of the story of the two Kenner politicians' public disdain for each other, with its racial overtones, and the growing threat of violence in the case even became news in other parts of the state. The *Daily Journal*, a local paper in Plaquemine, Louisiana, led off its remarks on the case with the headline "Will Lynch Him if Acquitted." The rural newspaper concluded its comments on the subject with a statement which encapsulated what many anti-Baumann supporters believed: "It is an open secret among the white people in Jefferson parish that if Baumann is acquitted of the charge they will lynch him."[40]

The increasing vitriol and threats against Baumann in Jefferson played into the hands of the Republican politician's attorneys. Shortly before Christmas, on the date set for the trial, Baumann's attorneys filed motions for a change of venue before Judge Emile Rost. After hearing witnesses from both sides, Rost agreed with Baumann's attorneys that "the accused had established the existence of prejudice in the parish." He ordered the case transferred to Orleans Parish. With the transfer of the trial out of Jefferson Parish and away from its district attorney and sheriff, the case against Baumann and the accused shooter Dennis Richards promptly fell apart. At the very first court appearance before New Orleans Judge John Ferguson,[41] M.J. Cunningham Jr. of the office of the state attorney general, who was now handling prosecution of the case, claimed in court that there was not enough evidence to support moving forward and entered a motion of *nolle prosequi* for both Baumann and Richards. Out of the grip of Jefferson law enforcement officials, both Richards and the witness Wilbert Williams, claiming that they had been beaten and forced to confess, renounced their testimony that had implicated Baumann. In spite of the good news that they were soon to be freed, both men and their attorneys strenuously opposed the motion stating that they wanted a trial so that the record would show an acquittal for them from the "criminal and infamous conspiracy" of the prosecution. The judge, noting that he had to rule on the state's motion before him, granted the request and both walked out of the courthouse as free men.[42] In spite of Baumann's final courtroom victory, politics in Kenner were changed forever. The once Republican stronghold had shifted allegiance to the Democrats. As to Baumann himself, he later summed up his situation befittingly when he recorded in his reminisces that as,

> a faithful, official and conscientious citizen . . . I have suffered more than any other man in the State of Louisiana from persecution, for no other reason than . . . I was a Republican by principle . . . . For devotion to the Republican principles and party, I was forced to lose all I had accumulated for years, with my life at stake on many occasions.[43]

The hard-knuckled political fight for control of Kenner politics had consequences greater than simply Baumann's personal loss and the political alliance of the city's residents. The use of violence and vigilantism in the struggle between the majority white Democratic Party and the majority black Republican Party proved to be a successful tactic. The use of violence by the Democrats in Kenner opened the door for the continued application of similar tactics in the rest of Jefferson Parish and parts of the rest of the state where race and social and political order remained contested. Although used by only a small segment of the white population, there was, nevertheless, a growing contagion of violence in the 1890s in Jefferson and the rest of Louisiana. Prior to the lynching of Henry Dixon in September 1892, there had been only one other lynching there in the prior twenty-seven-year-long-postwar period. However, after Dixon's murder there were an additional ten lynchings of blacks in Jefferson Parish during the next five years. Included among the murdered victims was Aleck Francis. A New Orleans resident, he was taken by a mob of approximately ten whites from the Kenner jail, where he had been placed after being arrested at the rail station for being a "dangerous character." His corpse, with a rope tied around his neck, was later located in the Mississippi River near Gretna, several miles downriver from Kenner. The message had been clearly sent to the African American population in Kenner and Jefferson Parish that the consequence for defying the defined political and racial order during the final years of the nineteenth century could be deadly.[44]

7

"A Parasite to the Rest of the Parish"

The long-standing political dispute between Republicans and Democrats as well as the years-long debate over education taxes and their collection and use in Kenner were only aspects of a greater decades-long struggle between the Kenner community and its neighbors in Jefferson Parish. Dating back to the very creation of Kennerville, a debate over the governance of the community continued for decades that (as discussed in the previous chapter) exacerbated other disputes that existed between the people of Kenner and Jefferson Parish. Within months of the end of the Civil War, the Jefferson Parish Police Jury in February 1866 informed Minor Kenner's widow that her husband's effort to establish a municipality at Kennerville had not been done in accordance with existing laws. Although the village had been electing officials for years, ever since the community had organized itself into the Kennerville community's first municipal government in order to obtain a much needed railroad depot, Minor Kenner and other village leaders never took the required legal steps to have the town officially authorized to incorporate. To address the issue, the police jury threatened the town with legal action if it did not submit immediately to the parish an acceptable plan of government. Community leaders responded quickly to address the legal oversight and worked with members of the state legislature to produce an acceptable plan of government. On March 27, 1867, Governor J. Madison Wells signed and approved Act 126 of the Louisiana legislature officially incorporating the town of Kenner. In addition to establishing the official name of the town as Kenner instead of Kennerville, the new charter provided that a mayor and five aldermen were to be elected every year. Ten days' notice was required before an election could be held. Town officials were empowered to levy taxes and impose fines up to one hundred dollars for violating town ordinances. As to the boundaries of the town, the plan, for the most part, followed a portion of the street design included in W. T. Thompson's original 1855 plan for the community. Only a fraction of the boundaries of modern-day Kenner, the town's limits extended from Fillmore Street on the east side to Butler Street on the west and from the river on the south to a distance of approximately six blocks to the north.[1]

This original charter quickly proved to be inadequate for the needs of the people of the town. Among the most disliked features of the document were the small boundaries established for the municipality and the short terms of office allowed its elected officials. To address the shortcomings of the 1867 charter, town leaders once again turned to the state legislature for assistance. However, the effort to update the charter ran into opposition in the legislature. Senator T.B. Stamps proposed the new reform legislation and introduced Senate Bill Number 27 on the second day of 1873 the session. The bill was referred to the Committee of Corporations where the legislation ran into determined opposition. After a month of review, the committee voted to report the bill unfavorably, an action which usually meant the death of proposed legislation. Stamps, an African American senator from Jefferson Parish, refused to accept the decision and worked to have the committee's unfavorable report rejected in the Senate. After pushing the issue for a couple of weeks, Stamps succeeded in having the bill made a special order for the day by the entire Senate, where it won approval. The legislation next moved to the House where it quickly won approval.[2]

On March 28, 1873, almost six years to the day after the community's first charter was approved, Governor William P. Kellogg signed Act 71 of the Louisiana Legislature granting the Kenner community its second municipal charter. The new document designated Kenner as a city and expanded the boundaries of the municipality approximately to the same as those which exist today. Under the new plan of government, a mayor and six councilmen held office for two-year terms. The mayor was granted veto power over council votes, but could be overridden by a vote of five council members. The new charter also allowed for the positions of treasurer, assessor, tax collector, street commissioner, and marshal, all of whom were appointed by the mayor and council.[3]

Although the new document was an improvement over Kenner's first governmental plan, issues soon developed with the new charter. Under sections six and twenty of the document, the City of Kenner was given the exclusive privilege of levying and collecting taxes. As a result of this exclusive right of taxation, the parish police jury lost all power to levy taxes within the Kenner city limits and its residents became exempt from paying their share of the general expenses of the courts, schools, and other obligations owed to Jefferson Parish. To resolve the issue, officials from the parish and city formed a committee, which included the president and one member of the police jury and the mayor and a city councilman. As Kenner's participation in the effort to determine the city's financial obligations to the parish was entirely voluntary, the city simply refused to pay whatever it considered to be an unfair assessment.[4]

Any chance of Jefferson Parish getting aid from the state in forcing Kenner to pay its share of taxes received a crushing setback in the Constitutional Convention of 1879. With the shifting of political power in Louisiana from the Radical Republicans to the Bourbon oligarchy that accompanied the national election of 1876 and the end of Reconstruction, political leaders had as a major objective replacing the 1868 Constitution, which had promoted social and political change in the state. The new state constitution enhanced the powers of the governor and placed inhibitions and limitations on the legislative branch of government. Some of the legislative restrictions extended to local governments. For example, Article 46 of the new constitution restrained the legislature from creating corporations or from amending any existing municipal charter, except as to that of the city of New Orleans.[5]

The constitutional restrictions placed upon Jefferson Parish did not stop the debate between the city and parish. The dispute dragged on for years. With their frustration growing, parish leaders decided to press the issue and turned to the courts for relief. They placed a tax levy upon Mrs. Rebecca Felix's property, which was located inside the city limits of Kenner. In turn, Mrs. Felix filed suit against the parish in the Twenty-Sixth District Court, claiming that the police jury had no power to tax in Kenner. On December 24, 1885, District Judge Emile Rost ruled in favor of Mrs. Felix and noted that she and the other residents of the city of Kenner were exempt from paying parish taxes. The parish appealed, and in April 1887 the Louisiana Supreme Court decreed that Judge Rost was correct in his opinion exempting the residents of Kenner from parish taxes.[6]

Having lost in court, parish leaders were not willing to give up their effort to get the people of Kenner to pay for the services they received from the parish. Though the constitution prohibited any amendments to the Kenner charter, it left open the possibility of an outright repeal of the entire document and legal dissolution of the municipality. The parish's legislative delegation first introduced a bill towards this aim in the 1884 session. The bill failed to win approval. Again in the 1886 session of the legislature, parish leaders worked for repeal of the Kenner charter. In an attempt to win support, they proposed that after the repeal of the existing charter, the city could immediately be re-incorporated with a new charter that did not repeat the errors of the of the 1873 legislation. The renewed effort received some support in the legislature, but in the end it fell short of the required number of votes needed for passage.[7]

As the legal debate between the city and parish over the charter and taxing power raged on, attitudes of the city's residents gradually changed. At first the residents of Kenner were happy about not having to pay taxes to the parish. At the time there was only a municipal tax of ten mills levied in the city, which was used almost entirely to pay the salaries of city officials. With the city not contributing anything towards the payment of the expenses associated with providing schools, levees, and roads located in Kenner, the parish cut off all of its support for the services it once offered. By 1883 the once successful public schools of the city were closed and other services were deteriorating. As conditions worsened, some of Kenner's residents began to reconsider their position on the tax issue. Discontent among the community's citizens increased to a point where the population of Kenner began to decline. Pressure and complaints from the city's residents led the two feuding governing bodies to return to negotiations. In September 1888, a special committee consisting of two police jury members and one member of the city council was established to determine the pro-rata for local expenses common to both the parish and city and to settle all other matters in dispute between the two entities.[8]

Unfortunately, the committee was not totally successful in its attempt to work out a solution to the tax debate that satisfied both sides. The feud continued to simmer for years and was made worse by the racist and rancorous status of politics in Jefferson Parish during the post-reconstruction period. Not until the legislative session of 1908 did the issue finally get resolved. At the legislative session, Representative F.A. Middleton of Jefferson Parish and a close ally to Sheriff L. H. Marrero—the chief proponent of the effort to get Kenner to pay a greater share of taxes,—introduced legislation revoking the city's charter. Middleton declared that because of its failure to pay its share of taxes, Kenner was "a parasite to the rest of the parish." He asked that the charter be revoked because the "Municipal methods of the town were antiquated" and pointed to the fact that Kenner depended on the parish for schools, courts, and other expenses and gave nothing in return. Denoting the racial tensions and the anti-Reconstruction feelings of the time of the majority of the people in the state, Middleton in a series of appearances before both Senate and House committees warned his legislative colleagues that the Kenner charter was antiquated and was "put on by the negroes [sic] during carpetbag times." During the debate over the proposal the Jefferson legislator complained that the town cost the parish $2,180 to operate schools in the city. He added that although in the negotiations between the city and the parish, the city had promised to pay $130 a year, no such payment had been received for the past four years. Whose fault was this problem? Middleton had an answer. According to him, "Thirty-six years incorporated, and living exempted from taxation, they [the people of Kenner] have not even now got a town hall. Where does the money they pay in municipal taxes go? To the Kenner office-holders!" Noting that salaries of city officials ranged from $480 to $1,000 a year, he dismissed the protest of some in the city against the effort to revoke the charter as simply an example of individuals being misled by the "municipal grafters" who wanted to continue to draw their salaries by continuing the old system. For example, he claimed that the secretary of the town council alone drew a salary that cost 10 percent of the town's revenues. Middleton added that "These Kenner office-holders have sucked the blood of the people for thirty-six years" and as a result the town had experienced a high crime rate and "the good people of Kenner themselves. . . fear a return of the things of the past." As he neared the conclusion of his fiery presentation before the House of Representatives' Judiciary Committee, Middleton summed up his position with the biting critique that "This place has been a pest hole. It has brought more disgrace to Jefferson Parish than any other one place."[9]

As with past efforts to revoke the charter, many in Kenner opposed the idea. When word of the effort reached the town, the residents held what the *Daily Picayune* labeled as "an indignation meeting." At the meeting the people present prepared a petition with 208 signatures that they sent with a delegation of thirty residents to the legislature.[10] To plead their side of the debate, they selected attorneys Colonel Emanuel A. O'Sullivan, a former district attorney, state senator, and city attorney for the city of New Orleans, and John E. Fleury. In his presentation to the judiciary committee, Colonel O'Sullivan cited the towns of Thibodaux, Houma, and Napoleonville as examples of incorporated communities in the state that, like Kenner, did not pay parish taxes. He claimed that the effort to revoke the charter was simply a case of political revenge by Jefferson Parish politicians against the people of Kenner. "This is not politics—if it is, it is the vilest sort of politics," he proclaimed. It was, according to O'Sullivan, an attempt by the supporters of Jefferson Parish Sheriff L. H. Marrero, "to wreck vengeance on the town for failing to support the 'ring' candidates in the recent election." Specifically, he noted that the people of Kenner had voted for John H. Language for clerk of court against the wishes of parish politicians and claimed, "Because Kenner asserted her manhood, this is the result." He also addressed the claim that Kenner was unsafe, in spite of the fact that, "the ten or twelve deputy sheriffs in Kenner who did not vote as Sheriff Marrero dictated had their commissions taken from them." He boasted, "Kenner is peaceful" and added, "Kenner is a model town, and I vouch for it." As to the claim that officials were misusing town revenues, O'Sullivan declared that the municipality maintained a fund balance of $6,000 in a local bank, without owing any debts, and that the town's mayor and council work without salary. He noted that those officials who did work on salary received reasonable salaries

Colonel Emanuel A. O'Sullivan was a distinguished former district attorney and state senator who represented before the state legislature the citizens of Kenner who opposed the revocation of the city's charter. In a subsequent election in Kenner following the legislative dispute, when he arrived at the polls, he was manhandled by a gang of opponents, bound, grabbed by his facial hair and had his beard sheared off.

which ranged from the city marshal who earned $75 a month to the tax collector who made $40 a month. Towards the end of his address to the legislative committee, O'Sullivan noted that the debate between Kenner and the parish had drawn the attention of people across that state: "You all know that the whole state is pointing the finger of shame at Jefferson Parish. Protect us against the whip of these men who are trying to chastise us for having exercised our rights as freemen and citizens."[11]

Though the debate in the legislative committees was labeled by the *Daily Picayune* as being "sensational," it was to little avail for the opponents of the revocation effort. The political influence of parish officials, including Sheriff L. H. Marrero, his son, District Attorney L. H. Marrero Jr., and Police Jury President F. L. St. Martin, along with the fact that several Kenner officials, including Mayor Paul Felix, Constable Fitzgerald, and Street Commissioner Centanni, spoke in favor of revocation, all led to swift approval by the legislature of the bill to take away Kenner's charter of incorporation. The bill was signed by Governor J. Y. Sanders and was promulgated as Act 74 of the legislature. The final act of disbanding the city's government came a few days later when on July 10, 1908, the *Daily Picayune* reported that the charter had been ordered annulled. Defeated in the legislature, a group of Kenner residents, claiming that the legislation ignored the will "of the majority of the people" and that it violated the state's 1898 Constitution by failing to give sufficient notice of the pending action revoking the charter, filed suit in court challenging the revocation. While the issue was battled in the courts, some city leaders attempted to carry on performing their duties. They even got Louisiana Secretary of State John T. Michel to promulgate an official ballot for an election for municipal officials they scheduled for November 3, 1908.[12]

The ballot for the November election, in addition to the disputed Kenner vote, included presidential electors and members of Congress. Having worked for years to control politics in Kenner, opponents to the effort to elect municipal leaders, in contradiction of the recent action by the state legislature to disband the city, were determined to see an end to Kenner's government. Many of the individuals who fought hard for the dissolution of the community's municipal government were among those who had participated in the successful effort to establish the political and social dominance of whites and the Democratic Party in the city. Having been successful in the past in achieving their political goals by means of intimidation and violence, the opponents of the Kenner vote were not adverse to once again using the same tactics to obtain their objectives. On election day the opponents of the municipal vote arrived at the polls armed and prepared to use force to influence the election's outcome. So brazen was their plan, that even the arrival of one of the well-known and respected leaders of the supporters of the vote, did not stop their intimidation of voters. Colonel E. A. O'Sullivan was an attorney of considerable reputation who had participated in the legislative debate over the abolition of Kenner's home rule charter. In spite of his respected stature and his being in his mid-sixties, when O'Sullivan arrived at the polls, he was confronted by the justice of the peace and former Kenner mayor Paul Felix who had with him a group of heavily armed men. O'Sullivan was seized by the gang and had his arms tied to his side. With O'Sullivan immobilized, William W. Stiles, a deputy sheriff and member of the group of men directed by Felix, grabbed him by his facial hair and took a scissors and cut the old gentlemen's beard off. The beard cutting was followed by a roughing up and degrading mocking that left O'Sullivan "cut, bruised, beaten, his face and eye blackened, his beard cut," and knocked senseless.[13] Humiliated and bruised, the tough old former district attorney was not intimidated. He filed Federal charges against the gang leaders that resulted in their being found guilty, fined, and given jail time. Desiring his own satisfaction against the culprits, O'Sullivan filed suit against the men for damages totaling $60,000. So determined was he to press his case that when it was dismissed for technical reasons by the lower courts, O'Sullivan carried it all the way to the U. S. Supreme Court. Nearly six years after the incident, the country's highest court in April 1914 dismissed Kenner's "whiskers" case for the final time on the technical grounds that the civil suit asking for damages had been filed after the deadline for filing such a claim.[14]

Although O'Sullivan and his fellow supporters of municipal government in Kenner were able to enjoy the personal satisfaction of knowing that at least some of the individuals who had intimidated voters were brought to justice for their misdeeds, their goal of saving home rule failed. Nothing came from the effort in Kenner to elect municipal officials in the November 1908 elections. After the passage of Act 74 by the state legislature, most local and state officials accepted the inevitable loss of home rule. At its first meeting in 1909, the Jefferson Parish Police Jury began the procedure for dismantling the municipal government of the community by assuming control of the financial affairs of "the late city." All creditors of the city were ordered to present their claims to the parish. After paying all debts owed by the city, the police jury ordered that any remaining funds collected from the Kenner treasury be transferred to the school board for use in schools located in the former city. The City of Kenner was no more.

Pictured are the members of the Italian Society of Kenner positioned in front of their social club on Hanson Street. Taken sometime during the early years of the twentieth century, the photograph includes 100 males members of the Kenner's Italian community.

8
Rebirth

With the resolution of the long debate over home rule in Kenner completed, residents of the little community enjoyed a period of peace and relative harmony. Unfortunately, the congruity of the community was not the result of a coming together of the various factions through a process of healing, compromise, and political give-and-take. Instead, the decline in the political disharmony that had long characterized community relations in the little settlement was the outcome of the establishment of political dominance by the Democratic Party in Jefferson Parish over its Republican counterpart. Contributing to the rise of Democratic dominance was the decline in the political influence of African Americans in both the parish and the state. With party allegiances largely paralleling racial identities, political contest in the parish carried with them strong racial overtones.

Dedicated to their belief in white supremacy, whites across the South looked to the Democratic Party as their vehicle for political and social dominance. Once Reconstruction had ended and Federal troops left the state, white Democrats were determined to end Republican and African American influence in Louisiana. As demonstrated by events discussed in the previous chapters, to obtain their objective of white supremacy, Democrats did not hesitate in the use of fraud, intimidation, and violence against their opponents. Until 1890, African Americans in Louisiana actually outnumbered whites as registered voters. However, to their detriment, Republicans and blacks in Jefferson and throughout most of the state were unwilling or unable to match the aggressiveness of the white Democratswho worked incessantly—and often violently—to re-establish white supremacy. Their efforts met fruition at the state's constitutional convention in 1898. At the convention, the white elites, or Bourbons, who controlled the writing of the new organic document were determined to disfranchise as many Negroes and as few whites as possible, while remaining in accord with the U.S. Constitution. Requiring that voters in the state had to prove their ability to read and write or show a property assessment of not less than $300—a sizeable sum for the day—and pay an annual poll tax, the 1898 Constitution accomplished its goal of limiting suffrage. Although the document reduced voting among some poor whites in Louisiana, it had a devastating consequence upon African American voters in the state. By 1904, the African American vote in the state had nearly evaporated, decreasing from 130,344 to a mere 1,342. Accompanying the effort to disfranchise black voter strength in Louisiana was an effort to strengthen the state's segregation laws. During most of the postwar era, whites in the state increasingly demanded the compulsory separation of the races. Legislation forcing the separation of races in the state continued to be a popular activity for state lawmakers well into the twentieth century.[1]

In the decades after the end of the Civil War, race relations in Kenner went through several phases, including the period of master/freedman tensions that followed immediately upon the emancipation of the area's slaves, the period of Radical Reconstruction when political influence in the area was dominated by freedmen and their Republican allies, and finally, the period of Bourbon ascendency when whites and their Democratic partners successfully re-acquired political control in Jefferson Parish. Another important factor that influenced the racial atmosphere in the community at the turn of the century was the growing power of the Italians in the region. Though it took years for the alliance to develop, the political alignment of the Italians in Kenner with the white-supremacist Democrats in the parish was instrumental in determining the social and cultural setting in the community during the first decades of the twentieth century. When they first settled in the region in the decades prior to the onset of the twentieth century, the new Italian residents in the area held little understanding of race relations in Louisiana and the South. Their failure to assimilate into the southern-race culture of the time, along with growing anti-immigrant feelings across America, soon resulted in the Italians also being targeted by white supremacists for retribution and social, political, and racial discrimination. The social harmony between the Italians and their African American neighbors led whites to stigmatize Italians as the socioeconomic equivalent of the region's black residents—thus largely stripping them of white status and subjecting them to some of the same prejudices and violence faced by the African American community. Escalating throughout the second half of the nineteenth century, the repression of Italians and blacks in the state reached its peak in the 1890s with the disfranchisement movement and the rise of anti-Italian violence, culminating with the lynching of Italians in several communities in Louisiana, including New Orleans. Because of the growing population of Italians in Kenner, the town was at times looked upon negatively by the area's press, which often ran prejudicial articles about the region's Italian and Sicilian residents. For example, during the emotional times following the October 1890 assassination of New Orleans Chief of Police David C. Hennessey, who proclaimed shortly before dying from wounds afflicted by an unknown assassin that, "The Dagoes did it," the *Daily States* newspaper, without citing any evidence, proclaimed that the body of an Italian found in the river near Kenner was "probably . . . a victim of the vendetta, or perhaps a witness, the assassins of Dave Hennessey desired out of the way." The paper then noted that this was likely because ". . . the mafia society are supposed to have a meeting place some where [*sic*] near Kennerville."[2] So serious became the prejudice against the region's Italian residents, that one historian of the period proclaimed that during the last decade of the nineteenth century the 25,000 to 30,000 Italian immigrants in the area at the time feared for their safety to such a degree that they lived under a "reign of terror."[3]

Although anti-Italian prejudice remained virulent in some parts of the state well into the new century, Italians worked to improve their acceptance by their neighbors. Realizing that to be accepted into southern white society they needed to distance themselves socially and culturally from the region's African Americans, many Italians in Kenner and elsewhere in Louisiana adopted the attitudes of the white supremacist concerning race. They also became more astute in handling political matters. As newcomers to America, first generation Italians were naive about politics in their new home. Realizing that political influence could give them power and increased social acceptance, Italians in New Orleans and elsewhere in the state gradually increased their participation in the political process. So it was with the Italians in the Kenner community, as they gradually assimilated with the residents of the region, their acceptance as viable members of the community increased.[4]

Whether by conscience choice, custom, or political pressure, Italian residents in Kenner increasingly associated themselves with the racial attitudes of the day in regards to African Americans. With anti-Italian sentiment running strong elsewhere in the state as evidenced by the incidents involving racial violence that took place in the community, many Italians in Kenner did not resist the efforts by the Bourbons, Democrats, and others to minimize the presence and influence of African Americans in their community. Similarly, with the number of Italian Americans in the area continuing to grow, thus giving them some political and economic clout, the Kenner Italians were among the first of their nationality in post-Reconstruction Louisiana to participate in the political arena. Most notably, in the long, drawn-out debate over the issue of home rule, Italian residents openly participated on both sides of the debate, including Italy native Joseph Maggiore—a strong supporter of Kenner homerule—and Michael Centanni, also a native of Italy, whoBin spite of his holding the position of City Street Commissioner, sided with Democratic leaders in the parish and supported the revoking of Kenner's home rule by the state. By the early years of the twentieth century, the political landscape in Kenner mirrored much of the rest of Louisiana. Most whites were united together in support of the white-supremacist Democrats who effectively eliminated the political opposition of the Republicans and their African American allies. Even in Kenner, where the 1910 Federal Census showed that blacks and mulattoes amounted to nearly 44 percent of the community's population of 922, African American political power and influence evaporated thanks to the effects of Jim Crowism and the determined disfranchisement effort in Louisiana. As white supremacists in the state gained power and placed limits on the ability of African Americans to contest the social order of disfranchisement and segregation, the black population in Kenner, either because of fear, powerlessness, or apathy, assumed a mostly inactive and passive role in resisting the white hegemony. The vile nature of the attitudes that poisoned the relations between the races in the community were evident in July 1900 when S.M. Cowen of Kenner participated in and addressed a deadly Negro-hunting mob roaming the streets of a portion of the city of New Orleans. Cowen proclaimed,

> Gentlemen, I am the Mayor of Kenner[5]. . . and I have come down to New Orleans tonight to assist you in teaching the blacks a lesson. I have killed a negro [sic] before and . . . I am willing to kill again. The only way you can teach these niggers a lesson and put them in their place is to go out and lynch a few of them as an object lesson . . . that is the only thing to do—kill them, string them up, lynch them. I will lead you if you will follow.[6]

Therefore with white residents largely united politically and the African American and Republican opposition threatened with violence, vanquished politically, and isolated socially, the long period of debate and conflict that dominated the area's politics and divided the community during the final decades of the nineteenth century ended with the white Democrats comfortably in control.[7]

With political power and control securely in the hands of the white Democrats in Jefferson Parish, residents in the former city of Kenner once again began an effort to get the city recognized by the state. After a little over five years under the authority of parish officials, community leaders relying upon provisions of Section 11 of Act No. 136 of the 1898 session of the Louisiana Legislature circulated a petition requesting the reincorporation of their city among the voters of the former municipality. Obtaining the signatures of two-thirds of the qualified electors who survived on the voters rolls following the disfranchising effort of the period, the people urged the governor of the state to take prompt action. On July 30, 1912, the Jefferson Parish Police Jury met in special session and officially supported the call of the citizens for municipal incorporation. On December 13, 1913, Governor Luther E. Hall responded to the people's plea for action and officially declared Kenner reincorporated.[8] However, as the new incorporation fell under the 1898 state statute commonly known as the Lawrason Act, the governor was required to designate the community a village. This was required because of the community's population of less than a thousand residents did not allow it to be classified as a town or city.[9]

The new governmental plan for the village provided for a mayor, five aldermen, and a marshal to be elected by the voters for a term of four years. Within days of the governor's proclamation, he appointed the town's first team of officials, who served until elected officials were chosen by the voters. Antoine Wattigney was named mayor and Philip Klees, V.L. D'Gerolamo, Dr. Wallace J. Babin, Ralph Part, and Sal Block were appointed aldermen. Finally, the governor appointed Angelo Maggiore as marshal, the village's law enforcement officer. The new plan of government offered by the Lawrason Act proved to be popular among the people of Kenner. With relatively few changes the organization of municipal government remained in place for decades. However, one area of disappointment for Kenner officials was the community's designation as a village. Immediately after its reincorporation, officials began a special census to establish an accurate count of the municipality's population. Just two months after being declared a village, Kenner officials certified to the state that their community had a population of 1,904 inhabitants,[10] qualifying it for a new designation. Responding to the new census, Governor Hall, on February 5, 1914, the same day he received the certified new population count, officially proclaimed Kenner to be a town. The community kept its designation as a town until 1952, when Governor Earl Long proclaimed Kenner a city.[11]

With its new legal status in place, the Kenner community also experienced important changes in the development of its infrastructure. Physically the little community at Kenner retained many of its antebellum physical characteristics—dusty and dirty when the sun was out and muddy when it rained. However, its strong agricultural economy continued to attract residents, and the community continued its slow steady gain in population that had started in the 1880s. As noted above, by 1914 the population of the town surpassed the 1,900 mark. The onset of the twentieth century also brought the final yellow fever epidemic to the town. For decades the disease called "Yellow Jack" had on occasion, as in 1853 when it took the lives of Butler Kenner and his son, brought death among the residents of Kenner. Although modern medical practices over time had reduced the frequency and mortality rate of the disease, the summer of 1905 marked the last time the mosquito-carried disease afflicted a large number of Kenner residents. With a mortality rate averaging as high as 20 percent, the Kenner community, with its close proximity to the mosquito laden swamps located in the northern portions of its boundaries, was among the hardest hit locations in the state by the epidemic. Fortunately, a determined effort in early 1906 by the State Board of Health to implement an ambitious sanitation program aimed at destroying the habitats where infected mosquitoes congregated effectively eliminated the threat of a second year of the epidemic. In spite of the occurrence of a case in Kenner which some thought was yellow fever, state medical officials determined a different explanation for the patient's illness, thus bringing to an end the Kenner community's long history of having to face the dreaded consequences of a deadly outbreak of "Yellow Jack."[12]

Also with the new century came the gradual arrival of many of the conveniences of the modern era. As in the previous century, the railroad was essential to the continued growth of the community. The New Orleans, Jackson and Great Northern Railroad had suffered damage and losses during the Civil War from which it was not able to recover fully. After years of struggling in the post-war period, the railroad became part of the Illinois Central Railroad in 1883. With new funds available, the railroad modernized its facilities in Kenner by constructing several large loading sheds, which encouraged new growth in the community by providing improved shipping facilities for the area's large truck farm and lumber industries. So successful became the Illinois Central Railroad that by 1950 it handled approximately one-third of the area's total inbound and outbound freight. The enlargement of the Illinois Central's facilities expanded the markets for Kenner's agricultural products to places as far away as Chicago and elsewhere in the Midwest. Complementing the Illinois Central's dominance of the Kenner market was the arrival of a second railroad through the community. In the 1890s the Louisiana Railway and Navigation Company completed a track bed through Kenner that connected New Orleans to Baton Rouge. Merging with the Louisiana and Arkansas Railroad after World War I, the joined railroad was acquired by the Kansas City Southern in 1939, which constructed additional loading facilities at

Kenner. [13] With the arrival of the railroad, the steamboat and river traffic and trade that once played a major role in the commerce to and from the Kenner area greatly diminished. Though the railroad provided an improved and effective way to ship the community's agricultural products, it did not meet all the transportation needs of the area's residents. Many farmers of the area wanted a convenient means of moving their crops, equipment, and livestock around the countryside without having to depend solely on the somewhat costly railroad or river transport. From as far back as colonial times, overland transit to and from the area had been limited. In the eighteenth century the Chemin Royal (Royal Road) passed through the area on its way to the German Coast. Over time the Royal Road running along the primitive levee system became known as the River Road and stretched on the east bank of the river from below New Orleans to Baton Rouge. The dirt road was usually dusty and rutted when dry and became almost impassible and muddy with rain. As the banks of the Mississippi River and the levees that lined it eroded and washed away with the shifting levels of the river's water, the location of the roadbed often was forced to shift to conform to the river's whims. Only with the arrival of the automobile in the early decades of the twentieth century did officials begin the process of covering the road with gravel. Except for the few streets laid out by W.T. Thompson when he first planned the layout of Kennerville, the River Road remained the only means of overland travel at the community. The road was primarily used in Jefferson Parish as a means of communication among the residents who resided along the river.[14]

As early as October 1871, parish leaders recognized the necessity for a second road to be constructed on the east bank of the river in Jefferson. A committee was created by the police jury to work on the construction of a public road from Carrollton to the junction of Short Street and Williams Avenue in Kenner. The road was to be financed by a special tax. However, the project was soon sidetracked when Joseph Kaiser petitioned parish officials to allow him to build, at his expense, an inter-urban railway which would connect Kenner to New Orleans. Seeing an opportunity to save the parish money, the police jury suspended work on the proposed new road. Unfortunately, the idea of a new inter-urban railway was premature and was soon abandoned because of the lack of resources. Leaders returned to the idea of a new road and in early 1874 the Louisiana State Legislature ordered that the roadway be built "from the western limits of the City of New Orleans to Williams street in the City of Kenner."[15] Originally the plan for the road called for it to follow the tract previously surveyed for the 1871 route. However, the plan was changed and it was decided to have the new roadbed follow a route similar to the long-existing River Road. A right of way sixty-feet wide inside of Kenner and one-hundred feet wide outside of the town was acquired. A price of $150 per arpent was paid for the needed land. Poor weather slowed construction for several months, but by the end of 1875 the new road was opened for traffic.[16]

At the time the police jury was working to improve the road transportation to the area, it also took steps to provide access for residents to the west bank of the Mississippi River opposite Kenner. In April 1870, the police jury authorized the creation of a ferry between Kennerville and the area on the west bank called South Kenner. The first franchise was issued to William Brown and Henry Brooks for a two-year term in exchange for payment of a $110 fee. After the initial franchise payment, subsequent franchises were auctioned to the highest bidder. At first, the ferry was only a simple skiff that held only one or two passengers, who were brave enough to be rowed across the turbulent river. With the passage of time and increased use of the service, the size of the ferry and the conditions of the trip across the river improved. Traveling between the head of Minor Street in Kenner on the east bank, the ferry crossed to a point on the opposite shore of the river at the upper limit of the Kennedy plantation. Although susceptible to the vagaries of weather, the ferry remained popular and experienced a growth in passenger use until the improved transportation systems, which arrived with the twentieth century, proved to be more popular alternatives to the boat ride across the river. The gradual decline that started in the new century continued until the 1930s when the little ferry was made obsolete and its service ended.[17]

Perhaps the most bothersome interruption to the ferry service came on Mardi Gras day in 1899. Residents of Kenner and New Orleans awoke on the morning of February 14 to a bitterly cold temperature of seven degrees and the ground covered with three inches of snow. However, for the people of the Kenner community, the greatest surprise of the day was not the rare snowfall and bitter cold or the fact that the weather forced the postponement of some of the scheduled activities planned for the holiday. Instead, it was the presence of the enormous ice floe choking the Mississippi River (discussed in chapter five) and its crushing of the little ferry and closing of the river to all vessel traffic.[18]

In addition to the improvements in the overland, railroad, and ferry services to the community, parish and town leaders continued to seek to bring other modern services to the people of Kenner. With the arrival of the widespread commercial use of electricity, new conveniences and services became available to the residents of Kenner. Among the first commercial applications of the electrical age to come to Jefferson Parish was a plan to establish an electric railway between New Orleans and Kenner. The first plans for an electric rail service were submitted by William L. Louque, president of the Jefferson Avenue Railway Company, to the Jefferson Parish Police Jury in late 1894. The plan called for the project to be completed within five years. Unfortunately, Louque and the police jury were overly optimistic in their plans and the project went unfulfilled during the allowed time frame. In spite of the failure of the project, interest in the plan remained high. The only road connecting the communities in East Jefferson to New Orleans continued to be a problem. Many citizens in both Jefferson and New Orleans complained that it was an all-day trip to travel and return between Kenner and the Crescent City. To push parish leaders to come up with a solution, the residents of East Jefferson and Kenner refused to let the issue die. On February 12, 1913, a petition signed by more than one-third of the property owners of Wards Seven, Eight, and Nine in Jefferson Parish was presented to the parish police jury requesting that a special election be called to authorize a special tax to finance an interurban railway connecting the east bank of Jefferson to the city. The ten-year property tax was put to the voters on April 1, 1913, and was approved by a margin of 153 for the levy and only four against. In January 1914, New Orleans Mayor Martin Behrman and the New Orleans Commission Council, along with the Kenner Town Council, approved the plans for the project. Shortly thereafter in March the Jefferson Parish Police Jury offered the franchise to build and operate an interurban electric railroad for sale. Both the police jury and Kenner Town Council awarded to the Orleans-Kenner Electric Railway Company the franchise to construct and operate an electric railway to Kenner where it would run "along and over Third Street." By early 1914, the project to build an electric railway was fully underway.[19]

First incorporated on January 7, 1913, by Harry K. Johnson, an individual who had previously constructed an electric interurban line the year before in New Iberia, Louisiana, the project reached the operational stage in March 1915 when the new railway began operating between New Orleans and Kenner's neighboring community of Harahan. It took several additional months of construction for the line to be completed to Kenner, reaching the town in time for Fourth of July celebrations. Known to all as the "O.K.," the Orleans-Kenner electric interurban line greatly improved transportation to New Orleans for the residents of Kenner. Extending sixteen miles from the intersection of Rampart and Canal streets in the city, the line followed a route that today traces Jefferson Highway to the Jefferson/St. Charles Parish line at the western-most edge of Kenner. Although a depot was built in Kenner near the carline's terminus at the parish boundary, the line's main car barn and storage yard was located near Harahan.[20]

The Harahan work barn where the cars of the Orleans-Kenner carline were housed and serviced.

The significance of the arrival of the electric carline connecting Kenner to New Orleans was not lost on the people of the community. During the early stage of the project the people of Kenner put together a grand celebration to mark the ceremonial dedication of the line. Praised by a New Orleans newspaper as the "biggest day in the history of Kenner," the event was headlined by Governor Luther E. Hall. The governor traveled to the town in a special nine-coach train and then was chauffeured, along with town Mayor Antoine Wattigney, in an open-air carriage pulled by four white horses to the corner of Williams and Third Streets for the ceremony. After giving a stirring speech, which the paper praised as, "one of the best speeches of his career," the governor officially dedicated the interurban line by driving a gold spike into the very first rail to be laid in the construction of the project. In honor of the event the entire town was gaily decorated and businesses and schools were closed. The grand celebration drew more than 1,500 residents, who turned out to cheer the governor and other dignitaries.[21]

In his remarks, the governor praised the people of Kenner and the parish for putting aside the factionalism that once dominated the political and social relations of the region to work together in making the interurban carline a reality. He accurately projected that the event marked "the beginning of new era of development" for the area and that the electric railroad would "bring splendid results to . . . [the] parish." Similarly, he saw Kenner as "the garden spot of south Louisiana" and envisioned in his "mind's eye" that in a few years "the land from New Orleans to Kenner would be filled with prosperous farms, country homes, with all the comforts of the city, good roads, and rapid transit . . . ."[22]

The governor's remarks soon proved to be prophetic. When completed, the O.K. line provided a much more convenient and economical means of getting back and forth to the city than did the traditional railroad lines and muddy roads that had serviced the Kenner community since its founding. The improved transportation facilities helped Kenner's farmers get their produce to markets in New Orleans much more efficiently and opened the door for new residents—both individuals and businesses—to settle in the area. In a little over a year after it started its operation, the Orleans-Kenner Electric Railroad Company reported that more than fifty new residential homes had been built along its track bed and the carline had brought more than a million

The 1914 dedication of the Orleans-Kenner electric car service was a major event and celebration in the lives of the people of Kenner. With the exception of seated Mayor Antoine Wattigny, the identities of these residents, dressed in their "Sunday best," and their roles in the celebration remain unknown.

Called by one newspaper "the biggest day in the history of Kenner," Governor Luther Hall's dedication in March 1914 of the Orleans-Kenner electric car service drew a large crowd of community residents to witness and participate in the celebration.

dollars worth of land and industrial value increases to the area.[23]

The Orleans-Kenner line brought to the people of Kenner new reliable hourly service and provided riders with "new, clean, airy, noiseless, and comfortable" cars to make their trips to and from New Orleans. Four regular cars were used until peak hours when one or two extra cars were added. The first car of the day began operating at five o'clock in the morning and the last one left the Rampart Street ticket office at midnight. Fares ranged from thirty cents one way to fifty cents for a round trip from Kenner to New Orleans. Regular commuters could also buy tickets at special rates, and riders to and from Harahan to the city paid only twenty cents each way. Riding the O.K. became a popular pastime among both city and rural residents. Orleanians commonly took Sunday excursions on the little streetcar out to buy fresh produce from the many farms and vegetable plots that lined the way. The "Old O.K." introduced many city dwellers to the pleasures of rural living while providing them easy access to the city for their employment or schools for their children.[24] The Orleans-Kenner Electric Railway Company was purchased by the Orleans-Kenner Traction Company, Inc., in 1918 and continued to operate successfully for another dozen years.[25]

In spite of its popularity and significance to the development of the Kenner area, the little interurban railway enjoyed a relatively short life span. The growing popularity during the early decades of the twentieth century of the automobile resulted in increased interest among local officials and residents alike in the construction of hard-surfaced roads. Even with a $7,500 a year subsidy that the parish gave for ten years to the interurban carline, it was not able to contend successfully with its automobile competitors. Somewhat ironically, the far-sighted design of the carline contributed to the success of its motorcar competition and expedited its demise. When plans for the electric railroad were originally approved by officials, a 100 foot-wide right-of-way from New Orleans to Third Street in Kenner was acquired for the project. The plan allotted thirty-five feet for the carline's use and thirty feet on both sides of the interurban's tracks for use by wheeled vehicles. As the popularity of the automobile increased, community leaders began plans for improving the areas' roadways. As early as 1926, the Jefferson Police Jury produced plans for the construction of the Jefferson Highway paralleling on both sides of the O.K.'s tracks. As soon as the new highway was opened to traffic the interurban carline began to lose money. Shortly thereafter the Jefferson Parish Police Jury created a committee to confer with officials in Kenner and Harahan over the possibility of discontinuing the carline. Efforts to keep the line in service, including having New Orleans Public Service take over operation of the line in 1927, proved unsuccessful. Riders continued to complain about fare hikes and what had become obsolete equipment. In 1930 community leaders decided that the electric carline was outmoded and had become inadequate in meeting the transportation needs of the area's residents. Officials decided it was time to end its historic service to the people of East Jefferson and Kenner. Later in the year, motorized buses using the Jefferson Highway roadway began replacing the once popular motorized rail-line. On New Year's morning of 1931, Motorman A.J. Gardner carried out the last run of the little rail cars from New Orleans to Kenner and at the end of his work shift parked the very last car of the Orleans-Kenner carline into the company's Harahan barn. By February 11, 1931, the Orleans-Kenner Traction Company started pulling up its tracks. The "Old O.K." was now history.[26]

Above: The old Centanni & Sons building, pictured here during the Great Depression, is located at the corner of Williams Blvd. and Third Street in Kenner's Rivertown development. This landmark structure remains today one of the very few buildings in the city that date back to the beginning of the twentieth century.

Below: Because of the long-standing disparity between the educational resources offered to the races in Kenner and elsewhere in Jefferson Parish, during the troublesome years of the Great Depression, the National Education Association worked with the Works Progress Administration to establish education programs for adult members of the African American community. Pictured is a depression era NEA night school in Kenner for African American adults.

9
Maturing as a Municipality

The paving in late 1926 of Jefferson Highway from the Orleans/Jefferson parish line to Williams Street and from there to the Louisiana Railway and Navigation Company tracks in Kenner was the first major road paving job to affect the people of the Kenner community. With its completion, New Orleans was now only a mere thirty-minute automobile drive from the vegetable farms of Kenner, a fact that soon brought both new residents and produce customers to the area. The Jefferson Highway project marked only the beginning of the arrival of paved roadways to the community. The modern road system for Kenner had its beginning in 1910 when the legislature created the Louisiana State Highway Department. At first the department was involved primarily with the building of gravel roads. However, as the automobile era came to age, it began an extensive paving program in and around New Orleans. Thus, at the same time that parish leaders were in the process of paving Jefferson Highway, a second road project was instigated to connect other parts of Jefferson with Kenner. The Jefferson Parish Police Jury began a project to construct a road between Shrewsbury Road at Metairie Ridge to Williams Street in Kenner. Since the plan called for the road to be constructed in a straight line, the project was given the name of Airline Road. Shortly after the new roadway was completed, the state highway department took over the road for the purpose of using it as a link in the newly planned New Orleans to Baton Rouge Airline Highway.[1]

As the Airline Highway progressed, planners decided to extend Jefferson Highway westward from Williams Street all the way to Baton Rouge. Because of the superior soil conditions along the river and the fact that the plans only called for a gravel road to be built, the project was able to progress quickly, and it became the first all-weather road between the state's capitol city and New Orleans. Meanwhile the work on the more substantive Airline Highway project progressed more slowly, with the first major paved section of the roadway opening in 1933. The new road stretched from Kenner to Bonnet Carré in St. Charles Parish and was later extended all the way to Baton Rouge.[2]

Not all of the roadway projects planned for the Kenner area at the time proved to be as successful as were the Jefferson and Airline projects. One of the most ambitious of the failed projects was an attempt by the Jefferson Parish Police Jury in 1926 to have a "ramp" built over the Mississippi River at Kenner. A feasibility study quickly proved the difficulties associated with any effort to span the river and the project was soon abandoned. An even greater disappointment involved the proposed New Orleans to Hammond, Louisiana Lakeshore link of the planned U.S. Route 33 which was to connect New Orleans with Chicago. The route was designed to run along an early levee along the Lake Pontchartrain shoreline which had been constructed in 1924 by the Fourth Jefferson Drainage District. The primitive-lake levee provided a 100 foot-wide-raised roadbed for the new road of four feet above the mean level of the lake's waters. Construction on the shell roadway was started in late 1927 and reached Williams Street in Kenner in late 1935. The opening of the highway was celebrated with great fanfare and motorcades and an expectation that the project would open the area along the lake's southern shore to residential development, which would be "unsurpassed in beauty and climatic condition." Unfortunately, soon after being opened for traffic, engineers realized that the road was in serious danger of failure because of the problem of high waters from the lake. Efforts were made to build an eight-foot-high protection levee between the lake and the roadbed. Unfortunately, the levee only partially protected the road. Plans to extend the road to Hammond were abandoned and an all-out effort at preserving the section of road already completed was put into place. Matters only got worse. In February 1937, the Bonnet Carré Spillway was opened allowing Mississippi River flood waters to enter the lake, causing the levels of the lake to rise. The rising lake waters caused the embankment of the road to sink another two feet, leading to even more flooding of the highway. The Louisiana State Highway Commission concluded that the only way the road could be saved was to construct a seawall along the lakefront. It was decided that the cost of saving the roadway was too great and the project and the road were abandoned. Although the ambitious project failed, it proved to be a valuable asset for the Kenner community. In order to provide a connection with the planned highway, Williams Street, now Boulevard, was extended from the Airline Highway north all the way to Lake Pontchartrain and its connection with the new lakeshore road. The extension of Williams Street (now Boulevard) to the lake opened, for the first time, vast areas of northern Kenner to future settlement and population growth and made the lakefront easily assessable to all of the area's residents. The demand for the newly opened lands gradually increased until by 1940 when real estate developers advertised land along the road in north Kenner at the rate of $600 a square.[3]

As the community worked during the early years of the new century to improve its road and rail access to Kenner, local officials also toiled to bring other modern services to the town. With the success of the new electric carline fresh in their minds, the town council worked to bring the new convenience of electric power to the people of Kenner. In February 1919 the town purchased a new $10,000 electric light plant. Because of its expertise and experience in operating the town's electric carline, the contract to operate the new plant was given to the Orleans-Kenner Traction Company. Shortly thereafter, the people of Kenner enjoyed the convenience of modern electricity. To advance the electrification of the town and its streets, a special discount of 6 percent per kilowatt hour was offered to residents and businesses who placed a light on the outside of their building.[4]

The new electrical system proved to be quite popular with the people of Kenner. Unfortunately, the system was very unreliable and efforts to address its problems were only partially successful, resulting in the system continuing to have problems throughout the entire time it was in operation. In spite of the problems with its operation, the erratic little plant remained in operation for ten years. In 1929, the

Louisiana Power and Light Company offered to purchase the plant and its distribution system from the town. A referendum was held to decide the fate of the plant, with the citizens voting 110 to seven in favor of selling the plant to the power company. Additionally, impressed with the resources of the company and taking advantage of newly elected Louisiana Governor Huey Long's push to force utilities to provide the natural resource to the New Orleans area at a cheap price, the town council, on March 5, 1929, also granted Louisiana Power and Light a franchise to supply the town with natural gas.[5]

The arrival of electricity in the town, with its poles and wires spread across the community, presented another opportunity for an additional service for the residents of Kenner. On December 4, 1919, the town council authorized L. Centanni and Company to install an expanded telephone system in the town.[6] Seven years later in August 1926, the Cumberland Telephone and Telegraph Company was authorized by the town council to install a new phone system throughout the town. Only a few months later, Cumberland Telephone was consolidated with the Bell Telephone Company, which continued to provide service to the town until modern times. However, it would not be until 1951 that the reorganized Southern Bell Telephone and Telegraph Company opened a new $500,000 facility in Kenner that the community's subscriber rates would be reduced to the same level as those of residents in New Orleans. Similarly, with the town making rapid progress into the modern age, town leaders looked to improve the quality of the community's supply of drinking water. As was customary for decades, in many communities of South Louisiana, drinking water was obtained by collecting rain water in large cisterns located near most houses. Though not used for drinking in the town, water for commercial activities and agriculture frequently was acquired through flumes which ran through the levee to the Mississippi River. In September 1925, town leaders began making plans for upgrading the community's water system. A $100,000 bond issue was approved by the voters, and by March of the following year the first houses were being connected to the new system. After a few years of successful operation, in September 1930, the town's waterworks were sold to the East Jefferson Water Works, operated by the parish. Since that time, Kenner's water system has been the responsibility of Jefferson Parish.[7]

Although Italians and others continued to migrate to the community during the early decades of the new century to establish vegetable farms, the arrival of modern civic improvements brought a new population of residents to Kenner. These new citizens were different from past groups who had settled in the town. Instead of the truck farmers and laborers of the earlier wave of post-Civil War migrants to the area, the new inhabitants mostly were people who lived in the town and commuted to work in the city or other parts of Jefferson Parish. They were the forerunners of the great migration from the city to the suburbs that would take place after the Second World War. The sudden onset of the Great Depression in 1929 imperiled the progress Kenner was enjoying at the time from the arrival of new residents. So serious was the economic downturn that by December 1929, the Jefferson Parish Police was forced to notify Kenner that it would no longer be able to repair the streets in the community and that the town would have to assume the job of roadway maintenance. Kenner leaders accepted the task and took additional steps to insure that the town's growth would not suffer from the depression. To continue the town's progress during the period of economic uncertainty, community leaders took the positive step of marketing the town's real estate opportunities to potential new suburbanites by running weekly advertisements in the New Orleans newspapers. The ads were similar to those run shortly before the stock-market crash for "Kenner Heights" which offered the buyer lots for $140 and up, with "electric lights, water and telephones" and "streets sixty feet wide," many of which "are already graveled."[8] By 1930, the population of Kenner reached 2,440, an increase of nearly 30 percent over its 1920 count of 1,882.[9]

As with the rest of the Unites States, the Great Depression had a negative effect on the economy of Louisiana and the New Orleans region. Though the great economic downturn resulted in declines in business and employment in New Orleans and its surrounding areas, the segment of Louisiana's economy that was most severely damaged by the Depression was the state's agricultural sector. Prices and acreage of the state's major cash crop of cotton declined drastically during the period. Fortunately, for the farmers of Kenner, whose efforts centered on providing the variety of vegetables needed by the residents of New Orleans and other large cities, demand for their crops did not suffer as greatly as that of the larger cash-crop enterprises in the state. Furthermore, several of the road and highway improvements discussed previously were completed during the Depression years. These road upgrades gave the farmers of Kenner an advantage in getting their goods to their markets over those living in more rural areas, who had to cope with a much more primitive system of unpaved roads.[10]

In addition to improving the farm to market experience for the areas' truck farmers, the new roads also benefited the community by opening new segments of Kenner to real estate development. The placement of Airline Highway to the north of the populated sections of Kenner and the construction of Williams Boulevard northward all the way to the shores of Lake Pontchartrain opened entirely new areas for residential and commercial development. Although the economic conditions brought about by the Depression resulted in slow progress at first, the existence of the new roads nevertheless made development in these areas relatively easy, once the economic situation improved. Eventually the newly opened areas in the northern section of the city would become the population center of Kenner. By 1972 more than eighty percent of Kenner's population was located in these areas which in the 1930s were mostly marsh lands, swamps, and woods. Among the earliest commercial endeavors to take advantage of the new access to the area near the lake was Loyola University, which owned radio station WWL. A pioneer in radio broadcasting, in 1922 Loyola was among the first to begin broadcasting to the general public. In December 1938 the radio station opened its new 50,000 watt clear-channel transmitter on university owned land near the Lake Pontchartrain shoreline in Kenner. The new transmitter made the station one of the most powerful in America and earned the town of Kenner national publicity when WWL was saluted by the Columbia Broadcasting System, of which the station was an affiliate, in a coast-to-coast radio broadcast. Using the nation-wide reach of the powerful transmitter in Kenner, the station grew to become the leading radio station in the South.[11]

Although the new roads that came to the area during the period of the Great Depression helped the farmers of Kenner from suffering as badly as other agricultural communities in the state, the area nevertheless remained in the grip of the national economic crisis. Widespread unemployment and low wages affected the lives of Kenner's citizens. As

Using its 50,000 watt clear-channel transmitter located near the lake in Kenner, WWL radio gained national recognition when it began broadcasting coast to coast in 1938.

was the case in the rest of Louisiana, many in Kenner lived at or near the poverty line. Across Louisiana the per capita income of families was $286, a figure considerably less than the national average at the time of $472. Similarly, two-thirds of employees in the state worked at unskilled jobs and only ten percent worked at the higher-paying white-collar employment. This was reinforced by the fact that the Louisiana education rate remained near the bottom among all states, with its illiteracy rate among adults surpassing the national average by approximately three fold. At the time, twenty percent of the entire adult population in the state received no schooling at all and over half of the remaining population progressed only as far as the fourth-grade level. Adding to the difficulties faced by the people of Kenner was the continuing presence of Jim Crow practices, which segregated the races in the community by both law and custom. Nowhere was the forced separation more consequential than in the area of education. Even at its best, Louisiana's educational efforts lagged far behind many other states. The situation was even worse when it came to the education of blacks across the state and in Kenner. Public education in the town remained the responsibility of the Jefferson Parish Public School system, which had a history of inconsistency in the operation of its white schools, much less its segregated black schools. Enormous disparities in the quality of public education offerings between white and black children remained, with approximately 25 percent of the state's African American adults having neither the ability to read nor write. Black parents were not satisfied with the situation and pushed officials to address the matter. Petition campaigns for better school facilities from the African American community were frequently submitted to parish school officials. Some effort was made by school officials to address the issue but the segregated nature of the system resulted in the area's black schools remaining incapable of addressing the schooling needs of its students. For example, even after four new "colored" schools were constructed in the parish, classrooms remained overcrowded. By 1924, Kenner had two schools for white children with a total of eleven teachers, while the black children of the town were crowded into one school which had a single teacher assigned to it. With the coming of the Depression, conditions in public education worsened. For several years salaries of school workers in Jefferson had to be reduced anywhere from five to twenty-five percent. The disparity between white and black education continued for decades. In 1940, black schools in Louisiana were funded at a rate that was only one-quarter of the amount allocated for white schools and black teachers made 64 percent of their white counterparts. So serious became the situation, particularly for the black families of Kenner, that groups such as the National Education Association, working in association with the Works Progress Administration, which managed all adult education in Jefferson Parish, sent teachers into the town to offer education classes to the adult African American community. However, among the positive aspects of education efforts in Kenner was the continued success of the school that had been opened towards the end of the previous century by the Archdiocese of New Orleans at its church parish of Our Lady of Perpetual Help. For a while, Salesian Missionary Sisters of the Sacred Heart traveled to Kenner a few times a week to help with the instruction of Italian children in the town. Eventually the academic program at the Catholic school was solidified and strengthened when the Religious Sisters of Mercy assumed management of the school in 1928 and began their long tenure of nearly eight decades of staffing the facility. The Sisters of Mercy continued to operate the school until 2005.[12]

Though the small truck farmers of Kenner enjoyed the benefits brought by improved roads, the long-running economic effects of the Great Depression eventually resulted in serious problems for the people of the town. Between 1900 and 1930 the population of the Kenner community had doubled, whereas in the ten years between 1930 and 1940, the population of the town actually decreased for only the second time in its history. The reduction in residents from 2,440 to 2,375 came as a consequence of one of the area's important factories shutting down because of the depressed economy. However, as with the nation as a whole, the economy of the Kenner community began to experience an economic revival with the coming of the 1940s. This financial upswing in the region was set in motion by two events that would change the history of Kenner forever. Of the events, the decision to construct a new airport within the boundaries of the town, discussed in detail in the next chapter, was the most locally dramatic and historic. The other significant occurrence which not only affected the history of Kenner forever but also that of the entire country and the world was the onset of World War II.[13]

Even before the United States officially entered the war at the end of 1941 after the bombing of Pearl Harbor, war activities by America's allies in Europe and Asia led to an increased demand for materials, which assisted the United States in its effort to shake off the effects of the Great Depression. With America's formal entry into the war, demand for war materials and agricultural produce grew rapidly. Between 1940 and 1943 alone, production on America's farms increased by 16 percent. The jump in production on the farms of America was accomplished in spite of a shortage of manpower. Though agriculture in general was given special consideration in the drafting of men for service in the armed forces of the nation, the farmers of Kenner had to deal with a shortage of manpower throughout the war. Many in the community heard the call of their nation and joined the military, while others were lost to the many war industries which operated in the area and paid wages superior to those of a farm worker. Regardless of their manpower shortages, the farmers of Kenner redoubled their efforts in answer to the wartime demands of the country for agricultural production and actually were able to increase farm acreage in the community to its highest point in history. As the war unfolded, city fathers continued to advertise the "splendid conditions" in Kenner for agricultural endeavors including "chicken raising," dairying, and growing vegetables year round.[14]

Many Kenner residents—both men and women—found employment in war-related civilian jobs. By 1943 there were a minimum of thirty-seven plants involved in producing war materials in Jefferson Parish. Many of these plants drew workers from Kenner. Among these included the growing oil and boat building industries on the west bank of the parish, including Avondale Marine Ways and the Allen Boat Company. On the east bank, some workers traveled to New Orleans to work in the many war industries located there, including the builder of America's legendary military landing craft, the Higgins boat, at Higgins Industries. Closer to Kenner, the Rheem Manufacturing Company located on Jefferson Highway near the foot of the Huey P. Long Bridge, which employed both men and women, produced military ordnance, including 105 millimeter artillery shell casings. Close by the Rheem plant was the sprawling Camp Plauche military facility.

Built in 1942 on land currently occupied by the Elmwood Industrial Park, the camp covered 425 acres and included more than 300 buildings and had a capacity to handle 30,000 inhabitants. Originally used as a training base, the camp later functioned as a camp for German and Italian prisoners of war.[15] Just a few minutes automobile drive along Jefferson Highway from Kenner, the large camp offered employment opportunities for many residents of the town. In Kenner itself, besides the determined efforts of the farmers of Kenner to increase their crop production, several local companies joined in the war effort by increasing their outputs, including Jill's Poultry Farm, which stepped up its egg and chicken production, the Louisiana Box and Lumber Company, and the Mancuso Barrel and Box Company. Perhaps the most involved local company in the production of war materials was the Ipik Plywood Corporation, which took pride in the fact that it was a major supplier of the mahogany plywood panels used by Higgins Industries in its production of its vitally needed landing craft and PT boats.[16]

With Japan's formal surrender in early September 1945, life in Kenner began the process of returning to a peacetime society and economy. Across the nation, including in Jefferson Parish and Kenner, once humming wartime industries quickly shut down following the cancellation of government's orders for war materials. With the closings and their subsequent layoffs of employees and the knowledge that large numbers of soldiers and sailors would soon be returning home and in need of employment, many feared that another economic depression could be in the making. Yet, much had changed for the better during the war for the people of Kenner. The Kenner of 1945 was not the community that it had been during the Depression and the early days of the war in Europe in 1939. Though farmers had enjoyed high demand for their crops during the war, employment opportunities in war-related businesses for the people of Kenner—men, women, whites, and blacks—presented many residents with opportunities and a refreshing degree of prosperity that they desired to continue in the postwar period. With the war emergency over, southern social norms returned to the forefront and both African Americans and women were forced to retreat, at least for the time being, from their wartime social and economic gains.[17]

An important wartime gain for the Kenner community, which

did not come to an end with the conclusion of the conflict, was the construction boom that accompanied the buildup in wartime projects. With workers drawn to the new war-related projects needing housing, beginning in 1940 home construction in Jefferson Parish jumped. In 1941 alone, the number of homes being built nearly doubled that of 1940. If anything, the end of the war accelerated the building boom in Kenner. Not only was there a growing demand for housing in the town caused by the return of large numbers of troops from the war who were anxious to start their families in homes of their own, there was also a need for the large workforce who were employed first with the construction and later the operations of the new airport in Kenner. The two postwar factors of an expanding new airport and a rapidly spreading residential community changed the town of Kenner forever. To make room for the expanding projects required developers to both change the use of lands that in the past had been dedicated as agricultural fields and to expand the size of the footprint of the town's developed lands. To accomplish the latter goal required officials and developers to drain large sections of Kenner lands that for centuries had remained natural woodlands, marshes and swamps. In order to convert the areas from their natural state, parish and town leaders looked to the methods used by the city of New Orleans during the early decades of the century to drain the city's back swamps. The draining of such a large area swampland was a major endeavor that required time, money, and the dredging of a system of drainage canals to drain the swamp water into Lake Pontchartrain. Levees and pumping stations added to the high cost of the project. [18] With the great majority of the region undeveloped and unprotected from storm surges, the people of Kenner had been among the first residents of East Jefferson to work towards the draining of the vast undrained lands along the lakeshore. The project started in 1913 when the Fourth Jefferson Drainage District created a sub-district to begin draining the Kenner area. Though the project ran into financing problems and had to be restarted on multiple occasions, by 1924 the drainage district had completed a crisscross pattern of large drainage canals and pumping stations on the east bank of Jefferson Parish that continues to serve as the backbone of parish's modern drainage system.[19]

Any debate over the need for improved flood protection was resolved in 1947 when the New Orleans area took a direct hit from a major hurricane.[20] A category two storm passed directly over the area at 9:30 in the morning of September 19, 1947. Pushing a flood surge of perhaps twenty-eight feet into Lake Pontchartrain, the storm overwhelmed the area's anemic drainage and storm controls and brought flood waters as deep as six feet to a large portion of Jefferson Parish north of Airline Highway. In Kenner, the storm surge reached within two hundred yards of Airline Highway, almost completely inundating the runways of the recently dedicated airport with between two and four feet of water. On at least one of the ranches in northern Kenner valuable livestock were drowned in the estimated ten feet of water that poured into the area.[21]

In spite of the widespread damage caused to the area by the storm, the growth in Kenner's postwar population and business community continued unabated. Although it had an agricultural-based economy throughout its history, within a decade of the end of Second World War, Kenner, like most of the east bank of Jefferson Parish, completely evolved to become overwhelmingly a residential and industrial community. Among the new commercial enterprises to move to the town during the postwar period was the Delta Match Corporation. Although the greater part of its holdings was located in neighboring St. Charles Parish, by 1951 the company acquired a sizeable portion of the old Oakland Plantation along the western boundary of Kenner. By the 1960s, Delta Match Corporation remained the only match manufacturer in the entire South. By 1968 the company changed its name to the Universal Match Corporation and boasted a daily production of 100 million matches. Unfortunately, because of decreasing demand for the product, in May 1991 the corporation closed its manufacturing operation. In regards to population changes in Kenner, by 1950 the population of the community had more than doubled from its 1940 count of 2,375. With the number of its residents now totaling 5,535, Kenner met the legal conditions for a change in its classification by the state. Thus on January 22, 1952, Governor Earl K. Long officially proclaimed Kenner a city.[22]

Although it offered mostly rudimentary facilities, when it was opened to use by commercial airlines in 1946, Moisant International Airport claimed the honor of being the largest civilian airport in America.

10
MSY: Kenner Takes to the Air

Coinciding with the economic growth of the area during the Second World War years was the arrival of large-scale commercial aviation and the construction of a new airport in Kenner. Since the decision in the 1850s to build a railroad through the area, no other single event has meant more to the development of the Kenner community than the locating of the region's major airport within the boundaries of the city. Over its history of approximately seven decades, the Kenner airfield has gone through several formal name changes. Originally named Moisant International Airport, the title was later changed to New Orleans International Airport—Moisant Field which it remained until 2001 when the name was changed again to its current designation of Louis Armstrong-New Orleans International airport. Given the official designation code of MSY,[1] the origin of the airport dates to the early days of aviation in Louisiana. As with other areas of the country, early interest in commercial aviation in New Orleans centered on its use as part of the postal service. Indeed, one of the earliest airmail flights in America occurred in 1912 when mail was sent to Baton Rouge from New Orleans by airplane. Early flights simply used open fields to take off and land. Increased interest in aviation led the Young Men's Business Club (YMBC) of New Orleans in 1925 to secure a tract of land on the west bank of the river in Plaquemine Parish for use as an airport. Named for Alvin Callender, the only flyer from New Orleans to be killed during World War I, the supporters of the new field began work on erecting a hanger and other facilities and undertook efforts to obtain government airmail contracts. With the success of Charles Lindbergh's 1927 historic flight across the Atlantic, enthusiasm for commercial aviation intensified markedly and Louisiana's first interstate airline, the St. Tammany Gulf Coast Airways, was given a federally subsidized route between New Orleans and Atlanta.[2]

The first airfield to be built near the Kenner area was opened in 1928 when J. C. Menefee, a New Orleans businessman and auto dealer, leased forty acres on Jefferson Highway a few miles from Kenner at the future site of Camp Plauche. At the location he laid out a landing strip and purchased two Lincoln-Page biplanes, which he hoped to use in the operation of a mail route. Within a year, Menefee's chief pilot and manager, James Wedell partnered with Harry P. Williams of Patterson, Louisiana, to inaugurate flights to both St. Louis and Shreveport, which included service to multiple locations in between the two cities. Even more significantly, the two partners opened an aviation school at the Menefee field on Jefferson Highway. In the 1930s, government policy changed, and instead of sprinkling contracts among many different small regional companies, the "big four" national airlines were given preference. Soon American Airlines had gained a foothold in the region and bought out the area's smaller companies. Nevertheless, improvements continued to be made on the community's airfields, with the Menefee airport obtaining the latest design in lights and a modern two-way radio telephone system.[3]

When plans developed in the 1920s to carry out a massive land reclamation project along the lakefront in New Orleans, authorization was obtained in 1928 to construct airfields as part of the project. An ambitious plan was hatched to build a modern full-service airport on land reclaimed from the lake. Under the direction of Abe Shushan and John Klorer, 315 acres were reclaimed from the lake's waters and four modern runways and a terminal were constructed. Opened in February 1934, the new airport was capable of handling the most modern planes flying at the time and was considered one of the finest airports in the nation. However, the rapid expansion of commercial aviation during the period soon resulted in the New Orleans Lakefront Airport becoming inadequate in handling the growing number of flights and passengers arriving in and departing from New Orleans. The development of the modern aircraft created an additional need for longer runways to deal with the higher landing and takeoff speeds and payload capacities.[4]

With the Lakefront Airport's inadequacies becoming increasingly evident, the City of New Orleans began a search for a site to build a new state-of-the-art airport. As the search continued, Congress authorized the expenditure of $40 million for the construction of new civil airports around the country. With the availability of new Federal funds, Jefferson Parish officials became interested in the effort to find a site for a new airport. By early 1941, they had selected a site in Kenner situated 3,000 feet from Airline Highway in the form of a parallelogram and measuring approximately one mile on each side. The site had many advantages over its competitors. It was believed to be remarkably free of fog, permitting year-round-all-weather flying, and was located near the two major transportation arteries of the Airline and Jefferson Highways. On the negative side, though the land consisted mostly of cultivated patches and unimproved real estate, the owners realized the value of the land as a future airport and demanded a price that officials considered to be unnecessarily high at $83.00 an acre. Needing at least six hundred acres for the new airfield, Civil Aeronautics Administration officials in Washington, D.C., though still interested in the Kenner site, began anew to look for cheaper land. Discussions continued for several more months over setting a fair price for the land.[5]

By September 1941, the City of New Orleans had also become interested in the Kenner site for its new airport. A law passed by the state legislature in 1936 allowed the city, with the consent of the local governing authority, to go outside of its geographical limits to buy, build, control, and maintain an airport. New Orleans Mayor Robert S. Maestri took the initiative to negotiate a settlement with the owners of the lands in Kenner. Negotiations with Jefferson officials did not go well, and the two sides failed to reach agreement on the value of the land. With the negotiations having failed and with the need for a new airport pressing, the City of New Orleans began expropriation proceedings against the land owners, paying them about $50.00 per acre for their land. It was planned that when the acquisition of the land was completed, workers from the W.P.A. (Works Progress Administration) would be used to clear the land and begin construction of the new airport. However, with America's entry into the World War in early December, work on W.P.A. and other Depression-era projects diminished, including the new airport where construction halted.[6]

Work at the airport site was not stopped for long. The military realized the strategic importance of the site and need for a new airport and stepped in and took over the project. Its location to the west of the city created a protective triangle around the city, with Lakefront Airport located on the north side of New Orleans and Alvin Callender Airport located to the south. Construction was accelerated. By November 1942, the first runway of 150 feet in width and 5,000 feet in length was completed to such a degree that military aircraft began using the facility. With the arrival of aircraft, the new field became fully operational. Mayor Maestri took advantage of the occasion and announced that the new airport would be named John B. Moisant Field. A world-famous aviator at the time that aviation was still in its infant stage, Moisant was born in Illinois to French Canadian parents. He had earned his renown by being the first to fly over the city of Paris with a passenger, and he was the first pilot to fly between Paris and London. He was among the first to fly around the Statue of Liberty in New York and was the first to build an all-metal aircraft. In late 1910, he spent several weeks in New Orleans putting on a series of flight demonstrations while preparing to participate in a competition for the $4000 Michelin Cup, an aviation prize which was to be awarded for the longest endurance flight for the year. While waiting the day for his tournament flight, the daring flyer wowed the residents of the Crescent City with flights around the city, from Mid-City along Canal Street across the river to Gretna and back to Audubon Park along St. Charles Avenue to Lee Circle and then dipping low over City Hall, then located in historic Gallier Hall. Waiting to the last day of the year to attempt his feat, Moisant, who was promoted in the New Orleans' newspaper as the "King of Aviators," took off on a preliminary flight from New Orleans to a field near the future site of Menefee Field at the village of Harahan, a short distance to the east of Kenner. Reaching the field where spectators awaited his arrival, he attempted to land but about twenty-five feet above the ground his plane suddenly became vertical and crashed, throwing its pilot violently to the ground where he suffered a broken spinal cord and died almost immediately.[7]

Construction continued on the facilities at the new airport in Kenner throughout the war. Nevertheless, because of the national emergency, both military and civilian aircraft used the facility. The first commercial aircraft flight to land at the field occurred on September 13, 1944, when a four-engine Pan American Clipper flew with a passenger load of local officials from the New Orleans Lakefront Airport to Moisant field to mark the start of commercial aviation at the facility. However, civilian passengers who used the airport during its early days of operation found only rudimentary facilities available. Nearly all structures were of temporary construction and consisted mostly of military style Quonset huts. While construction continued, officials worked to increase the size of the footprint of the project. Originally planned in 1940 as a 600 acre tract, its area was enlarged to 800 acres in 1941 and to 1,010 acres in 1944. By the time the war ended, the facility neared completion and had converted to mostly civilian use. In 1946 the airport was again increased in size to 1,360 acres, thus making it four times the size of Alvin Callender Airport and, at the time, twice the size of either the airport at Chicago or New York City's LaGuardia Field and larger than 99 percent of all other civilian airports in the United States.[8]

Though the facility was used extensively by the armed forces during the war, the City of New Orleans continued to develop the project for commercial use. In September 1943 the New Orleans Aviation Board was organized and given authority to administer, operate, and maintain the two municipal airports at Callender and Moisant. Additionally, the board was given the responsibility of appointing an Aviation Director, whose duty was to manage the airports. A month later the taxpayers of New Orleans joined in the effort to build a modern state-of-the-art facility by passing a bond issue that provided $5,000,000 in bonds to cover the cost of the continued construction of updated facilities at the city-owned airports. With the end of the war, the city assumed total responsibility for the facility. Early in the new year of 1946, city leaders organized a grand two-day celebration to mark the official dedication of the airport. On Saturday and Sunday, January 12 and 13, 1946, Lt. General James H. "Jimmy" Doolittle, the hero of the daring raid on Tokyo in 1942 and a Medal of Honor recipient, officially dedicated the airport. Thousands of New Orleanians

Illinois born, John Bevins Moisant, was a pioneer in American aviation. Learning to fly in Europe, Moisant was the first to fly passengers over Paris and made the first Paris to London flight. Shortly thereafter he retuned to the United States where he won the Statue of Liberty race in New York. A few weeks later he in arrived in New Orleans where he planned to compete for the $4000 Michelin Prize, which was to be awarded for the year's longest endurance flight. On December 31, 1910, on the first phase of the competition while attempting a landing near Harahan, he was thrown from his aircraft and killed. Decades later, the newly constructed airport at Kenner was named in honor of the daring aviator.

Full page advertisement from January 12, 1946 announcing the dedication ceremonies of the new airport in Kenner.

and Jeffersonians celebrated the dedication with activities that ranged from banquets and a military parade on Canal Street to static displays of military equipment and aircraft and flight demonstrations. A mock amphibious invasion by a detachment of U.S. Marines was performed on the river levee in Kenner not far from the new airport. At the time of the dedication, Moisant consisted of four 150 foot-wide concrete runways, one 7,000 foot-long and three other runways of 5,000 feet each. Hangar and administration buildings still consisted of the wartime Quonset huts. In spite of the military structures, the airport's facilities were considered to be equal to any other terminal in the country. Promoted as the "air hub of the Americas," the city boasted that its new airport was the largest in the country and was capable of handling the largest commercial airliners in use at the time. Operating with fifty flights a day out of the field, by early spring, all six major airlines operating from the Lakefront Airport had transferred their operations to Moisant. From that time forward, the smaller lakefront field focused mostly on general aviation (non-scheduled and private flights).[9]

As was the case in general with commercial aviation across the nation, services and facilities at Moisant expanded quickly to keep pace with growing demand by the public for flights to and from the New Orleans area. During the first year of operation after its official dedication, 180,000 passengers used the airport. In 1948 the facility continued to claim itself to be the largest commercial airport in America. Two years later, nine airlines were flying 122 flights a day in and out of the airport and the number of passengers jumped to 380,000. By 1952 the number of passengers using the airport reached 635,000. By the early 1970s nearly 3.7 million passengers a year were using the facility. With the increase in the number of passengers and with the arrival of the new jet age in commercial aviation, there came a growing need to replace the World War II period buildings that had been in use since the airport opened. To address the need, the Aviation Board, in the late fifties, began a $23 million improvement program designed to handle the equipment and facilities necessary for the new larger and heavier jet aircraft. The first commercial jet to use the airport, a Capitol Airline Viscount, took off on a flight to New York City in 1956. A few months later, New Orleans Mayor deLesseps S. Morrison laid the cornerstone for a new $7.5 million terminal. The new building was formally opened on November 11, 1959. Among the changes included in the expansion project was the construction of a new state-of-the-art ten-story high control tower to replace the original World War II-era one. The new terminal building, with its modern design of glass, concrete, marble, and steel, had more than ten times the space of the old structures it replaced. With the completion of its expansion program in 1961, the New Orleans City Council, following a trend throughout the country of having airports named for the cities they serviced, officially changed the name of the facility to New Orleans International Airport (Moisant Field).[10]

Coinciding with the increase in passenger travel through the airport was a growth in the air-freight industry. To meet the needs of the expanding freight business, the Aviation Board, working with the airlines and local businesses, developed a concept that led to the nation's first off-airport air-cargo depot. Called the LaFon Air Park, the facility was built entirely with private funds and was situated adjacent to the airport, approximately one mile west of the main facility. Constructed so that it could be easily expanded to meet future needs, as originally constructed the LaFon Air Park offered more than 100,000 square feet of modern warehousing and represented more than a fivefold increase in the airport's capacity to handle air freight. Designed to handle as many as eight of the new jumbo jets that were joining the nation's air fleet at the time, the new air park was planned to handle the freight needs of the community for decades.[11]

The expanding passenger and freight demands along with advances in airplane design led to the use of a new generation of commercial aircraft—the jumbo jet. Beginning in late 1972, National Airlines introduced jumbo-jet service to the airport with its daily DC-10 flights to Los Angeles. To keep pace with the changing demands, officials once again extensively remodeled the facility. The terminal building was enlarged by adding a new concourse specifically designed to handle the jumbo jets. Indeed, the fact that the air transportation industry is dynamic and constantly in a state of change has required that airports in America build and remodel their facilities on an almost perpetual cycle. So has been the case with the airport in Kenner. Updating of the terminal, runways, and other facilities at the airport has continued off and on to contemporary times. In 1977 a new access road, which provided speedy vehicular entrance to the airport, was completed, and in 1995 a new $10 million state-of-the-art tower, which at 209 feet was twice the height of the old structure it replaced, was put into service. Even into the twenty-first century, airport managers have continued to upgrade the facility as demonstrated by the addition of a new automobile garage, which increased the number of parking spaces at the facility to 2,500 when it opened to the public in 2003. One additional change brought to the facility was another new name designation. On August 2, 2001 the airport officially changed its name to Louis Armstrong New Orleans International Airport following a July vote by the New Orleans City Council. The new name honoring New Orleans native and jazz great Louis "Satchmo" Armstrong was given to the facility by the council as part of what was thought to be at the time a growing, but short lived, custom in the country of naming airports for a famous son, such as John Wayne Airport in California and Will Rogers Airport in Oklahoma City.[12]

The effort to keep the airport's facilities current with the offerings of its competing airports and the demands of the aviation industry has not been cheap and has at times strained the resources of the City of New Orleans. Under Federal Aviation Administration law, all monies earned at the airport have to be used there, thus although a vital resource for the City of New Orleans, the airport provides few direct financial benefits to the city at times of fiscal distress. New Orleans Mayor Maurice "Moon" Landrieu was among the first to propose a solution to the issue. In 1977 he floated the idea of the city selling the airport to the state. He set the value of the facility at $100 million dollars and promised that money obtained by the sale would be used for the city's capital needs. Landrieu's successor, Dutch Morial, at first opposed the plan but in 1985 changed his mind and bought into the idea. However, he did not set a price for the facility. Yet, in spite of the idea being supported by two mayors of New Orleans and a 1979 study by the airport's Aviation Board which concluded the state should control the facility, the amount of resources it would have required the state to dedicate to the project was too great for it to commit to the effort and thus the plan never moved beyond the discussion stage.[13]

Complicating the discussion on the viability of a state takeover of the airport was a longstanding dispute between the City of New

Orleans and the communities neighboring the airport. Although the airport was a welcome arrival to the Kenner community at time the decision was made to build the facility at its present location, the unique relationship between the airport, a wholly owned property of the City of New Orleans, and the legal entities of the City of Kenner and Jefferson Parish has at times resulted in strained relations between the governmental entities. Over the years of its existence, the airport has produced millions of dollars' worth of construction and business projects, as well as jobs for thousands of area residents. However, because the airport is legally part of the City of New Orleans, as a subsidiary of a subdivision of the state it enjoys tax exempt status from all local and parish taxes. Not unexpectedly, early in the history of the airport, Kenner and Jefferson Parish made a determined effort to have the facility added to the tax rolls. At first the parish tax assessor refused to do so on the grounds that the airport could not be taxed as it was the property of the City of New Orleans. Not being satisfied with the decision of the assessor, politically powerful Sheriff Frank J. Clancy of Jefferson Parish in April 1946 overruled the assessor and threatened to seize the airport's land for back taxes. Though the land was quickly added to the tax rolls at a value of a half million dollars, it did not remain there for long. The City of New Orleans took the issue to court and won back its tax exempt status.[14]

The debate over the airport's tax status was not the only dispute over the facility to take place between the City of New Orleans and the airport's neighbors. In early 1956 simmering feelings of animosity between New Orleans officials and leaders in Jefferson Parish and Kenner concerning the future of the airport burst into public view when plans by New Orleans to make the airport ready for use by commercial jet airliners resulted in the Federal Housing Administration and Veterans Administration suspending home-loan guarantees for all construction in a two mile area around the Kenner airport. The loan ban was implemented because of the potential of the new jets causing noise problems which could potentially lower property values, thus making homes in the area financial risks. The order endangered millions of dollars of construction projects and alarmed local officials, housing developers, home owners, and prospective homeowners in Kenner. Local officials placed as much blame for the damaging ban on officials of the City of

New Orleans for planning to bring jets to the airport as they did on the local Federal administrators who actually imposed the restrictions. State Representative John F. Rau Jr. complained that "To let New Orleans do as she wished would be to abandon oversight of government in Jefferson Parish." Sheriff Clancy of Jefferson Parish took an even blunter position by stating that,

> The serious trouble caused by this affair can be laid at the foot of irresponsible officials. First, the mayor of New Orleans [deLesseps Morrison] was irresponsible in not investigating the possible effects of the use of jet aircraft at Moisant—a city owned airport. [And] second the local FHA and VA officials presumably did not investigate the matter before invoking the ban.[15]

He concluded his remarks with the resentful observation that "no New Orleans official has approached the duly constituted officials of Jefferson Parish to offer aid in fighting the . . . ban they helped bring about."[16] When the local Federal authorities refused to rescind their ban, both the Kenner City Council and the Jefferson Parish Police Jury took action to protect the residents of Kenner by introducing ordinances designed to eliminate any noise problems by barring jets from landing or taking off in both Kenner and Jefferson Parish. With so much riding on the issue, Federal authorities in Washington D.C., including Congressman Hale Boggs, became involved, quickly overruled the Federal administrators in New Orleans, and rescinded the suspension of the home-loan guarantees. The ban was permanently lifted and the anti-jet ordinances were repealed when the airlines convinced both sides that the noise from the new jets would be no louder than the planes already in service at the airport.[17]

Unfortunately, within weeks of the hostile debate over the noise issue, the two sides again found themselves publicly at odds with one another. Once again the airport's effort to accommodate the new generation of commercial jets upset the residents of Kenner. When the airport made plans to expand its runways in order to be able to handle the new jets, Kenner and Jefferson Parish officials as well as residents of Kenner publicly opposed the improvements. As with the previous incident, local officials complained that there was a "careful concealment of [the] expansion plans by the aviation board" and that "New Orleans [was] . . . acting selfishly and arrogantly [and was] willing to connive with Federal agencies in a deliberate attempt to by-pass state authority . . . ." Jefferson Parish Police Jury member John G. Fitzgerald proclaimed that the sub-rosa plans for the airport's modifications were proof that New Orleans was "assuming governmental functions which are inherently functions of Jefferson Parish and Kenner." Kenner residents joined in the debate at a city council meeting and urged officials to not only oppose the expansion plans of the airport but to work towards the outright removal of the facility altogether. In a remark made at a council meeting, Director of the New Orleans City Planning Commission Louis Bisso proclaimed that New Orleans had "a lot of authority" on the question of expansion. His comments also touched upon the sensitive issue of airport control and local authority. Taking offense at the comment, Kenner Mayor Joseph S. Kopfler responded with a challenge of his own by noting, "Well, we'll just see how much authority we have." He then requested and received a motion of the Kenner City Council aimed at preventing the future expansion of the airport.[18]

The two sides eventually reached agreement by increasing the size of the Aviation Board from five to nine members and including among the membership representatives from Jefferson and St. Charles parishes. It was felt that the new expanded board membership gave the airport's neighbors input into all future plans. With the concession from New Orleans to allow representation from other parishes on the Aviation Board, the modernization project moved forward. Nevertheless, with the mayor of New Orleans remaining the appointing authority to the board, competition between New Orleans and its neighbors over the control of the airport remained an issue of concern for years to come. In the late 1970s an effort was made to resolve the issue once and for all by having the state acquire ownership of the airport. At the same time, officials in Kenner and Jefferson Parish began a multi-year effort to acquire some degree of legal oversight of the airport. The issue returned to public view during the 1982 city election in Kenner when candidate and parish councilman Aaron Broussard made the state takeover of the airport an important part of his successful campaign for mayor. An influential member of the Jefferson Parish Council at the time he was a candidate for mayor, Broussard enjoyed the support of other members of the parish-lawmaking body. Hence in the days leading up to the Kenner election, the parish council voted to ask the Jefferson Parish legislative delegation and the governor in Baton Rouge to consider the reactivation of a legislative committee, which dated back to the time when New Orleans Mayor Moon Landrieu had originally discussed selling the airport, in order to consider anew the possible transfer of ownership of the airport to the state. The Jefferson officials maintained that a state takeover would not only give Kenner and Jefferson fairer treatment in regards to the airport but also would provide additional revenues to the City of New Orleans. The people of Kenner increasingly experienced a love-hate relationship with their airport. On one hand, the airport was among the region's largest employers, even elected Kenner officials such as Mayor Larry Hooper worked at the facility. Nevertheless, on the other side of the issue, many residents and officials thought that the city, with approximately 15 percent of its territory occupied by the facility, should have received a larger portion of the airport's revenues. However, with the arrival of jet aircraft, the issue most complained about by Kenner residents was the high noise levels experienced by those who resided in neighborhoods close to the airfield. Kenner officials even recommended that new north-south runways be constructed on the western side of the field so takeoffs and landings would take place over the uninhabited swamp lands of St. Charles Parish. In making the proposal for new runways to the west of Kenner and demonstrating the frustration that many in Kenner held towards the airport, City Councilman Kenneth Hipp proclaimed that, "We should not allow the city of Kenner to become hostage to the city of New Orleans for their facility."[19]

State Representative Quentin Dastugue of Jefferson Parish took the lead in the effort to change control, if not ownership, of the airport. Over the next three years, Dastugue led an effort in the legislature to modify the control of the airport. Among the proposals concerning the airport's control discussed by the legislature was the outright transfer and sale of the airport to the state, the joining together of the airport in Kenner with the Lakefront airport under the Orleans Levee Board, and the allocation of seats on the Aviation Board to Jefferson Parish, Kenner, and St. Charles Parish. Nearly all efforts to legislate new management for the airport were opposed by the City of New Orleans and the Aviation Board. However, in the 1983 legislative session, the supporters of change finally succeeded in passing a law that required the nine-member Aviation Board to include members not only from New Orleans but also Kenner, Jefferson Parish, and St. Charles Parish. Opponents of the law immediately filed suit and within months of its passage, the law was ruled illegal by Civil District Judge Gerald P. Fedoroff because it violated the home-rule charter of the City of New Orleans. With the court siding with the City of New Orleans and its control of the airport, those seeking to change the management of the facility began to work towards getting New Orleans to cooperate by pointing out that as a state entity many of the problems then being faced by the airport would be resolved. Most notably, the desperate need of the airport to extend its main runway into St. Charles Parish would be much easier to address as a state facility. Although state law permitted the City of New Orleans to own the airport in another parish, another state law denied the city and its Aviation Board the authority to expropriate land in another parish. Hence, with St. Charles Parish resisting the vital expansion of runways westward into its lands, state ownership of the facility would permit expropriation of the needed land. Eventually the merits of the plan for state ownership began to take hold and led to the surprise change of position on the issue by New Orleans Mayor Dutch Morial from opposition to acceptance. In spite of the fact that the City of New Orleans dropped its opposition to the possibility of a state takeover of the airport, control of the facility remains largely under the control of the City of New Orleans. A 1984 analysis of the value of the airport estimated that the city had an overall bonded investment in the facility of over $200 million, while others set the value at $500 million to $1 billion, a cost that at the time the state found to be beyond its means.[20]

The operation of any large commercial airport with thousands of takeoffs and landings and millions of passengers using the facility annually is by its very nature a potentially dangerous operation. As has many of its competing airfields, the airport in Kenner has had a mixed safety history. During the first twenty years of its operation there were no fatal accidents involving commercial aviation at the airport. The first fatal accident occurred during World War II—shortly after the airport first opened—when a military plane while attempting to land clipped a limb of a tree and killed the copilot of the aircraft. In spite of the damage to his plane, the pilot managed to land the aircraft successfully. It was another twenty years before a major incident occurred at the Kenner facility.[21] On February 25, 1964, Eastern Airlines flight 304 was heading from New Orleans to Atlanta on the second leg of a flight that originated in Mexico City. The DC-8 jet took off from the airport at 2:01 a.m. and nine minutes later mysteriously disappeared from the facility's radar. It was later discovered that the plane with fifty-one passengers and seven crew members for an unknown reason had plunged into the choppy waters of Lake Pontchartrain five to seven miles south of Mandeville on the north shore and five miles east of the Causeway bridge. No distress call was heard from the doomed aircraft. For forty-fives days officials worked to recover pieces of the aircraft and the remains of the victims, of which twenty-six were never found. Following an investigation of the accident, officials noted the poor weather conditions at the time of the flight and listed the cause of the crash as being a "degradation of aircraft stability characteristics in turbulence." A follow-up investigation later determined that the tragic crash was caused by the failure of a single mechanical part called a "pitch trim compensator," which could be raised or lowered to control the plane's speed. Investigators found the device to be in the wrong position as the aircraft gained height to 1500 feet, resulting in the loss of control by the crew and devastating crash into the fifteen-foot deep lake.[22]

Just three years later the airport experienced a second DC-8 disaster.[23] On the night of March 29-30, 1967, while on a routine training flight with a crew of five and a Federal Aviation Agency inspector onboard, a Delta Airlines plane turning on its final approach to the airport slammed into the ground and crashed through two Kenner homes on Worth Street and cartwheeled into the rear of the Hilton Inn Motel on Airline Highway. Spreading wreckage and flaming jet fuel as it skidded along the ground and across a railroad embankment, the crash injured eleven and killed a total of nineteen individuals, including the plane's crew, a mother and her thirteen year-old son, who were in their home on Worth Street, two employees of the Hilton, and nine high-school girls from the Midwest who were guests at the motel while they were visiting New Orleans on their senior class trip. Investigators eventually determined that the cause of the crash was pilot error among the crew members on the training flight.[24]

Almost two years later to the day, on March 20, 1969, airport officials were forced again to deal with a fatal crash. At 7:02 in the morning a World War II era DC-3 twin-engine propeller airplane on a charter flight from Memphis, Tennessee, to British Honduras with twenty-seven individuals on board attempted a landing for refueling at the airport in a thick fog. Landing hard, the pilot lost control of the aircraft, which broke apart and burst into flames. Sixteen of the people on board the flight died in the crash and subsequent fire.[25]

As tragic as these accidents were, they would pale in comparison to the catastrophic events of July 9, 1982. On this most tragic of days in the history of the Kenner community, death would be visited upon the the city in numbers as never before. Like so many other summertime days, that Friday began in typical fashion with high humidity and temperatures rising into the low 90 degree range. Expectation was for a 40 percent chance of afternoon thundershowers—showers which were typically welcomed by many for they brought cooling breezes and rain that helped to break the oppressive heat of July in south Louisiana. So it was in the small Roosevelt subdivision, nestled within walking distance of city hall and situated between the thoroughfares of Roosevelt Boulevard to the east and Williams Boulevard to the west. By afternoon the predicted thunderstorms appeared over the little subdivision and the eastern edge of the airport. Some residents of the neighborhood, including Evelyn Pourciau and Veral Crocker decided to take advantage of the cooling breezes that accompanied the afternoon rainstorm by sitting outside under covered patios at their houses. At about the same time, a little over a mile away, Capt. Kenneth L. McCullers was sitting in the cockpit of his Pan American Boeing 727 making final preparations for takeoff on his flight to Las Vegas, Nevada, and then on to San Diego in California. His plane was filled to capacity, so much so that five women had to be bumped from the flight at the last minute before boarding. On board were a seven-person crew, an additional airline mechanic, 137 passengers and a full load of jet fuel—making the takeoff a heavy lift.[26]

As Veral Crocker sat under her patio watching the afternoon thunderstorm and Evelyn Pourciau brushed her dog on her patio, at

4:07 and fifty-nine seconds, Capt. McCullers and his crew, upon receiving final clearance for takeoff, powered up his plane's engines and began the takeoff of Pan Am Flight 759. As the plane jumped forward and headed eastward down the runway, the rain clouds over Roosevelt subdivision and the eastern end of the runway continued to poor rain. The storm stood in the path of the fully-loaded aircraft. People who lived near the eastern edge of the airport were accustomed to hearing the sounds of takeoffs. Many could, even before seeing the planes, recognize the type of aircraft involved by simply listening to the sound of the engines of the plane that was taking off. Evelyn Pourciau would remember years later that as she brushed her dog there was a unique sputtering and popping of the jetliner's engines, which caused her to look up to see the plane as she had done hundreds of times before. This time she was shocked to hear trees cracking and could see the huge blue and white Pan American aircraft zoom past just a few feet away from her. Within a second or two she could see the left wing down and witnessed it begin to cut a path of destruction and death through her neighbors' homes. Later investigation showed that the time was 4:09 and five seconds when the huge plane began its devastating death cartwheel through the quiet Kenner subdivision of small ranch-style bungalows. As the aircraft disintegrated and spewed its contents of passengers, fuel, and pieces of itself, it devastated a four-block area of the small Kenner neighborhood. As it plowed through the neighborhood, houses exploded and added their charred contents to the hellish scene. Jet fuel poured from the aircraft's ruptured tanks inflaming houses to the sides of the plane's path of destruction, causing Evelyn Pourciau to remember years later that the scene "looked like Hades had turned loose." A handful of yards away from the exploding plane careening across Fairway Street and through her neighbor's homes, Veral Crocker, who moments before had been sitting on her patio watching the afternoon rain storm, barely escaped being another casualty of the disaster as two pieces of metal from the ill-fated plane crashed through the aluminum awning over her head and landed within a few feet from where she was seated. Not all of Veral's neighbors in her subdivision were so fortunate. Though some survived for a while after being rushed to local hospitals, the killer crash eventually took the lives of eight residents of the subdivision. Of those killed on the ground, two were mothers at home with their youngsters and six were young children ranging in ages from four months to eleven years. In addition to those Kenner residents who lost their lives in the devastation, nine others were seriously injured in the incident, including the neighbor of Evelyn Pourciau who she recalled seeing running from her burning house with her burned skin hanging from her body like a "sheet of wax." Later, the body of the neighbor's young daughter was located in the ruins of her destroyed house. Another nearby neighbor, nineteen year-old Charles Watson Jr. reported seeing shortly after the crash, "people . . . running through the streets on fire. They were screaming."[27]

In a single minute or so, starting at 4:07 and fifty-nine seconds and ending with the impact of the Pan American aircraft with the ground at 4:09 and five seconds, the plane traveled a mere 4,610 feet from the runway where it had taken off and gained a maximum altitude of only 163 feet. The post-crash investigation by the National Transportation Safety Board determined that the plane, during the lift-off and initial climb phase of the flight, encountered a "microburst-induced wind shear which imposed a downward draft and a decreased headwind," which caused the plane to lose altitude rapidly. It struck trees at a height of approximately fifty feet along Williams Boulevard and shortly thereafter crashed into the ground. The devastation caused by the crash was far greater than simply the airliner and the houses it crushed. In addition to the deaths of the residents of the subdivision, all 145 on board the plane perished. Of those, ninety passengers had boarded the aircraft in New Orleans and joined the forty-nine individuals who had boarded the flight at its previous stop in Miami, Florida. The destruction of Flight 759 also brought lasting trauma and regrets to not only the relatives and friends of those killed but also to the nearly two hundred first responders and rescue workers from thirty-five different agencies who reported to the site in an almost fruitless effort to rescue survivors. Over three decades after the event, individuals involved in the rescue and recovery effort continue to recount vivid and traumatic memories of the tragic scene. Former Kenner Police Chief Nick Congemi, who at the time was a police lieutenant and also worked for Pan American Airlines at the airport, related in newspaper interviews how even after three decades he was aware of, "some people who still have thoughts and dreams about what they saw there." He

The Times-Picayune
The States-Item

THE CRASH OF FLIGHT 759

Pan Am jet slams into Kenner; more than 148 are feared dead

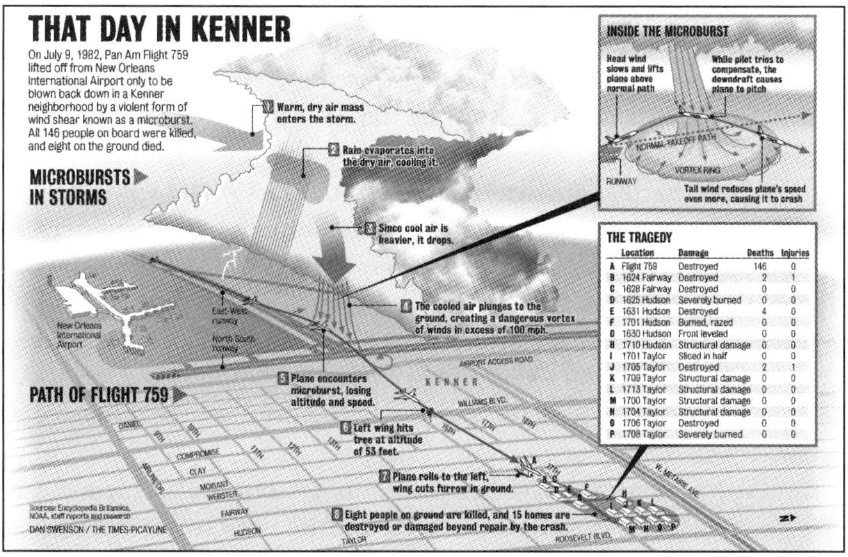

	Location	Damage	Deaths	Injuries
A	Flight 759	Destroyed	146	0
B	1624 Fairway	Destroyed	2	1
C	1628 Fairway	Destroyed	0	0
D	1625 Hudson	Severely burned	0	0
E	1631 Hudson	Destroyed	4	0
F	1701 Hudson	Burned, razed	0	0
G	1630 Hudson	Front leveled	0	0
H	1710 Hudson	Structural damage	0	0
I	1701 Taylor	Sliced in half	0	0
J	1705 Taylor	Destroyed	2	1
K	1709 Taylor	Structural damage	0	0
L	1713 Taylor	Structural damage	0	0
M	1700 Taylor	Structural damage	0	0
N	1704 Taylor	Structural damage	0	0
O	1706 Taylor	Destroyed	0	0
P	1708 Taylor	Severely burned	0	0

The most tragic event in Kenner's long history, the devastating crash of Pan American flight 759.

added that, "When you walk through something like that, it gives you, I think, a good idea of what it looks like to walk through hell. . . with flames all around you and people yelling, screaming."[28]

Although fate handed the people of Kenner a quarter-mile path of gruesome death and destruction across 17th, Fairway, Hudson, and Taylor streets, before the day would end there would be one more turn of fate—this time of good fortune. Rescue workers from across the region raced to the site to assist in the rescue and recovery effort. Upon arriving at the scene rescuers quickly realized that there would be no survivors of the crash. For hours, they fought the fires that covered much of the quarter-mile-long site and searched through the piles of debris, which included pieces of the plane, destroyed houses, and burned-out cars and boats, looking for the bodies and pieces of bodies of the unfortunate victims. So gruesome was the task that rescue workers did not have enough body bags for their task and had to have more flown in from Dallas, Texas. Yet, after three and a half hours of the gruesome and depressing recovery work, all present at the deadly site were stunned to hear at approximately 7:45 p.m. the shout by a deputy sheriff: "We've got a survivor!" Demonstrating fate's fickle and unpredictable nature, Jefferson Parish Deputy Sheriff Gerald Hibbs inexplicably saw movement among the wreckage of what once was a home. Lying under the mattress to her bed was sixteen-month-old Melissa Trahan. Suffering only minor burns, the young child had miraculously survived a near direct hit by the doomed plane on her house. Her mother had placed her in her baby bed at the rear of her house on Taylor Street. As fate determined, her mother, to be with Melissa's four year old sister Bridget, then moved to the front of the home where both mother and child were when their home was broadsided by the doomed jetliner. Bridget and her mom were killed instantly; however, young Melissa in her baby bed was spared by what rescuers believed to have been the fortunate event of having her bed flipped over with the mattress landing on top of her and protecting her from the carnage that occurred all around her.[29]

At the time, the 154 deaths resulting from the accident made the event the second-worst air disaster in American history. It was an event that affected not only the lives of the families of the residents of Kenner who were killed, nor just the lives of the hundreds of rescuers who carried out the gruesome task of recovery, affected the lives of people across Kenner and a large portion of Louisiana and even the world. Among those who lost their lives in the incident included elderly people, young children, and entire families. Though many lived in Louisiana, there were others from all over the United States as well as the Bahamas, Uruguay, Switzerland, Hong Kong, and elsewhere. Aaron Broussard, who had been mayor of Kenner for a total of eight days at the time of the crash, moved quickly to clear the disaster. So much contamination of aviation fuel and blood soaked the area that machinery was brought in to remove three feet of dirt from across the site and replace it with new soil.

During the months and years after the crash the neighborhood was gradually rebuilt, leaving few physical reminders of the event that changed Kenner forever. However, the mental trauma that so many experienced has left permanent scars upon the memories and history of the Kenner community. Other consequences of the disaster have had more positive results. Because of the role wind shear played in the downing of the jetliner, the crash led to extensive research and detection technology into the issue of wind shear at airports. Research resulting from the disaster led to improvements in technology and airport procedures that greatly reduced the danger of a repeat event at other airports. Similarly, the crash in the middle of a populated area enabled local authorities to undertake reforms to address the long-standing issue of the extension of the New Orleans airport's east-west runway westward into the swamp lands in St. Charles Parish. Although the state's 1983 effort to require legislatively representation for Kenner and neighboring parishes on the Aviation Board was ruled unconstitutional by the courts, with the memories of Pan American Flight 759 still fresh in the minds of many, officials continued to work on ways to improve safety at the facility and were eventually able to reach an agreement on the long-standing issues of airport management and westward expansion. The leaders of New Orleans, the New Orleans Aviation Board, St. Charles Parish, and the City of Kenner signed on to the Airport Expansion Agreement in 1985. The agreement established the procedure by which Kenner and St. Charles Parish would each designate a member to the Aviation Board to the mayor of New Orleans, who would then nominate the individual for approval by the New Orleans City

Council. In exchange for their representation on the aviation board and $135,000 in annual compensation, St. Charles Parish agreed to grant the use of land for airport improvements, including runway expansion and the filling of forty-eight acres of wetlands, and the City of Kenner agreed on sharing a percentage of sales and use-tax monies. The construction of the longer runway that followed the agreement allowed takeoffs to begin sooner on the important east-west runway, which kept aircraft from flying low over residential neighborhoods and fulfilled Mayor Broussard's prediction that the new runway would stop "planes taking off over rooftops."[30]

Although the agreement that allowed the expansion of the airport into St. Charles Parish addressed many of the issues involving airport safety and governance, it did not resolve all of the concerns the people of Kenner had with the facility. Many of the issues resulted from the rapid population growth experienced by the Kenner community in the decades following the end of World War II. As Kenner grew, its residential area expanded rapidly and like a rising tide flooding a beach, new subdivisions and homes eventually surrounded the facility to its east and north, greatly restricting the airport's growth potential and bringing the needs of residents increasingly in conflict with the needs of the airport. This led Kenner officials to take a more restrictive attitude towards authorizing airport projects. Such was the situation in the 1990s when Kenner residents sued the airport over noise issues. The dispute eventually led to the airport buying and tearing down hundreds of homes near the facility, which resulted in wide areas of the Kenner community remaining vacant for decades.[31]

Additionally, the size limitations forced on the airport by the population growth in Kenner also placed the facility at a serious disadvantage in its competition with other airports in the South and Southwest. Houston, Memphis, Miami, Charlotte, and Atlanta all greatly expanded their airport facilities to meet the demands of the growing airline industry. As its competitor cities expanded and improved their airports, New Orleans, faced with growing financial problems in the late twentieth century, found it increasingly difficult to keep pace with the expensive demands of the industry for bigger and better designed airports. Nevertheless, New Orleans and airport leaders throughout the decades of the 1980s, 1990s, and 2000s spent millions of dollars to expand and modernize the facility in Kenner. Appreciating the problems faced by the airport and the facility's importance to the economic well-being of metropolitan New Orleans and the entire state of Louisiana, community and state leaders have for decades explored possible alternatives to the current airport arrangement. Over the years, multiple studies and plans for the construction of a completely new regional airport which could have been located somewhere between Baton Rouge and the Mississippi Gulf Coast were considered and rejected by officials because of high costs and feasibility problems. With the failure of the effort to build a new regional facility, leaders examined other options to upgrade the airport dramatically, including expanding the footprint of the existing facility westward into the marshlands of St. Charles Parish, state takeover of the airport, and turning control of the installation over to private operators. To date, all such options have been rejected by the Aviation Board and community leaders.[32]

Though the debate over the future of the airport and its relationship with its neighbors continues from time to time, the vital role that the facility plays in the wellbeing of the region was dramatically demonstrated during the Katrina disaster of 2005. When the deadly hurricane roared out of the warm waters of the Gulf of Mexico during the early hours of August 29, its category five storm surge punched through poorly designed canal walls resulting in the inundation of large sections of New Orleans and its surrounding communities. With the city flooded and the area's utilities, streets, highways, and bridges damaged or destroyed, desperation quickly set in among the thousands who failed to heed the pre-storm orders to evacuate the region before the storm arrived. As the nation watched in stunned amazement and concern over the slow reaction of officials to the spreading catastrophe, it was the presence of the airport in Kenner that opened the door to help and relief. In spite of damage sustained to the facility's roof, hangars, and fences, the airport was sufficiently repaired to reopen to humanitarian flights on August 31, just two days after the storm struck. The airport soon handled 3,800 takeoffs and landings a day. Though most activities involved helicopters, hundreds of commercial and military aircraft made daily trips into the facility to bring relief crews, military personnel, and supplies and to evacuate thousands of refugees to other cities. In the first week alone, between fifty and seventy-five thousand evacuees passed through the airport on their way to safe havens. The refugees came from all areas of the region with many coming from overloaded staging areas including the Superdome and Ernest N. Morial Convention Center in New Orleans. Many others came to the airport on helicopters after being picked off the roofs of their flooded homes. Of these thousands of rescued individuals, approximately thirty thousand were flown out by military aircraft, with thousands more being transported out of the airport to safety by busses. For many long days after the storm, the airport remained the base for as many as 2,500 military and medical personnel who worked exhaustive schedules in the triage and care of the thousands of refugees who passed through the mud-caked and people-jammed structure with very limited sanitary facilities caused by the loss of sewage services. In the end at least twenty individuals died at the airport during the storm emergency. In addition, a large portion of the airport's vacant land in south Kenner was commandeered by Jefferson Parish and the U.S. Army Corps of Engineers for use as a temporary dump staging area for tons of collected storm debris from around Kenner and East Jefferson parish.[33]

As with the community as a whole, the passage of time allowed for operations at the airport in Kenner eventually to return to near pre-storm levels. By the end of 2011, a little over six years after Katrina's devastating visit, the airport was operating with nine airlines and approximately 125 flights a day at the facility. The facility continued to show growth. In 2012 it handled a total of 8,600,989 passengers. However, it would take until 2014, when 9,785,000 people used the airport, that passenger numbers exceeded pre-Katrina figures, falling slightly short of the all-time airport record of 9.8 million travelers in the year 2000. Today the facility handles the business of thirteen airlines and offers more non-stop flights to destinations than any time in its history. In regards to the airport's freight and mail handling, the numbers have not been as promising. Though the installation handled 48,463.59 metric tons of material in 2011, the figure represent an 8.1 percent decrease from the previous year's total. When all of its flights are taken into consideration, Louis Armstrong International Airport accounts for more than 80 percent of the air traffic in Louisiana and remains a driving force in the economy of the region.[34]

Although the airport ranked as low as fifty-sixth busiest facility in the country at the time of Katrina, it currently ranks thirty-ninth among the nation's domestic airports. Nevertheless, in spite of its improving rank, the future of the airport in Kenner remains uncertain. With the terminal building pushing nearly double the average life span of a typical American airport terminal, passengers using the Kenner facility pay fees roughly 21 percent more per ticket compared to the average fees charged at most other domestic airports. Providing approximately 12,400 jobs and $2.6 billion in revenues to the region through its operations and impact on the tourism industry, community leaders are aware of the role a successful airport plays in improving a community's national stature and its standing in related economic activities. As with mayoral administrations previous to his, New Orleans Mayor Mitch Landrieu in recent times has announced plans for a major overhaul of the airport. Set forth in the long-term strategic plan for the facility, in April 2013, Landrieu and the members of the New Orleans Aviation Board announced that they had decided on an $826 million redevelopment plan for the airport that would result in the construction of a new thirty-gate terminal with three concourses being constructed on the north side of the current facility's footprint. The bold plan also includes a new power station and a new ramp from the airport to the nearby interstate highway. Under the plan, no new runways would be constructed and the old terminal would be remodeled and modified for other airport uses, including a lucrative reuse of the existing terminal as a cargo transit hub that would permit the airport to connect more efficiently with other modes of shipping including the nearby Mississippi River barge and vessel traffic, trucking facilities and highways, and railroad lines. Ironically, though the new plan would result in a state-of-the-art facility with consolidated security checkpoints, new and more efficient and profitable concession stands, and modern automated baggage handling systems, the new terminal will actually be almost half the size of the current facility. The efficiency of the new building is expected to increase the airport's financial standing. After decades of public debate over the airport and its future, community leaders voice the belief that they realize that time is short for the airport to find its place in today's modern aviation world. Hoping to avoid some of the missteps of earlier efforts to upgrade airport facilities, New Orleans and airport leaders have brought their counterparts in Kenner and the surrounding parishes into discussions concerning the new long-range plans for the facility. Kenner officials have expressed support for the revitalization plans, with Kenner Mayor Mike Yenni proclaiming that, "If it benefits Kenner, we're anxious and willing and ready to move on this."[35] Only time will tell if this latest plan to modernize Kenner's greatest economic asset will make the airport once again a world-class facility capable of competing in today's aviation industry. The airport's long history of petty internecine battles among community leaders of New Orleans, the state, and surrounding communities, along with a history of insufficient financial support from the state and the airport's owner, and the failure of the community as a whole to insist that their airport return to its status as one of the country's leading facilities of its kind, all cast a long shadow over the chances of a true transformation of Louis Armstrong Airport occurring anytime soon. When questioned about the long history of disappointment associated with reforming the facility, New Orleans Mayor Landrieu noted that in regards to plans for modernization of the airport, "There was a complete and total commitment on my behalf of the people of this city to make this happen." He concluded: ". . . we've got to get this done. Failure is not an option."[36]

Artist concept of the new Armstrong International Airport terminal which has an estimated completion date of 2018.

11
Suburban Metamorphosis

The end of World War II brought more changes to the Kenner community than just the commercialization and expansion of the new airport. As with many other large metropolitan regions of the country, the New Orleans area in the postwar period experienced a population shift from its urban center to suburban areas located on its outskirts. With the end of the war, communities across the country experienced the return of thousands of veterans. Anxious to return to civilian life and to start their own families, veterans and their new spouses faced a postwar housing shortage. Wartime needs and material shortages resulted in limited construction opportunities for civilian housing during the conflict, thus making the need for new housing among the nation's most pressing needs in the postwar period. So it was in New Orleans, where on occasion during the early postwar period dozens of anxious home seekers would show up to bid on newly listed vacant homes or apartments. To address the housing shortages, builders across America turned to the open spaces of the suburbs to expand the nation's stock of affordable housing. In New Orleans, suburban expansion to the west into Jefferson Parish had its roots in the years leading up to World War II, when home construction along Metairie Road became popular. However, after the war ended and the resulting housing shortage, the numbers of families looking for homes in Jefferson Parish grew rapidly. At first, the new dwellings were limited to areas serviced by the few existing improved major roads in Jefferson Parish. In Kenner this meant

A photo of the author's childhood home, the structure is an example of the cement-slab suburban ranch-style home build by the thousands in subdivisions across Kenner between the 1950s and the 1980s.

that the earliest postwar structures appeared along and near Airline Highway. Many of the first postwar immigrants to arrive in Kenner were involved with work at the new and expanding airport. One of the first postwar subdivisions to be started in Kenner even went so far as to mimic the name of the airport and called itself "Moisant Place."[1]

With the demand for new housing strong, it was not long before developers in the region adopted construction philosophies which had proven successful in other parts of the United States and began the building of large-scale modern subdivisions. In this new and mostly postwar phenomenon, standardized construction components and design were employed to create the suburban subdivision. With houses in these residential tracts being virtually the same, they could be constructed quickly and relatively cheaply. Equipped with the modern conveniences now becoming increasingly available in the new consumer-driven postwar economy, the new homes carried attractive price tags of approximately $6,000 to $15,000, typically payable over thirty years on a FHA (Federal Housing Administration) or GI Bill home mortgage. These financial devices allowed veterans to purchase homes with no down payments and monthly mortgage payments as low as

$50. The new subdivision architecture of the period spread across the country and became the norm in the suburban areas of New Orleans. The suburban ranch-style house for the most part abandoned the traditional New Orleans construction practice of building homes above the ground on raised piers of some sort. Instead, the great majority of suburban ranch-style houses were built on concrete slabs, just a few inches off of the ground. The design of the ranch home was such that it was successfully applied to the construction of modest, inexpensive dwellings for first-time buyers, as well as upscale-custom-built houses in the more tawny neighborhoods of Kenner and its surrounding region. Horizontal in appearance with a low, wide facade, floor plans in the ranch-style home were most often either rectangular or L-shaped with hipped or gabled roofs. Ceiling heights in most of the new ranch homes were fairly standardized at eight feet. Commonly, large picture windows graced the main living room, which were often flanked by ornamental shutters that served only a decorative purpose for they were typically too small to cover the glass area. The suburban ranch-home dominated the architectural styling of the new homes built in Kenner for decades.[2]

Early in the postwar period, most of the new homes in Kenner were either constructed on speculation or custom built by small contractors. Within months of the end of the war, Kenner began to see an influx of new construction and new families moving to the community. In 1947 alone, 150 new houses were completed in Kenner—an impressive number when compared to housing starts during the depression and war years, but just a sampling of the future. The rising demand for more housing soon led developers and community leaders to think big and plan large-scale projects. Among the first of Kenner's larger postwar housing efforts began construction in December 1949 when developers broke ground on the $8 million Pope Park. Consisting of the modest prewar-raised-bungalow style homes and the increasingly popular ranch-style homes, the tract, located just off of Williams Blvd. a little over a mile north of Airline Highway, eventually contained more than 1,100 single family dwellings. The success of the Pope Park venture and the continued demand for suburban housing resulted in other developers flocking to Kenner. Over the next few decades a series of large subdivision developments spread northward across the wooded and grassland expanses of Kenner. With acres of subdivisions appearing like pieces of grand mosaic, Kenner's once largely ignored areas located to the east and north of the sprawling airport lands quickly transformed into neighborhoods of single family homes. Among the new subdivisions the new residents of Kenner called home were Susan Park, Greenlawn Terrace, Westgate, Holly Heights, Highway Park, Driftwood Park, Redwood Park, Lincoln Manor, Wentwood, University City, Chateau Estates, Cannes Brûlées, Woodlake Estates, and Grand Lake Estates. So dynamic was the spread of the developments that as early as 1954 a thousand homes a year were being constructed in the city, earning Kenner the title of "Fastest Growing City in the State."[3] Population figures of the period demonstrate the remarkable growth that occurred in postwar Kenner. In 1942, when the airport was in its early stages of construction, the population of Kenner was only 2,300. Ten years later the number of residents in Kenner had more than doubled to 7,000. Yet, just one year later in 1953, the population of the rapidly growing community jumped nearly 29 percent to more than 9,000 people. The growth continued, and by 1960 the population of Kenner vaulted to 17,037 or triple its 1950 count of 5,535. The new Kenner was somewhat different from its historic predecessor. By 1960, the population of community was 78.2 percent white as compared to the prewar white population of 66.2 percent. The median family income at the time was $5,609, slightly below the national average of $5,660 and somewhat higher than the state average of $4,272. Indeed, Jefferson Parish, as a whole, soon claimed the title of being the parish with the highest per capita income in Louisiana. Thus by 1960, the old sleepy days of Kenner's little vegetable farms and modest growth were gone forever. The census of that year revealed that only eight families in all of Kenner still made their living by farming. Modern subdivisions had replaced the truck farms of earlier times.[4]

The need for postwar housing was only one factor in the rapid growth in population of Kenner—and East Jefferson Parish as a whole. The attraction of the suburban lifestyle with its brand new homes with their modern appliances, large yards for children to play, and other recreational activities drew others from what one historian has labeled "the frayed urban fabric" of America's large cities.[5] An aspect of the urban fabric fraying which contributed to the on-going migration of city dwellers to the new suburbs was the growing racial tension in New Orleans during the 1960s and 1970s that played an important role in bringing whites to the homogeneous suburbs. As was the situation in cities across the South, the changes in race relations brought on by the civil rights movement, Federal legislation, and court challenges created uncertainty, fear, and anger among many whites. Most notably, forced school desegregation resulted in large-scale resistance among urban whites and fueled suburbanization. Hence by the early 1970s housing patterns in New Orleans and its surrounding suburbs, including Kenner, reflected an increased racial polarization. In 1960 New Orleans was less segregated than the average American city. Ten years later, following the start of the "white flight" suburban exodus, New Orleans defied the national trend in America's large cities of decreased segregation to becoming one of rising segregation among its neighborhoods and schools. Builders and community planners aware of the racial aspects of the suburbanization movement in the New Orleans region did not hesitate to take advantage of the situation. It was not uncommon across the region and the South, including in Jefferson Parish, for deed covenants in the new subdivisions to prohibit specifically home sales and rentals to African Americans. As early as 1954, exemplifying the racial attitudes of the time, long-time Kenner Mayor Joseph S. Kopfler made it clear that the new housing coming to his community would be racially segregated by announcing that plans were in place that would bring during the next two years, "over 2000 new homes for whites" while 1000 new homes would also be "erected for colored families." He added that the homes for Kenner's new African American residents were to be constructed in a specified area "in back of Moisant Airport."[6]

Though in times past there had been periods of animosity, tension, and violence between the races in Kenner, in the post-World War II era race relations in the community remained cordial. African America residents of the community remained concentrated in the older, poorer sections of the city located along the railroad tracks that traversed the city not far from the Mississippi River levees. Many of the residents of the area were poor and made their living as day laborers and domestics. A close-knit community, where residents felt as if they were members of one large extended family, for much of the postwar period most blacks in Kenner, either by choice, custom, or circumstance, remained largely apolitical.[7]

Perhaps the best published description of life in Kenner's African American community during the period of the civil rights movement can be found in the autobiography of Donna Brazile. A native of Kenner who grew up on Filmore Street in the older section of the city between Airline Highway and the Mississippi River, Brazile as an adult would become one of America's leading political operatives and media commentators. As a prominent national-campaign strategist, she served as the national campaign manager for candidate Vice President Al Gore in his 2000 bid for the presidency and later became the Interim Chair of the Democratic National Committee. According to Brazile, during the early years of the modern civil rights movement, many Kenner blacks were either afraid to discuss civil rights or were simply uninterested in or unaware of the movement. In spite of the passage of new civil rights legislation by Congress and the consequent fading of segregation as law, Brazile found in her childhood that segregation remained very much in practice in Kenner for, "There was definitely a White Kenner and a Black Kenner."[8] She added that in spite of efforts in other communities to promote "civil rights, justice, freedom, and equality," in her hometown ". . . no one had a clue in Kenner. If they did, they didn't dare utter the words. . . It was like they were asleep."[9]

Brazile found a change in attitudes begin to take place in the spring of 1968 following the assassination of Dr. Martin Luther King, Jr. People began to desire to see a change in the opportunities for Kenner's blacks and for the first time African American political organizations sprang up. People became more vocal and started to talk about the long-standing social problems that plagued their community. Among the earliest to begin the process of organizing Kenner's blacks was the Rev. Arthur Paul Clay. The pastor of Mt. Zion Missionary Baptist Church and local leader of the Southern Christian Leadership Conference (SCLC), Clay worked tirelessly to get the blacks of Kenner to organize and demand their rights. Until his death in 1992, Clay remained the most prominent African American leader in Kenner and even was popularly known as "the Little Black Mayor of Kenner." Among the first African Americans in modern times to hold a political position in Kenner's municipal government, Clay was appointed in 1965 by Mayor Edward D'Gerolamo to the city's Zoning and Appeals

Board. The appointment quickly raised the ire of racists in the region who began a campaign of threats and intimidation. Clay received numerous threatening phone calls and had "KKK" painted on the door of the Oakland Baptist Church where he also served as pastor. Harassment escalated to include the burning of a cross on the lawn of his house and a casket being delivered to his Little Zion Church containing a chicken heart and an effigy of a man with a nail driven through the heart. Included in the casket was a threat that Clay would be killed on January 1, 1966. When the date arrived, a wreath of flowers was delivered to Clay's wife. Finally, harkening back seventy-five years to when Judge Baumann's house was attacked by unknown gunmen, in June six shots were fired by unidentified individuals into the pastor's home. However, demonstrating how matters had changed in Kenner, instead of Clay and the other African American activists giving up in fear, neighbors and other residents began a process of standing guard outside of the pastor's home to protect him and his family from further threats and intimidation.[10]

Over time, others in Kenner's African American community followed Rev. Clay's leadership and worked to organize the black community's political influence. Among them were Arthur and Shirley Burton, whose pharmacy located in south Kenner became a popular gathering place where members of the black community discussed and kept up with the latest local political news. The organizing efforts of the Burtons were joined by Rosemary Minor, who took the dramatic step of filing suit against the city to force the officials to provide the black children of Kenner with public recreation facilities similar to those being constructed in the white sections of the community. With the organizational and legal efforts meeting with some success and with increasing numbers of blacks moving into the city, the political power of Kenner's African American community grew. In the municipal elections of 1970 for the first time a concerted effort was made by Kenner's white politicians to win the support of black voters. Candidate for mayor Joseph Yenni realized that his challenge against the incumbent mayor would fail without his getting the votes of Kenner's African Americans. With Yenni promising, if elected, to provide the black community in Kenner with the playground facilities it had long requested, Rosemary Minor and other activist used their organizational skills to support Yenni.

Demonstrative of the new recognition by Kenner's white politicians of the growing political power of the city's black community, Minor's garage at her house on Taylor Street was used as the Yenni campaign headquarters in old Kenner. Building upon its power and influence it demonstrated in the successful Yenni campaign, the African American community in Kenner continued to organize and build its political influence. The growing influence of the community's African American citizens was demonstrated in the summer of 1979. When the District One seat on the city council became vacant that year, city leaders chose long-time activist in Kenner's black community, the Rev. Henry "Teddy" Stewart to serve as interim councilman until the seat could be filled by election later in the year, thus making Stewart the first African American to serve on Kenner's law-making body in modern times. In December of that same year, less than a decade after the Yenni campaign first recognized the needs of Kenner's African American citizens, long-time community leader Shirley Burton became the first African American in modern times to be elected to the Kenner City Council. Burton's election to the District One council seat also marked the first time a female was chosen to serve on the Kenner council.[11]

Yenni's and Burton's elections were not the only examples of the changing racial attitudes of the time. Federal legislation and court decisions also led to major societal changes in the segregated ways of the South. As exemplified by the desegregation in the region's housing, some of these changes occurred gradually over a period of time and were accompanied by relatively little social upheaval. A social change not accomplished without controversy took place in the months prior to the 1972 mayor's election. Court decisions forced local school officials to step up their desegregation efforts by introducing the busing of students around the parish to achieve racial balance in their schools' populations. Though absent the deadly violence of earlier civil-right efforts in the parish, the busing issue did release anew racial tensions in the Kenner and Jefferson Parish communities. Donna Brazile was a young junior high school student at the time of the introduction of busing. She was bussed from her local, predominantly African American neighborhood school she loved, Washington Elementary, four miles to T.H. Harris Junior High in predominantly white Metairie. At the Metairie school she was forced to deal with the racial tensions and white protest of the time. Tensions were high, and the kids from Kenner found their new school an unwelcoming place. Crowds of angry whites met the newly bussed African American children with cries of anger, curse words, and racial epitheths. On occasion, rocks, eggs, and tomatoes were tossed by angry adults at the young black students. Fortunately, the racial tensions and incidents that accompanied the onset of bussing in Jefferson Parish gradually faded away. By the time Brazile moved on from her junior high to Grace King High School, also in Metairie, attitudes, including her own, changed, with both races becoming more accommodating to the other. The gradual improvement of race relations in the schools was soon duplicated in the community, including in the integration of the neighborhoods of Kenner and the rest of the parish.[12]

The practice of segregated housing continued until the end of the 1960s and early 1970s, when the Federal Fair Housing Act of 1968, which barred racial discrimination in the sale and rental of housing, began to take effect. At first, small numbers of blacks and other minorities began moving into formerly all-white neighborhoods across Kenner. Because white flight had played a part in the exodus of residents from New Orleans to the suburbs, some feared that the integration of neighborhoods would have a negative effect upon growth in the city. Events proved that the end of segregated housing had no discernable negative effect upon Kenner's skyrocketing growth. In 1970, shortly after the Federal housing law went into effect, Kenner's population reached 29,858. Ten years later in 1980, the size of the city more than doubled to 66,382. In 1979, the year before the Federal decennial population count, a special census taken by the City of Kenner found the city to be 83 percent white, 12 percent black, 4 percent Hispanic, and 1 percent other ethnic groups.[13]

Accompanying the end of segregated-housing covenants in Kenner was an arrival of large numbers of immigrant families. Beginnings in the 1960s and gradually inreasing over the years, immigrant families from Latin America found the availability of affordable housing in Kenner to their liking. Though the Hispanic community in the metropolitan New Orleans area was diverse with large numbers of residents being migrants from Cuba, Honduras, Nicaragua, and Guatemala, in Kenner the immigrant community was dominated by Hondurans—so much so that sections of north Kenner became known as "Little Honduras." So robust was the growth in immigrant residents that by 1980, 7 percent of the city's residents labeled themselves as being Hispanics. By 1990 the number of immigrant residents increased to 10 percent, by 2000 to 14 percent, and by 2010 the number reached 22 percent. The influx of Hispanic residents so changed the population dynamics of the city that Kenner today is included among the most ethnically diverse populations in the region. Federal census authorities determined in their 2010 count that sections of Kenner possessed the highest concentration of Hispanic residents in Louisiana, with a population density of 41 percent.[14]

Though welcome and sought after by community leaders at the time, the rapid and massive influx of developers, builders, and new residents into Kenner was not problem free. The skyrocketing growth in many ways overwhelmed the city's resources. Anxious to accommodate those developers who were willing to invest millions of dollars in Kenner and having limited resources to plan adequately for the city's rapid expansion, city leaders allowed builders and developers great leeway in the placement and design of their new subdivisions. The building boom at times was uncontrolled and lacked proper community planning. Such haphazard development multiplied the tasks of local officials in bringing modern city services to Kenner's residents. From the earliest days of the postwar building boom, Kenner's community leaders worked to keep pace with the growth. In 1950, for the first time since the post office was originally established in Kenner in 1870, daily delivery of the mail to homes began. A year later Southern Bell Telephone and Telegraph Company opened a modern telephone exchange that finally reduced the rates for telephone service in Kenner to match those in New Orleans. To meet the expanding size of Kenner government a new municipal complex was built. The $400,000 complex, which included both the city hall and the city's main fire station, was constructed on Williams Boulevard at 18th Street. The new structure marked the first time that a municipal building was constructed north of Airline Highway and not in the original footprint of old Kennerville. The construction of a new main fire station marked the city's commitment of providing the city's residents with a professional and modern fire department and has led to multiple fire stations being constructed across the city. The modern stations and their equipment continued a long tradition by city fathers of providing residents effective fire protection dating back to the very earliest days of the community when the pre-Civil War village had but one well and pumper to fight fires and had in place the agreed upon practice that when the fire-bell rang, the first horse or mule team to arrive at the pumper station got $5.00 and the job of hauling the pumper to the fire.[15]

Improved fire protection was not the only demand placed upon city resources by the rapid suburbanization of Kenner. The community's police department had to be enlarged and modernized. Gone were the days of 1914, when Kenner's police force consisted of six part-time officers who were paid one dollar for every arrest they made. In its place the citizens of Kenner for decades have supported a modern police force and facilities. Officials also began free trash pickup, improved street lighting, and in 1966, a shuttle-bus service designed to assist residents moving around Kenner. The latter service eventually transitioned into the larger Louisiana Transit Company service, and in April 1985 the service, now called the Kenner Loop, was placed under the operation of the Regional Transit Authority, which also operates public transit in New Orleans.[16]

Essential to the success of the population movement from urban centers to suburban communities was the presence of streets and highways that made daily commuting in the family automobile to the city for employment and other life necessities prompt and convenient. From its earliest days, the people of Kenner realized the importance of convenient transportation to and from the business district in New Orleans. Hence during the prewar period in the 1930s, community leaders worked with parish and state officials to improve both Jefferson and Airline highways access into Kenner. With the arrival of the new subdivisions in the city during the postwar decades, Kenner officials struggled to keep up with providing adequate roadways for the rapidly expanding new neighborhoods. As developments moved to previously unused areas of the city, roadbeds were laid out which consisted mostly of clam shells dredged from the bottom of Lake Pontchartrain. Determined to upgrade the quality of its neighborhood streets, in the 1960s Kenner officials initiated a $1,000,000 program to provide paved streets for the newly developed areas of the city. Years before they committed to upgrading the city's residential streets, Kenner and Jefferson Parish officials, at the early stages of the suburban migration movement, realized that if the vast areas of woods, swamps, marsh lands, and grasslands covered with scrub trees which made up the majority of northern Kenner and East Jefferson parish were to be successfully developed and suburbanized, a major access roadway needed to be cut into the virgin-land areas. Though possible, access from New Orleans to the developing areas of Kenner could only take place by taking either the Jefferson or Airline highways in south Kenner to Williams Boulevard and then north towards the lake where the new subdivisions were going up. Parish and city leaders worked to alleviate the long roundabout trip. A series of major roadways designed to spur development of the open areas of East Jefferson Parish and Kenner were constructed. Major road building went on for decades. Included among the major roads constructed during this period were the east/west traveling West Metairie Avenue, West Esplanade Avenue, Vintage Drive, and Joe Yenni Boulevard (originally called Sunset Boulevard). The most important of the new east/west thoroughfares was the Veterans Memorial Highway. Designed in the early 1950s as a modern, fast access highway, Veterans Memorial Highway was to cut across East Jefferson Parish from the Orleans/Jefferson boundary into St. Charles Parish, where it would connect with Airline Highway and provide a second route to the airport. Although the roadway was completed through Kenner up to the levee that borders St. Charles Parish, it never quite achieved its status as a fast access thoroughfare or even rightly as a "highway," though it was officially called such for decades until it was re-labeled as a boulevard in the early 1970s. Nor has the road been connected to Airline Highway as originally planned. Unfortunately, while parish and city leaders were working to provide access to the newly developing areas in the northern sections of East Jefferson by constructing new east/west roadways, community leaders virtually ignored the need for additional roadways to connect the northern and southern sections of Kenner. Only one road, Williams Boulevard, ran the length of the city from the river to the lake, thus assuring future significant traffic problems for Kenner's residents attempting to travel between the northern and southern sections of the city.[17]

The new roads achieved their goal of expediting the development of the northern sections of Kenner. Within ten years of its construction, Veterans Highway became completely overloaded with its daily flow of traffic—so much so that even with all of the improvements in transportation and roadways, by the mid-1960s it took longer for a commuter from Kenner to get to the business district in New Orleans than it did his father in 1940. Kenner's commuter problems were somewhat alleviated in the early 1970s when Interstate 10 was completed through the city. Although the interstate highway provided some relief to the region's commuters, the respite was relatively short lived, for the new highway soon opened regions to the west of Kenner to development. Over time, subdivisions to the west of Kenner in St. Charles and St. John the Baptist parishes funneled new commuters onto Interstate 10, which once again slowed the commute for Kenner's residents to and from New Orleans.[18]

Transportation and other infrastructure improvements were not the only issues that needed to be addressed by the Kenner community as a result of its transformation from small agricultural settlement snuggled up against the Mississippi River to a modern suburban community that reached all the way to the Lake Pontchartrain shoreline. Early in the postwar suburban metamorphosis of Kenner, community leaders began to think that the urbanization of the city would require new and more governmental services and that a modification of the city's municipal government was in order. Although the 1898 Lawrason Act, which defined the format of Kenner's government, permitted considerable organizational leeway to municipal governments in Louisiana, shortly after being officially designated a city in 1952 and again in 1961, leaders in the community proposed the updating and reorganization of Kenner's municipal government. Neither proposal went very far because of popular suspicions of the new plans. Much of the opposition to the proposals came from the older families of Kenner whose roots dated back to earlier times and who believed that the city had in the past always been managed by local amateurs and that such management would be fine for the future. Other residents felt that a new plan of government would simply cost the taxpayers of the community more and not improve the situation.[19]

By the mid-1950s, Kenner's municipal government had evolved into a somewhat unique governmental organization. As set forth in the Lawrason Act, Kenner's elected officials included a mayor, five aldermen, and a marshal. For the most part, the city's alderman enacted ordinances and established public policy with the mayor serving as the city's chief administrator. The marshal was responsible for handling law enforcement. Among the weaknesses of the government was the fact that although the city's mayor and marshal had the responsibility of directing the activities of their employees, the city council actually possessed the authority to hire and fire all city workers. Complicating the matter further was the issue that over time, as the city grew, mayors began to delegate some of their administrative duties to others. For example, there existed a quasi-official arrangement in which each of the city's five aldermen were assigned a city department to administer. Hence at times, administrative authority—including hiring and firing decisions—in the city was divided among seven (mayor, five aldermen, and marshal) different people. It is easy to imagine the confusion that sometimes existed because of the lack of clarity among citizens when it came to determining responsibility for shortcomings in the way the city was operated.[20]

With the rapid increase in the city's population during the 1960s, calls for reforming Kenner's municipal government steadily gained support. With the City of New Orleans having formally reformed its own plan of government in the mid-1950s and since a large percentage of the community's new residents were recent migrants from the Crescent City, many of Kenner's new residents generally looked favorably on the effort to bring governmental reform. The push for reform came to a head in the municipal election of 1970. The population of Kenner had increased to nearly thirty thousand residents and there was growing support for reform. In the election, a political ticket under the leadership of mayoral candidate Joseph S. Yenni ran on a platform of governmental reform. The voters responded to the call for reform and pushed aside an eight-year incumbent administration in favor of the Yenni reform ticket. Shortly thereafter in September 1971, the new city council created a fifteen-member citizen's committee to review Kenner's plan of government.[21]

After the review, the committee determined that the state's 1898 Lawrason Act did not provide enough flexibility for local voters to update adequately Kenner's plan of government. The committee concluded that the old law provided for overlapping of governmental responsibilities, including a serious lack of separation of powers resulting from the mayor possessing certain legislative and judicial duties and members of the council performing administrative acts. As authorized by the city council, the governmental-study committee began work on a new home-rule charter for the city. After approximately a year of work, the committee, under the chairmanship of attorney T. Robert Lacour, presented a new home-rule charter that provided for a modified strong-mayor-council form of government. The new plan called for a mayor, with veto authority, and seven councilpersons, two from at-large seats and five from single-member districts. The modified nature of the plan involved the office of police chief being independently elected instead of being appointed by the mayor as is common in traditional strong-mayor-council governmental plans. The new plan also removed all administrative duties from councilmen and judicial and legislative responsibilities, except for the veto, from the mayor, thus clarifying areas of governmental responsibility for the citizens of Kenner. When the proposal was placed on the ballot for citizen review, the voters of the city responded to the call for charter reform by voting by an almost two-to-one margin in favor of adoption of the new home rule charter.[22]

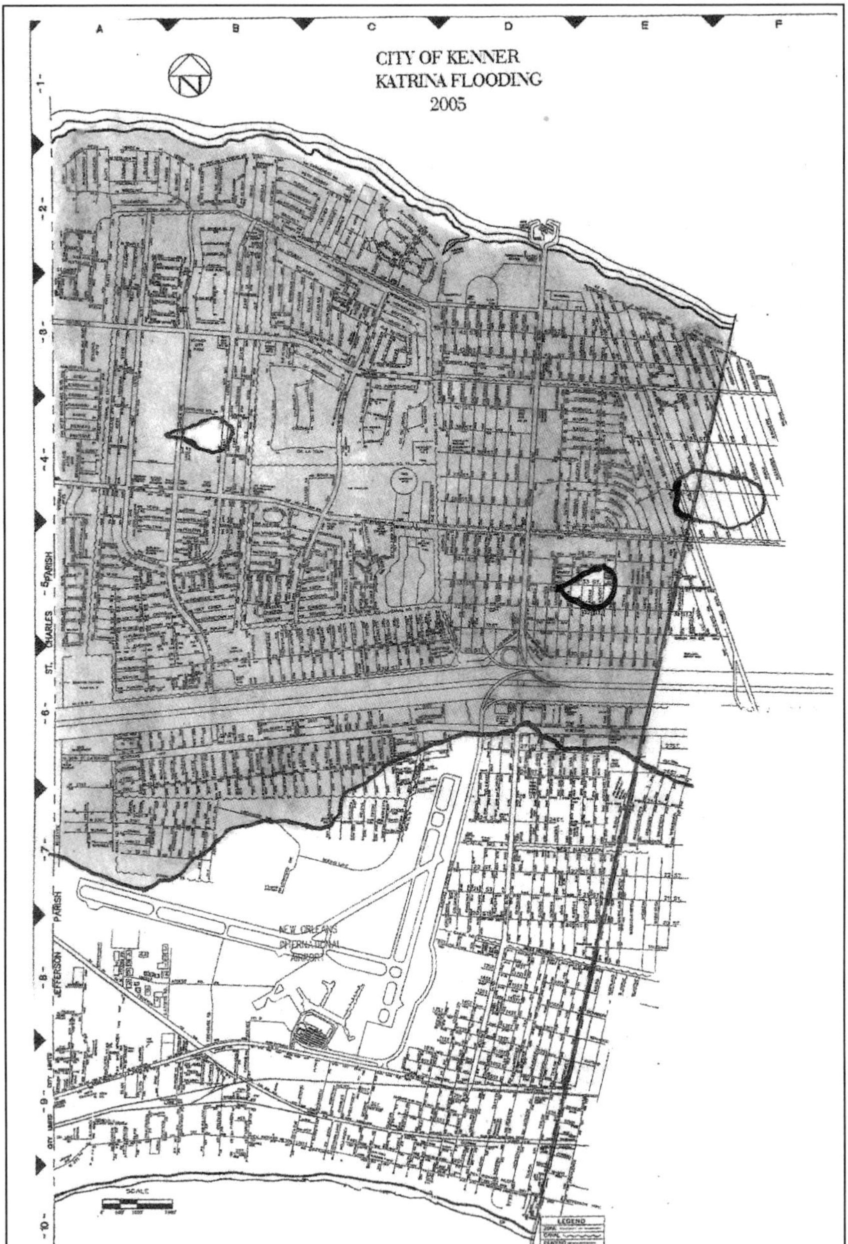

City map showing the extent of coverage by hurricane Katrina flooding in 2005. The map reveals that with the exception of a few areas next to the protection levees, after the storm, there were only a few small islands of dry land in all of northern Kenner which avoided floodwaters.

12

"This wasn't an act of God. It was an act of stupidity."

Since being approved by voters in 1973, the city's new charter has passed the test of time. Though it has been amended several times over the years by the city's citizens, the basics of the charter as it was first presented remain in place. With its new home-rule charter and the completion of the new Interstate-10 and its two interchanges at Williams and Loyola boulevards in the city, Kenner's population continued to skyrocket. By 1980, the city's 1970 population of 29,858 had more than doubled to 66,382, making that ten-year period among the fastest growing decades in Kenner's history and making the municipality the sixth-largest city in Louisiana. The rapid expansion of the city's population was indeed a sign of a vibrant and rapidly expanding community that offered builders, developers, and local business persons opportunities to make quick fortunes. The frantic speed of development and growth also brought a deluge of planning and design challenges that overwhelmed city leaders. The seemingly ceaseless efforts by community leaders to promote business growth and the expansion of the city's tax base were important ingredients in Kenner's exploding development. Unfortunately, although the rapid growth brought with it many pluses for the city and its residents, it did not come without a sizable cost. Perhaps most notable among the negative costs was the incapacity of city leaders to design a well-planned pattern of growth and development. For example, though Kenner's growth and prosperity earned it the title as Louisiana's fastest growing city, its leaders at the time, working with state officials, designed a roadway plan for the city that allowed for only a single thoroughfare for the city that ran its full length from the river to the lake. Less than adequate community planning also resulted in the development of commercial corridors across Kenner that demonstrated little in the way of sophisticated design or character and mostly consisted of block upon block of cheap-boxlike structures. Over time, many of these cheap, look-alike boxed structures evolved to become little more than strips of commercial blight. One important exception to the haphazard design and placement of commercial properties in the city took place in 1973 with the construction of Kenner's first high-rise building. Located near the corner of Veterans and Williams boulevards, the modern nine-story Sheraton Motor Inn (now the DoubleTree by Hilton) was of a style and class that over the years since its opening has only rarely been repeated by other commercial ventures in the city.[1]

The growing presence of ugly look-alike commercial strip malls along the city's major thoroughfares was not the only issue that affected the quality of life in the rapidly developing areas of northern Kenner. The postwar surge of people from the inner city to the suburbs opened the floodgates of residential development in areas of the city that had been marsh and swamp lands. The lands once served as the historic shoreline of Lake Pontchartrain. In the early decades of the twentieth century, officials built levees along the shoreline and drained and dried out the lands of the area and opened the region to residential development. In the rush to promote development and expansion on these portions of the city, little thought was given to the suitability of the geology of the area for residential and commercial development. Not until 1972 when Louisiana State University's Center for Wetland Resources released a study on the issue was it learned by local officials across the metropolitan New Orleans region that the ancient soils that bordered Lake Pontchartrain possessed serious inadequacies for development. Since the time that the lake's levees were constructed and the water which historically saturated the lands that bordered the lake was pumped out, thousands of acres of land near the lakefront across metropolitan New Orleans presented what appeared to be good land for development. However, as the 1972 study and others after it revealed, the areas's acreage was covered with only a veneer of organic surface soils. These soils were subject to severe limitations for the purpose of building residential and commercial structures. Given the name "Kenner soil" by geologists, this type of soil is considered the worst in the region for construction purposes. Consisting of between five to twelve feet of organic materials over clayey layers, "Kenner soil" is extremely susceptible to subsidence. Bloated by high water content in its natural state of marsh and swamp land, as the water is drained away, the soil volume contracts resulting in the organic matter disintegrating. As the soil particles settle under their own weight, subsidence is created. Furthermore, once dried, the soil will swell anew when it again becomes wet and shrink as it dries again. Over time, the continued shrinking and swelling of the soil caused severe damages to properties built on top of it across the region. Structures on concrete slabs, the most common construction method during the years of suburban expansion, were susceptible to the worst subsidence damage. When the "Kenner soil" subsides it typically settles away from slab structures resulting in driveways no longer connecting to garages and homes. Pockets of air frequently open up beneath slab foundations and yards sometimes fall below the level of adjacent streets, opening properties to flooding. Gas and sewerage lines are subject to separation from structures, potentially creating explosive pockets of gas.[2]

The discovery of the unsuitable nature of the "Kenner soils" did not halt the construction of new buildings. Although studies revealed that in some areas of Kenner subsidence exceeded ten feet, community leaders across the region readily determined that considering the many thousands of acres that were comprised of the poor-quality soils, it simply was not practical to abandon the vast areas or even to stop new construction on them. To address the problem, soil scientists recommended that officials find ways to keep the area's water table high enough to keep the organic soils moist so as to limit their oxidation and breakdown and thus reduce subsidence. Individual property owners were urged to take care to fill their lots with mineral soils like river sand, which is readily available and relatively inexpensive. When applied in suitable depth around a structure, the mineral soil forms a seal over the upper levels of organic soil, cutting off oxygen to the deteriorating organic materials and thus controlling or even eliminating future subsidence. Although a common practice in the region for decades, the practice of ordering a "load of sand" to spread across a residential lot has resulted in an annual occurrence (usually in the spring or early summer before the heavy heat of the season sets in) of parades of dump trucks loaded with yards of river sand delivering their payloads across Kenner and much of the metropolitan region to homeowners who thus spend a weekend of back-numbing work of shoveling, wheelbarrowing, and spreading their newly acquired "good soil" around their homes. Though the awareness of the dangers of subsidence and the need to "fill" individual lots has led to a more-or-less successful management of the subsidence problem, the issue remains a major consideration for builders and community leaders, for subsidence remains an important factor for new construction projects in the region and the all-important question of flood control. For example, a study in 2000 of the levee-protected soils of the New Orleans region found that the levee-protected land of northwest Kenner, with its organic "Kenner soil" had subsided below nearby un-leveed marshes. The levee-protected Kenner neighborhoods in the city's northwest quadrant where "Kenner soil" predominates the soil classification was found to be 5.5 feet below sea level (the level of the lake and marshes on the outside of the levee system).[3]

The subsidence problem and the resulting lowering of the elevation levels of large sections of the city is a particularly acute problem for community leaders in handling drainage and flood control issues. This is especially important during the times when the Kenner area is affected by tropical storms. Like all communities located along the Gulf Coast of the United States, the Kenner area is frequented by tropical weather, including the occasional hurricane. Though affected by tropical weather on a relatively frequent time table, since the end of World War II, Kenner has had to deal on three occasions with powerful tropical storms that, more or less, directly struck the city. Two of the direct hits came before the northern sections of the city experienced the rapid development of the 1970s and 1980s. As discussed in chapter nine, an unnamed category two hurricane struck the community on the morning of September 19, 1947. The lack of levees and other flood protections in the area along the lake allowed for waters from the powerful storm's flood surge to advance nearly all the way to Airline Highway. However, though flood waters were quite deep in parts of northern Kenner, except for the new airport most of the land north of the highway was undeveloped, thus minimizing the damage to Kenner's residential areas, which were located closer to the river.[4]

Eighteen years later, Kenner was again threatened by a large hurricane that had the metro New Orleans region in its bull's-eye. In 1965, the city was in the early stages of its massive suburban growth-surge; hence, there was only limited development at the time in the northern sections of the Kenner. Forming in late August as a tropical depression approximately five hundred miles off the coast of Surinam in South America, the weather disturbance quickly grew to become the second named tropical storm of the hurricane season—"Betsy." On September 8, 1965, after meandering in the Atlantic waters for days, the now hurricane crossed Key West in Florida, entered the Gulf of Mexico, and moved northwestwardly at the rapid rate of twenty knots towards New Orleans. The modern practice of mass evacuation of hurricane-threatened land areas did not exist. The lack of adequate transportation systems, including the unfinished interstate highway system, limited any possibility of a large-scale evacuation. Community storm preparation included moving residents of low-lying areas to New Orleans. New Orleanians and their suburban neighbors in Jefferson Parish and Kenner generally prepared for the event by "boarding up" or by moving to Red Cross and Civil Defense structures, including schools and public buildings, for safe keeping during the duration of the high winds and water. [5]

As the massive storm approached the Louisiana coast on the early evening of September 9, its winds were estimated to be as high as 155 to160 miles per hour, the maximum strength for a category 4 storm. By 10:00 p.m. the center of Betsy crossed the coast slightly to the west of Grand Isle with a tide of 8.8 feet above mean sea level and a barometer reading of 28.00 inches. After making landfall the storm continued to move in a northwestward path that roughly paralleled the west bank of the Mississippi River. Eventually the powerful storm passed approximately thirty-five miles to the west of New Orleans and Kenner. The path of the hurricane west of the metropolitan region meant that the northeast sector of the storm, where the fiercest winds of a hurricane are located, crossed directly over Kenner and the east bank of Jefferson Parish. Although its overland track had helped to moderate its powerful wind gusts, by the time the storm reached Kenner it still packed a mighty wallop. As with most major storms, the wind and rain levels varied from place to place in the city. The storm's official data for the community was recorded on the instruments located at Moisant Airport. There the barometric pressure was measured shortly before midnight to be 28.63 inches and rainfall during the storm totaled 4.09 inches. The wind speed was calculated out of the east at 85 miles per hour and wind gusts at the airport ran as high as 112 miles per hour.[6]

Although Hurricane Betsy was a huge storm and one of the worst on record at the time it struck Louisiana in 1965, the residents of Kenner survived the event in relatively good shape. With the exception of having to hunker down in their homes for several hours of angst-filled noise and house shuddering as Betsy's wind and rain pounded against the structures, Kenner and most of Jefferson Parish suffered relatively minor damage compared to the damage caused by the storm elsewhere in the state. Having the good fortune of avoiding much of the serious damage that ravaged other areas in South Louisiana, Kenner, and particularly the airport, played an important role in assisting the region's recovery. Within hours of the passing of the storm, the airport resumed service allowing assistance to begin to flow into the city. Among those who arrived to survey the damage was President Lyndon B. Johnson who landed at the airport in Kenner on the evening of September 10. Accompanied by several ranking officials of his administration, the president drove in a motorcade to the heavily damaged and flooded areas of New Orleans. Though brief, his presence proved essential in expediting Federal assistance that was essential in the state's rebuilding effort. Kenner had escaped the worse of Betsy's damage, but others in the metropolitan area were not so fortunate. When fully tallied, the cost of Betsy's visit was huge. The storm claimed the lives of eighty-one Louisianans, injured an additional 17,600 individuals, and caused $372 million (in 1965 dollars) in damage, with most of the damage taking place in the Lower Ninth Ward areas of New Orleans. Unfortunately, one of the great losses of the Betsy experience was that of a lost opportunity to learn from the event. Community leaders on all levels—federal, state, and local—failed to use fully the lessons of Betsy to prepare for the region's next great storm.[7]

The philosopher and poet George Santayana once noted that,

"Those who do not learn from history are doomed to repeat it." So it was in mid-summer of 2005 for the residents of metropolitan New Orleans. Many of the hard-earned lessons taught by hurricane Betsy four decades before concerning flood control and levees in an area where normal land levels are either below or slightly above encroaching sea levels went unheeded by officials who had as their responsibility protecting the residents of the New Orleans region from winds and waters. The 1965 storm had shown the devastating consequences that would be visited during a powerful storm to areas where levees and pumping stations were not properly constructed or maintained. Forty years later the people of Kenner and the rest of southeast Louisiana as well as the Mississippi Gulf Coast relearned the tragic lessons of unpreparedness and poor planning.

Towards the end of August 2005, meteorologists warned the people along the Atlantic and Gulf Coast of the presence of a new tropical storm in the warm waters of the western Atlantic over the southeastern Bahamas—a position of little worry for the residents of Kenner and the region. Over the next few days the stormed grew into a tropical storm and shortly thereafter into a Category 1 hurricane named Katrina. Although the storm slammed into southern Florida in the north Miami area and traveled across the Florida peninsula into the Gulf of Mexico, computer models predicted the future path of the storm to be up the western side of Florida. In spite of its location in the Gulf, the forecast track did not seem to pose a threat to the residents of Kenner. However, as the hours passed, Katrina refused to follow its script as written by the National Hurricane Center and instead moved ominously to the west. As it traveled westward across the warm waters of the Gulf of Mexico, it gathered new energy and power, and by Sunday, August 28 it reached the frightening classification of a Category 5 hurricane with winds hitting 175 miles per hour. By late Sunday the monster storm moved sufficiently westward that most storm prognosticators held a consensus that the New Orleans area would, as the *Times- Picayune* headlined, be "Ground Zero" for the hurricane's landfall. With so many of the earlier track predictions having projected that the storm was likely to make landfall to the east of the city, the people of the New Orleans region were surprised when the city became the projected target of Katrina. By Saturday morning area residents were in full-hurricane-preparation mode, with most individuals choosing to evacuate the area for higher, safer ground.[8]

At a few minutes after 6:00 a.m. of August 29, 2005, Katrina made landfall over Louisiana's Barataria Basin between Grand Isle and the mouth of the Mississippi River. It advanced northeastward over parts of Plaquemine and St. Bernard parishes, with its eye passing just to the east of New Orleans. Although the winds of the giant storm had decreased to Category 2 levels when it moved over land, Katrina's Category 5 level storm surge remained and continued its momentum up the region's numerous waterways. In the waters of the Gulf, waves swelled ten to thirty feet above normal sea level, with some waves offshore reaching heights of one hundred feet. Near Kenner, in the waters of Lake Pontchartrain, waves rose to between nine and twelve feet above normal levels. In addition to the rising sea levels the storm-effected region also had to handle an immense amount of rainfall. Radar data collected during the storm showed that during the 24-hour duration of the storm as much as 13.6 inches of rain fell in some parts of the metropolitan area. Its intense winds, rainfall, waves, and storm surges made Katrina one of the strongest hurricanes ever to hit the coast of the United States. In spite of the fact of the lessons offered by the experience of Hurricane Betsy forty-years earlier and the investment of millions of dollars by federal, state, and local officials to protect against the next "big one," post-Katrina evaluation showed that much of the area's flood protection was under-designed because of "engineering and engineering-related policy failures."[9] The combination of the intense forces that Katrina brought to bear soon overwhelmed parts of the metropolitan New Orleans flood protection system. Fairly early on the morning that the storm struck the New Orleans area, several of the protections system's I-walls and levees that lined the area's lakes and waterways failed. By the end of the storm, more than fifty locations in the hurricane protection system were either overtopped or breached by storm waters, allowing massive amounts of water to pour into parts of New Orleans and St. Bernard Parish. By September 1, 2005, over 80 percent of the New Orleans region was flooded.[10]

Fortunately for the residents of Kenner, the section of the hurricane protection system that separated the city from the Katrina-produced storm surge and wind-pushed raging waters of Lake Pontchartrain held throughout the storm, saving the area from the catastrophic destruction incurred in New Orleans, where billions of gallons of lake and canal waters surged into the city as a result of broken levees and canal walls. Although spared from the deep-water flooding that inundated so much of New Orleans, parts of Old Metairie, and St. Bernard Parish, the people of Kenner nonetheless suffered great damage from Katrina's visit. Much of Kenner's destruction included, as would be expected from a near direct hit of a major hurricane, large numbers of downed trees and utility lines, lost roofing shingles, completely destroyed roofs, blown-out storefronts, and downed billboards. In addition to widespread wind damage in neighborhoods across the city, more than 50 percent of the homes and businesses in Kenner were flooded due to the storm's massive rainfall. The worst flooding took place in the northern sections of the city between Veterans Boulevard and the lake, where parts of the University City, Driftwood Park, and Chateau Estates neighborhoods experienced as much as six to eight feet of water. Even in parts of south Kenner near the river and along Kenner Avenue had flood waters as deep as three and four feet. The flooding, the worst in the city's history, and the wind damage was so extensive that it led Kenner Mayor Phil Capitano to lament that it appeared that every structure in the city suffered some type of damage from the storm. Final tally of the storm's effects showed that approximately 2,800 homes were damaged in Kenner with additional multi-millions of dollars of damage being afflicted upon city-owned facilities and infrastructure.[11]

Recovery for the people of Kenner from Katrina was long and tedious. Local authorities were overwhelmed by the magnitude of the storm damage and the task of returning things to normal. With Jefferson Parish President Aaron Broussard having declared martial law, the hundreds of thousands of residents from all over the metropolitan area who had evacuated before the arrival of the storm were blocked from a quick return to their homes. Flood waters had to be pumped away and debris removal had to take place before the roads would be safe for citizens to return. It took nearly a week—until September 5—for Broussard to begin to allow the residents of Jefferson Parish and Kenner to begin their return to their homes. Much remained to be done. The first citizens to return found a site reminiscent of a war zone, with hundreds of buildings and homes destroyed or damaged, trees down on houses and across many streets and thoroughfares, electricity outages across the entire area, and very low water pressure, which limited firefighting and the treatment of sewage and wastewater. Most traffic controls were nonexistent. Most devastating of all the damage was the vast numbers of homes flooded by storm waters. The official re-entry plan called for the evacuated residents to be allowed to return upon showing proof of residency at police roadblocks, assess the damage to their property and then leave the community so that the authority's recovery efforts could proceed without hindrance. However, upon returning and discovering the water damage in their homes and the stench caused by soaked carpets and wallboard, standing water, and the colonies of black mold and mildew that quickly established themselves in the intense humidity of the closed-up houses of the post-storm period, many residents ignored officials' requests to re-evacuate and remained to begin saving and repairing their residences.[12]

Throughout the Katrina disaster, evacuees from Kenner and their Jefferson Parish neighbors experienced a wide range of response emotions. First waiting for the storm to arrive and then waiting for days to be allowed back into their homes to see how they survived resulted in an extended period of extreme apprehension for the area's evacuees. Once allowed back home, residents faced a crippled community and, for many, flooded and storm-damaged homes. Apprehension quickly gave way to depression and the realization of the task that lay ahead before "normalcy" would return to their lives. Once residents returned to Kenner in large numbers, progress in making repairs to the damaged community infrastructure services proceeded fairly quickly, but in spite of the progress, residents increasingly experienced a growing sense of anger and outrage. One source of anger resulted from the looting in the community that followed the passing of the storm. Though the looting in the area did not approach the levels experienced in New Orleans, where wholesale and organized looting of businesses and homes took place, Kenner was not immune from the problem. In spite of a large and active law-enforcement presence in the city by Kenner police, during the first week following the storm seventy-nine individuals, including thirteen juveniles, were arrested for looting in the city.[13]

As depressing and angst causing as the damage caused by Hurricane Katrina was, residents of Kenner and Jefferson Parish accepted that living in the region brings with it a vulnerability to the wrath of nature, as do most residents living along the Gulf Coast. Storms coming inland from the Gulf, with their high winds and torrential rains, are part of the life and history of the region. With that knowledge and the expectation that nature, which normally provides the area with such beauty and bountiful resources from the sea, would from time-to-time demonstrate its darker side and power through its tropical storms and hurricanes, the people of Southeast Louisiana have a sense of acceptance and reasonableness concerning hurricanes. However, the stoic attitude of the returning Katrina evacuees to Kenner and the rest of Jefferson Parish soon shifted from begrudging acceptance of their plight and the conditions of their damaged property to one of disbelief and anger. The outrage focused especially on Jefferson Parish President Aaron Broussard and his Director of Emergency Operations, Walter S. Maestri. The anger towards the two men developed when the residents of Kenner and Jefferson Parish learned that the two Jefferson officials had ordered the evacuation from the parish of more than two hundred pump-station operators from the parish's vital flood-control pumping stations. The order resulted in the shutting down of the parish's pumping stations just as Hurricane Katrina neared the Louisiana coast. With parish officials operating the drainage system for the entire parish, including municipalities such as Kenner, once the parish workers were evacuated and the pumps were shut down, Kenner, like most of the parish, was left unprotected from the torrential rains of the hurricane. Word of the pump-workers' evacuation and shutdown spread across the parish and Kenner just at the time that thousands of residents were in the process of ripping out and discarding mountains of soggy carpet, flood-soaked and moldy wallboard, ruined furniture, and destroyed appliances in huge piles along the curbs in the front of their homes.[14]

The reaction and feelings of the people once they found out that the multi-million dollar system of new and updated stations that federal, state, and parish governments had spent decades promoting as state-of-the-art flood control had simply been turned off at the height of the storm by parish authorities was aptly reported by the *Times-Picayune* when it quoted Jefferson resident Danny Callahan, who in frustration proclaimed, "This wasn't an act of God. It was an act of stupidity."[15]

The outrage over the pumping station shutdown was not limited to the general public. Kenner's officials also proclaimed that they were caught unaware until August 28, the very last minute before the arrival of the storm, of the parish's plan to abandon the pumps. Stunned by the parish's action, Kenner Councilman Marc Johnson proclaimed disbelief that the very idea of "bailing out of the pumping station was ever an option."[16] Exacerbating the situation was the fact that although Kenner officials were informed of the decision to abandon the area's pumping stations only hours before Katrina arrived, the parish's plan to take such action had actually been around for years and no one thought that it was important enough to present it to the municipal officials in Kenner so that preparations for such a controversial and threatening action could be considered. The failure by parish officials to inform city authorities in advance of the plans to shut down pumping stations was not the only breakdown in Jefferson Parish's hurricane preparedness. In spite of Parish President Broussard's vociferous and frequent defense of the plan to evacuate pump-station workers in order to save their lives, several months after the storm, when he had to give sworn testimony in the legal defense of his actions and decisions during Katrina, Broussard testified under oath that he, either as president or a member of the parish council, had never seen, discussed, or knew about in advance of the plan to shut down the parish's drainage pumps during powerful hurricanes such as Katrina! Although Broussard's testimony was met with a great deal of skepticism by both the press and public, his statements concerning the lack of planning and sharing of information among community leaders of what was called the "Doomsday Plan" reveals just how bizarre and incompetent was Jefferson Parish's plan and management for handling hurricane emergencies.[17]

Thus, the worst flooding in the history of the city of Kenner resulted from the implementation by Jefferson Parish officials of a poorly designed and scarcely vetted plan. Officially known as the "Catastrophic Weather Event Doomsday Plan," it was originally prepared by Walter Maestri, director of the parish's Emergency Management Department, in 1998 during the administration of Parish President Tim Coulon. Under the Broussard administration, the plan was revised by Maestri in March of 2005 to switch the sheltering of essential public workers, including approximately one hundred pump-station operators from

Louis Armstrong International Airport in Kenner to a location more than one hundred miles away to an area north of Lake Pontchartrain in the town of Mount Hermon, near the border with Mississippi. As a result of the evacuation, in which a total of 1,100 parish workers and 700 vehicles were pulled out of the parish during the storm, the pump stations of Jefferson Parish sat vacant for thirty-six hours while the residents of the area dealt with one of the most powerful and dangerous hurricanes in history. Post-Katrina analysis revealed just how damaging and poorly conceived was Maestri's "Doomsday Plan." Not only did it leave the people of Kenner and the rest of Jefferson Parish without drainage capacity during one of the great rain events of the era, by leaving the pumping stations abandoned it also resulted in unintended reverse flow of water from Lake Pontchartrain passing through some of the pumps into the parish's system of canals, further raising their levels and increasing the danger of the flooding. Furthermore, Broussard's long-held contention that keeping workers in Jefferson Parish during a storm like Katrina would have been tantamount to a death sentence was discredited by the simple fact that hundreds of first responders, including the members of the Jefferson Parish Sheriff's Department and the Kenner Police and Fire Departments, Kenner's municipal officials, medical personnel at area hospitals, and more than five hundred people at the airport in Kenner, all stayed during the storm so that they could provide their needed services as soon as the storm subsided. To avoid a repeat of the problem, several months after Katrina, city and parish leaders instituted a plan of cross-training Kenner public-works personnel with parish pump-operators, so in any future parish manpower shortage, city employees will be available to keep Kenner's two pumping stations in operation. The inept design and implementation of the ill-fated doomsday plan by Jefferson Parish officials marks a sad betrayal of the public trust unmatched in Kenner's modern history.[18]

Google Earth satellite view of modern Kenner, showing the footprints of the airport, Laketown developments and the clear demarcation of the levee protected areas and neighboring lake and marshlands.

13
Yesterday, Today, and Tomorrow

The hurricane Katrina catastrophe changed the metropolitan area of New Orleans forever. From the almost total destruction of vast sections of the city of New Orleans and St. Bernard Parish to the partial flooding of thousands of homes in Jefferson Parish and Kenner, permanent change to life in the region as it had existed before the arrival of Katrina went along hand-in-hand with the area's effort to recover. For tens of thousands of those residents who lived through the great storm and its aftermath, a new benchmark was added to their life spectrum—now there are birthdays, wedding days, the day a child is born, and the time pre and post Katrina. A decade after the storm, there are billions of dollars worth of new and strengthened flood control systems protecting the region. However, in spite of the rebuilding and repairing of much of the destruction suffered by New Orleans and nearly all of the damage inflicted upon the residents of East Jefferson and Kenner, the region continues to experience population loss as a result of the arrival of Katrina. At the time of the great diaspora of residents from the metro-New Orleans area that accompanied the arrival and recovery periods of the storm, most refugees from the storm-affected community evacuated to areas across the rest of Louisiana and the United States. The sheer size of the numbers involved in the largest mass exodus in American history forced thousands to move far away from their homes for extended periods of time. Many simply never returned to their pre-Katrina homes in the metro New Orleans area.

The U.S. Census Bureau analysis of the population change in the area showed that in 2010 a total of 1,191,189 residents lived in the New Orleans metropolitan area. This number equaled only 90 percent of region's pre-Katrina census count. Although not all of the loss can be attributed to Katrina, the storm, by far, was the dominant reason for the area's out migration. Not unexpectedly, the greatest loss in population came from the areas that experienced the most devastating flooding, including parts of Orleans, Plaquemine, and St. Bernard parishes. In Kenner, which had mostly avoided the storm's severest flooding, the post-Katrina population losses were not as bad as elsewhere. Nevertheless, the Katrina catastrophe did mark the first time in decades that the population of Kenner actually decreased. In 2000, the population of the city reached its all-time high of 70,517. By time of the next Federal census in 2010, the population dropped to 66,702, a decrease of 5.4 percent. As noted below, the population shift in Kenner from the pre to the post Katrina periods was also accompanied by important demographic changes highlighted by a growing number of Hispanics moving to the city.[1]

The post-Katrina population decline and the lengthy recovery created many problems for the Kenner community. The drop in population along with storm-related damage to many of the city's commercial operations led to losses of tax revenues. Most prominent of the commercial losses was the closing for an extended period of a large portion of the city's premier retail center, the Esplanade Mall and its leading anchor, Macy's department store. Also heavily damaged by the storm was Kenner's largest multi-family complex, the Redwood Apartments. Opened in 1976 as a four hundred-unit complex on a fifteen acre tract located on West Esplanade Avenue, the apartments had gradually declined over the years and in recent times became a problem area for police and city officials. Severely damaged structures, including the large Redwood Apartment complex, were torn down and removed. Repairing and rebuilding began in Kenner immediately after the storm. Across the city, house by house, business by business, the community went to work rebuilding. Other structures and businesses took time to recover from the storm and its consequences. Macy's anchor store at the Esplanade Mall did not reopen until November 2008, over three years after Katrina ravished the region. Although during the

Table 2:
Pre/Post-Katrina Census Data for Kenner, Louisiana

	2000	2010	Change
Total Population	70,517	66,702	-3815 (-5.4%)
Whites	68%	61.6%	-6.4%
Blacks	22.6%	24%	1.4%
Hispanics	13.6%	22.4%	8.8%

long post-Katrina recovery period emphasis remained on repair and rebuilding, development of some new projects also went forward. Excluding the massive government sponsored flood-control projects that continued for years, perhaps the grandest of the privately sponsored post-Katrina projects in Kenner involved the continued development of the multimillion-dollar-upscale Gabriel subdivision located on the city's lakefront.

The large gated development actually had its start in the years before Katrina, when community leaders began to look to Kenner's lakefront area as place for development. For decades the city's lakefront had been dominated by a poorly functioning public boat launch, a levee area composed mostly of a barren strip of silt and riprap materials, and on the inner side of the levee, acres of asphalt parking places surrounding the once popular Jefferson Downs racetrack. Situated on approximately ninety acres of some of the most valuable real estate in Kenner, the racetrack occupied the location of the old WWL radio transmitter. The track moved to its Kenner location from its original location in Jefferson Parish, where the site is today the location of Lafreniere Park. After Hurricane Betsy damaged the facility beyond repair, it moved to Kenner and reopened in 1971, where it remained in operation until 1992, when it was closed for financial reasons. The final months of the Kenner horse track coincided with the revitalization of the city's lakefront. The project was pushed by Kenner's civic and political leaders, including then-Mayor Aaron Broussard. Given the name of Laketown in 1994 by Broussard, the project to redevelop the lake area had its nascence with Louisiana's rapid expansion of legalized gambling and the floating casino industry. The first step in the redevelopment project took place in 1990 with the opening of Kenner's multipurpose Pontchartrain Center on land leased from the city. Kenner's floating casino, the Treasure Chest, began operating on Labor Day in 1994 and the city, using revenues from the casino, expanded the public areas around the casino's dock into an enlarged park area with a neatly landscaped jetty with playgrounds, picnic pavilions and new fishing pier. With its popularity growing, the Laketown development was again improved in late 1999 when construction of a new $9 million, 121-room hotel was started near the Pontchartrain Center. As the Laketown development progressed, the nearby Jefferson Downs racetrack was closing. The owners of the track, Marie Krantz and her son Bryan, wanting to see the track's land used in such a way as would not clash with the neighborhood, had a feasibility study performed that supported their plans for an upscale residential project they called Gabriel. Promoted by its developers as "a living paradise," when opened for business in the months before Katrina, the large-gated development offered 219 lots near the lake, within a short walk of Laketown. Beginning in size at 7000 square feet, the vacant lots in the plush development carried a range of costs from $150,000 to as much as $500,000. The new subdivision quickly met with success, and by the time Hurricane Katrina struck the area, the one-time horse track and barns had blossomed into the crown jewel of residential neighborhoods in Kenner and one of Jefferson Parish's most affluent developments. Today, as demonstrated by the moving to the area of the popular Coconut Beach sport facility, city and community leaders continue to work on developing Laketown and Kenner's lakefront area to their economic potentials as a way to provide the city of Kenner with new sources of revenue and to offer the people of the community new recreational opportunities.[3]

Laketown was not the only effort by city leaders to revitalize underused assets of the Kenner community. Years before the Laketown project began to take shape, community leaders looked to revitalize the oldest portion of the city—the original location of Kennerville.

However, somewhat inexplicably, officials, instead of capitalizing on the area's heritage, history, and name, labeled their revitalization project Rivertown U.S.A. The project was born in the months leading up to the 1984 World's Fair in New Orleans. Local merchants and civic groups in Kenner looking for ways to capitalize on the six-month fair, which was expected to bring thousands of visitors to the metropolitan region, developed a plan for a permanent and hopefully profitable tourist attraction. As with the Laketown project, Rivertown was vigorously promoted by then-mayor Aaron Broussard. As originally planned, the project was to include the redevelopment of a small number of blocks in area of Williams Boulevard and the Mississippi River. Containing the city's oldest structures, many of which dated to the late 1800s and early 1900s, the project called for the recreation of a Victorian village, including a reconstructed train depot, museums, restaurants, a pedestrian mall, and a new river landing and overlook known as La Salle's Landing. In support of the effort, the Kenner City Council in April 1983 voted to designate the Rivertown area as the Kenner Historical District. Over the three-plus decades of its existence, community and city leaders have placed considerable resources into the project. Since its formation, more than eight different museums, a performing arts center, and the sophisticated Louis J. Roussel Jr. Laser Planetarium operated at Rivertown. Unfortunately, the project's success has been limited. Although festivals such as the springtime Festa Italiana and the fall's Oktoberfest bring sizeable crowds to the area, on too many other occasions the area appears almost as a ghost town. The limited public interest, and an inability or unwillingness to provide the resources to keep the various museums fresh and up-to-date led Mayor Ed Muniz to slash the number of museums by half, leaving primarily exhibits associated with the planetarium and disappointedly closing those associated with telling the history of the region. Among the galleries and museums that operated at one time in the historic district but have been closed for good were the Toy Train Museum, closed in 2009; the Wildlife and Fisheries and Native American Galleries; the Kenner Museum (located in the former home of Sheriff Frank Clancy on Third Street); the New Orleans Saints Hall of Fame (moved to a location in the Louisiana Superdome); and finally the Mardi Gras Museum, which shut its doors for good in 2012. Today, in spite of promises and plans of multiple mayoral administrations to revitalize the project, Rivertown remains an area of unique cultural offerings in search of an identity and use design that meets and fulfills its potential as a centerpiece of the Kenner community. In the summer of 2013, the area was officially designation by the state as a Cultural District. The new designation is designed to provide incentives for redevelopment of the area by providing tax credits for artists and the rehabilitation of historic structures.[4]

As noted in the pages of this book, the history of the Kenner community is essentially the story of the people of Kenner. Laboring singularly or in cooperation with others, it was the many generations of individuals whose dedication and hard work have created the modern city of Kenner. Whenever the identities are known of those individuals who made contributions and changes to the ongoing story of Kenner, their stories have been included here. Included among those residents who have contributed to the history of Kenner, there are those individuals whose societal contributions extend beyond Kenner to include the parish, state, and nation. Some of these notable Kenner residents have been discussed previously, including the various members of the Kenner family who in their time were widely respected and held political, economic, and social influence across the region and state.

Among those notable and influential Kenner residents deserving of recognition is Frank James Clancy. The son of John Clancy, who was a native of New York, a leading organizer of the Kenner vegetable growers, and a minor Jefferson Parish politician, Frank was born in Kenner on September 8, 1892. The third of six children, he earned a law degree from Tulane University Law School. A semi-pro baseball player, he married Vera Wattigney, the daughter of Antoine Wattigney, the first mayor of Kenner following its 1913 incorporation. Upon completing his law studies, he practiced in Kenner and soon entered politics. Serving first as an attorney for the City of Kenner and later as alderman, he eventually won election as the Jefferson Parish Clerk of Court. After eight years as clerk, in 1928 he was elected Jefferson Parish Sheriff, a position he held for twenty-eight years, or seven terms—making him the longest serving sheriff in the history of Jefferson Parish. Although others from Kenner before him had been elected to parish offices, Clancy was the first Kenner resident to obtain political dominance of

Although a native of Kenner who gained parish-wide political influence, Frank J. Clancy obtained an unmatched degree of political influence and dominance in Jefferson Parish. Holding office from 1928 to 1956, Clancy's tenure remains unmatched in the history of the parish in both length and influence.

politics in Jefferson Parish. During his long term in office, Clancy expanded both his political and economic power. He was among the first to realize the economic potential of the vast grass and marshlands along the lake in north Kenner and East Jefferson. Acquiring large sections of the open lands, he established a sprawling beef farmstead. The Clancy ranch eventually grew to 1,940 acres, which included large portions of Kenner and East Jefferson. Similar to his acquisition of his land holdings, Clancy went about building his political fortunes. Having learned organizational skills from his father, Frank effectively distributed patronage to build support across the parish for himself. Popular among the people, he did not hesitate to use the iron-hand of political authority to get his way. He soon dominated the politics of Jefferson Parish and earned the nicknames of "The Irishman" and the "King." Clancy did little to curb the thriving illegal gambling industry in the parish. During the years of the Great Depression and World War II there was little public complaint about the gambling. However, by the 1950s national attention became focused on Jefferson's gambling situation and its association with organized crime. The situation took a dramatic change when U.S. Senator Estes Kefauver's Special Committee to Investigate Organized Crime in Interstate Commerce held meetings broadcast live on the area's fledgling television station. With the national spotlight now shining on events in Jefferson, Clancy reversed his long-standing position on the issue of wide-open gambling and began shutting down its operations in the parish. The issue of his association with gambling and organized crime remained a political liability for Clancy, and in a stunning upset he was defeated in his 1956 effort at reelection. A founder and first president of the Louisiana Sheriffs' Association, Clancy died in December 1960.[5]

It took over two decades before another native of Kenner would assume a similar position of political prominence in Jefferson Parish. Though he would become the most popular and dominant political figure in the parish, Joseph S. Yenni achieved his power and prominence not through the distribution of patronage and questionable deal making, as was all too common in Jefferson politics, but rather by establishing a reputation of integrity, optimism, and sound leadership. Joe, to all who knew him, grew up poor in the older section of Kenner. His mother died when he was a young boy. His father was a railroad maintenance employee. An exceptional athlete, his skills helped him obtain a college education at what is now the University of Southern Mississippi and later a master's degree at Loyola University in New Orleans. A naval communications officer during World War II, upon returning home he made a career of three decades as an educator and coach in the public schools of Jefferson Parish. His political career began in 1962 when Governor Jimmie Davis appointed him to a seat on the Kenner Board of Aldermen. Losing his first effort to win a seat on the Jefferson Parish Council, he refocused his attention on the politics of Kenner. From that time forward, Yenni's path to political power and influence was steady and constant. In 1966 he won election and returned to the city's Board of Aldermen. In 1970, at age fifty-two, Yenni, as one of the leaders of a reform ticket of candidates, defeated the incumbent to become mayor of Kenner. His election set the historic precedent of marking the first election in modern times that a white candidate actively worked for the support of and made commitments to the African American community in Kenner.[6]

In his campaign for mayor, Yenni strongly promoted a proposal to update Kenner's plan of government. After his victory, he carried through with his promise and supported charter reform for the city. Appointing a citizen's charter study commission, a new home-rule charter was written and presented to the voters of the city who approved the new plan of government by an over-whelming margin. As mayor, he held the reigns of city government during a challenging period of growth and expansion unsurpassed in the history of Kenner. He reorganized city government, improved efficiency, and established a confident and personal standard that the people of Kenner found reassuring and dependable. As mayor he enjoyed the trust and popularity of the people of Kenner while at the same time in greater Jefferson Parish a series of scandals, frauds, and kickback schemes involving parish leaders resulted in investigations by Federal prosecutors and serious protest and anger by parish residents. Hence, after serving as mayor for nearly three terms, in 1979 he announced his plans to run for the position of parish president. In the 1980 election, his reputation for integrity and competence as mayor led to a landslide win with 77 percent of the vote, making him the first native-born parish president. His strong work ethic, basic honesty, energy, and optimism was eagerly accepted by the electorate. After a period of years of voters venting their anger against Jefferson's ineffective leadership by voting down nearly all tax renewals and proposals, soon after taking office Yenni got both voters and parish leaders to enter into massive programs of much needed drainage and other public works improvements. Proving the cogency of Chicago mayor Richard Daley's remark that "good government is good politics," when Yenni ran for reelection in 1983, he was elected without opposition. Unfortunately, Yenni did not have the opportuni-

Joseph S. Yenni was a popular mayor of Kenner who became the first native-born Jefferson Parish President. Known for his integrity, he was among the most influential and popular politicians in Kenner and Jefferson Parish.

ty to complete his second term as parish president. In the summer of 1986, he was diagnosed with a deadly brain cancer which took his life on March 16, 1987. An all-too-rare politician who inspired trust and loyalty of people from across the political spectrum, Yenni's efforts and many contributions to both the City of Kenner and Jefferson Parish made him perhaps the most respected and liked elected leader in the history of both the parish and Kenner.[7]

Among the legacies Joe Yenni's left the people of Jefferson was the his name. So respected and revered was Yenni that the depth of the goodwill of the people of Jefferson towards him was shared by other members of his family, including his son Michael J. Yenni. Following the death of the popular two term parish president, most political movers in the parish decided that Councilman Willie Hof would be the individual who would take over and complete Yenni's term. To the surprise of nearly everyone in the parish, Joe's son Michael (Mike), claiming to be outraged by the political deal-making that was in the process of handpicking his father's successor, announced he was running to fill his dad's unfinished term. Like his father, he was a native and resident of Kenner. But unlike his dad, he had previously showed no interest in running for elective office. Although he lacked the management and political experience and know-how of his father, Mike shared with his father a reputation of personal integrity. In an unexpected upset, the neophyte politician narrowly defeated Hof, the candidate supported by most of the parish's political establishment. Upon taking office, young Yenni at times stumbled in his new job. However, despite a sometime rocky relationship with the council, his administration proved popular with the people of Jefferson and brought about several major reforms. Among his successes was an effort, approved by the voters, to amend the parish's home-rule charter to give the parish president veto power over council actions and to implement term limits for most elected officials in the parish. His most important accomplishment was a $200 million urban flood protection program. Incredibly, the devastating event faced by his family with the loss of his father to a deadly disease during his term as parish president tragically repeated itself. Soon after winning reelection and taking office for a second term, Michael Yenni was struck by the serious bone-marrow disease myelofibrosis. After a ten month battle with the deadly illness, Yenni, three weeks shy of his forty-fifth birthday, died at his home in Kenner, with his wife and three children by his side.[8]

The untimely passing of Joe and Michael Yenni did not bring to an end to the dominance of Kenner natives in the politics of Jefferson Parish. A political contemporary of the Yennis, Aaron Broussard spent three-and-a-half decades in Jefferson Parish politics. Born in Marksville, Louisiana, in 1949, Broussard moved as a young boy to Kenner in 1958. After graduating from the University of New Orleans and earning a law degree from Loyola University in New Orleans, Broussard, at the young age of twenty-five, entered the local political realm by winning a seat on the Jefferson Parish School Board. Just three years later he won a special election and assumed a seat on the Jefferson Parish Council as the representative of the 3rd District, which included a large portion of the city of Kenner. His keen sense of humor and gregarious personality made him a natural politician and popular among the voters. Although a Democrat in the largely conservative Republican Jefferson Parish, over his thirty-five year political career Broussard managed to win every election in which he appeared on the ballot.[9]

When Joe Yenni moved from Kenner's mayor's office to the parish presidency in 1980, Broussard ran for the office in the 1982 mayoral election. That particular race to become Kenner's mayor became legendary for its cost and bitter nature. Forced to face two other well-financed candidates, Raoul "Skip" Galan and Kernan "Skip" Hand, the campaign, for the time, quickly became one of the most expensive local elections in Louisiana history. The three candidates combined spent more than $1 million—an amount unprecedented for a community of fewer than 70,000 residents. Broussard won and eventually went on to win three additional terms. As mayor, he soon earned a reputation for innovativeness, vision, a strong work ethic, showmanship, and political consensus building to obtain his objectives. The positive aspects of his character were amply demonstrated when, as noted in chapter ten, just a few days after becoming mayor, he had to handle the devastating crash of Pan American World Airways flight 759 into a Kenner neighborhood within walking distance of his office in city hall. The disaster claimed the lives of 154 passengers and Kenner citizens. As mayor, Broussard also won praise for his work in improving relations with New Orleans and St. Charles Parish in regards to long-standing issues concerning the airport. Other issues and events during his time as mayor which earned him praise included his support for the acquisition of the Treasure Chest Casino on Lake Pontchartrain and his vision and support for the building of the Pontchartrain Center at the lake, as well as the development of the Rivertown and Laketown projects at the southern and northern ends of Williams Boulevard. With his popularity running high at home, in 1990 Broussard surprised many by his announcement that he was entering the race for governor. Unfortunately, his ambitious effort to become the state's chief executive never really caught on with the voters in other areas of Louisiana. After nearly eight months on the campaign trail and before his name ever appeared on the ballot, he withdrew from the race, which ended when the controversial Edwin Edwards later defeated the former Klansman David Duke in a runoff election.[10]

His disappointing run for governor did not discourage Broussard in his desire to achieve higher political office. Winning reelection for a fourth term as Kenner's mayor in 1994, just one year later in 1995 he ran for and was elected to the politically powerful Chairmanship of the Jefferson Parish Council; he thus gave up his long-held position of mayor. After easily winning re-election in 1999, Broussard was elected parish president in 2003. Finally achieving his long-sought position as one of the parish's most influential political leaders, Broussard's fall from grace soon began. Having sharpened his administrative skills during his four terms as mayor, it surprised many that as parish president a series of administrative decisions soon led to a dramatic loss of support among parish residents. In spite of the complex nature and size of parish government, Broussard looked upon the position of parish president as a part-time job. He also kept several of his predecessor's staff in his administration, including his top aide Tim Whitmer who he made his chief administrative officer and vested with broad authority and power.[11]

In a little over a year after assuming the position of parish president in 2004, Broussard's leadership was severely tested with the arrival of Hurricane Katrina. The widespread flooding, as discussed in chapter twelve, that accompanied the storm devastated large portions of East Jefferson. When the post-storm analysis revealed that much of the flooding in Jefferson Parish was the result of the implementation of the parish government's poorly designed "Doomsday Plan," which required the vital drainage pumps to be abandoned during the storm and their operators evacuated one hundred miles away from their duty stations, parish homeowners became outraged and furiously blamed Broussard for the disaster in Jefferson. Broussard's defense of the evacuation only enraged citizens more. So damaged was his standing that two years later he barely eked out a re-election win against two political unknowns. His problems continued into his second term. In 2009 reports from local news media outlets and the Metropolitan Crime Commission led to an FBI investigation and eventual indictment of Tim Whitman, Broussard's chief administrative officer, for illegal contracting and insurance practices with government agencies. The investigation eventually spread to include other parish officials, including Broussard himself, revealing that the standards of integrity set by Joe and Mike Yenni clearly had been abandoned. Following months of investigation and in a move that caught nearly everyone by surprise, on January 8, 2010, Broussard abruptly resigned from his office, ending a career of thirty-five uninterrupted years in public office. After over three years of investigation by Federal authorities Broussard eventually pled guilty to series of criminal acts committed while he was parish president, including payroll fraud, conspiracy, wire fraud, and theft. In late February 2013, the onetime most influential politician in Jefferson Parish appeared before a Federal judge and was sentenced to forty-six months in prison, leading the acting United States Attorney Dana Boente to claim, "The sad end to Aaron Broussard's career is a self-inflicted wound resulting from his venality, corruption, and deceit."[12] In addition to taking a bribe from a local businessman in exchange for parish business, Broussard's guilty plea for payroll fraud resulted from the employing of his then fiancée in a high-paying parish government job for which she was not qualified and at which she rarely worked. As he was sentenced to prison, Broussard accepted full responsibility for his downfall and apologized to the people of Jefferson for the shame he brought to his office and concluded with the lament that "I will pay for that dishonor for the rest of my life."[13]

No discussion of influential Kennerites would be complete without a mention of two individuals who have gained national recognition for their political sapience. As noted in chapter eleven, Donna Brazile

Among Kenner's accomplished natives, Donna Brazile is one of America's most prominent political analysts who is frequently seen on national television programs and currently serves as the vice Chairwomen of the Democratic National Committee.

grew up in the predominantly African American neighborhoods of old Kenner located between Airline and Jefferson highways. Having cut her political teeth as a young girl in municipal campaigns in Kenner, Brazile has risen to become the first African American to manage a presidential campaign. Today she continues as a Democratic political strategist on the national scene. She also remains one of the most influential political commentators and a frequent on-air contributor to the national news networks of CNN and ABC. Among her many awards and recognitions she has been named by *O, The Oprah Magazine* as one of its twenty "remarkable visionaries," *Essence* magazine has included her among their list of the "Top 50 Women in America," and she has received the Congressional Black Caucus Foundation's highest award for political achievement.[14]

Of all the notable and influential political figures who have called Kenner home, perhaps the individual who has acquired the most power and political notoriety is Bobby Jindal. The only resident of Kenner and the first Indian-American to be elected governor in the United States, Jindal's rise to prominence is an impressive story of achievement. However, his rise to power actually had relatively little to do with the Kenner community. Except for the happenstance of residency at the time of his election to the governorship, Jindal's association with Kenner was somewhat brief. The son of immigrants from India, Jindal was born and reared in Baton Rouge. A graduate of Brown University and a Rhodes Scholar at Oxford University, while in his early twenties he entered public service by becoming the secretary of the Louisiana Department of Health and Hospitals. In 2001, President George W. Bush appointed him as assistant secretary of the U.S. Department of Health and Human Services. In 2003, he failed in his first effort at state-wide elected office when he was defeated by Kathleen Blanco in a runoff for governor. It was only at that point that Jindal became associated with Kenner. A short time after his failed effort at winning the governorship, a vacancy became open in the First Congressional District when Representative David Vitter was elected to the U.S. Senate. Seeing an opportunity for political advancement, Jindal and his family moved from his native Baton Rouge to Kenner, which is located within the boundaries of the district. Using the contacts and resources he had mustered in his ill-fated race for governor, Jindal overpowered his opposition and won election to the U.S. Congress. After serving two terms in the Congress, in 2007, he again ran for governor. With no incumbent in the race, he was able to outdistance his opposition and captured the state's highest elected office. Popular with voters at the end of his first term, Jindal easily won reelection with only token opposition in 2011. His popularity and leadership style won him recognition by national Republican Party leaders and led to national media attention. Because of term limits, Jindal was legally prohibited from running for a third term as governor. His frequent absences from the state to participate in national Republican activities, including an ill-fated attempt in 2015 to win the Republican nomination for president, at the time he was implementing draconian budget balancing policies that resulted in services to state hospitals, universities and colleges, and the mentally ill and disabled being severely cut resulted in a dramatic decline in his polling popularity in Louisiana. The politically-opportune nature of Jindal's residency in Kenner was confirmed when at the end of his governorship he chose to not return to the city and instead resettled in his native Baton Rouge.[15]

The political arena is not the only area where Kenner residents have obtained regional and national prominence. During the decades following the end of World War II many social and cultural changes made their way into post-war American society. Among the most dramatic of these social changes came in the area of popular music with the birth of rock and roll. An amalgamation of the traditions of the rhythm and blues of the black community and white country music, the new music sound was quickly embraced by young people in Kenner and across America. Considering the relatively small size of the African American population that resided in the city during the early postwar decades, Kenner's African American community made an impressive contribution to America's growing interest in the world of rhythm and blues and rock and roll music. Among the residents of Kenner who made notable contributions to America's music culture during the formative years of rock and roll were such standouts as Henry Gray, King Floyd, Chris Kenner, and Lloyd Price. Born in Kenner in 1925 and moving as a youth near Baton Rouge, Henry Gray eventually traveled to Chicago where he joined the band of blues legend Howlin Wolf as pianist. He remained in the band until 1968, after which he played with many of the great rhythm and blues musicians of his time, including such notables as Muddy Waters, B.B. King, and Guitar Slim. Over his career Gray received two Grammy nominations and was named a National Endowment for the Arts Heritage Fellow. King Floyd's history is somewhat the opposite of that of Gray's in that he was born in New Orleans in 1945 and moved to Kenner where he spent his formative years. Getting his start by singing on street corners, Floyd's most famous work, his 1970 song "Groove Me," became a national hit, selling more than five-million records.[16]

Another son of Kenner who drew national attention during the formative years of rock and roll in America was Chris Kenner. Born in 1929, Kenner was schooled in his youth in gospel; however, as he grew older his interest increasingly shifted to rhythm and blues. Not particularly talented in the showmanship aspects of the music business, Kenner presented poorly in the live venues of his day. His talent lay in his writing and composing. Working with music legend Dave Bartholomew, his first big break in music happened in 1957 when together they recorded "Sick and Tired," which met with much local acclaim and a year later became a national hit when the great Fats Domino recorded it. Kenner's greatest success came shortly thereafter when he teamed with Allen Toussaint to produce his biggest hit song "I Like It Like That." The song surged to number two on the national pop charts and earned a Grammy nomination and a spot on the popular national television show *American Bandstand.* Kenner continued to write popular songs, such as "Packin Up" and "Something You Got." In 1962 he released "Land of 1,000 Dances." The song was not received well either locally or at the national level. Eventually it reached a respectable number seventy-seven on the pop charts. But that was not its end. Strapped for money, 50 percent of the song was sold to Fats Domino for $2,000. Other artists, including Domino, began recording the song and its popularity increased. Popularized by more than thirty artist from other cities, including Jimi Hendrix, Tom Jones, and Roy Orbison, with the most popular version of the song by Wilson Pickett, "Land of 1,000 Dances" eventually became one of the most lucrative New Orleans song copyrights. Unfortunately, Kenner, who held a day job as a longshoreman, squandered a great deal of his money. Convicted of statutory rape, he spent time in Angola prison. An attempted comeback was not successful and although his music was recorded by many artists and produced millions of dollars of revenue for others, Kenner tragically died of an apparent heart attack in a transient rooming house on Jackson Avenue in New Orleans. He is buried in an unknown location.[17]

Among Kenner's music men of the early rock and roll era none obtained the level of national recognition and success of Lloyd Price. Born on March 9, 1933, he grew up in a residence at 323 Butler Street in a mostly African American neighborhood of south Kenner. The seventh of eleven children born to Louis, a laborer at the nearby woodbox factory, and Beatrice Price, young Lloyd was exposed to the artists of the time through the jukebox his mother had in her small fish-fry business. Anxious to try his hand at the music business, in 1944 Price jumped at the opportunity to join with other kids from his neighborhood in the Kenner Community Band. Founded by long-time Kenner civil-rights activist Henry "Teddy" Stewart, the band gave its young members an opportunity to learn music and to become acquainted with musical instruments. Shortly thereafter Lloyd and his younger

The Kenner Community Band pictured here in the mid-1940s was organized by community leader Henry "Teddy" Stewart (upper left). An important component in Kenner's African American community, the band introduced many youth of the community to the music scene, including R&B star and Kenner native Lloyd Price.

brother Leo, who was one year his junior and who later went on to be a songwriter in his own right, including co-writing "Send Me Some Lovin" for rock-and-roll star Little Richard, formed their own band to play at local venues. His music and singing soon caught the attention of leaders among the New Orleans music scene. In March 1952 at age nineteen, with Fats Domino accompanying him on piano, he recorded "Lawdy Miss Clawdy." The song shot to the top of the R&B charts and remained there for seven weeks and was later named the Song of the Year. The song eventually was recorded by many other leading rock and roll artists, including such greats as Fats Domino, Little Richard, Conway Twitty, Paul McCartney, John Lennon, and Elvis Presley. The song became so popular that it was included by the Rock and Roll Hall of Fame as one of the "500 Songs That Shaped Rock and Roll." The talented Price quickly followed up on his early success with four more top ten R&B songs in 1952 and 1953, including "Oooh, Oooh,

Lloyd Price was born in south Kenner in 1933. At an early age he began to write and perform R&B songs. By age nineteen his song "Lawdy Miss Clawdy" was at the top of the R&B charts. The first teenager in history to sell one million records, he was chosen a member of the Louisiana Music Hall of Fame, and in 1998 was inducted into the national Rock and Roll Hall of Fame.

Oooh" (number four), "Restless Heart" (number five), "Tell Me Pretty Baby" (number eight), and "Ain't It A Shame" (number four). Drafted into the army for a three-year hitch, he was forced to take a multi-year hiatus from his music career.[18]

Upon Price's release from the army, he returned to his career and was soon producing hits that once again placed him at the top of the music charts. Over the next few years he released a long list of successful songs, including "Stagger Lee" (number1), "Where Were You (On Our Wedding Day?)" (number 4), "I'm Gonna Get Married" (number 1), "Come into My Heart" (number 2), "Lady Luck" (number 3), "Question" (number 5), and several others hits including a popular release of Errol Garner's "Misty" (number 11). Unlike some of his contemporaries who started their careers in music on the streets of south Kenner, Price was astute in his business operations and managed his money effectively. As he aged and his hits came further apart, Price expanded his interest to other areas of the music industry. He became a glitzy nightclub owner in New York, formed his own record label, and worked as a songwriter, producer, bandleader, booking agent, and promoter. His entrepreneurial success soured in 1969 when his business partner and friend, Harold Logan, was murdered. Price moved to Africa and pursued new ventures, including joining with one of the premier pitchman of his time, Don King, to promote such international events as the 1974 Muhammad Ali versus George Foreman fight in Zaire—"the Rumble in the Jungle"—and the Ali/ Joe Frazier contest in the Philippines—"the Thrilla in Manila." In the 1980s he returned to the United States, where he performed on a limited basis, including regular headline performances at the Jazz & Heritage Festival back in New Orleans. In 1994, Price was honored by his hometown with the naming of a street near his former home in honor of the entertainer. Also that year, as the first teenager in history to sell one million records, the Rhythm & Blues Foundation awarded the Kenner native the prestigious Pioneer Award. In 1998 Price was honored with induction into the Rock and Roll Hall of Fame—quite a journey for a young Kenner teenager of the 1940s and 1950s to have made it from his mother Beatrice's Fish n' Fry to America's Rock and Roll Hall of Fame![19]

Even today, Kenner's tradition of producing amazingly talented musicians continues. The most recent Kenner native to rise to national acclaim and recognition is the jazz musician Jon (Jonathan) Batiste. A member of a large local musical family, Batiste began performing at age eight and released two albums by time he was seventeen. He attended the New Orleans Center for Creative Arts and later moved to New York City to obtain both undergraduate and graduate degrees from the renowned Julliard School. Comfortable playing a wide range of instruments, he developed a kinetic hybrid style of jazz that has taken him to perform in more than forty countries and has led to collaborations with such performers as Prince, Lenny Kravitz, and Wynton Marsalis. He has been one of the largest draws at the National Jazz Museum in Harlem, where he has also served as the artistic director. Though only in his late twenties, Batiste's record of impressive accomplishments led to his being selected in 2015 for the highly-sought-after position of musical director for the CBS network's "The Late Show with Stephen Colbert," where, as the show's bandleader, he and his group Stay Human get to perform five nights a week before a national television audience.[20]

Today the city of Kenner remains an integral part of the metropolitan New Orleans area. As with most suburban communities positioned fairly close to its central-city neighbor, Kenner's identity as a bedroom community and its economic fortunes rely heavily upon the fate of New Orleans. Hence, as the metropolitan New Orleans area has rebuilt after the devastation of Katrina, the city of Kenner has also worked to recover from the historic storm. Though most of the physical scars from the storm have been repaired, the community continues to suffer from a reduction in population. No doubt the problems visited upon the community by Hurricane Katrina are a factor in Kenner's population loss, they are not the only factors involved. The 2010 census of Kenner showed a population of 66,702, a 7.4 percent decrease from the city's 1990 record total of 72,033 residents. The population decline is also the result of a social and cultural malaise now taking affect in today's post-Katrina Kenner. Across America suburban communities like Kenner are experiencing the same general uneasiness in their expectations for future growth and prosperity. Like their larger and older neighboring central cities, suburban areas are beginning to enter a cycle of decline. This trend of suburban decline now challenges the Kenner community to make changes. One recent study initiated by Kenner officials determined that the city is at an "inflection point," meaning that time is short for the community to take steps to reverse the ongoing decline.[21]

Kenner's boom years of the 1960s, 70s, and 80s are forever over. The large tracts of undeveloped land waiting for the arrival of bulldozers to begin cutting paths for the development of another new subdivision of modern homes and paved streets, which in the past served as the economic engine for the city, are mostly gone. Nevertheless, there still remains a supply of developable properties in the northwestern portion of the city. However, symptomatic of issues facing the community as a whole, real estate activity in Kenner is currently in a state of serious decline. The median value of owner-occupied housing in the city has declined when compared to the rest of Jefferson Parish and the metropolitan area. The same is true in regards to rental property, where rental rates, which historically have stood at the same level as those in the overall region, are now drifting lower. There is no one single reason for Kenner's malaise. As in other areas of the country, suburban decline in Kenner has a multitude of causes, some of which had their origins during the boom days of several decades ago. In a detailed analysis of

Kenner's strengths and weaknesses prepared for the administration of Mayor Michael S. Yenni,[22] consultants and city planners determined that the city's lack of growth and stagnant property values are the consequence of Kenner's inability to attract a new generation of residents. Today's new younger generation of home buyers is typically focused more on quality-of-life issues than past generations. Among the issues needing to be addressed by the leaders and residents of Kenner are: a less-than-satisfactory system of public education, outdated zoning laws; the slow redevelopment of areas around Armstrong Airport; how to transform the city's developments at both Rivertown and Laketown into vibrant, mixed-used, pedestrian-friendly areas with offerings designed to attract young home owners; an upgrade of the city's major retail center located at and around the Esplanade Mall; and both aesthetic and engineering improvements for the city's major thoroughfares.[23]

Finally, the mayor's study found what every citizen and visitor to Kenner for decades has known: there is a need to redevelop and modernize the traffic flow and aesthetic character of the city's major commercial corridors. Largely laid out and constructed during the boom periods of decades ago when the goal of developers was expansion and financial profits—not aesthetics—the older thoroughfares, including Airline Drive, Veterans Boulevard, and, perhaps worst of all, Williams Boulevard, are all characterized by design and aesthetic shortcomings that deter newcomers from wanting to make Kenner their home. Nearly all of Kenner's major roadways provide horrible lasting impressions to residents, visitors, and investors. Scant landscaping; tangled power lines; ugly and oversized signage; cheaply constructed, architecturally void box-shaped buildings; long traffic delays; and poor signal-light coordination, make any trip down Kenner's corridors an affront to aesthetic taste and comfort of most individuals. According to the city's planning study of the problem, the current status of the community's thoroughfares places the city "at a tremendous competitive disadvantage in appealing to outside residents and businesses."[24]

Fortunately, the decline in population, stagnant economic growth, and stigma of suburban decline that currently undermines Kenner's potential is not necessarily a predictor of the city's future. The same study that identified the list of negatives which have contributed to the city's decline also recognized that Kenner continues to possess

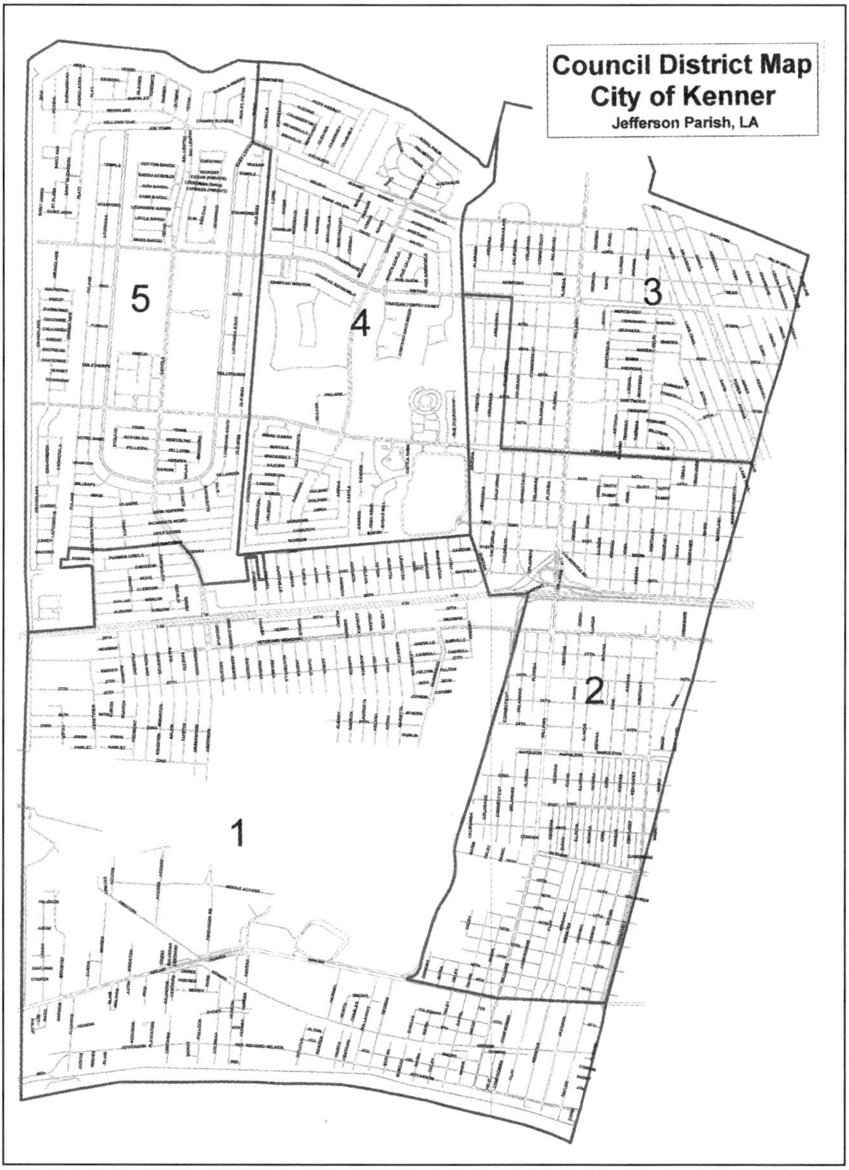

Street and council districts map of modern Kenner

an array of strengths and opportunities that can be used to build a new and better Kenner. Among the strengths found in the city that can be used in the future to create a modern and attractive community include the continued location of the region's main airport within its boundaries; a wealthier population than other communities in the region; an attractive and affordable housing stock of properties and an abundance of quality and well-maintained neighborhoods; ample recreational amenities and opportunities; a convenient location that allows for reasonable commutes; an effective system of public safety; a lower unemployment and poverty rate than its neighbors; a higher percentage of residents with college degrees than its neighbors; and a racially and ethnically diverse population today of 61 percent white, 24 percent African American, 11 percent Hispanic, and 4 percent Asian.[25]

As in its historic past when the people of Kenner joined together to create a village government to accommodate the demands of the railroad in order to get a community depot or when the community accepted the placement of a major airport within its boundaries, or when after World War II the community opened its vacant lands and welcomed widespread and rapid development of its vast open spaces, the community has been faced in the past with making hard, challenging choices that changed the future of Kenner. Today the city is again at a crossroads that could determine its future for decades to come. The boom times of the past few decades when rapid expansion of housing and new neighborhoods drove the economics and identity of Kenner are now over. In spite of its many attributes and for whatever reasons, Kenner's reputation has declined, and it no longer enjoys a favorable impression among people throughout the region. The slow but continued pattern of decline of the past few years has brought Kenner to the current situation where the people and leaders of the community must decide what they want for the future of their community. Suburban areas around the country facing similar declines in their fortunes as Kenner is currently facing have successfully reversed the trend of decline and disinvestment. However, to bring about the needed change in fortune will require prompt forceful action by both city fathers and residents. As noted in the strategic planning study on Kenner's future, the key to reversing suburban decline is "overcoming an aging housing stock, aging commercial corridors, and aging infrastructure to attract a new generation of residents and businesses."[26] Kenner's future does not have to be one of continued decline. This once "untractable country" has grown, matured, and prospered beyond the wildest dreams of those first Europeans to visit the area and even far beyond the hopes and visions of the members of the Kenner family who first foresaw a residential community at the site of modern Kenner. If this amazing journey of growth and prosperity that has been such an important part of Kenner's past is to be the story of its future, the people and community leaders of today's Kenner must make it so.[27]

Appendix:
Mayors of Modern Kenner

Mayor	Term
Paul Felix	1905-1908
Antoine Wattigny	1913-1916
Paul Felix	1916-1920
George Thompson	1920-1921
August Cristina	1921-1922
Angelo Maggiore	1922-1924
Emile Deshautreaux	1924-1928
Anthony Centanni	1928-1930
Victor D'Gerolamo	1930-1942
Dr. Joseph S. Kopfler (died in office)	1942-1957
Mrs. Joseph S. Kopfler (filled husband's term)	1957-1958
Joseph S. Maggiore	1958-1962
Edward J. D'Gerolamo	1962-1970
Joseph S. Yenni	1970- 1980
Larry Hooper	1980-1982
Aaron Broussard	1982-1996
Terry McCarthy (acting mayor)	1996
Louis Congemi	1996-2003
Dominic Weilbacher (acting mayor)	2004
Phil Capitano	2004-2006
Ed Muniz	2006-2010
Mike Yenni	2010-Jan. 2016
Mike Sigur (acting mayor)	Jan. to Nov. 2016

Notes

CHAPTER 1

1. Henry C. Bezou, *Metairie: A Tongue of Land* (Gretna, La.: Pelican Publishing Company, 1973), 4.

2. Fred B. Kniffen, Hiram F. Gregory, George A. Stokes, *Tribes of Louisiana: From 1542 to the Present* (Baton Rouge: Louisiana State University Press, 1987), 28.

3. Ibid., 30; Tristram R. Kidder, "Making the City Inevitable: Native Americans and the Geography of New Orleans" in *Transforming New Orleans and Its Environs: Centuries of Change*, ed. Craig E. Carlton, (Pittsburgh: University of Pittsburgh Press, 2000), 12; Bennet H. Wall, Judith Kelleher Schafer, Edward F. Haas, and Michael L. Kurtz, *Louisiana: A History*, 4th ed. (Wheeling, Ill.: Harlan Davidson, Inc., 2002), 6.

4. Richard Campanella, *Bienville's Dilemma: A Historical Geography of New Orleans* (Lafayette: Center for Louisiana Studies, University of Louisiana at Lafayette, 2008), 77-78.

5. Betsy Swanson, *Historic Jefferson Parish: From Shore to Shore* (Gretna, La.: Pelican Publishing Company, 1975), 3; Peirce F. Lewis, *New Orleans: The Making of an Urban Landscape* (Cambridge: Ballinger Publishing Company, 1976), 21-22; Bezou, *Metairie*, 3-4.

6. Bezou, *Metairie*, 5; Swanson, *Historic Jefferson Parish*, 38; Pierre de Charlevoix, *Journal of a Voyage to North-America*, vol. 2 (London: R. And J. Dodsley, 1861; Ann Arbor, Mich.: University Microfilms, Inc., 1966), 286.

7. In some translations, the last part of the passage reads "they remove the bones and bury the flesh." See Swanson, *Historic Jefferson Parish*, 39.

8. The French term for Canadian geese.

9. Probably snow or blue geese.

10. Richebourg Gaillard McWilliams, ed. and trans., *Fleur de Lys and Calumet: Being the Penicaut Narrative of French Adventure in Louisiana* (Tuscaloosa: The University of Alabama Press, 1981), 110-12.

11. Kidder, "Making the City Inevitable," 19-20; Craig A. Bauer, "From Burnt Canes to Budding City: A History of the City of Kenner, Louisiana," *Louisiana History* 33 (Fall 1982): 353-54; Edna Freiberg, *Bayou St. John in Colonial Louisiana: 1699-1803* (New Orleans: Harvey Press, 1980), 24, 348.

12. There is no evidence that the community of the same name obtained it from the notary. See Bezou, *Metairie*, 4.

13. Quoted in Bezou, *Metairie*, 5. For a slightly different edition and translation of the passage see William J. Foster, ed., *The La Salle Expedition on the Mississippi: A Lost Manuscript of Nicolas de La Salle, 1682*, trans. Johanna L. Warren (Austin: Texas State Historical Association, 2003), 134.

14. The term league is an ancient form of linear measurement. The French in Iberville's time considered a marine league to be approximately three miles in length; whereas, a land league was approximately 20 percent shorter than the marine measurement.

15. Carl A. Brasseaux, ed. and trans., *A Comparative View of French Louisiana, 1699 and 1762: The Journals of Pierre Le Moyne d'Iberville and Jean-Jacques-Blaise d'Abbadie* (Lafayette: Center for Louisiana Studies, University of Southwestern Louisiana, 1979: revised ed., 1981), 44.

16. There are some who believe that instead the waterway was possibly the extinct "Tiguayn River." See Kidder, "Making the City Inevitable,"18-19; and Bezou, *Metairie*, 8.

17. McWilliams, *Fleur de Lys and Calumet*, 14-15.

18. Ibid., 14.

19. Quoted by Bezou, *Metairie*, 8.

20. Ibid., 8-10.

21. Ibid., 16-17; Bauer, "From Burnt Canes to Budding City," 354-55; Edwin Adams Davis, *Louisiana: A Narrative History* (Nashville: Bensen Printing Co., 1965), 53.

22. Roger Baudier, *The Catholic Church in Louisiana* (New Orleans: Roger Baudier, 1939), 43; Craig A. Bauer, "The History of the City of Kenner, Louisiana" (master's thesis, Southeastern Louisiana University, 1973), 3; Charles Gayarre, *History of Louisiana: The French Domination,* 2nd ed. (New York: William J. Widdleton, Publisher, 1867), 241.

23. The arpent was an French measurement of land which varied somewhat from locality to locality. Usually lineal, it typically measured .84 to 1.28 acres and referred to the length of one side of a square.

24. Bezou, *Metairie*, 20-21; McWilliams, *Fleur de Lys and Calumet*, 242; Charlevoix, *Journal of a Voyage to North-America,* vol. 2, 286; Helmut Blume, *The German Coast During the Colonial Era 1722-1803*, ed. and trans. Ellen C. Merrill (Destrehan, La.: The German-Acadian Coast Historical and Genealogical Society, 1990), 35.

25. There were actually three d'Artaguiette brothers involved in the French colonial experience in Louisiana. Martin was joined in his colonial venture by both his

younger brother Bernard Diron and a third brother Pierre d'Itouralde, who assisted Diron at the d'Artaguiette concession at Baton Rouge. McWilliams, *Fleur de Lys and Calumet*, 121; Henry C. Bezou, "Jefferson Parish's Gallic Roots," *Jefferson History Notebook* 1 (December 1979), 2.

26. This reference is almost certainly to Martin d'Artaguiette and not his younger brother Bernard Diron, who in addition to working the Cannes Brûlées concession also possessed a concession of his own and is considered to be the first European settler at today's Baton Rouge. See Bezou, "Jefferson Parish's Gallic Roots," 3.

27. Quoted by Bezou, "Jefferson Parish's Gallic Roots,"1.

28. Bezou, *Metairie*, 21; McWilliams, *Fleur de Lys and Calumet*, 243; Bezou, "Jefferson Parish's Gallic Roots," 2; Blume, *The German Coast*, 35.

29. Blume, *The German Coast*, 35.

30. Ibid., 32-33.

31. Rene Le Conte and Glenn R. Conrad, trans., "The Germans in Louisiana in the Eighteenth Century," *Louisiana History* 8 (Winter 1967): 81; Glenn R. Conrad, *The First Families of Louisiana* (Baton Rouge: Claitor's Publishing Division, 1970), ii.

32. Charlevoix, *Journal of a Voyage to North-America*, vol. 2, 286.

33. Ibid.; Baudier, *The Catholic Church in Louisiana*, 43-46;

34. Baudier, *The Catholic Church in Louisiana*, 117-18; Bezou, *Metairie*, 28, 30, 56.

35. Quoted by Bezou, *Metairie*, 58-59.

36. Kidder, "Making the City Inevitable," 13.

37. Quoted by Swanson, *Historic Jefferson Parish*, 37-38.

38. Francois Xavier Martin, *The History of Louisiana: From the Earliest Period* (Gretna, La.: Pelican Publishing Company, 1975), 162; Lawrence N. Powell, *The Accidental City: Improvising New Orleans* (Cambridge: Harvard University Press, 2012), 84-85.

39. Lillian C. Bourgeois, *Cabanocey: The History, Customs and Folklore of St. James Parish* (New Orleans: Pelican Publishing Company, 1957), 7-9.

40. Edna F. Campbell, "New Orleans in Early Days," *Geographical Review* 10 (July 1920): 32; Martin, *The History of Louisiana*, 168; N. M. Surrey, "The Development of Industries in Louisiana During the French Regime 1673-1763," *The Mississippi Valley Historical Review* 9 (December 1922): 229-30; John Hebron Moore, "The Cypress Lumber Industry of the Lower Mississippi Valley during the Colonial Period," *Louisiana History* 24 (Winter 1983): 27; Bezou, *Metairie*, 39.

41. Quoted in U.S. Army Corps of Engineers, *Cultural Resource Survey and Testing of the East Jefferson Parish Levee Gap Closure, Jefferson Parish, Louisiana*, Report No. Coelmn/PD-92/0Z (April 1992), 16-21.

42. Surrey, "The Development of Industries," 230-31; Campbell, "New Orleans in Early Days," 34.

43. The overgrazing by cattle of the cane during the early years of the colony led to a weakening of the natural levees where the cane grew most abundantly and helped to hold the soil of the river banks together.

44. Campbell, "New Orleans in Early Days," 33; Christopher Morris, "Impenetrable but Easy" in *Transforming New Orleans and Its Environs: Centuries of Change*, ed. Craig E. Carlton (Pittsburgh: University of Pittsburgh Press, 2000), 28, 31; Blume, *The German Coast*, 35.

45. Quoted by Christopher Morris, "Impenetrable but Easy," 32.

46. Powell, *Accidental City*, 42-45, 50, 93, and 127.

47. Ibid., 29.

48. Ibid., 29-30; Campbell, "New Orleans in Early Days," 33.

49. The problem with growing tobacco at Cannes Brûlées and other areas along the river near New Orleans was the crop's lack of tolerance to the occasional flooding that beset the settlement during high-water periods of the Mississippi River. Blume, *The German Coast*, 14.

50. Surrey, "The Development of Industries," 232-33; Campbell, "New Orleans in Early Days," 34; Bauer, "The History of the City of Kenner, Louisiana," 8.

51. Surrey, "The Development of Industries," 234; Campbell, "New Orleans in Early Days," 33; Edwin Adams Davis, *Louisiana: A Narrative History* (Nashville: Bensen Printing Co., 1965), 73.

52. Campbell, "New Orleans in Early Days," 33-34; Bauer, "The History of the City of Kenner, Louisiana," 9; Glenn R. Conrad and Ray F. Lucas, *White Gold: A Brief History of the Louisiana Sugar Industry 1795-1995* (Lafayette: Center for Louisiana Studies, 1995), 3.

53. Moore, "The Cypress Lumber Industry," 28; Percy Viosco Jr., "Bayoulands of Jefferson," *Jefferson Parish Yearly Review* (1943): 50.

54. Campbell, "New Orleans in Early Days," 35; Blume, *The German Coast*, 9.

CHAPTER 2

1. Thomas N. Ingersoll, *Mammon and Manon in Early New Orleans: The First Slave Society in the Deep South, 1718-1819* (Knoxville: University of Tennessee Press, 1999), 28.

2. The practice of pulling vessels upriver with ropes was known by the settlers as lining or cordelling. N. M. Miller Surrey, "The Commerce of Louisiana During the French Regime, 1699-1763" (Ph.D. dissertation, Columbia University, 1916), 57, 67; E. S. Pennebaker, "Transportation in Jefferson," *Jefferson Parish Yearly Review* (1960): 56; Fred B. Kniffen, *Louisiana: Its Land and People* (Baton Rouge: Louisiana State University Press, 1968), 125-26; Lyle Saxon, *Father Mississippi* (New York: The Century Co., 1927), 243.
3. Bauer, "The History of the City of Kenner, Louisiana," 72; Davis, *Louisiana: A Narrative History*, 85; Surrey, "The Commerce of Louisiana During the French Regime, 1699-1763," 92, 96; Bezou, *Metairie*, 37; Mary Ann Sternberg, *Along the River Road: Past and Present on Louisiana's Historic Byway* (Baton Rouge: Louisiana State University Press, 2001), 43-44.
4. Years later when Louisiana became a territory of the United States, the Territorial Legislature established a fifty-foot right-of-way along the southern bank of the bayou from Bayou St. John to Cannes Brûlées to expand the roadway. This action made the Chemin des Chapitoulas an official roadway and remains today the highly used Metairie Road, making it the oldest continuous in use roadway in the state. Swanson, *Historic Jefferson Parish*, 127; Bezou, *Metairie*, 60; Campanella, *Bienville's Dilemma*, 203-204.
5. Lewis, *New Orleans: The Making of an Urban Landscape*, 34; Davis, *Louisiana*, 85.
6. Davis, *Louisiana*, 86.
7. Ibid.; Swanson, *Historic Jefferson Parish*, 67.
8. Though no first name was listed, the Meuillon noted was probably Louis-Augustin Meuillon, a planter and property owner who resided in neighboring St. Charles Parish.
9. The Bell Grove Plantation at Kenner should not be confused with the grander house of the same name which was located near White Castle, Louisiana. The house in Kenner remained in existence until it was destroyed by fire early in the morning of March 19, 1870. *Daily Picayune*, March 19, 1870; Swanson, *Historic Jefferson Parish*, 73-74; U.S. Army Corps of Engineers, *Cultural Resource Survey*; U.S. Congress, *Journal of the Senate of the United States*, Vol. 21, *List of Acts and Resolutions Passed at the First Session of the Twenty-Second Congress*, 533-34; Fred Daspit, *Louisiana Architecture 1714-1830* (Lafayette: Center for Louisiana Studies, University of Southwestern Louisiana, 1996), 215-16.
10. Little else is known of William Kenner's early life in Virginia. Throughout his life, William never spoke of his relatives and family roots in his home state. Inquiries by his children only received the response that he was "born in Staunton a month before the Declaration was signed." This suggests that his migration from Virginia may not have been on pleasant terms. However, his quick acquisition of

wealth and acceptance by the political and social elite in Natchez suggest that his departure from Virginia was possibly a result of errant family feelings instead of any questionable or illegal activities. Genealogists and other researchers have for years attempted to determine the background to William's Virginia roots. The most plausible link to his heritage is that William was the son of Sarah Kenner (later Carter). Sarah was a landowner of a sizeable 1791 Spanish land claim of five hundred acres in Adams County, Mississippi near Natchez, where William lived. This proximity raises the possibility that she was a relative, perhaps his mother or even a sister. The likelihood of a relationship between William and Sarah increases when one takes into consideration that young Kenner was able to gain the hand in marriage of the daughter of the high-ranking and respected Spanish official, Stephen Minor. The Minors had migrated to the Adams County region from Monogahela County in Virginia. Now in West Virginia, the area was once part of Augusta County in Virginia—the home county of the city of Staunton, where William claimed he was born. Hence, since both the Minors and Kenners were from the same general region in Virginia, it is plausible that they had some kind of relationship prior to their move to Mississippi. If Sarah was indeed William's mother, tracing her back to Virginia could reveal William's father. Unfortunately, the lack of records makes this task impossible. However, in a privately printed genealogical study titled *Houston and Allied Families* compiled by Thomas H. Bateman, the author of the work contends that a review of period documents show that "the only Kenner found in Virginia at the proper time with a wife Sarah, was Rodham [Kenner]." Rodham married Sarah (surname unknown) on May 28, 1773. It is to this marriage that William is thought to have been born on June 4, 1776.

Finally, it must be observed that in spite of the plausibility of a relationship between Sarah Kenner Carter and William Kenner questions concerning William's heritage remain. For example, if Sarah Kenner Carter was William's mother, it seems likely that Stephen Minor, Spanish official and father of William's bride, would have had some knowledge of the relationship. It also is likely that either Stephen Minor or some other member of the Minor family would have at some time shared this information with William Kenner's children so that after his death, they would have had more knowledge of their heritage than their father's simple statement that he was from Staunton, Virginia. See Thomas H. Bateman, *Houston and Allied Families* (New York: privately printed for Samuel Frederic Houston by the American Historical Company, Inc., 1950), 93-94; Craig A. Bauer, *A Leader Among Peers: The Life and Times of Duncan Farrar Kenner* (Lafayette: Center for Louisiana Studies, University of Southwestern Louisiana, 1993), 3, 292; Philip Chadwick Foster Smith and G. Gouverneur Meredith S. Smith, *Cane, Cotton, & Crevasses: Some Antebellum Louisiana and Mississippi Plantations of the Minor, Kenner, Hooke, and Shepherd Families* (Bath, Maine: The Renfrew Group, 1992), 22-23; The Natchez Court Records, 1767-1805,

Ancestry.com, available from http://search.ancestry.com/browse/bookvew.aspx-?dbid'48049&iid 'NatchezCourtRec-00 (accessed April 12, 2012).

11. Bauer, *A Leader Among Peers*, 4-6.

12. Ibid., 6; Smith, *Cane, Cotton, & Crevasses*, 23.

13. Bauer, *A Leader Among Peers*, 6.

14. Clement Eaton, *A History of the Old South* (London: The Macmillan Company, 1966), 297; Bauer, *A Leader Among Peers*, 7; Dunbar Rowland, compiler and editor, *The Mississippi Territorial Archives 1798-1803: Executive Journals of Governor Winthrop Sargent and Governor William Charles Cole Claiborne* (Nashville: Brandon Printing Company, 1905), 175.

15. Though it was common for southern women to marry at a young age, marriage at age fourteen was somewhat unusual. Historian Catherine Clinton's study of women in the Old South found that the median age of marriage for women (based upon a sample of planters born between 1765 and 1815) was twenty, and twenty-eight for men. Only .5 percent of southern females in Clinton's study married at Mary's young age of fourteen. See Catherine Clinton, *The Plantation Mistress: Women's World in the Old South* (New York: Pantheon Books, 1982), 60, 233; Bauer, *A Leader Among Peers*, 8; John G. Clark, *New Orleans 1718-1812: An Economic History* (Baton Rouge: Louisiana State University Press, 1970), 351; Smith, *Cane, Cotton, & Crevasses*, 23.

16. Bauer, *A Leader Among Peers*, 9.

17. Ibid.; Smith, *Cane, Cotton, & Crevasses*, 24; Clark, *New Orleans 1718-1812*, 272-74, 303, 306-307; *Louisiana Gazette*, June 5, 1810; *Orleans Gazette*, June 5, 1810; *Le Courrier de la Louisiane*, January 11, 1811, at LOUISdigital Library; Kenner and Henderson, New Orleans to Colonel Sam Fulton, December 31, 1808, at LOUISdigital Library; *Orleans Gazette*, August 4, 1819; Thomas Curry, *Reports of Cases Argued and Determined in the Supreme Court of the State of Louisiana,* vol. 19 (New Orleans: E. Johns & Co., 1842), 155-60.

18. William Kenner to Stephen Minor, June 20, 1812, William Kenner Papers, Special Collections, Hill Memorial Library, Louisiana State University, Baton Rouge, Louisiana.

19. Quoted in U.S. Army Corps of Engineers, *Cultural Resource Survey*, 19.

20. Charles Vincent, "'Of Such Historical Importance . . .': The African American Experience in Louisiana," *Louisiana History* 50 (Spring 2009): 139; *Orleans Gazette*, July 5, 1806; Charles H. Wesley, "Manifests of Slave Shipments Along the Waterways, 1808-1864," *The Journal of Negro History* 27(April 1942): 161; Clark, *New Orleans 1718-1812*, 318; Ulrich Bonnell Phillips, *American Negro Slavery: A Survey of the Supply, Employment and Control of Negro Labor as Determined by the Plantation Regime* (New York: Appleton and Company, 1918), 196-97.

21. Clark, *New Orleans 1718-1812*, 341, 344, 348; *Times-Picayune*, April 3, 1921; Bauer, *A Leader Among Peers*, 15; Smith, *Cane, Cotton, & Crevasses*, 24; Lawrence N. Powell, *The Accidental City: Improvising New Orleans* (Cambridge: Harvard University Press, 2012), 206.

22. Bauer, *A Leader Among Peers*, 14-15.

23. Quoted by Ory G. Poret, "History of land Titles in the State of Louisiana," 1972, State Land Office, Division of Administration, State of Louisiana, Baton Rouge, Louisiana, 26.

24. Quoted by Bauer, *A Leader Among Peers*, 13.

25. Ibid.

26. Ibid., 14.

27. Ibid., 16; Clark, *New Orleans 1718-1812*; Smith, *Cane, Cotton, & Crevasse*, 36.

28. U.S. Army Corps of Engineers, *Cultural Resource Survey*, 21; Jefferson Parish Court House, Gretna, Louisiana, Succession of William and Mary Minor, his wife, 1826; Smith, *Cane, Cotton, & Crevasses*, 25; Clark, *New Orleans 1718-1812*, 344; *The Times-Democrat* (New Orleans), October 23, 1892; *Louisiana Gazette*, September 5, 1810.

29. Bauer, *A Leader Among Peers*, 15; Conrad and Lucas, *White Gold*, 5-6.

30. Smith, *Cane, Cotton, & Crevasses*, 25, 34; Dan'l Dennett, *Louisiana As it Is* (New Orleans: Eureka Press, 1876), 270; U.S. Army Corps of Engineers, *Cultural Resource Survey*, 20-21; Bauer, *A Leader Among Peers*, 15-16.

31. William Kenner to Stephen Minor, May 10, 1813, William Kenner Papers, Special Collections, Hill Memorial Library, Louisiana State University, Baton Rouge, Louisiana.

32. Bauer, *A Leader Among Peers*, 16; Succession of William and Mary Minor, his wife, 1826, Jefferson Parish Court House, Gretna, Louisiana.

33. Succession of William and Mary Minor, his wife, 1826; Bauer, *A Leader Among Peers*, 17, 25; Smith, *Cane, Cotton, & Crevasses*, 25-26.

34. Bauer, *A Leader Among Peers*, 17.

35. Ibid., 18.

36. Craig A. Bauer and Mark LaFlaur, "Duncan F. Kenner," *Dictionary of American National Biography* (New York: Oxford Press, 2002); Craig A. Bauer, "The Last Effort: The Secret Mission of the Confederate Diplomat, Duncan F. Kenner," *Louisiana History* 22 (Winter 1981): 67-95.

37. Bauer, *A Leader Among Peers*, 17.

38. Campanella, *Bienville's Dilemma*, 309; John M. Barry, *Rising Tide: The Great Mississippi Flood of 1927 and How It Changed America* (New York: Simon &

Schuster Paperbacks, 1997), 40.

39. William D. Reeves, *De La Barre: Life of a Creole Family in Louisiana* (New Orleans: Polyanthos, 1980), 80-81

40. The exact number of participants remains unknown. Documentary evidence at the time produced evidence against 124 individuals, whereas, eyewitness accounts estimated the number of slave participants to have been between 200 and 500. Most historians put the numbers between 200 and 300 participants. See Daniel Rasmussen, *American Uprising: The Untold Story of America's Largest Slave Revolt* (New York: Harper Collins Publishers, 2011), 128; Glenn R. Conrad, *The German Coast: Abstracts of the Civil Records of St. Charles and St. John the Baptist Parishes 1804-1812* (Lafayette: Center for Louisiana Studies, 1981), 107.

41. At the time of the event, the property at Cannes Brûlées still belonged to the Kenner and Henderson partnership. The establishment of William's Oakland Plantation would take place later in 1811. Henderson went on to focus his efforts on his ownership of the large Destrehan Plantation located a short distance up river from the Cannes Brûlées property.

42. Nathan A. Buman, "To Kill Whites: The 1811 Louisiana Slave Insurrection" (master's thesis, Louisiana State University, 2008), 73; James H. Dorman, "The Persistent Specter: Slave Rebellion in Territorial Louisiana," *Louisiana History* 18 (Autumn 1977): 394-99; Henry E. Yoes III, *Louisiana's German Coast: A History of St. Charles Parish* (Lake Charles, La.: Racing Pigeon Digest Company, Inc., 2005), 85-89; Adam Rothman, *Slave Country: American Expansion and the Origins of the Deep South* (Cambridge: Harvard University Press, 2005), 111-12; Rasmussen, *American Uprising*, 95, 126-37.

43. Quoted by Rasmussen, *American Uprising*, 127.

44. There remain some discrepancies in the records of the identities of the Kenner and Henderson slaves who died as a result of the revolt. A St. Charles Parish court record dated March 7, 1811, lists the names and ages of Kenner and Henderson slaves lost in the uprising, including the executed individuals: Joseph (28), Harry (25), Lindor (28), Charles (25), Noutoun (22), and Smillet (28). Jerry (30), Major (18), and Elisha (28) were "shot by the militia on the plantation to which they belonged," with Jerry and Major being "shot accidentally." Peter (24) was said to have been killed "by the brigands at Cabaret's place," with Croaker (22) being killed in the fighting between the militia and slaves. Conrad, *The German Coast*; 108; Rasmussen, *American Uprising*, 127; Albert Thrasher, *"On to New Orleans:" Louisiana's Heroic 1811 Slave Revolt*, 2nd ed. (New Orleans: Albert Thrasher, 1996), 62, 64-65.

45. Andry, after narrowly escaping death when the slave rebellion started at his estate, crossed the Mississippi River and organized a force of well-armed volunteers who again crossed the river to join in the attack against the rebel force.

46. The quote was by Manuel Andry who had escaped the early stages of the rebellion on his plantation to give warning of the revolt and to organize a counterattack by volunteers and militiamen. Quoted by Rothman, *Slave Country*, 113.

47. The exact number of Kenner and Henderson participants in the revolt remains somewhat uncertain. Different names and spelling of names of slaves attributed to Kenner and Henderson appear on different lists prepared at the time. The official list promulgated on March 5, 1811, and signed by Judge P.B. St. Martin lists the names of eleven slaves owned by Kenner and Henderson killed in the rebellion. However, as noted in the text, current historiography on the revolt identifies by name twelve different members of the Kenner and Henderson slave force as active members in the revolt. Rothman, *Slave Country*, 111-12, 114-15; Thrasher, *"On to New Orleans,"* 62, 64-65, 216, 219; Nathan A. Buman, "Historiographical Examinations of the 1811 Slave Insurrection," *Louisiana History* 53 (Summer 2012): 328; Conrad, *The German Coast*, 101-102; Powell, *The Accidental City*, 344-45.

48. Quoted by Rothman, *Slave Country*, 114.

49. Ibid., 114-15.

50. Dorman, "The Persistent Specter"; Yoes, *Louisiana's German Coast*, 86-87; Thrasher, *"On to New Orleans,"* iii, 62, 65, 216, 219; Rasmussen, *American Uprising*, 87,127.

51. Although the disturbance and loss of slaves resulting from the ill-fated rebellion caused Kenner and his planter neighbors considerable financial costs, matters could have been much worse. For in spite of the armed nature of the slave force, it appears from the lack of reports of damage that relatively little damage was done to the Kenner and Henderson property at Cannes Brûlées. Though the event has been re-examined multiple times by historians, no clear explanation has yet evolved to explain why the rebels, who were supposedly determined to use force in their effort to get to New Orleans, left several large plantation homes and support buildings filled with valuables undamaged, including the Destrehan plantation house.

52. Quoted in Davis, *Louisiana*, 5; Smith, *Cane, Cotton, & Crevasses*, 25.

53. William Kenner to Stephen Minor, June 19, 1814, William Kenner Papers; R. Claque to Stephen Minor, October 7, 1814, Kenner Family Papers, Special Collections, Hill Memorial Library, Baton Rouge, Louisiana; Bauer, *A Leader Among Peers*, 19; Trist Wood notes (typescript page B-III-1a), Bringier and Related Families Papers, Williams Research Center, The Historic New Orleans Collection, New Orleans, Louisiana.

54. Bauer, *A Leader Among Peers*, 20-23; Smith, *Cane, Cotton, & Crevasses*, 27.

55. William Kenner to John Minor, December 1, 1819, William Kenner Papers, Special Collections, Hill Memorial Library, Louisiana State University, Baton

Rouge, Louisiana.

56. Papers at the time and subsequent published materials about Oldham's actions often claim that he "absconded" with the company's resources. However, as he remained an active partner in the business until it was dissolved over two years after William's death, it appears that his actions were merely bad business decisions and not an illegal absconding of the company's resources. See *Louisiana State Gazette*, June 5, 1826 for the company's dissolution announcement with Claque and Oldham listed as partners and the *Louisiana Advertiser*, December 2, 1826.

57. Bauer, *A Leader Among Peers*, 25; *Louisiana Advertiser*, December 2, 1826, and November 3, 1827.

58. *Louisiana State Gazette*, June 12, 1826; Bauer, *A Leader Among Peers*, 26.

59. Ibid.; Smith, *Cane, Cotton, & Crevasses,* 26-27; *Baltimore Patriot*, June 3, 1824.

CHAPTER 3

1. Smith, *Cane, Cotton, & Crevasses,* 27; Bauer, *A Leader Among Peers*, 28; *Louisiana State Gazette*, June 12, 1826; Stanley C. Arthur and George C. Huchet de Kernion, *Old Families of Louisiana* (1931; repr., Baton Rouge: Claitor's Publishing Division, 1971), 158.

2. Last Will and Testament of William Kenner, July 23, 1823, Will Book Number 4, New Orleans Public Library, New Orleans.

3. Succession of William Kenner and Mary Minor, his wife, 1826; *Louisiana Advertiser*, March 1, 1827; Smith, *Cane, Cotton, & Crevasses,* 27.

4. Smith, *Cane, Cotton, & Crevasses,* 27; Bauer, *A Leader Among Peers*, 32-34.

5. Their younger brother Duncan having sold his share of the property to them in 1832. Swanson, *Historic Jefferson Parish*, 108.

6. U.S. Army Corps of Engineers, *Cultural Resource Survey*, 22; Swanson, *Historic Jefferson Parish*, 108.

7. In later years, Minor acquired almost forty-one acres in the resort community of Beersheba, Tennessee. By 1858, he had constructed on the site a large house with a steep roof and pointed gables. Equipped with servant quarters, the property offered a grand view of the Tarlton Valley and contained a fine spring for recreation. Minor and his family used the property as their summer vacation home. They continued to visit the property until the outbreak of the Civil War, during which the house was ransacked and in 1865 was lost in a sheriff's sale. Margaret Brown Coppinger, Herschel Gower, Samuel H. Howell, Georgianna D. Overby, *Beersheba Springs: 150 Years 1833-1983: A History of a Celebration* (Beersheba, Tenn.: Beersheba Springs Historical Society, 1983), 110.

8. Minor Kenner's plantation at Cannes Brûlées should not be confused with the more famous Bell Grove Plantation located on Bayou Lafourche. The plantation was located approximately at the spot where today's Williams Boulevard and Jefferson Highway intersect. Belle Grove was operated by William Davis until his death in 1819. Two years after his passing, his widow Maria married John R. Holliday, who managed the property until his death in 1827. Though heavily mortgaged by Holliday, the plantation grew to include a slave force of seventy-eight workers. U.S. Congress, Senate, *A Bill Confirming the Claim of Maria Holliday to a Tract of Land in Louisiana*, S. 46, 22nd Cong., 1st sess., January 5, 1832, 1; Curry, *Reports of Cases Argued*, 155-56.

9. U.S. Congress, *A Bill Confirming the Claim of Maria Holliday*, January 5, 1832, 1; Curry, *Reports of Cases Argued*, 155-156; Swanson, *Historic Jefferson Parish*, 108; Bauer, "From Burnt Canes to Budding City," 361.

10. Conrad and Lucas, *White Gold*, 12; Bauer, *A Leader Among Peers*, 48; J. Carlyle Sitterson, *Sugar Country: The Cane Sugar Industry in the South, 1753-1950* (Lexington: University of Kentucky Press, 1953), 60-61.

11. Smith, *Cane, Cotton, & Crevasses,* 28; Richard Follett, *Documenting Louisiana Sugar 1845-1917* (Sussex, England: University of Sussex, 2008), database online at www.sussex.ac.uk/louisiana/index.php; Conrad and Lucas, *White Gold*, 27; Bauer, "The History of the City of Kenner, Louisiana," 15.

12. *Daily Picayune*, February 26, 1851; Follett, *Documenting Louisiana Sugar 1845-1917*.

13. *The Davenport Gazette*, July 5, 1849.

14. Swanson, *Historic Jefferson Parish*, 91; Richard Campanella, *Geographies of New Orleans: Urban Fabrics Before the Storm* (Lafayette: Center for Louisiana Studies, 2006), 82.

15. Quoted in Mel Leavitt, *Kenner: An Historical Sketch by Mel Levitt* (Kenner, Louisiana: by the Merchants Trust and Savings Bank, no date), np.

16. Smith, *Cane, Cotton, & Crevasses,* 28-29; Follett, *Documenting Louisiana Sugar 1845-1917.*

17. The Louisiana legislature had officially created Jefferson Parish on February 11, 1825. The area was carved out of Orleans Parish.

18. Roger W. Shugg, *Origins of Class Struggle in Louisiana: A Social History of White Farmers and Laborers During and After, 1840-1875,* paperback ed. (Baton Rouge: Louisiana State University Press, 1967), 155; Historical Records Survey, *Transcription of Parish Records of Louisiana; Number 26, Jefferson Parish (Gretna), Series I, Police Jury Minutes* (Baton Rouge, 1939-1941), June 8, 1835 and February 6, 1838. Hereinafter cited as Jefferson Parish Police Jury Minutes; Charles S. Sydnor, "The Development of Southern Sectionalism, 1819-1848," in *A History of the South,* vol. 5, ed. Wendell Holmes Stephenson and E. Merton

Coulter (Baton Rouge: Louisiana State University Press and the Littlefield Fund for Southern History at the University of Texas, 1948), 34-35, 39.

19. Smith, *Cane, Cotton, & Crevasses,* 28; *Old Families of Louisiana*, 159.

20. Smith, *Cane, Cotton, & Crevasses*, 29; Bauer, "The History of the City of Kenner, Louisiana," 18.

21. Joan B. Garvey and Mary Lou Widmer, *Beautiful Crescent: A History of New Orleans,* 7th ed. (New Orleans: Garmer Press, Inc., 1994), 110-11; Davis, *Louisiana*, 235; Smith, *Cane, Cotton, & Crevasses,* 29; *Daily Picayune*, September 11, 1853.

22. Smith, *Cane, Cotton, & Crevasses,* 29-31.

23. United States of America, Bureau of the Census, *Eighth Census of the United States, 1860,* Washington, D.C.: National Archives and Records Administration, 1860.

24. Merl E. Reed, "Government Investment and Economic Growth: Louisiana's Ante Bellum Railroads," *The Journal of Southern History* 28 (May 1962): 186-87; George B. Davis, Leslie J. Perry, Joseph W. Kirkley, *The Official Military Atlas of the Civil War* (New York: Barnes & Noble Books, 2003), 220.

25. Quoted by U.S. Army Corps of Engineers, *Cultural Resource Survey*, 23; John G. Clark, "New Orleans and the River: A Study in Attitude and Responses," *Louisiana History* 8 (Spring 1967): 125; Pie Dufour, "A La Mode: 'Minor' Error on Kenner for it was Minor Kenner who Founded the Town," *New Orleans States*, March 4, 1955; Merl Reed, "Boom or Bust: Louisiana's Economy during the 1830's," *Louisiana History* 4 (Winter, 1963): 42; Merl E. Reed, *New Orleans and the Railroads: The Struggle for Commercial Empire 1830-1860* (Baton Rouge: Louisiana State University Press, 1966), 93; *Daily Picayune*, September 12, 1852.

26. E.S. Pennebaker, "Transportation in Jefferson," 79; *New York Times*, April 1, 1858.

27. Garvey and Widmer, *Beautiful Crescent*, 110-12; Davis, *Louisiana*, 235; Jo Ann Carrigan, "Yellow Fever in New Orleans, 1853: Abstractions and Realities," *Journal of Southern History* 25 (August 1959): 343; Bauer, "The History of the City of Kenner," 19-20.

28. Bauer, "The History of the City of Kenner," 19-20.

29. *The Times Democrat,* October 23, 1892; Bauer, "The History of the City of Kenner," 20-21; Swanson, *Historic Jefferson Parish*, 108; Copy of March 28th, 1855, map based on W.T. Thompson's plan titled "Important Sale of Lots, Squares & Tracts of Land in the Town of Kenner," provided to the author by Mr. J. P. Walker, Metairie, Louisiana.

30. Map titled "Important Sale of Lots, Squares & Tracts of Land in the Town of

Kenner," March 28, 1855.

31. Originally published in the *Daily Picayune*, June 11, 1854, the quotation cited is a paraphrased version of the original as published in Swanson, *Historic Jefferson Parish*, 108.

32. Ibid., 109; *The Times-Democrat*, October 23, 1892; Bauer, "The History of the City of Kenner," 21; *Daily True Delta*, January 1, 1861. A story persists in several modern accounts that the Coleman Foundry produced cannons and cannonballs during the Civil War. Since no reference to the foundry and any arms or weapons it was producing are mentioned in the many surviving war records and accounts written at the time, it is doubtful that the stories of weapons production at the facility are accurate.

33. *Daily Picayune*, November 26, 1858.

34. Reminisces of Judge James C. Baumann in James Connor Prescott Family Papers in the possession of J. Brown, Tucson, Arizona.

35. Ibid.

36. Ibid.

37. Mayor Joseph S. Kepfler Sr., "Kenner's Centennial Celebration Address," March 2, 1955, copy available at Jefferson Parish Library, Kenner, Louisiana.

CHAPTER 4

1. Abraham Lincoln was considered a radical and represented what the New Orleans *Crescent* called the "irrepressible conflict." So unpopular was his position that not a single vote was recorded for him in Louisiana. Perry H. Howard, *Political Tendencies in Louisiana: Revised and Expanded Edition* (Baton Rouge: Louisiana State University Press, 1971), 89, 443.

2. Ibid., 91; Davis, *Louisiana*, 245.

3. Davis, *Louisiana*, 246-47; Bauer, *Leader Among Peers*, 176; W. Motthoff, President Police Jury, Jefferson Left Bank to Major General Benjamin Butler, May 29, 1862 in *Private and Official Correspondence of Gen. Benjamin F. Butler During the Period of the Civil War*, ed. Jessie Ames Marshall (Norwood, Mass.: The Plimpton Press, 1917), 526.

4. Quoted in Davis, *Louisiana*, 249.

5. Other units organized in Jefferson Parish included the following: Jefferson Artillery, Jefferson Blues, Jefferson Cadets, Jefferson Chasseurs, Jefferson Confederate Guards, Jefferson Fire Guards, Jefferson Guards, the Carrollton Guards of Jefferson Parish, and the Jefferson Light Guards. An unknown number of units under the names of their organizing officers could also have been mustered from Jefferson Parish. See A.B. Booth, "Louisiana Confederate Military Records,"

Louisiana Historical Quarterly 4 (January 1921): 393 and John D. Winters, *The Civil War in Louisiana* (Baton Rouge: Louisiana State University Press, 1963), 75.

6. Born in 1841, Minor was the youngest son of Minor and Eliza Kenner.
7. Jefferson Parish Police Jury Minutes, December 1, 1860; *The Times-Democrat,* October 23, 1892; Napier Bartlett, *A Soldier's Story of the War: Including the Marshes and Battles of the Washington Artillery and of other Louisiana Troops* (New Orleans: Clark and Hofeline, 1874), 149-50; *The Daily Picayune,* March 7, 1862; Andrew B. Booth, *Records of Louisiana Confederate Soldiers and Louisiana Confederate Commands* (New Orleans, 1920), 11.
8. Charles L. Dufour, *The Night the War Was Lost* (Lincoln: University of Nebraska Press, 1994), 40, 42.
9. Jefferson D. Bragg, *Louisiana in the Confederacy* (Baton Rouge: Louisiana State University Press, 1941), 73-77; Swanson, *Historic Jefferson Parish*, 93; Winters, *The Civil War in Louisiana*, 80.
10. Chester G. Hearn, *The Capture of New Orleans 1862* (Baton Rouge: Louisiana State University Press, 1995), 237-38, 243; Davis, *Louisiana*, 255; U.S. Department of War, *The War of the Rebellion: A Compilation of the Official Records of the Union and Confederate Armies* (Washington, D.C.: United States Government Printing Office, 1880-1901), series I, vol. 6, 566, hereinafter cited as *Official Records.*
11. *Official Records*, series I, vol. 18, 700 and vol. 6, 579.
12. Smith, *Cane, Cotton, & Crevasses,* 31; *Daily True Delta*, May 21, 1862..
13. In spite of things being quiet on her plantation, Ruhamah was not comfortable with the situation at Kennerville. Within weeks she left Louisiana to stay with a married daughter who lived in Philadelphia. She remained there until December 1867. *Official Records*, series I, vol. 15, 22-23; quoted by Smith, *Cane, Cotton, & Crevasses,* 31.
14. *Private and Official Correspondence of Gen. Benjamin F. Butler*, 481-82, 493, 632.
15. Bauer, "The History of the City of Kenner," 27-29; Allan Nevins, *Ordeal of the Union: Selected Chapters* (New York: Charles Scribner's Sons, 1973), 386-87.
16. *Private and Official Correspondence of Gen. Benjamin F. Butler*, 524-25; *Official Records*, series I, vol. 15, 446-47.
17. *Private and Official Correspondence of Gen. Benjamin F. Butler*, 524-25;
18. Ibid.
19. Colonel Charles Everett to Captain Wage, February 19, 1865, "Letters Sent, November, 1864-March 1865, Kenner, Louisiana," U.S. Army Continental Commands-Department of the Gulf, National Archives, Washington, D.C.;

Bauer, "The History of the City of Kenner," 28-29; *Official Records*, series I, vol. 48 (part 1), 464.

20. Alfred A. Rigby, "Union Soldier's Diary, 1862-1865," June 20, 1864, Special Collection Department, Emory University, Atlanta, Georgia; A Guide to the Papers of Edward Jameson ca. 1862-1871, Special Collections, The University of Virginia Library, Charlottesville, Virginia, available from http://ead.lib.virginia.edu/vivaead/published/uva-sc/viu03875.document, accessed January 2, 2010; "Oaths of Allegiance Administered, September, 1862-July, 1863, Cavalry Camp of Instruction and Distribution at Kenner, Louisiana," U.S. Army Continental Commands, Department of the Gulf, National Archives and Records Service, Washington, D.C.; J.G. Randall and David Donald, *The Civil War and Reconstruction*, 2nd ed. (Lexington, Mass.: D.C. Heath and Company, 1969), 514-15; Winters, *The Civil War in Louisiana*, 140.

21. *Official Records*, series I, vol. 48 (part 1), 648.

22. Alfred A. Rigby, "Union Soldier's Diary," 1862-1865, June 20, 1864.

23. Ibid.

24. Civil War Diary of Henry Carl Ketzle, 37th Illinois Volunteer Infantry, Company A, 1861-1865, available from http//w.w.w.ketzle.com/diary/1865.html, accessed January 2, 2010.

25. Letter from John J. Bigbee, Kennerville, Louisiana, January 7, 1865, available from http://w.w.w.groantiques.com/detail,indiana-47th-infantry,1946164.html, accessed January 6, 2010.

26. Notes for Elias P. Risshel, January 2 and February 8, 1865, available from http://familytreemaker.genealogy.com/users/s/i/n/David-R-Sinn/GENE1-001.html, accessed January 6, 1865.

27. *Official Records*, series I, vol. 48 (part 1), 648.

28. Ibid., 737.

29. The other garrisons involved in securing the region were New Orleans, Algiers, Camp Parapet, Carrollton, Greensville, Lakeport, Proctorville, Ship Island, Fort Jackson, Plaquemine, Fort Saint Philip, Fort Pike, Fort Macomb, Fort Livingston, Donaldsonville, Napoleonville, Thibodaux, Brashear City, Bonnet Carre!, and Terre Bonne. See *Official Records*, series I, vol. 48 (part I), 464.

30. For example, it appears that it was illness that took the life of twenty-one year-old David Banford of the 11th New York Cavalry who died at Kennerville on August 5, 1864. See *Annual Report of the Adjutant-General of the State of New York for the year 1894 Vol III: Registers of the 9th, 10th, 11th, and 12th Regiments of Cavalry, N.Y. Vols, in War of the Rebellion* (Albany: James B. Lyon, State Printer, 1895), 676.

31. *Official Records*, series I, vol. 15, 283; Thomas Hamilton Murray, *History of the*

Ninth Regiment, Connecticut Volunteer Infantry, "The Irish Regiment," in the War of the Rebellion, 1861-65 (New Haven: The Price, Lee & Adkiss Co., 1903), 161-62; Bauer, "From Burnt Canes to Budding City," 366; William E. Perrin Jr., "Civil War Military Operations In and Around Ponchatoula, Louisiana," *Louisiana History* 13 (Spring 1971): 127-31.

32. General Steele was a combat veteran of several campaigns in Arkansas, Missouri, Mississippi, and Tennessee, including commanding a division at Vicksburg. After commanding at Kenner, he later led a division in the Union campaign to capture Mobile, Alabama. See Patricia L. Faust, ed. *Historical Times Illustrated Encyclopedia of the Civil War* (New York: Harper & Row Publishers, 1986), s.v. "Steele, Frederick," by Jeffrey D. West.

33. The exact number of troops stationed at the camp is not known. Ideally a regiment during the Civil War totaled about one thousand men. However, because of attrition, most units functioned under strength. Therefore, because of the number of support units associated with providing supplies and services to the field regiments at the camp, the total of troops at Kennerville in early 1865 may have approached twenty thousand. *Official Records*, series I, vol. 48 (part 1), 648; U.S. Army Continental Commands, Department of the Gulf, "Letters Sent, November, 1864-March 1865, Kenner, Louisiana;" Ian Drury and Tony Gibbons, *The Civil War Military Machine: Weapons and Tactics of the Union and Confederate Armed Forces* (New York: Smithmark Publishers, Inc., 1993), 22.

34. *Official Records*, series I, vol. 48 (part 1), 409-410, 464; Col. Charles Everett to Captain F. Speed, November 30, 1864, U.S. Army Continental Commands, Department of the Gulf, Letters Sent, November 1864-March 1865, Kenner, Louisiana; Bauer, "From Burnt Canes to Budding City," 367.

CHAPTER 5

1. John D. Winters, *The Civil War in Louisiana* (Baton Rouge: Louisiana State University Press, 1963), 428-29; John F. Stover, "Southern Ambitions of the Illinois Central Railroad," *The Journal of Southern History* 20 (November 1954): 505.

2. Sitterson, *Sugar Country*, 226; Smith, *Cane, Cotton, & Crevasses,* 31.

3. Ibid., 32; Roger W. Shugg, *Origins of Class Struggle in Louisiana: A Social History of White Farmers and Laborers during Slavery and After, 1840-1875* (1939; repr., Baton Rouge: Louisiana State University Press, 1972), 193; John B. Boles, *The South Through Time: A History of an American Region* (Englewood Cliffs, N.J.: Prentice Hall, 1995), 369.

4. Ruhamah Riske Kenner to Philip Minor Kenner, August 23, 1868, Kenner Family Papers.

5. Follett, *Documenting Louisiana Sugar 1845-1917.*

6. *The Daily Picayune*, May 11, 1870; Nathaniel F. Belloni Jr., "The Great Mace-Allen Fight: When Kenner was the World's Boxing Capital," *Jefferson History Notebook* 1 (August 1979): 1-4.

7. The Mace/Allen fight was not the first large-scale fight to take place at Kennerville. In late January 1867, the *New Orleans Times* reported that four participants agreed to participate at Kennerville in the "manly art of self defence [*sic*]" by mutual consent "and for a stated amount . . . agreed to give each other a good pummeling after the most approved fashion of the prize ring." To see the seven-round fight between Bill Davis and Ned Burnett spectators were brought to the town by steamers. The number of spectators was not detailed other than to say that there were "quite a number of spectators." See the *New Orleans Times*, January 25, 1867.

8. Quoted by Belloni in "The Great Mace-Allen Fight," 3.

9. *Daily Picayune*, June 23, 1901.

10. Ibid., 3-4; *Daily Picayune*, May 11, 1870; Leavitt, *Kenner*, np; Davis, *Louisiana*, 329.

11. Ruhamah Riske Kenner to Philip Minor Kenner, August 23, 1868, Kenner Family Papers.

12. Quoted by Smith, *Cane, Cotton, & Crevasses,* 32.

13. Duncan's assistance to Philip Minor Kenner was not in vain. The situation at the Roseland Plantation improved to such a state that in February 1878, Philip Minor was able to acquire Duncan's interest in the property and assume ownership of the estate. C.K. Harding to P.M. Kenner, 20th day of an unidentified month in 1871 and Roseland Plantation Account Book, Kenner Family Papers; Bauer, *A Leader Among Peers*, 245.

14. Quoted by Smith, *Cane, Cotton, & Crevasses,* 32.

15. Ibid.

16. Ibid., 33.

17. Quoted by Bauer, *A Leader Among Peers*, 245.

18. Though most of the Oakland estate was lost at the time of the sheriff's sale, Ruhamah did retain a small strip of land three-arpents wide located down river from the plantation and reaching from the Mississippi River back to the lake. She obtained no revenues from its ownership and died nearly destitute at age seventy in 1885. Smith, *Cane, Cotton, & Crevasses,* 34; The Historical Records Survey, "A Brief History of Jefferson Parish," *Jefferson Parish Yearly Review* (1939): 159; Follett, *Documenting Louisiana Sugar 1845-1917*; U.S. Army Corps of Engineers, *Cultural Resource Survey*, 24.

19. *Daily Picayune*, March 19, 1870; Follett, *Documenting Louisiana Sugar 1845-1917*; A. Bouchereau, *Statement of the Sugar and Rice Crops Made in Louisiana*

in 1877-1878 (New Orleans: Pelican Book and Job Printing, 1878), 39; Davis, *Louisiana*, 296-297; U.S. Army Corps of Engineers, *Cultural Resource Survey*, 24.

20. Sitterson, *Sugar Country*, 255; *Daily Picayune*, October 9, 1885 and December 24, 1886.

21. *Daily Picayune*, March 19, 1870.

22. Joe Gray Taylor, *Louisiana Reconstructed: 1863-1877* (Baton Rouge: Louisiana State University, 1974), 317.

23. *Daily Picayune*, September 9, 1892.

24. The 1870 census was the first population count that listed Kennerville as a community. Because the census of that year only listed names and not addresses it is not possible to determine how many of the individuals counted actually lived in the village or resided in nearby areas. The census count focused on the individuals who used the Kenner post office, so the numbers undoubtedly included individuals who resided outside of the town. A population of over two thousand people would have made the town one of the largest population centers in the state. This is highly unlikely to have been the situation in 1870.

25. U.S. Department of the Interior, Bureau of the Census, *Ninth Census of the United States: 1870, Jefferson Parish;* Baudier, *The Catholic Church in Louisiana*, 449; Bezou, *Metairie*, 147-48.

26. There were several waves of Italian immigration to America during the nineteenth and twentieth centuries. The largest group of Italian immigrants and the one which populated Kenner took place during the period between 1880 and 1920. Mary Lou Widmer, *New Orleans 1900 to 1920* (Gretna, La.: Pelican Publishing Company, 2007), 21, 104; *Times-Picayune*, November 9, 1981.

27. Campanella, *Bienville's Dilemma*, 175; Elizabeth Fussell, "Contructing New Orleans, Constructing Race: A Population History of New Orleans," *The Journal of American History* 94 (December 2007): 849-50; John Fredrick Nau, *The German People of New Orleans, 1850-1900* (Leiden: E.J. Brill, 1958), 59; Joseph S. Kopfler, "Kenner Means Business," *Jefferson Parish Yearly Review* (1952): 172-73; Bauer, "History of the City of Kenner, Louisiana," 38-39.

28. Kopfler, "Kenner Means Business," 172-73; Bauer, "The History of the City of Kenner," 38; *Times-Picayune*, April 26, 1981.

29. Mayor Joseph S. Kopfler Sr., "Kenner's Centennial Celebration," Jefferson Parish Public Library, Kenner, Louisiana; Martel McNeely, "Jefferson Parish Food Production," *Jefferson Parish Yearly Review* (1943): 162; Leavitt, *Kenner*, np; *Daily Picayune*, May 4, 1913.

30. Kopfler, "Kenner's Centennial Celebration;" Martel McNeely, "Jefferson Parish Food Production," *Jefferson Parish Yearly Review* (1943): 162; *Daily Picayune*,

May 4, 1913.

31. U.S. Army Corps of Engineers, *Cultural Resource Survey*, 24; Lyle Saxon, "A Tourist Looks at Jefferson," *Jefferson Parish Yearly Review* (1941): 126; Kopfler, "Town of Kenner," *Jefferson Parish Yearly Review* (1943): 162; *Daily Picayune*, July 25, 1908; *Times-Picayune*, April 26, 1981.

32. *The Daily Item* (New Orleans), October 11, November 7 and 10, December 12, 1894; *The Daily Picayune*, November 7, 9, and 11, 1894.

33. Taylor, *Louisiana Reconstructed*, 86, 193, 319; Jefferson Parish Police Jury Minutes, August 1, 1877; *New Orleans Times*, October 9, 1866; Campanella, *Geographies of New Orleans*, 82; *The City News* [Kenner], March 7, 1970.

34. *Daily Picayune*, February 7 and May 5, 1880, May 17, 1892.

35. *Daily Picayune*, February 14, 1899; Leavitt, *Kenner*, np.

36. Bauer, "The History of the City of Kenner," 40; Leavitt, *Kenner*, np; Lyle Saxon, Edward Dreyer, and Robert Tallant, *Gumbo Ya-Ya: Collection of Louisiana Folk Tales* (Baton Rouge: Louisiana Library Commission, 1945), 107-120; *Times-Picayune*, September 11, 1976; Raphaella Maggiore, "Raphaella Says," *The City News* (Kenner), September 12, 1975.

37. Bauer, "The History of the City of Kenner," 40; Leavitt, *Kenner*, np.; *Daily Picayune*, September 10, 1900; *Times-Picayune*, September 11, 1976 and September 12, 2010; Maggiore, "Raphaella Says," *The City News*, September 12, 1975; John J. Holtgreve, "Just Around the Corner of Time," *Jefferson Parish Yearly Review* (1954): 107.

38. *Daily Picayune*, May 28, 1871.

39. *Daily Picayune*, February 23, 1872.

CHAPTER 6

1. Taylor, *Louisiana Reconstructed*, 65-66.

2. Kenneth M. Stampp, *The Era of Reconstruction: 1865-1877* (New York: Vintage Books, 1965), 79.

3. John Hope Franklin, *From Slavery to Freedom*, 3rd ed. (New York: Alfred A. Knopf, 1967), 303.

4. Bauer, "The History of the City of Kenner," 32; Davis, *Louisiana*, 266-67; Bauer, *A Leader Among Peers*, 263; C. Van Woodward, *The Strange Career of Jim Crow*, 9th ed. (New York: Oxford University Press, 1963), *23*.

5. *New Orleans Daily Crescent*, November 1, 1865.

6. Melinda Meek Hennessey, "Race and Violence in Reconstruction New Orleans: The 1868 Riot," *Louisiana History* 20 (Winter, 1979): 77, 82.

7. Eric Foner, *Reconstruction: America's Unfinished Revolution 1863-1877* (New York: Harper & Row Publishers, 1988), 276-78; Perry H. Howard, *Political Tendencies in Louisiana,* rev. and enl. ed. (Baton Rouge: Louisiana State University Press, 1971), 124-25, 127; Bauer, *A Leader Among Peers*, 268-69.

8. Hennessey, "Race and Violence in Reconstruction New Orleans," 82-83; James K. Hogue, *Uncivil War: Five New Orleans Street Battles and the Rise and Fall of Radical Reconstruction* (Baton Rouge: Louisiana State University, 2006), 66; Taylor, *Louisiana Reconstructed*, 177; Justin A. Nystrom, *New Orleans After the Civil War: Race, Politics, and a New Birth of Freedom*, (Baltimore: Johns Hopkins University Press, 2010), 75-76.

9. Taylor, *Louisiana Reconstructed*, 151, 154.

10. George Cecil Daul, *The Administration of the Public Schools of Jefferson Parish Since the Civil War (1860-1940)* (Metairie, La.: Jefferson Parish Historical Commission, 1981), 1-3, 7; John W. Blassingame, *Black New Orleans 1860-1880*, (Chicago: University of Chicago Press, 1973), 109; Howard A. White, *The Freedmen's Bureau in Louisiana* (Baton Rouge: Louisiana State University Press, 1970), 168, 172.

11. Quoted by Daul, *Public Schools of Jefferson Parish*, 9, 11.

12. *Daily Picayune*, May 23, 1874; Daul, *Public Schools of Jefferson Parish*, 11.

13. Daul, *Public Schools of Jefferson Parish*, 11, Baudier, *The Catholic Church in Louisiana*, 478; *Daily Picayune*, June 4, 1908.

14. Jefferson Parish Police Jury Minutes, January 14, 1881; Kenner Town Council Minutes, September 3, 1914.

15. Howard, *Political Tendencies in Louisiana*, 142-43, 145, 149-50; Shugg, *Origins of Class Struggle in Louisiana,* 217.

16. Michael J. Pfeifer, "Lynching and Criminal Justice in South Louisiana, 1878-1930," *Louisiana History* 40 (Spring 199): 156; Howard, *Political Tendencies in Louisiana*, 141, 149-50, 157; William Ivy Hair, *Bourbonism and Agrarian Protest: Louisiana Politics 1877-1900* (Baton Rouge: Louisiana State University Press, 1969),116c.

17. *Cincinnati Daily Gazette*, January 2, 1875; *New Orleans Times*, January 3, 1875.

18. *New Orleans Times*, January 3, 1875.

19. *Cincinnati Daily Gazette*, January 2, 1875.

20. Reminisces of Judge James C. Baumann.

21. Ibid.

22. Ibid.

23. Ibid.

24. Ibid.; *Daily Picayune*, March 17, 1880.

25. Frank King, Edward Steward, Harris Williams (an African American), Benjamin Felix, Joseph Marona, and Peter Schneckerberger Jr. were elected as councilmen.

26. Reminisces of Judge James C. Baumann.

27. Ibid.

28. Called "L.H." throughout his political life, Louis Herman Marrero Sr.'s career in Jefferson politics extended from 1884 until 1920, including six terms as parish sheriff. See Frank J. Borne Jr., "Jefferson Parish Sheriffs: A Collection of Biographies of Jefferson Parish's Chief Law Enforcement Officers," *Jefferson History Notebook* 8 (Jefferson Parish, La.: Jefferson Historical Society, February, 2004), 11-12.

29. Ibid.

30. As noted in the previous chapter, it was at this time in 1889 that Baumann and John Deloss Rouse acquired the Oakland Plantation property and held it for two months before selling the land to The Oakland Land Company.

31. Ibid.; *Daily Picayune*, December 22, 1892.

32. Ibid.

33. *Daily Picayune*, July 23, 1892.

34. Gretna is a municipality on the west bank of the Mississippi River in Jefferson Parish several miles distant from Kenner. It is also the parish seat of government.

35. *Daily Picayune*, August 5, 1892.

36. *Daily Picayune*, September 9, 1892; Michael J. Pfeifer, "'. . . the already scarlet record of Jefferson Parish': Analysis of a Lynching Syndrome, 1892-1897," paper presented at the Southern Historical Association's Annual Meeting, New Orleans, Louisiana, November 17, 2001.

37. *Daily Picayune*, September 9, 1892.

38. *Daily Picayune*, September 25, 1892.

39. *Daily Picayune*, September 29, 1892 and December 14, 1892.

40. *Daily Journal* (Plaquemine, Louisiana), December 19, 1892.

41. The judge would soon obtain national notoriety as a named party to the 1896 historic United States Supreme Court decision of *Plessy v. Ferguson* that recognized the legality of racially segregated facilities in America.

42. *The Daily City Item*, January 25, 1893.

43. *Daily Picayune*, December 23, 1892 and January 26, 1893; Reminisces of Judge James C. Baumann.

44. Pfeifer, ". . . the already scarlet record of Jefferson Parish'"; *Daily Picayune*, Sep-

tember 27, 1895; Michael J. Pfeifer, "Louisiana Lynchings 1878-1946," (Olympia, Wash.: Evergreen State College), database available from http://academic.evergreen.edu/p/pfeiferm/home.htm.

CHAPTER 7

1. *Daily Picayune*, February 11, 1866; Louisiana, *Acts Passed by the General Assembly of the State of Louisiana* (Baton Rouge, 1867).
2. Charles Vincent, *Black Legislators in Louisiana During Reconstruction* (Baton Rouge: Louisiana State University Press, 1976), 160-61; *Daily Picayune*, February 11, 1873; A. E. Perkins, "Some Negro Officers and Legislators in Louisiana," *The Journal of Negro History* 14 (October 1929): 523.
3. Louisiana, *Acts Passed by the General Assembly of the State of Louisiana* (Baton Rouge, 1873).
4. Ibid.; Jefferson Parish Police Jury Minutes, November 3, 1873, May 7, 1877.
5. Hair, *Bourbonism and Agrarian Protest*, 100-101; Sigur Martin, *History of Our Local Government and the Development of Parishes, Municipalities and Political Subdivisions in Louisiana, and Their Power and Authority to Incur Debt and Issue Bonds* (Sigur Martin, 1966), 21.
6. Jefferson Parish Police Jury Minutes, June 16, 1886, May 4, 1887; *Daily Picayune*, June 24, 1884; *Felix v. Wagner*, 39 La. Ann. 391 (La. 1887).
7. Jefferson Parish Police Jury Minutes, June 16, 1886; *Daily Picayune*, June 1 and 23, 1886.
8. *Daily Picayune*, September 12, 1888.
9. *Daily Picayune*, June 4 and 11, 1908.
10. Among those who opposed the effort to revoke the charter were some of the town's leading citizens, including A. Wattigny, Joseph Christina (a councilman), Ed. Stoulig, H. J. Langhauser, J.R. Strickland, E.J. Deshautreaux, Joseph Maggiore, and R.V. Degury (a councilman). *Daily Picayune*, June 4, and 18, 1908.
11. *Daily Picayune,* June 4, 1908.
12. *Daily Picayune*, June 11, 18, July 10, 21, 1908, January 7, 1909; Louisiana, *Acts of State of Louisiana*, Regular Session 1908; *Felix et al. v. Michel,* Secretary of State, 122 La. 352 (1908).
13. *O'Sullivan v. Felix*, 233 U.S. 318; 34 S. Ct. 596, 58 L. Ed. 980 (1914).
14. Ibid.; *Daily Picayune*, March 20, 1914.

CHAPTER 8

1. Hair, *Bourbonism and Agrarian Protest*, 76; Howard, *Political Tendencies in Louisiana*, 142-43, 150, 188; Woodward, *The Strange Career of Jim Crow*, 23, 28; Henry C. Dethloff and Robert R. Jones, "Race Relations in Louisiana, 1877-98," *Louisiana History* 9 (Fall 1968): 308, 321; Wall, *Louisiana History*, 242-244.

2. Quoted by John V. Baiamonte Jr., "'Who Killa de Chief' Revisited: The Hennessey Assassination and Its Aftermath, 1890-1991," *Louisiana History* 33 (Spring 1992): 122, 125; John Higham, *Strangers in the Land: Patterns of American Nativism 1860-1925* (New Brunswick: Rutgers University Press, 1955), 90-92; Alan G. Gauthreaux, "An Inhospitable Land: Anti-Italian Sentiment and Violence in Louisiana, 1891-1924," *Louisiana History* 51 (Winter 2010): 41-42, 52-54, 56, 60; Roselyn Bologna Boneno, "From Migrant to Millionaire: The Story of the Italian-American in New Orleans, 1880-1910" (Ph.D. dissertation, Louisiana State University, 1986), 142.

3. Quoted by Earl F. Niehaus, "Catholic Ethnics in Nineteenth-Century Louisiana," in *Cross, Crozier, and Crucible: A volume Celebrating the Bicentennial of a Catholic Diocese in Louisiana*, ed. Glenn R. Conrad (New Orleans: The Roman Catholic Church of the Archdiocese of New Orleans, 1993), 66.

4. Ibid.; Gauthreaux, "An Inhospitable Land," 41-42, 52-54, 56, 60.

5. In actuality Cowen was only the mayor protempore of Kenner. See William Ivy Hair, *Carnival of Fury: Robert Charles and the New Orleans Race Riot of 1900* (Baton Rouge: Louisiana State University Press, 1976), 151, 189, 199.

6. Although indicted on a charge of unlawful assembly, the charge was later dropped and Cowen was never punished for his actions. Hair, *Carnival of Fury*, 151, 189, 199.

7. Howard, *Political Tendencies in Louisiana*, 193-97; *Thirteenth Census of the United States, 1910*. Records of the Bureau of the Census, record Group 29, National Archives, Washington, D.C. (Ancestry.com on-line database); Greta de Jong, *A Different Day: African American Struggle for Justice in Rural Louisiana, 1900-1970* (Chapel Hill: University of North Carolina Press, 2002), 4-5, 7; Dethloff and Jones, "Race Relations in Louisiana," 318-19.

8. Jefferson Parish Police Jury Minutes, July 30, 1912; The boundaries of the new municipality were fairly close to the modern city, with the Mississippi River to the south, the St. Charles Parish boundary to the west, Lake Pontchartrain to the north and Filmore Street to the east. See Luther E. Hall, Proclamation Declaring the Incorporation of the Village of Kenner, Louisiana, December 13, 1913.

9. Hall, Proclamation Declaring the Incorporation of the Village of Kenner; Bauer, "The History of the City of Kenner, Louisiana," 61; *Daily Picayune*, December 11 and 17, 1913.

10. The cause of the wide difference between the 1900 Federal Census (922 people) and the 1914 special census (1,904 inhabitants) is not clear. Most likely explanations suggest that the Federal count was limited to the old Kennerville boundaries; whereas, the special count included the extended boundaries of the modern municipality.

11. Kenner Village Council Minutes, January 21, 1914; *Daily Picayune*, December 17, 25, 1913, and February 19, 1914; A.Wattigny, Population certification of the "Village of Kenner," February 5, 1914; Luther E. Hall, Proclamation Declaring Kenner to be a Town, February 5, 1914; Earl K. Long, Proclamation Declaring Kenner a City, January 22, 1952.

12. Gordon E. Gillson, *Louisiana State Board of Health: The Progressive Years* (Baton Rouge: Moran Industries, 1976), 168, 186-87.

13. Stover, "*Southern Ambitions of the Illinois Central Railroad,*" 510; Swanson, *Historic Jefferson Parish*, 109; *New Orleans Item*, June 10, 1952; Kenner Town Council Minutes, January 21, 1914; Bauer, "The History of the City of Kenner," 71-72; Pennebaker, "Transportation in Jefferson." 79; Leavitt, *Kenner*, n.p.

14. Davis, *Louisiana*, 301; Sternberg, *Along the River Road*, 44; Bauer, "The History of the City of Kenner, Louisiana," 72-73.

15. Jefferson Parish Police Jury (Left Bank) Minutes, March 3, 1874.

16. Jefferson Parish Police Jury (Left Bank) Minutes, October 16, 17, November 6, 17, 1871, March 3, 18, April 15, June 15, July 20, 1874, February 4, May 17, September 6, 1875; *The City News* [Kenner], March 5, 1970; *Daily Picayune*, May 6, 1874.

17. Jefferson Parish Police Jury Minutes, April 3, 1870, February 6, 1889, January 7, May 1, 1896, March 1, 1902, and December 5, 1930; Kenner Town Council Minutes, December 5, 1930.

18. Leavitt, *Kenner*, np; *Daily Picayune*, February 14, 1899.

19. *Daily Picayune*, November 15, 1894; Kenner Town Council Minutes, January 21, 1914; Bauer, "The History of the City of Kenner," 75-76; Robert Tallant, "From Cockfights to Commerce," *Jefferson Parish Yearly Review* (1952): 90, 97.

20. U.S. Army Corps of Engineers, *Cultural Resource Survey*, 25-28; Swanson, *Historic Jefferson Parish*, 109; Leavitt, *Kenner*, n.p.; *Daily Picayune*, March 20, 2012; Bauer, "The History of the City of Kenner, Louisiana," 79.

21. *Daily Picayune*, March 20, 1914.

22. Ibid.

23. Advertisement from New Orleans Press Club, 1916, reproduced in U.S. Army Corps of Engineers, *Cultural Resource Survey*, 29; *Daily Picayune*, May 4, 1913.

24. Tallant, "From Cockfights to Commerce," *Jefferson Parish Yearly Review*, 90, 97.

25. Ibid.

26. Ibid.; Jefferson Parish Police Jury Minutes, October 8, 1930; Swanson, *Historic Jefferson Parish*, 109. Leavitt, *Kenner*, n.p.

CHAPTER 9

1. Regional Planning Commission, *History of Regional Growth of Jefferson, Orleans, and St. Bernard Parishes, Louisiana* (New Orleans: Regional Planning Commission, 1969), 77; Kenner Town Council Minutes, May 10, 1927; Jefferson Parish Police Jury Minutes, March 14, 1928; *The New Orleans Item*, June 10, 1952.

2. *Times-Picayune*, June 6, 1954.

3. Jefferson Parish Police Jury Minutes, July 12, 1926, September 14, 1927, October 23, 1935; Kenner Town Council Minutes, May 10, 1927, December 19, 1935; Justin F. Bordenave, "Wanted—One Seawall," *Jefferson Parish Yearly Review* (1940): 156-60; *Times-Picayune*, April 14, 1940.

4. Kenner Town Council Minutes, January 7, 1918, February 19, 1919, June 18, 1919, and March 19, 1920.

5. Kenner Town Council Minutes, September 27, 1920, May 4, 1922, March 5, 1929, April 2, 1929, and May 1, 1929; Allan P. Sindler, *Huey Long's Louisiana: State Politics, 1920-1952* (Baltimore: The Johns Hopkins Press, 1956), 25, 42.

6. Limited telephone service was available in Kenner as soon as the early 1890s.

7. Kenner Town Council Minutes, December 4, 1919, September 16, 1925, March 2, 1926, August 3, 1929, September 6, 1930, and October 7, 1930; Jefferson Parish Jury Minutes, December 11, 1929; Bauer, "The History of the City of Kenner, Louisiana," 47.

8. *Times-Picayune*, August 11, 1929.

9. Kenner Town Council Minutes, January 21, 1914, August 6, 1929, November 5, 1929; Bauer, "History of the City of Kenner, Louisiana," 45-46, 61; *The City News* [Kenner], March 5, 1970; Wall, *Louisiana: A History*, 327.

10. Wall, *Louisiana: A History*, 327-28; Roman Heleniak, "Local Reaction to the Great Depression in New Orleans, 1929-1933," *Louisiana History* 10 (Fall 1969): 301, 306.

11. Bauer, "The History of the City of Kenner," 80; C. Joseph Pusateri, "Radio Broadcasters and the Challenge of Television: A New Orleans Case," *The Business History Review* 54 (Autumn 1980): 304, 322; Nancy McKenzie Dupont, "The German Priest, the Banana Boats, and the Origins of Broadcasting in New Orleans," *Louisiana History* 40 (Spring 1999): 219-20; *Times-Picayune*, December 1, 1938.

12. The race-based disparities in the quality of education in Jefferson at the time are

demonstrated in the school-board's salary schedule for 1937. For example, in the schedule new white bachelor-level teachers were paid a yearly salary of $950; whereas, a black teacher with the same qualifications was paid $60 a month. In addition to being considerably less than the salary for white teachers, the fact that the salaries for African American teachers were based on a monthly rather than yearly schedule, implied less of a long-term commitment to black education than white. Wall, *Louisiana: A History*, 305, 327-331; Daul, *Public Schools of Jefferson Parish*, 51, 57-59, 62, 65-67; "National Education Association-Negro Night School in Kenner," series 47.03, WPA Photographs-Parishes Outside Orleans, Series 47.03, New Orleans Public Library, New Orleans, Louisiana; Lem Higgins, "Expansion is Keynote of Public School System," *Jefferson Parish Yearly Review* (1940): 98; *Daily Picayune*, May 31, 1900; Bezou, *Metairie*, 148; Sr. Mary Jeremy Buckman, RSM to the author, April 12, 2012.

13. *Times-Picayune*, June 11 and 16, 1940.

14. Jacob J. Kaufman, "Farm Labor During World War II," *Journal of Farm Economics* 31 (February 1949) 131-32; J. S. Kopfler, "Town of Kenner," *Jefferson Parish Yearly Review* (1943): 162; George T. Geiger Jr., "A Silver Lining," *Jefferson Parish Yearly Review* (1942): 136; Jerry Purvis Sanson, *Louisiana During World War II: Politics and Society 1939-1945* (Baton Rouge: Louisiana State University, 1999), 198-99; Vic D'Gerolamo, "Town of Kenner," *Jefferson Parish Yearly Review* (1942): 164.

15. Shortly after the end of the war, in 1946 a part of the sprawling facility was used as the first location of Ochsner Foundation Hospital. Not the ideal setting for a hospital, the old wooden barracks used by the facility soon earned the nickname of "Splinter Village" by the nurses and medical staff who worked at the site. See Paul F. Stahls Jr., *Jefferson Parish: Richer Heritage, Promising Future* (San Antonio: Historical Publishing Network, 2009), 124.

16. Ray M. Thompson, "Industry!" *Jefferson Parish Yearly Review* (1943): 10, 18; J. H. Bull, "Shipbuilding in Jefferson," *Jefferson Parish Yearly Review* (1942): 102-106; Sanson, *Louisiana During World War II*, 217-19; Dorothy Dix, "Women in War," *Jefferson Parish Yearly Review* (1942): 26, 28; Ipik Plywood Corporation advertisement, *Jefferson Parish Yearly Review* (1943): 41; *Gambit* (New Orleans), August 7, 2009.

17. Sanson, *Louisiana During World War II*, 273-74, 284.

18. W.R. Toledano, "Streamlined for War," *Jefferson Parish Yearly Review* (1942): 7; Lewis, *New Orleans—The Making of an Urban Landscape*, 62; *Times-Picayune*, September 20, 21, 1947.

19. Justin F. Bordenave, "Fourth Jefferson Drainage District," *Jefferson Parish Yearly Review* (1938): 187-91.

20. At the time of the 1947 storm, the Weather Bureau had not begun the modern

practice of naming tropical storms.

21. Toledano, "Streamlined for War," 7; Lewis, *New Orleans—The Making of an Urban Landscape*, 62; *Times-Picayune*, September 20, 21, 1947; David Roth, "Louisiana Hurricane History," (Camp Springs, Md.: National Weather Service, 2010), 36, available from www.hpc.ncep.noaa.gov/research/lahur.pdf (accessed June 10, 2012); Leavitt, *Kenner*, np.

22. U.S. Army Corps of Engineers. *Cultural Resource Survey*, 30-31; *Times-Picayune*, March 21, 1991; Earl K. Long, Proclamation Declaring Kenner a City, January 22, 1952; Kenner Town Council Minutes, July 6, 1951.

CHAPTER 10

1. The airport code of MSY, which has remained the same throughout the airport's existence, originally was an abbreviation of Moisant Stock Yards. So named because of the cattle that pastured on the fields in the Kenner/Harahan area that sometimes were used as landing sites by early aviators. See Campanella, *Geographies of New Orleans*, 19; *Times-Picayune*, December 31, 2010.

2. Ibid.; John A. Heitmann, "Getting Places in a Hurry: The Development of Aviation in Long-Era South Louisiana," *Louisiana History* 39 (Fall 1988): 327, 329, 331; Davis, *Louisiana*, 362.

3. Heitmann, "Getting Places in a Hurry," 334.

4. Ibid., 336-38; Leavitt, *Kenner*, np; Regional Planning Commission, *History of Regional Growth of Jefferson, Orleans, and St. Bernard Parishes, Louisiana*, 85.

5. *Jefferson Democrat*, January 11 and 18, August 2, May 24, 1941; D. O. Langstaff, "The Airport Situation Today," *Jefferson Parish Yearly Review* (1941): 146; Joseph S. Kopfler, "Kenner Takes to the Air," *Jefferson Parish Yearly Review* (1946): 167.

6. Kenner Town Council Minutes, September 19, 1941; *Times-Picayune*, January 25, 1953, *Jefferson Democrat*, September 13, November 8, December 6, 1941; Leavitt, *Kenner*, np.

7. *Jefferson Democrat*, November 21, 22, 1942; *Daily Picayune*, January 1, 1911, January 6, 1946; *New Orleans Item*, October 31, December 24, 1910, *Times-Picayune*, December 31, 2010.

8. *Times-Picayune*, September 13, November 7, 1944, January 12, 1946; *States-Item*, November 10, 1959; Joseph S. Kopfler, "Town of Kenner," *Jefferson Parish Yearly Review* (1944): 176; *The Jefferson Democrat*, January 11, November 22, 1941.

9. *Times-Picayune*, March 31, 1944, January 12, 13, 14, 1946, January 29, 2012; Bauer, "The History of the City of Kenner, Louisiana," 89-90; Regional Planning Commission, *History of Regional Growth*, 85; *Times-Picayune*, November 20, 2011.

10. *Times-Picayune*, January 25, 1953; Bauer, "The History of the City of Kenner, Louisiana," 91; New Orleans Aviation Board, "Two Billion Dollars: New Orleans International Airport's Contribution to the Growing Economy of Greater New Orleans in the 1970's," np.; Davis, *Louisiana,* 363; "Moisant International Airport," *Jefferson Parish Yearly Review* (1960): 91; *The States-Item*, December 14, 1961.

11. *Times-Picayune*, September 5, 1970; New Orleans Aviation Board, "Two Billion Dollars," np.

12. *Times-Picayune*, January 28, 1973, July 6, 1977; September 16, 1980, January 31, 1993, July 21, 1995, July 4, 1998, August 3, 2001, August 23, 2003, October 13, 2003.

13. *Times-Picayune*, May 9, 1983; June 12 and 14, 1984; May 22, 26, 1985.

14. Kenner Town Council Minutes, October 30, 1944; *States-Item*, November 10, 1959; Bauer, "A History of the City of Kenner, Louisiana," 94-95.

15. *Times-Picayune*, January 28, 1956.

16. Ibid.

17. *Times-Picayune*, January 28 and 29, 1956; *States-Item*, November 10, 1959.

18. *Times-Picayune*, March 13, 1956; Kenner City Council Minutes, March 12, 1956.

19. *Times-Picayune*, March 18, July 10, 1982, May 9, and 15, October 25, May 5, 1984, January 29, May 22, 1985.

20. *Times-Picayune*, March 18, 1982, May 9 and 15, October 25, and May 5, 1984, May 22 and 26, 1985; James D. "Buddy" Caldwell, Louisiana Attorney General, Opinion 12-0060, July 17, 2012.

21. On November 16, 1959, a National Airlines DC-7 flight from Tampa, Florida, to New Orleans crashed in the Gulf of Mexico with the loss of all forty-two persons on the flight. The cause of the incident was never determined. See *Times-Picayune*, November 17, 1959.

22. *Times-Picayune*, March 31, 1967, February 26, 1964, February 26, 2014; *States-Item*, February 25, 1964; Flight Safety Foundation, Aviation Safety Network Database available at www.flightsafety.org.

23. Because Eastern Airlines flight 304 had reached its flight path away from the airport before it crashed, the *Times-Picayune* newspaper and others do not associate the incident with the Kenner airport. To them the 1967 crash was the first to involve the airport. See *Times-Picayune*, March 31, 1967.

24. *Times-Picayune*, March 31, 1967; Flight Safety Foundation, Aviation Safety Network Database.

25. *Times-Picayune*, March 21, 1969; Flight Safety Foundation, Aviation Safety

Network Database.

26. *Times-Picayune*, July 10, 11, 12, 1982 and July 8, 2012; National Transportation Safety Board, "Aircraft Accident Report: Pan American World Airways, Inc., Clipper 759, Boeing 727-235, N4737, New Orleans International Airport, Kenner, Louisiana, July 9, 1982," 2-5, 18, 20.
27. *Times-Picayune*, July 10, 11, 12, 1982 and July 8, 2012; National Transportation Safety Board, "Aircraft Accident Report: Pan American World Airways, Inc., Clipper 759, Boeing 727-235, N4737, New Orleans International Airport, Kenner, Louisiana, July 9, 1982," 2-5.
28. National Transportation Safety Board, "Aircraft Accident Report: Pan American World Airways, Inc., Clipper 759, Boeing 727-235, N4737, New Orleans International Airport, Kenner, Louisiana, July 9, 1982," ii, 20; *Times-Picayune*, July 8, 2012 and July 11, 1982.
29. *Times-Picayune*, July 10, 11, 1982 and July 8, 2012.
30. *Times-Picayune*, July 27, 1985, July 8, 2012; Caldwell, Opinion 12-0060, July 17, 2012.
31. *Times-Picayune*, October 1, 2010, January 29, 2012.
32. *Times-Picayune*, May 5, 1984, February 5, 1992, July 21, 1995, August 9, 1998, February 11, 2000, June 22, 2001, August 31, 2005, May 16, 2008, June 24, 2009, September 22, 2009, July 6, 2010; October 21, 2010; Chamber of Commerce/New Orleans, *Community Report*, December 1973.
33. Campanella, *Geographies of New Orleans*, 28; *Times-Picayune*, August 31, September 7, 10, October 19, 2005.
34. Jeffrey Sigmon, New Orleans Aviation Board to the author, September 24, 2012; *Times-Picayune*, March 8 and 27, 2013; *New Orleans Advocate*, January 31, 2015.
35. *Times-Picayune*, August 18, 2011.
36. *Times-Picayune*, March 27, April 17, 2013, January 17, 2014.

CHAPTER 11

1. Irwin Unger, *These United States: The Question of Our Past* (Upper Saddle River, N.J.: Prentice Hall, 1999), 677; Mary Lou Widmer, *New Orleans in the Forties* (Gretna, La.: Pelican Publishing Company, 1990), 109; Swanson, *Historic Jefferson Parish*, 131; R.W. Hartshorn, "The Home Frontier," *Jefferson Parish Yearly Review* (1948): 61.
2. Unger, *These United States*, 677; Becky M. Nicolaides, "Suburbia and the Sunbelt," *OAH Magazine of History* 18 (October 2003): 22, 24; Widmer, *New Orleans in the Forties*, 127; Lloyd Vogt, *New Orleans Houses: A House-Watcher's Guide*

(Gretna, La.: Pelican Publishing Company, 1992), 165; Joseph S. Kopfler, "Kenner 'Fastest Growing City in the State,'" *Jefferson Parish Yearly Review* (1954): 182..

3. Hartshorn, "The Home Frontier," *Jefferson Parish Yearly Review* (1948): 61; Kenner Town Council Minutes, July 20, 1950; Kopfler, "Kenner 'Fastest Growing City in the State,'"183.
4. Kopfler, "Kenner 'Fastest Growing City in the State,'" 182; Kenner Town Council Minutes, July 6, 1951; Public Affairs Research Council of Louisiana, *A Statistical Profile of Jefferson Parish* (Baton Rouge: Public Affairs Research Council of Louisiana, Inc., 1965), 23-26; Lewis, *New Orleans: The Making of an Urban Landscape*, 76.
5. Nicole Stelle Garnett, "Suburbs as Exit, Suburbs as Entrance," *Michigan Law Review* 106 (November, 2007): 284.
6. Kopfler, "Kenner 'Fastest Growing City in the State,'" 182; Garnett, "Suburbs as Exit, Suburbs as Entrance," 284-85; Campanella, *Geographies of New Orleans*, 309; Nicolaides, "Suburbia and the Sunbelt," 24; Arnold R. Hirsch, "New Orleans: Sunbelt in the Swamp," in *New Orleans and Urban Louisiana, Part C: 1920 to Present*, ed. Samuel C. Shepherd Jr., The Louisiana Purchase Bicentennial Series in Louisiana History (Lafayette: Center for Louisiana Studies, 2005), 511, 530-31; Numan V. Bartley, *The New South: 1945-1980* (Baton Rouge: Louisiana State University Press, 1995), 378.
7. Donna Brazile, *Cooking With Grease: Stirring the Pots in American Politics* (New York: Simon & Schuster, 2004), 1, 4.
8. Ibid., 2, 22.
9. Ibid., 22; *Times-Picayune*, August 4, 1992.
10. Brazile, *Cooking With Grease*, 25, 31.
11. Ibid., 32, 34; *Times-Picayune*, August 2, September 11, and December 9, 1979.
12. Ibid., 40-43, 47-49, *Times-Picayune*, August 31, 1971.
13. Garnett, "Suburbs as Exit, Suburbs as Entrance," 284-85; Campanella, *Geographies of New Orleans*, 309; Nicolaides, "Suburbia and the Sunbelt," 24; Hirsch, "New Orleans: Sunbelt in the Swamp," 511, 530-31; Kopfler, "Kenner 'Fastest Growing City in the State,'" 182; Numan V. Bartley, *The New South: 1945-1980* (Baton Rouge: Louisiana State University Press, 1995), 378; *East Bank Guide*, June 27, 1979.
14. Campanella, *Geographies of New Orleans*, 16, 21, 378, 380; *Times-Picayune*, July 9, 2001 and June 16, 2011.
15. Hirsch, "New Orleans: Sunbelt in the Swamp," 512; Kenner City Council Minutes, April 13, 1955; Bauer, "History of the City of Kenner," 47, 49-50.

16. Bauer, "History of the City of Kenner," 49; Kenner City Council Minutes, February 12, 1973; *East Bank Guide*, December 27, 1972; *Times-Picayune*, January 9, 1991, October 24, 2006.

17. Bauer, "History of the City of Kenner," 48, 83; Bezou, *Metairie*, 140; Lewis, *New Orleans—The Making of an Urban Landscape*, 76; *States-Item*, March 26, 1973; *Times-Picayune*, November 30, 2011.

18. *States-Item*, March 26, 1973; Lewis, *New Orleans: The Making of an Urban Landscape*, 76.

19. Kenner City Council Minutes, August 1, 1952; *Times-Picayune*, January 11, 1961; Lane W. Lancaster, *Government in Rural America* (Princeton, N.J.: D. Van Nostrand Company, Inc., 1952), 105.

20. Author's interview with Kenner City Councilman Thomas LeBlanc, May 5, 1971.

21. *Kenner City News*, March 5, 1970; *States-Item*, February 13, 1973.

22. *East Bank Guide*, November 1 and November 8, 1972; Kenner, Louisiana, *Home Rule Charter of the City of Kenner, Louisiana*, November 7, 1973.

CHAPTER 12

1. Lewis, *New Orleans: The Making of an Urban Landscape*, 76; Leavitt, *Kenner*, np; *Times-Picayune*, January 28, 1973.

2. *Times-Picayune*, November 1, 1972, February 13, October 3, 1977; Campanella, *Geographies of New Orleans*, 61-62.

3. Craig E. Colten, "Reintroducing Nature to the City: Wetlands in New Orleans," in *New Orleans and Urban Louisiana 1920 to Present*, ed. Samuel C. Shepherd Jr., The Louisiana Purchase Bicentennial Series in Louisiana History (Lafayette: Center for Louisiana Studies, 2005), 548; *Times-Picayune*, July 28, 1974 and October 3, 1977; United States Soil Conservation Service, "Greater New Orleans' Unique City Unique Soils: Soil Information For Homebuyers and Homebuilders," undated pamphlet issued sometime in the late 1970s; Campanella, *Geographies of New Orleans*, 63.

4. *Times-Picayune*, September 20, 21, 1947; David Roth, "Louisiana Hurricane History"; Leavitt, *Kenner*, np.

5. Campanella, *Bienville's Dilemma*, 321;

6. Ibid.; U.S. Army Engineering District, New Orleans, *Report on Hurricane Betsy, 8-11 September 1965* (New Orleans: Corps of Engineers, November 1965), 4, 49; Frank J. Borne Jr., "Remembering Hurricane Betsy on Her 40th Anniversary: Recollections of a Storm that Affected a Generation," *Jefferson History Notebook* 9 (Jefferson Parish, La.: Jefferson Historical Society of Louisiana, October

2005), 3.

7. U.S. Army Engineering District, *Report on Hurricane Betsy*, 35; Borne, "Remembering Hurricane Betsy on Her 40th Anniversary: Recollections of a Storm that Affected a Generation." 25-26; Campanella, *Bienville's Dilemma*, 323.

8. Campanella, *Bienville's Dilemma*, 329-30; *Times-Picayune*, August 29, 2005.

9. American Society of Civil Engineers, *The New Orleans Hurricane Protection System: What Went Wrong and Why* (Reston, Va.: American Society of Civil Engineers, 2007), 55.

10. Campanella, *Bienville's Dilemma*, 331-32; American Society of Civil Engineers, *The New Orleans Hurricane Protection System*, 19, 22, 24, 35, 39, 73.

11. *Times-Picayune*, September 4 and 9, 2005, August 31, 2014.

12. *Times-Picayune*, August 30, September 2, 3, and 6, 2005.

13. *Times-Picayune*, September 2 and 9, 2005.

14. *Times-Picayune*, October 7, 8, and 12, 2005.

15. *Times-Picayune*, October 7, 2005.

16. *Times-Picayune*, October 8, 2005.

17. *Times-Picayune*, January 24, 27, April 23, 29, 2008, September 4, 2013, and January 19, 2014; *USA Today*, April 29, 2008; Videotaped Deposition of Aaron Broussard, 24th Judicial District Court for the Parish of Jefferson, State of Louisiana, Chicago Property Interests, L.L.C. and Zoe Aldige Individually and on Behalf of Those Similarly Situated Versus Aaron Broussard Personally and in His Capacity as President of Jefferson Parish and Jefferson Parish, November 28, 2007, available from http://blog.nola.com/news_impact/2008/01/Broussard%20 deposition .pdf, accessed March 20, 2013.

18. In February 2014, in a civil suit over the Katrina flooding, a Jefferson Parish jury issued a complicated and contradictory finding that the parish was negligent in how it handled its "doomsday plan" during the great storm. However, because the jury also found that there was no "willful misconduct" by Broussard and other parish officials, under state law Broussard and the parish could not be found liable for the flood damages. The jury did not rule on the wisdom or competence of the parish's doomsday plan of hurricane protection. *Times-Picayune*, September 7, 2005, October 8, 2005, April 11, 2006, April 17, 23, 29, 2008, and February 7, 2014; American Society of Civil Engineers, *The New Orleans Hurricane Protection System*, 68; Douglas Brinkley, *The Great Deluge: Hurricane Katrina, New Orleans, and the Mississippi Gulf Coast* (New York: Harper Collins, 2006),

CHAPTER 13

1. *Times-Picayune*, February 6, 2011; Greater New Orleans Community Data Center, "Who Lives in New Orleans and the Metro Area Now?" September 20, 2012, available from https://gnocdc.s3.amazonaws.com/reports/GNOCDC_WhoLivesinNewOrleansAndThe MetroAreaNow.pdf (accessed April 5, 2012); United States Census Bureau, State and County Quikfacts, Kenner, Louisiana, available from www.quickfacts.census.gov/qfd/states /22/ 2239475.htm (accessed April 7, 2013).
2. *Times-Picayune*, October 13, 1990, September 27, 2007, and December 6, 2012.
3. Ibid., June 9, 1994, October 13, 1999, May 30, 2000, May 25, 2002, March 7, 2004, February 25 and 27, 2013; *Gambit* (New Orleans), February 26, 2008; *Kenner Star*, June 2011 and September 2012.
4. *Times-Picayune*, December 10, 1982, March 6, 1983, February 13, 2012, an July 7, 2013; *The City News: Rivertown, USA Special Edition,* ND, 1984; *The Advocate* (New Orleans Edition), November 25, 2012 and July 3, 2013; Dawn Achee, "Rivertown: A Hidden Collection of Culture Emerges" (master's thesis, University of New Orleans, 2002), 2; Stahls, *Jefferson Parish: Rich Heritage, Promising Future*, 55.
5. Holtgreve, "Just Around the Corner," 107; Leavitt, *Kenner*, np; Borne, "Jefferson Parish Sheriffs," 9-11; Stahls, *Jefferson Parish: Rich Heritage, Promising Future*, 45-46.
6. *Times-Picayune*, February 23, 1966, April 1, 1970; March 17, 1987; Brazile, *Cooking With Grease*, 31-34; Joseph Maselli and Dominic Candeloro, *Images of America: Italians in New Orleans* (Charleston: Arcadia Publishing, 2004), 85.
7. Bauer, "The History of the City of Kenner, Louisiana," 63-64; *Times-Picayune*, February 17, 1980 and March 17, 1987.
8. *Times-Picayune*, October 6, 1995.
9. *Times-Picayune*, January 10, 2010; James Gill, "The Election That Turned Into a Perp Walk," *Times-Picayune*, March 3, 2013.
10. *Times-Picayune*, January 10, 2010; Gill, "The Election That Turned Into a Perp Walk."
11. *Times-Picayune*, January 10, 2010.
12. Quoted in the *Times-Picayune*, February 27, 2013.
13. Ibid.; *Times-Picayune,* January 10, 2010; *New Orleans Advocate*, December 22, 2015.
14. Donnabrazile.com (accessed February 22, 2014).
15. *Times-Picayune*, January 31, February 4 and 7, August 22, 2004; Dawn Ruth,

"Calculating the Big Picture: Hard Times for Higher Ed," *New Orleans Magazine* 47 (August 2013): 34-36; Office of the Governor, State of Louisiana. "Bobby Jindal." available from http;//lousiana.gov/index.cfm?md'pagebuilder&tmp'home&na (accessed July 17, 2013); *New Orleans Advocate*, December 22, 2015.

16. James Kirby Martin, Randy Roberts, Steven Mintz, Linda O. McMurry, and James H. Jones, *America and Its People: A Mosaic in the Making* (New York: Pearson Longman, 2004), 777; David C. Roller and Robert W. Twyman, eds., *The Encyclopedia of Southern History* (Baton Rouge: Louisiana State University Press, 1979), s.v. "Music, Jazz, and Popular," by William H. Young; Tom Aswell, *Louisiana Rocks! The True Genesis of Rock & Roll* (Gretna, La.: Pelican Publishing Company, 2010), 138, 181-82.

17. Jeff Hannusch, "Classic Songs of Louisiana—Land of 1,000 Dances," *Offbeat* 19 (May 2006): 40-41; Jeff Hannusch, "Reviews: Chris Kenner," *Offbeat* 21 (August 2008): 38; Oscar Garza, "'Land of 1000 Dances,' An R&B Fable," *Popular Music* 24 (October 2005): 429-30.

18. Aswell, *Louisiana Rocks*. 59-61; Bureau of the Census, *Sixteenth Census of the United States, 1940*, Washington, D.C.: National Archives and Records Administration, 1940; Bill Dahl, "Lloyd Price Biography," Allmusic.com, available from www.allmusic.com/artist/lloyd-price-mn0000827250/biography (accessed August 24, 2013); Troy A. Broussard and Frank J. Borne Jr., *Images of America: Kenner* (Charleston: Troy A. Broussard and Frank J. Borne, Jr., 2012), 118; William "Dollar Bill" Waller, "The Lloyd Price 'Did U Know' Trivia Facts," available from www.Lawdymissclawdy.com/Lloyd%20Price%20Bio%20as%20as%of%20Oct%201,%202010%20%and%20YESTERDAY%20and%TODAY.pdf (accessed September 3, 2013).

19. Aswell, *Louisiana Rocks*, 59-61, 405-406; Dahl, "Lloyd Price Biography;" *Times-Picayune*, March 4 and 19, 1994; Waller, "The Lloyd Price 'Did U Know' Trivia Facts."

20. ARTINFO's 30 Under 30/Jonathan Batiste, Pinterest.com, accessed May 17, 2016; Eliza Berman, "Meet Jon Batiste Bandleader for The Late Show with Stephen Colbert," available from time.com/3907726/jon-baptiste-bandleader-stephen-colbet, June 4, 2015, accessed May 17, 2016; Amanda Wicks, "Jon Batiste-Bandleader, the late show with stephen colbert, New York City via kenner," available from Http://www.myneworleans.com/Louisiana-Life/January-February-2016/Louisianians-of-the Year/, accessed May 17, 2016.

21. "Kenner 2030: Strategic Plan for a Prosperous Future-Executive Summary," n.d., available from www.kenner.la.us/2/kenner2030.pdf (accessed August 24, 2013).

22. Michael S. Yenni is not the son of Joseph Yenni discussed previously. He is the grandson of Joseph Yenni who followed in his grandfather's steps by first being

elected mayor of Kenner and in October 2015 was elected parish president.

23. "Kenner 2030: Strategic Plan for a Prosperous Future," n.d., 5, 9-10, 95, available from www.kenner.la.us/2/kenner2030.pdf (accessed August 24, 2013).

24. Ibid., 73.

25. "Kenner 2030: Strategic Plan for a Prosperous Future-Executive Summary," 7, 17.

26. "Kenner 2030: Strategic Plan for a Prosperous Future," 121.

27. Perhaps signifying the beginning of a renaissance for the community, as the writing of this manuscript neared completion, Kenner Mayor Mike Yenni initiated an ambitious $47 million plan for a series of city-wide projects designed to improve the major traffic corridors of the city. The proposal included new bicycle paths, public art, better lighting, landscaping, pedestrian crosswalks, and road and drainage work. In October of 2015, Mike Yenni continued the practice of Kenner mayors winning parish-wide political office. As his grandfather and cousin before him, Mike Yenni was elected with 52 percent of the vote to the office of Parish President. See *Times-Picayune*, April 5, 14, 2013 and October 24, 2015, *The Advocate*, March 1, 2013.

Bibliography

Primary Source Materials and public Documents

Annual Report of the Adjutant-General of the State of New York for the year 1894 Vol III: Registers of the 9th, 10th, 11th, and 12th Regiments of Cavalry, N.Y. Vols, in War of the Rebellion. Albany: James B. Lyon, State Printer, 1895.

Atlanta, Georgia. Emory University Library. Special Collections Department. Alfred A. Rigby: Union Soldier's Diary, 1862-1865.

Baton Rouge, Louisiana. Special Collections, Hill Memorial Library. Louisiana State University.

William Kenner Papers.

Kenner Family Papers.

Caldwell, James D. "Buddy." Louisiana Attorney General, Opinion 12-0060, July 17, 2012.

Felix v. Wagner, 39 La. Ann. 391 (1887).

Felix et al. V. Michel, Secretary of State, 122 La. 352 (1908).

Gretna, Louisiana. Jefferson Parish Court House.

Succession of William Kenner and Mary Minor, his wife, 1826.

Jefferson Parish Police Jury (Left Bank) Minutes.

Jefferson Parish Police Jury Minutes.

Hall, Luther E. Proclamation Declaring the Incorporation of the Village of Kenner, Louisiana, December 13, 1913.

______. Proclamation Declaring Kenner to be a Town, February 5, 1914.

Historical Records Survey, *Transcription of Parish Records of Louisiana; Number 26, Jefferson Parish (Gretna), Series I, Police Jury Minutes*, Baton Rouge, 1939-1941.

"Important Sale of Lots, Squares & Tracts of Land in the Town of Kenner."March 28, 1855. Provided to the author by Mr. J. P. Walker, Metairie, Louisiana.

Kenner, Louisiana. *Home Rule Charter of the City of Kenner, Louisiana*. November 7, 1973.

Kenner, Louisiana. Jefferson Parish Public Library. Mayor Joseph S. Kepfler Sr. "Kenner's Centennial Celebration Address." March 2, 1955.

Kenner, Louisiana. Kenner City Hall Archives.

Kenner City Council Minutes

Kenner Town Council Minutes

Kenner Village Council Minutes

Long, Earl K. Proclamation Declaring Kenner a City, January 22, 1952.

Louisiana, *Acts Passed by the General Assembly of the State of Louisiana* (Baton Rouge, 1867).

Louisiana, *Acts Passed by the General Assembly of the State of Louisiana* (Baton Rouge, 1873).

Louisiana, *Acts of State of Louisiana*, Regular Session 1908.

O'Sullivan v. Felix, 233 U.S. 318; 34 S. Ct. 596, 58 L. Ed. 980 (1914).

National Transportation Safety Board. "Aircraft Accident Report: Pan American World Airways, Inc., Clipper 759, Boeing 727-235, N4737, New Orleans International Airport, Kenner, Louisiana, July 9, 1982."

New Orleans, Louisiana. Historic New Orleans Collection. Williams Research Center.

Bringier and Related Families Papers.

New Orleans, Louisiana. New Orleans Public Library.

Last Will and Testament of William Kenner, July 23, 1823, Will Book Number 4.

WPA Photographs-Parishes Outside Orleans.

Regional Planning Commission. *History of Regional Growth of Jefferson, Orleans, and St. Bernard Parishes, Louisiana.* New Orleans: Regional Planning Commission, 1969.

Thirteenth Census of the United States, 1910. Records of the Bureau of the Census, record Group 29. National Archives, Washington D.C. (Ancestry.com on-line database).

Tucson, Arizona. James Connor Prescott Family Papers including the Reminisces of Judge James C. Baumann, in the possession of J. Brown.

United States of America, Bureau of the Census. *Eighth Census of the United States, 1860.* Washington, D.C.: National Archives and Records Administration, 1860.

U.S. Congress, *Journal of the Senate of the United States.* Vol. 21. *List of Acts and Resolutions Passed at the First Session of the Twenty-Second Congress.*

U.S. Congress. Senate. *A Bill Confirming the Claim of Maria Holliday to a Tract of Land in Louisiana.* S. 46, 22nd Cong., 1st sess., January 5, 1832.

U.S. Department of War. *The War of the Rebellion: A Compilation of the Official Records of the Union and Confederate Armies.* 128 vols. Washington, D.C.: United States Government Printing Office, 1880-1901.

U.S. Department of the Interior. Bureau of the Census. *Ninth Census of the United States: 1870, Jefferson Parish.*

Washington, D.C. National Archives.

Bureau of the Census. *Sixteenth Census of the United States, 1940.* Washington,

D.C.: National Archives and Records Administration, 1940.

U.S. Army Continental Commands, Department of the Gulf. "Letters Sent, November, 1864-March 1865, Kenner, Louisiana."

U.S. Army Continental Commands, Department of the Gulf. "Oaths of Allegiance Administered, September, 1862-July, 1863, Cavalry Camp of Instruction and Distribution at Kenner, Louisiana."

Wattigny, A. Population certification of the "Village of Kenner." February 5, 1914.

Newspapers

Advocate (New Orleans Edition), 2012, 2013, 2015.

Baltimore Patriot, 1824.

Cincinnati Daily Gazette, 1875.

The Daily City Item, 1893.

Daily Picayune, 1851-1854, 1858, 1862, 1866, 1870-1874, 1880, 1884-1886, 1892, 1893, 1895, 1899-1901, 1908, 1909, 1911, 1913, 1914.

Daily True Delta, 1861, 1862.

Davenport Gazette, 1849.

Gambit, 2008-2009.

Jefferson Democrat, 1941, 1942.

Jefferson Parish East Bank Guide, 1972, 1979.

The City News (Kenner), 1970, 1984.

Kenner Star, 2011, 2012.

Louisiana Advertiser, 1826, 1827.

Louisiana Gazette, 1810.

Louisiana State Gazette, 1826.

New Orleans Advocate, 2015

New Orleans Daily Crescent, 1865.

New Orleans Item, 1910, 1952.

New Orleans States-Item, 1959, 1961, 1964, 1973.

New Orleans Times, 1866, 1867, 1875.

New York Times, 1858.

Plaquemine Daily Journal, 1892.

Orleans Gazette, 1810.

Times-Democrat, 1892.

Times-Picayune, 1921, 1944, 1946, 1953, 1956, 1959, 1961, 1964, 1967, 1969,

1970-1974, 1977, 1980-1984, 1987, 1990-1995, 1998, 2000-2002, 2004-2015.

USA Today, 2008.

Interviews

Author's interview with Kenner City Councilman Thomas LeBlanc, May 5, 1971.

Correspondence

Buckman, RSM, Sr. Mary Jeremy to the author, April 12, 2012.

Sigmon, Jeffrey, New Orleans Aviation Board to the author, September 24, 2012.

Books and Articles

Achee, Dawn. "Rivertown: A Hidden Collection of Culture Emerges." master's thesis, University of New Orleans, 2002.

American Society of Civil Engineers. *The New Orleans Hurricane Protection System: What Went Wrong and Why.* Reston, Va.: American Society of Civil Engineers, 2007.

Arthur, Stanley C. and George C. Huchet de Kernion. *Old Families of Louisiana.* 1931; Reprint ed., Baton Rouge: Claitor's Publishing Division, 1971.

Aswell, Tom. *Louisiana Rocks! The True Genesis of Rock & Roll.* Gretna, La.: Pelican Publishing Company, 2010.

Baiamonte, John V., Jr. "'Who Killa de Chief' Revisited: The Hennessey Assassination and Its Aftermath, 1890-1981." *Louisiana History* 33 (Spring 1992): 117-46.

Barry, John M. *Rising Tide: The Great Mississippi Flood of 1927 and How It Changed America.* New York: Simon & Schuster Paperbacks, 1997.

Bartlett, Napier. *A Soldier's Story of the War: Including the Marshes and Battles of the Washington Artillery and of other Louisiana Troops.* New Orleans: Clark and Hofeline, 1874.

Bartley, Numan V. *The New South: 1945-1980.* Baton Rouge: Louisiana State University Press, 1995.

Bateman, Thomas H. *Houston and Allied Families.* New York: privately printed for Samuel Frederic Houston by the American Historical Company, Inc., 1950.

Baudier, Roger. *The Catholic Church in Louisiana.* New Orleans: Roger Baudier, 1939.

Bauer, Craig A. *A Leader Among Peers: The Life and Times of Duncan Farrar Kenner.* Lafayette: Center for Louisiana Studies, University of Southwestern Louisiana,

1993.

______. "From Burnt Canes to Budding City: A History of the City of Kenner, Louisiana." *Louisiana History* 33 (Fall 1982): 353-81.

______. "The History of the City of Kenner, Louisiana." master's thesis, Southeastern Louisiana University, 1973.

______. "The Last Effort: The Secret Mission of the Confederate Diplomat, Duncan F. Kenner." *Louisiana History* 22 (Winter 1981): 67-95.

______ and Mark LaFlaur. "Duncan F. Kenner." *Dictionary of American National Biography*. New York: Oxford Press, 2002.

Belloni, Nathaniel F., Jr. "The Great Mace-Allen Fight: When Kenner was the World's Boxing Capital." *Jefferson History Notebook* 1 (August 1979): 1-4.

Bezou, Henry C. "Jefferson Parish's Gallic Roots." *Jefferson History Notebook* 1 (December 1979): 1-4.

______. *Metairie: A Tongue of Land to Pasture.* Gretna, La.: Pelican Publishing Company, 1973.

Blume, Helmut. *The German Coast During the Colonial Era 1722-1803*. Edited and translated by Ellen C. Merrill. Destrehan, La.: The German-Acadian Coast Historical and Genealogical Society, 1990.

Boneno, Roselyn Bologna. "From Migrant to Millionaire: The Story of the Italian-American in New Orleans, 1880-1910." Ph.D. dissertation, Louisiana State University, 1986.

Boles, John B. *The South Through Time: A History of an American Region.* Englewood Cliffs, N.J.: Prentice Hall, 1995.

Booth, A.B. "Louisiana Confederate Military Records." *Louisiana Historical Quarterly* 4 (January 1921): 369-418.

Booth, Andrew B. *Records of Louisiana Confederate Soldiers and Louisiana Confederate Commands*. New Orleans, 1920.

Bordenave, Justin F. "Fourth Jefferson Drainage District." *Jefferson Parish Yearly Review* (1938): 187-91.

______. "Wanted–One Seawall." *Jefferson Parish Yearly Review* (1940): 156-62.

Borne, Frank J., Jr. 'Jefferson Parish Sheriffs: A Collection of Biographies of Jefferson Parish's Chief Law Enforcement Officers." *Jefferson History Notebook* 8. Jefferson Parish, La.: Jefferson Historical Society of Louisiana, February, 2004.

______. 'Remembering Hurricane Betsy on Her 40th Anniversary: Recollections of a Storm that Affected a Generation." *Jefferson History Notebook* 9. Jefferson Parish, La.: Jefferson Historical Society of Louisiana, October 2005.

Bouchereau, A. *Statement of the Sugar and Rice Crops Made in Louisiana in 1877-1878.* New Orleans: Pelican Book and Job Printing, 1878.

Bourgeois, Lillian C. *Cabanocey: The History, Customs and Folklore of St. James Parish.* New Orleans: Pelican Publishing Company, 1957.

Bragg, Jefferson D. *Louisiana in the Confederacy*. Baton Rouge: Louisiana State University Press, 1941.

Brasseaux, Carl A., ed. and trans. *A Comparative View of French Louisiana, 1699 and 1762: The Journals of Pierre Le Moyne d'Iberville and Jean-Jacques-Blaise d'Abbadie*. Lafayette: Center for Louisiana Studies, University of Southwestern Louisiana, 1979: revised ed., 1981.

Brazile, Donna. *Cooking With Grease: Stirring the Pots in American Politics.* New York: Simon & Schuster, 2004.

Brinkley, Douglas. *The Great Deluge: Hurricane Katrina, New Orleans,and the Mississippi Gulf Coast.* New York: Harper Collins, 2006.

Broussard, Troy A. and Frank J. Borne Jr. *Images of America: Kenner.* Charleston: Troy A. Broussard and Frank J. Borne Jr., 2012.

Buman, Nathan A. "Historiographical Examinations of the 1811 Slave Insurrection." *Louisiana History* 53 (Summer 2012): 318-37.

______. "To Kill Whites: The 1811 Louisiana Slave Insurrection." master's thesis, Louisiana State University, 2008.

Blassingame, John W. *Black New Orleans 1860-1880.* Chicago: University of Chicago Press, 1973.

Bull, J. H. "Shipbuilding in Jefferson." *Jefferson Parish Yearly Review* (1942): 102-106.

Campanella, Richard. *Bienville's Dilemma: A Historical Geography of New Orleans.* Lafayette: Center for Louisiana Studies, University of Louisiana at Lafayette, 2008.

_______. *Geographies of New Orleans: Urban Fabrics Before the Storm.* Lafayette: Center for Louisiana Studies, 2006.

Campbell, Edna F. "New Orleans in Early Days." *Geographical Review* 10 (July 1920): 31-36.

Carrigan, Jo Ann. "Yellow Fever in New Orleans, 1853: Abstractions and Realities." *Journal of Southern History* 25 (August 1959): 339-55.

Clark, John G. "New Orleans and the River: A Study in Attitude and Responses." *Louisiana History* 8 (Spring 1967): 117-35.

Clinton, Catherine. *The Plantation Mistress: Women's World in the Old South.* New York: Pantheon Books, 1982.

Chamber of Commerce/New Orleans. *Community Report*. December 1973.

Charlevoix, Pierre de. *Journal of a Voyage to North-America*. Vol 2. London: R. and J. Dodsley, 1861; Ann Arbor: University Microfilms, Inc., 1966.

Clark, John G. *New Orleans 1718-1812: An Economic History*. Baton Rouge: Louisiana State University Press, 1970.

Colten, Craig E. "Reintroducing Nature to the City: Wetlands in New Orleans." In *New Orleans and Urban Louisiana, 1920 to Present*, edited by Samuel C. Shepherd Jr., 538-58. The Louisiana Purchase Bicentennial Series in Louisiana History. Lafayette: Center for Louisiana Studies, 2005.

Conrad, Glenn R. *The First Families of Louisiana.* Baton Rouge: Claitor's Publishing Division, 1970.

______. *The German Coast: Abstracts of the Civil Records of St. Charles and St. John the Baptist Parishes 1804-1812.* Lafayette: Center for Louisiana Studies, 1981.

______ and Ray F. Lucas. *White Gold: A Brief History of the Louisiana Sugar Industry 1795-1995.* Lafayette: Center for Louisiana Studies, 1995.

Coppinger, Margaret Brown, Herschel Gower, Samuel H. Howell, and Georgianna D. Overby. *Beersheba Springs: 150 Years 1833-1983: A History of a Celebration.* Beersheba, Tenn.: Beersheba Springs Historical Society, 1983.

Curry, Thomas. *Reports of Cases Argued and Determined in the Supreme Court of the State of Louisiana.* Vol. 19. New Orleans: E. Johns & Co., 1842.

D'Gerolamo, Vic. "Town of Kenner." *Jefferson Parish Yearly Review* (1942): 162, 164.

Daspit, Fred. *Louisiana Architecture 1714-1830.* Lafayette, La.: Center for Louisiana Studies, University of Southwestern Louisiana, 1996.

Daul, George Cecil. *The Administration of the Public Schools of Jefferson Parish Since the Civil War (1860-1940).* Metairie, La.: Jefferson Parish Historical Commission, 1981.

Davis, Edwin Adams. *Louisiana: A Narrative History.* Nashville: Bensen Printing Co., 1965.

Davis, George B., Leslie J. Perry, and Joseph W. Kirkley. *The Official Military Atlas of the Civil War.* New York: Barnes & Noble Books, 2003.

De Jong, Greta. *A Different Day: African American Struggle for Justice in Rural Louisiana, 1900-1970.* Chapel Hill: University of North Carolina Press, 2002.

Dennett, Dan'l. *Louisiana As it Is.* New Orleans: Eureka Press, 1876.

Dethloff, Henry C. and Robert R. Jones. "Race Relations in Louisiana, 1877-98." *Louisiana History* 9 (Fall 1968): 301-23.

Dix, Dorothy. "Women in War." *Jefferson Parish Yearly Review* (1942): 25-33.

Dorman, James H. "The Persistent Specter: Slave Rebellion in Territorial Louisiana." *Louisiana History* 18 (Autumn 1977): 389-404.

Dufour, Pie (Charles L.). "A La Mode- 'Minor' Error on Kenner for it was Minor Kenner who Founded the Town." *New Orleans States*, March 4, 1955.

______. *The Night the War Was Lost.* Lincoln: University of Nebraska Press, 1994.

Dupont, Nancy McKenzie. "The German Priest, the Banana Boats, and the Origins of Broadcasting in New Orleans." *Louisiana History* 40 (Spring 1999): 211-21.

Eaton, Clement. *A History of the Old South.* London: Macmillan Company, 1966.

East Jefferson General Hospital, *Examiner*, June 1987.

Faust, Patricia L., ed. *Historical Times Illustrated Encyclopedia of the Civil War.* New York: Harper & Row, Publishers, 1986. S.v. "Steele, Frederick," by Jeffrey D.

West.

Foner, Eric. *Reconstruction: America's Unfinished Revolution 1863-1877.* New York: Harper & Row Publishers, 1988.

Foster, William J., ed. *The La Salle Expedition on the Mississippi: A Lost Manuscript of Nicolas de La Salle, 1682.* Translated by Johanna L. Warren. Austin: Texas State Historical Association, 2003.

Franklin, John Hope. *From Slavery to Freedom.* 3rd ed. New York: Alfred A.mKnopf, 1967.

Freiberg, Edna. *Bayou St. John in Colonial Louisiana: 1699-1803.* New Orleans: Harvey Press, 1980.

Fussell, Elizabeth. "Constructing New Orleans, Constructing Race: A Population History of New Orleans." *The Journal of American History* 94 (December 2007): 846-55.

Garnett, Nicole Stelle. "Suburbs as Exit, Suburbs as Entrance." *Michigan Law Review* 106 (November 2007): 277-304.

Garvey, Joan B. and Mary Lou Widmer. *Beautiful Crescent: A History of New Orleans.* 7th ed. New Orleans: Garmer Press, Inc., 1994.

Garza, Oscar. "'Land of 1000 Dances,' An R&B Fable." *Popular Music* 24 (October 2005): 429-37.

Gauthreaux, Alan G. AInhospitable land: Anti-Italian Sentiment and Violence in Louisiana, 1891-1924." *Louisiana History* 51 (Winter 2010): 41-68.

Gayarre, Charles. *History of Louisiana: The French Domination.* 2nd. ed. New York: William J. Widdleton, Publisher, 1867.

Geiger, George T., Jr. "A Silver Lining." *Jefferson Parish Yearly Review* (1942): 130-36.

Gill, James. "The Election That Turned Into a Perp Walk." *Times-Picayune*, March 3, 2013.

Gillson, Gordon E. *Louisiana State Board of Health: The Progressive Years.* Baton Rouge: Moran Industries, 1976.

Hair, William Ivy. *Bourbonism and Agrarian Protest: Louisiana Politics 1877-1900.* Baton Rouge: Louisiana State University Press, 1969.

______. *Carnival of Fury: Robert Charles and the New Orleans Race Riot of 1900.* Baton Rouge: Louisiana State University Press, 1976.

Hannusch, Jeff. "Classic Songs of Louisiana, 'Land of 1,000 Dances.'" *Offbeat* 19 (May 2006): 40-41.

______. "Reviews: Chris Kenner." *Offbeat* 21 (August 2008): 38.

Hartshorn, R.W. "The Home Frontier." *Jefferson Parish Yearly Review* (1948): 55-63.

Hearn, Chester G. *The Capture of New Orleans 1862.* Baton Rouge: Louisiana State University Press, 1995.

Heitmann, John A. "Getting Places in a Hurry: The Development of Aviation in

Long-Era South Louisiana." *Louisiana History* 39 (Fall 1988): 325-42.

Heleniak, Roman. "Local Reaction to the Great Depression in New Orleans, 1929-1933." *Louisiana History* 10 (Fall 1969): 289-306.

Hennessey, Melinda Meek. "Race and Violence in Reconstruction New Orleans: The 1868 Riot." *Louisiana History* 20 (Winter, 1979): 77-91.

Higgins, Lem. "Expansion is Keynote of Public School System." *Jefferson Parish Yearly Review* (1940): 90-98.

Higham, John. *Strangers in the Land: Patterns of American Nativism 1860-1925*. New Brunswick: Rutgers University Press, 1955.

Hirsch, Arnold R. "New Orleans: Sunbelt in the Swamp." In *New Orleans and Urban Louisiana, 1920 to Present*, edited by Samuel C. Shepherd Jr., 508-37. The Louisiana Purchase Bicentennial Series in Louisiana History Lafayette: Center for Louisiana Studies, 2005.

Historical Records Survey. "A Brief History of Jefferson Parish." *Jefferson Parish Yearly Review* (1939): 127-83.

Hogue, James K. *Uncivil War: Five New Orleans Street Battles and the Rise and Fall of Radical Reconstruction*. Baton Rouge: Louisiana State University, 2006.

Holtgreve, John J. "Just Around the Corner of Time." *Jefferson Parish Yearly Review* (1954): 2-15, 81-119.

Howard, Perry H. *Political Tendencies in Louisiana.* Rev. and enl. ed. Baton Rouge: Louisiana State University Press, 1971.

Ingersoll, Thomas N. *Mammon and Manon in Early New Orleans: The First Slave Society in the Deep South, 1718-1819*. Knoxville: University of Tennessee Press, 1999.

Ipik Plywood Corporation advertisement, *Jefferson Parish Yearly Review* (1943): 41.

Kaufman, Jacob J. "Farm Labor During World War II." *Journal of Farm Economics* 31 (February 1949): 131-42.

Kidder, Tristram R. "Making the City Inevitable: Native Americans and the Geography of New Orleans." In *Transforming New Orleans and Its Environs: Centuries of Change*, edited by Craig E. Carlton, 9-21. Pittsburgh: University of Pittsburgh Press, 2000.

Kniffen, Fred D., Hiram F. Gregory, and George A. Stokes. *Tribes of Louisiana: From 1542 to the Present*. Baton Rouge: Louisiana State University Press, 1987.

______. *Louisiana: Its Land and People.* Baton Rouge: Louisiana State University Press, 1968.

Kopfler, Joseph S. "Kenner Means Business." *Jefferson Parish Yearly Review* (1952): 172-75.

______. "Kenner 'Fastest Growing City in the State.'" *Jefferson Parish Yearly Review* (1954): 182-86.

______. "Kenner Takes to the Air." *Jefferson Parish Yearly Review* (1946): 167-69.

______. "Town of Kenner." *Jefferson Parish Yearly Review* (1943): 162, 170.

______. "Town of Kenner." *Jefferson Parish Yearly Review* (1944): 176.

Lancaster, Lane W. *Government in Rural America.* Princeton, N.J.: D. Van Nostrand Company, Inc., 1952.

Langstaff, D. O. "The Airport Situation Today." *Jefferson Parish Yearly Review* (1941): 146.

Le Conte, Rene and Glenn R. Conrad, trans., "The Germans in Louisiana in the Eighteenth Century." *Louisiana History* 8 (Winter 1967): 67-84.

Leavitt, Mel. *Kenner: An Historical Sketch by Mel Leavitt.* Kenner, La.: Merchants Trust and Savings Bank, n.d.

Lewis, Peirce F. *New Orleans: The Making of an Urban Landscape.* Cambridge: Ballinger Publishing Company, 1976.

Maggiore, Raphaella. "Raphaella Says." *The Kenner City News*, September 12, 1975.

Marshall, Jessie Ames, ed. *Private and Official Correspondence of Gen. Benjamin F. Butler During the Period of the Civil War.* Norwood, Mass.: Plimpton Press, 1917.

Maselli, Joseph and Dominic Candeloro. *Images of America: Italians in New Orleans.* Charleston: Arcadia Publishing, 2004.

Martin, Francois Xavier. *The History of Louisiana: From the Earliest Period.* Gretna, La.: Pelican Publishing Company, 1975.

Martin, James Kirby, Randy Roberts, Steven Mintz, Linda O. McMurry, and James H. Jones. *America and Its People: A Mosaic in the Making.* New York: Pearson Longman, 2004.

Martin, Sigur. *History of Our Local Government and the Development of Parishes, Municipalities and Political Subdivisions in Louisiana, and Their Power and Authority to Incur Debt and Issue Bonds.* Sigur Martin, 1966.

McNeely, Martel. "Jefferson Parish Food Production." *Jefferson Parish Yearly Review* (1943) 106-26.

McWilliams, Richebourg Gaillard ed. and trans. *Fleur de Lys and Calumet: Being the Penicaut Narrative of French Adventure in Louisiana.* Tuscaloosa: University of Alabama Press, 1981.

Mississippi River Commission, Mississippi River, Sheet Number 28, 1896.

"Moisant International Airport," *Jefferson Parish Yearly Review* (1960): 91-93.

Moore, John Hebron. "The Cypress Lumber Industry of the Lower Mississippi Valley during the Colonial Period." *Louisiana History* 24 (Winter 1983): 25-47.

Morris, Christopher. "Impenetrable but Easy." In *Transforming New Orleans and Its Environs: Centuries of Change*, edited by Craig E. Carlton. Pittsburgh: University of Pittsburgh Press, 2000.

Murray, Thomas Hamilton. *History of the Ninth Regiment, Connecticut Volunteer Infantry, "The Irish Regiment," in the War of the Rebellion, 1861-65.* New Haven: The Price, Lee & Adkiss Co., 1903.

Nau, John Fredrick. *The German People of New Orleans, 1850-1900.* Leiden: E.J. Brill, 1958.

Nevins, Allan. *Ordeal of the Union: Selected Chapters.* New York: Charles Scribner's Sons, 1973.

New Orleans Aviation Board. "Two Billion Dollars: New Orleans International Airport's Contribution to the Growing Economy of Greater New Orleans in the 1970's." n.p.

Nicolaides, Becky M. "Suburbia and the Sunbelt." *OAH Magazine of History* 18 (October 2003): 21-26.

Niehaus, Earl F. "Catholic Ethnics in Nineteenth-Century Louisiana." In *Cross, Crozier, and Crucible: A Volume Celebrating the Bicentennial of a Catholic Diocese in Louisiana,* edited by Glenn R. Conrad, 48-69. New Orleans: Roman Catholic Church of the Archdiocese of New Orleans, 1993.

Nystrom, Justin A. *New Orleans After the Civil War: Race, Politics, and a New Birth of Freedom.* Baltimore: Johns Hopkins University Press, 2010.

Pennebaker, E. S. "Transportation in Jefferson." *Jefferson Parish Yearly Review* (1960): 56-64, 71-89, 215-19.

Perkins, A. E. "Some Negro Officers and Legislators in Louisiana." *The Journal of Negro History* 14 (October 1929): 523-28.

Perrin, William E., Jr. "Civil War Military Operations In and Around Ponchatoula, Louisiana." *Louisiana History* 12 (Spring 1971): 123-36.

Pfeifer, Michael J. "Lynching and Criminal Justice in South Louisiana, 1878-1930." *Louisiana History* 40 (Spring 1999): 155-77.

______. "'. . . the already scarlet record of Jefferson Parish': Analysis of a Lynching Syndrome, 1892-1897." Paper presented at the Southern Historical Association's Annual Meeting. New Orleans, Louisiana, November 17, 2001.

Phillips, Ulrich Bonnell. *American Negro Slavery: A Survey of the Supply, Employment and Control of Negro Labor as Determined by the Plantation Regime.* New York: Appleton and Company, 1918.

Powell, Lawrence N. *The Accidental City: Improvising New Orleans.* Cambridge: Harvard University Press, 2012.

Poret, Ory G. "History of Land Titles in the State of Louisiana." Baton Rouge, Louisiana. State Land Office, Division of Administration, State of Louisiana, 1972.

Public Affairs Research Council of Louisiana, *A Statistical Profile of Jefferson Parish.* Baton Rouge: Public Affairs Research Council of Louisiana, Inc., 1965.

Pusateri, C. Joseph. "Radio Broadcasters and the Challenge of Television: A New Orleans Case." *The Business History Review* 54 (Autumn 1980): 303-29.

Randall, J.G. and David Donald. *The Civil War and Reconstruction.* 2nd ed. Lexington, Mass.: D.C. Heath and Company, 1969.

Rasmussen, Daniel. *American Uprising: The Untold Story of America's Largest Slave*

Revolt. New York: Harper Collins Publishers, 2011.

Reed, Merl. "Boom or Bust: Louisiana's Economy during the 1830's." *Louisiana History* 4 (Winter 1963): 35-53.

Reed, Merl E. "Government Investment and Economic Growth: Louisiana's Ante Bellum Railroads." *The Journal of Southern History* 28 (May 1962): 183-201

______. *New Orleans and the Railroads: The Struggle for Commercial Empire 1830-1860*. Baton Rouge: Louisiana State University Press, 1966.

Reeves, William D. *De La Barre: Life of a Creole Family in Louisiana*. New Orleans: Polyanthos, 1980.

Roller, David C. and Robert W. Twyman, eds. *The Encyclopedia of Southern History*. Baton Rouge: Louisiana State University Press, 1979. S.v. "Music, Jazz, and Popular," by William H. Young.

Rothman, Adam. *Slave Country: American Expansion and the Origins of the Deep South*. Cambridge: Harvard University Press, 2005.

Rowland, Dunbar, compiler and ed. *The Mississippi Territorial Archives 1798-1803: Executive Journals of Governor Winthrop Sargent and Governor William Charles Cole Claiborne*. Nashville: Brandon Printing Company, 1905.

Ruth, Dawn. "Calculating the Big Picture: Hard Times for Higher Ed." *New Orleans Magazine* 47 (August 2013): 34-36

Sanson, Jerry Purvis. *Louisiana During World War II: Politics and Society 1939-1945*. Baton Rouge: Louisiana State University, 1999.

Saxon, Lyle. "A Tourist Looks at Jefferson." *Jefferson Parish Yearly Review* (1941): 122-44.

______. *Father Mississippi*. New York: The Century Co., 1927.

______. Edward Dreyer, and Robert Tallant. *Gumbo Ya-Ya: Collection of Louisiana Folk Tales*. Baton Rouge: Louisiana Library Commission, 1945.

Shugg, Roger W. *Origins of Class Struggle in Louisiana: A Social History of White Farmers and Laborers During and After, 1840-1875*, paperback ed. Baton Rouge: Louisiana State University Press, 1967.

Sindler, Allan P. *Huey Long's Louisiana: State Politics, 1920-1952*. Baltimore: Johns Hopkins Press, 1956.

Sitterson, J. Carlyle. *Sugar Country: The Cane Sugar Industry in the South, 1753-1950*. Lexington: University of Kentucky Press, 1953.

Smith, Philip, Chadwick Foster, and G. Gouverneur Meredith S. Smith. *Cane, Cotton, & Crevasses: Some Antebellum Louisiana and Mississippi Plantations of the Minor, Kenner, Hooke, and Shepherd Families*. Bath, Maine: Renfrew Group, 1992.

Stahls, Paul F., Jr. *Jefferson Parish: Richer Heritage, Promising Future*. San Antonio: Historical Publishing Network, 2009.

Stampp, Kenneth M. *The Era of Reconstruction: 1865-1877*. New York: Vintage Books, 1965.

Sternberg, Mary Ann. *Along the River Road: Past and Present on Louisiana's Historic Byway*. Baton Rouge: Louisiana State University Press, 2001.

Stover, John F. "Southern Ambitions of the Illinois Central Railroad." *The Journal of Southern History* 20 (November 1954): 499-510.

Surrey, N. M. Miller. "The Commerce of Louisiana During the French Regime, 1699-1763." Ph.D. dissertation, Columbia University, 1916.

______. "The Development of Industries in Louisiana During the French Regime 1673-1763." *The Mississippi Valley Historical Review* 9 (December 1922): 227-35.

Swanson, Betsy. *Historic Jefferson Parish: From Shore to Shore.* Gretna, La.: Pelican Publishing Company, 1975.

Sydnor, Charles S. *The Development of Southern Sectionalism, 1819-1848*. In *A History of the South.* Vol. 5, edited by Wendell Holmes Stephenson and E. Merton Coulter. Baton Rouge: Louisiana State University Press and the Littlefield Fund for Southern History at the University of Texas, 1948.

Tallant, Robert. "From Cockfights to Commerce." *Jefferson Parish Yearly Review* (1952): 88-101.

Taylor, Joe Gray. *Louisiana Reconstructed: 1863-1877.* Baton Rouge: Louisiana State University, 1974.

Thompson, Ray M. "Industry!" *Jefferson Parish Yearly Review* (1943): 9-30.

Thrasher, Albert. *"On to New Orleans:" Louisiana's Heroic 1811 Slave Revolt.* 2nd ed. New Orleans: Albert Thrasher, 1996.

Toledano, W. R. "Streamlined for War." *Jefferson Parish Yearly Review* (1942): 5-8.

Vincent, Charles. "'Of Such Historical Importance . . . :' The African American Experience in Louisiana." *Louisiana History* 50 (Spring 2009): 133-58.

U.S. Army Corps of Engineers. *Cultural Resource Survey and Testing of the East Jefferson Parish Levee Gap Closure, Jefferson Parish, Louisiana*. Report No. Coelmn/PD-92/0Z. R. Christopher Goodwin & Associates, Inc., April 1992.

U.S. Army Engineering District, New Orleans. *Report on Hurricane Betsy, 8-11 September 1965.* New Orleans: Corps of Engineers, November 1965.

United States Soil Conservation Service. "Greater New Orleans: Unique City Unique Soils: Soil Information For Homebuyers and Homebuilders." undated pamphlet issued sometime in the late 1970s.

Vincent, Charles. *Black Legislators in the Louisiana During Reconstruction.* Baton Rouge: Louisiana State University Press, 1976.

Viosco, Percy, Jr. "Bayoulands of Jefferson." *Jefferson Parish Yearly Review* (1943): 42-58.

Vogt, Lloyd. *New Orleans Houses: A House-Watcher's Guide.* Gretna, La.: Pelican Publishing Company, 1992.

Wall, Bennet H., Judith Kelleher Schafer, Edward F. Haas, and Michael L. Kurtz.

Louisiana: A History, 4th ed. Wheeling, Ill.: Harlan Davidson, Inc., 2002.

Wesley, Charles H. "Manifests of Slave Shipments Along the Waterways, 1808-1864." *The Journal of Negro History* 27 (April 1942): 155-74.

White, Howard A. *The Freedmen's Bureau in Louisiana.* Baton Rouge: Louisiana State University Press, 1970.

Widmer, Mary Lou. *New Orleans 1900 to 1920.* Gretna, La.: Pelican Publishing Company, 2007.

______. *New Orleans in the Forties.* Gretna, La.: Pelican Publishing Company, 1990.

Winters, John D. *The Civil War in Louisiana.* Baton Rouge: Louisiana State University Press, 1963.

Woodward, C. Van. *The Strange Career of Jim Crow.* 9th ed. New York: Oxford University Press, 1963.

Yoes, Henry E., III. *Louisiana's German Coast: A History of St. Charles Parish.* Lake Charles, La.: Racing Pigeon Digest Company, Inc., 2005.

Digital Materials

Flight Safety Foundation. Aviation Safety Network Database. Available from www.flightsafety.org (accessed July 8, 2012).

A Guide to the Papers of Edward Jameson ca. 1862-1871. The University of Virginia Library, Charlottesville, Virginia. Special Collections. Available from http://ead.lib.virginia.edu/vivaead/published/uva-sc/viu03875.document (accessed January 2, 2010).

Civil War Diary of Henry Carl Ketzle, 37th Illinois Volunteer Infantry, Company A, 1861-1865. Available from http//w.w.w.ketzle.com/diary/1865.html (accessed January 2, 2010).

Dahl, Bill. "Lloyd Price Biography." *Allmusic.com.* Available from www.allmusic.com/artist/lloyd-price-mn0000827250/biography (accessed August 24, 2013).

Donnabrazile.com (accessed February 22, 2014).

Follett, Richard. *Documenting Louisiana Sugar 1845-1917.* Sussex, England: University of Sussex, 2008. Available from www.sussex.ac.uk/louisiana/index.php (accessed between January 2010 and August 2010).

Greater New Orleans Community Data Center. "Who Lives in New Orleans and the Metro Area Now?" September 20, 2012. Available from https://gnocdc.s3.amazonaws.com/reports/ GNOCDC_WhoLivesinNew OrleansAndThe MetroAreaNow.pdf (accessed April 5, 2013).

"Kenner 2030: Strategic Plan for a Prosperous Future,"n.d.. Available from www.kenner.la. us/2/kenner2030.pdf (accessed August 24, 2013).

"Kenner 2030: Strategic Plan for a Prosperous Future-Executive Summary," n.d. Available from www.kenner.la.us/2/kenner2030.pdf. (accessed August 24, 2013).

Kennerville, Louisiana. Letter from John J. Bigbee, January 7, 1865. Available from http://w.w.w.groantiques.com/detail,indiana-47th-infantry,1946164.html (accessed January 6, 2010).

LOUISiana Digital Library

Kenner and Henderson, New Orleans to Colonel Sam Fulton, December 31, 1808.

Le Courrier de la Louisiane, January 11, 1811.

Natchez Court Records, 1767-1805. Ancestry.com. Available from http://search.ancestry.com/browse/bookvew.aspx?dbid=48049&iid=NatchezCourtRec-00 (accessed April 12, 2012).

Notes for Elias P. Risshel, January 2 and February 8, 1865. Available from http://familytreemaker.genealogy.com/users/s/i/n/David-R-Sinn/GENE1-001.html (accessed January 6, 2010).

Office of the Governor, State of Louisiana. "Bobby Jindal." Available from http;//lousiana.gov/index.cfm?md=pagebuilder&tmp=home&na (accessed July 17, 2013).

Pfeifer, Michael J. "Louisiana Lynchings 1878-1946." Olympia, Wash.: Evergreen State College. Available from http://academic.evergreen.edu/p/pfeiferm/home.htm (accessed February 1, 2011).

Roth, David. "Louisiana Hurricane History." Camp Springs, Md.: National Weather Service, 2010. Available from www.hpc.ncep.noaa.gov/research/lahur.pdf (accessed June 10, 2012).

United States Census Bureau, State and County Quikfacts, Kenner, Louisiana. Available from www.quickfacts.census.gov/qfd/states /22/ 2239475.htm (accessed April 7, 2013).

Videotaped Deposition of Aaron Broussard. 24th Judicial District Court for the Parish of Jefferson, State of Louisiana, Chicago Property Interests, L.L.C. and Zoe Aldige Individually and on Behalf of Those Similarly Situated Versus Aaron Broussard Personally and in His Capacity as President of Jefferson Parish and Jefferson Parish, November 28, 2007. Available from http://blog.nola.com/news_impact/2008/01 /Broussard%20deposition.pdf (accessed March 20, 2013).

Waller, William "Dollar Bill." "The Lloyd Price: Did U Know? Trivia Facts.: Available from www.Lawdymissclawdy.com/Lloyd%20Price%20Bio%20as%20as%of%20Oct%201,%202010%20% and%20YESTERDAY%20and%TODAY.pdf (accessed September 3, 2013).

Image Credits

Courtesy of the City of Kenner, pages: xiv, 30, 42, 50 , 104, 108 (top), 108 (middle), 115 (top), 159, 161 (both), 257.

Courtesy of the Library of Congress, pages: 22, 64, 82 (both), 92 (top), 98, 164 (top), 184 (top).

From the *New Orleans Times-Picayune*: 114 (top), 145, 184 (bottom), 197 (both).

Courtesy of the author, pages: 206, 220.

Page 9, from: Alcee Fortier. *A History of Louisiana.* (New York: Manzi, Joyant, & Co., 1904).

Page 57, from: Philip Chadwick Foster Smith and G. Gouverneur Meredith S. Smith. *Cane, Cotton, & Crevasses: Some Antebellum Louisiana and Mississippi Plantations of the Minor, Kenner, Hooke, and Shepherd Families.* (Bath, Maine: the Renfrew Group, 1992).

Page 72-73: courtesy of J.E. Walker.

Page 92 (bottom): from: Thomas Hamilton Murray, *History of the Ninth Regiment, Connecticut Volunteer Infantry, "The Irish Regiment," in the War of the Rebellion, 1861-65* (New Haven: The Price, Lee & Adkiss Co., 1903).

Page 108 (bottom): from *Kenner City News.*

Page 114 (bottom): from report of Mississippi River Commission (1896).

Page 115 (bottom): courtesy of the Jefferson Convention and Visitor's Bureau, Inc.

Page 132: courtesy of Mrs. Shirley Hay.

Page 148: courtesy of former Kenner mayor, Louis Congemi.

Page 164 (bottom): courtesy of the New Orleans Public Library.

Page 171: courtesy of the State Library of Louisiana.

Page 178: from www.stuckattheairpor.com.

Page 204: courtesy of the City of New Orleans.

Page 234: from Google Earth.

Page 241: from the *Jefferson Parish Yearly Review.*

Page 243: from the *East Jefferson General Hospital Examiner.*

Page 248: courtesy Donna Brazile.

Page 252: courtesy Honorable Marc E. Johnson.

Page 253: promotional still shot.

Index

About the Author

CRAIG BAUER is Professor of History at the University of Holy Cross in New Orleans where he currently holds the Nancy O'Neill Endowed Professorship III in History. In addition to his current work *An Untractable Country: The History of Kenner, Louisiana*, he is author of *Creole Genesis: The Bringier Family and Antebellum Plantation Life in Louisiana*, published in 2011, and *A Leader Among Peers: The Life and Times of Duncan Farrar Kenner*, published in 1993. He has also published several journal and periodical articles on Louisiana history and the juvenile justice system.